al Epic

 the

The Allegorical Epic

Michael Murrin

The Allegorical Epic

Essays in Its Rise and Decline

The University of Chicago Press
Chicago and London

Michael Murrin is professor of English at the University of Chicago. He is the author of *The Veil of Allegory: Some Notes toward a Theory of Allegorical Rhetoric in the English Renaissance* (1969).

The University of Chicago Press, Chicago 60637
The University of Chicago Press, Ltd., London

84 83 82 81 80   5 4 3 2 1

Library of Congress Cataloging in Publication Data

Murrin, Michael.
   The allegorical epic.

   Includes bibliographical references and index.
   1. Epic poetry—History and criticism.
2. Allegory. I. Title.
PN1329.M8   809.1′3   79–20832
ISBN 0–226–55402–3

For my parents, Francis and Rose,
my sister, Marilyn,
and my brothers, John and David

Contents

Preface

I have designed this book as a companion volume to *The Veil of Allegory*, practical criticism to complement the theory, and the book preserves the same format. They both begin historically in the classical world. *The Veil* concentrates on the late classical theories which the Florentines revived and reaches back to Jeremiah and biblical prophecy. *The Allegorical Epic* starts with Virgil and the tradition of Homeric allegory, extending backward to the fifth century B.C. They both end around 1800, *The Veil* with an epilogue on two English romantics and *The Allegorical Epic* with a discussion of the disintegrationist criticism of Homer, particularly with that of F. A. Wolf, who separated allegory from Homer and gave to the method its first history. *The Allegorical Epic*, therefore, begins and ends with Homer, where allegory itself began and ended.

This book at the same time "corrects" the *Veil*, since it shows the differences and vagaries of practical application and so balances the clear structures of the earlier study. There, for example, I chose the more elaborate paradigms for the allegorical levels, those of Harington and Pico, which were the most exhaustive classifications and could account for any literary work. In actual practice, however, allegory is often simpler. Boiardo and Tasso have no theological allegory in the sense in which I define that level in *The Veil*. Similarly, in biblical study the exegete did not rigidly follow his three- or fourfold method. Origen in his practical criticism used a different schema from that which he outlined in the *Periarchon*.[1] Such constructs, be they three- or sevenfold, registered believed historical ideals, norms which guided the individual critic or writer but which he did not simply reflect. In this volume only the chapter on Spenser presents all the levels discussed in *The Veil*.

This book was also designed to complement the other comparative studies in epic, those by Greene, Durling, and Giamatti, but my commitment to historicism, to a criticism determined by strictly historical data, produced a different result. The reader will not find here a reflection and development of twentieth-century opinion on various authors. I have tried, rather, to present those allegories which can be recovered by the historian, an analysis of what some critics actually wrote in the Renaissance, or a direct reading of those poems where we have sufficient data to determine the kind and method of the allegory. With the exception of a Spenser or Dante, however, the literary historian has hardly studied practical allegorical criticism. Where biblical allegory has attracted distinguished scholars like de Lubac, Smalley, and Daniélou, the older and parallel secular tradition which stems from classical epic has not. This study is therefore selective. It does not, for example, include the *Furioso,* the *Adone,* or the influence of the *Divina commedia* and its allegories. While our knowledge of secular allegory remains so limited, a true survey of the major epics is not possible. On the other hand, each chapter of this book makes claims which to varying degrees are unique to the criticism of that field or writer. I contend that Virgil invented polysemous allegory for the epic, perhaps for all literature; that the old critics who Platonized Virgil had textual support in the *Aeneid;* that Boiardo and Tasso are susceptible to classical rules for allegorical interpretation. None of these claims is received opinion. For the romance writers, where there is little hard evidence, I had to use hypothesis in the end: the Mongols in Boiardo and theological allegory in Spenser. This newness is accidental. It comes not from unique insight but from the choice of an area of research completely different from those which the students of epic normally follow. References to contemporary criticism, therefore, are few and mostly confined to footnotes.

Historicism likewise distinguishes this work from most other studies in secular allegory. I assume that allegory began and ended in our historical past, and three of the seven chapters are concerned with its genesis and death. I would not otherwise have included a chapter on Milton, for example; but a historical understanding of allegory required a discussion of the heavenly war in *Paradise Lost.* Allegory began with Homer's quarrelsome deities, and Milton helps to close its story when he deliberately prevents an allegorical reading of his heavenly scenes.[2] The inclusion of such material separates this book from those by critics who consider allegory to be a genre or something atemporal. While allegory may indeed respond to something permanent in the mind, I think that this something manifested itself differently both before the Greeks started arguing about Homer's theology and today. It is not the object of the literary historian to speculate about the mind. He can only study its expressions. This book, therefore, has nothing to do with the modern or romantic definition of allegory, the play of personifications which express our passions;[3] nor is it concerned with modern experiments which critics have felt to be mythic or allegorical. If Kafka uses a similar form, he does so with different suppositions and for alien purposes. The reader who thinks in these ways or who wants a new method which he can use on contemporary literature will find this book a disappointment.

He may, however, find a challenge. Most practical criticism today is at once theoretical and scholarly, and this in-between character can encourage a misuse of older writers. The critic is tempted to exaggerate those ideas which correspond to his own or to decorate a modern theory with historical footnotes. The historian, on the other hand, prevents these abuses, forces a critic to separate his theory and mind-set from that of a Spenser or Virgil. He tries to make the assertion of human communality difficult and shows the chameleon-like nature of our thinking. The challenge can be exhilarating. As I said in another context, "to read Spenser or Boiardo properly, we must understand poets who wrote when astrology and witchcraft were more than poetic fictions and who read a mass of literature we no longer know: long medieval romances and mythographic encyclopedias like *Genealogie deorum gentilium*. Boiardo lived when the world was half unknown, and *The Faerie Queene* embodies a poetic theory which denies some of the most crucial assumptions of modern form criticism. Only in this totality can we treat the *Orlando innamorato* or *The Faerie Queene* fairly and perhaps reeducate ourselves. For, if we consider erroneous vast areas of thought which formed their world view, we might learn something about our own. The enounter with a text or with a culture should go two ways, and Boiardo or Spenser might force us to recognize that our linguistic assumptions, our model of the human psyche, our current literary theories, most of them recent, fifty or a hundred years old in a human history which can be traced back thousands of years, that these mind-sets or thought frames may be as delusive as that of the Ptolemaic spheres. The recognition, however unpleasant, might help us grow. Aeneas had to discard most of his preconceptions before he found Latium."[4]

Finally, it is the pleasure of the historian to revive writers previously forgotten or ignored, in this case Landino and Boiardo. The former has always been outshone by Ficino and Pico, but in any other system he would be its sun. Similarly, the reputation of Ariosto has obscured that of Boiardo, justifiably if we think of characterization and style, unjustifiably if we think of invention. The wondrous fantasy of the Orlando romance is Boiardo's and in these scenes he showed himself one of the great allegorical poets of the Renaissance.

The reader can see in the footnotes what scholars I have used, but I wish to thank here those who read or helped in the writing of this book. At the University of Chicago, these are Robert Kaster, Bernard McGinn, Janel Mueller, Jay Schleusener, Richard Strier, John Wallace, George Walsh, Elissa Weaver, and John Woods. Elsewhere, I thank David Quint at Princeton; Charles Ross at Purdue; Fredi Chiappelli, director of the Center for Medieval and Renaissance Studies at UCLA; and the two readers for the University of Chicago Press, one of whom was Raymond Waddington of the University of Wisconsin. I also wish to thank the University of Chicago, which granted me two quarters' leave for research, and the Guggenheim Foundation. The latter's grant allowed me to study in Rome, to write the middle part of this book, and generally to attempt the more ambitious project which I had dreamed of earlier but which I had not believed practical.

Classical

1   The Goddess of Air

Allegory began with Homer's gods, and we can best estimate its qualities through a deity like Hera. A dominant figure in the *Iliad,* she links Homer with Virgil. Through her we can see a complex development: how the allegorical interpreter turned Homer's divine scenes into philosophical poetry, one which used symbols rather than syllogisms, and how Virgil in turn made such symbols polyvalent and started the multileveled allegory familiar to us from the medieval and Renaissance periods.

My concern will not be with the history of this interpretation. Félix Buffière has done this already in *Les mythes d'Homère et la pensée grecque* (1956). Rather, I want to understand the methodology of this early allegory, *why* it existed, the problems it created for itself, how it solved them. The ancients wished to explain away the scandal of Homer's gods. Hera seduces her husband out of doors on a mountain top, boxes the ears of Artemis, and generally acts in a fashion unacceptable for the great goddess whom the Greeks worshiped. Allegory removed the scandal, and the figures in such scenes were read philosophically, as symbols for hidden processes—physical and chemical in the case of Hera, moral and psychological in the case of Athena. The gods then functioned as intermittent commentary on the epic action, occasional forays into ethics and physics which helped the audience to comprehend the human events of the *Iliad* and the *Odyssey*. This method in turn created its own set of problems. The exegete wanted to standardize Homer's symbolism, give it the consistency of a philosophical vocabulary; but he found the divine scenes difficult to harmonize, separated as they were from each other by whole books, and different in tone. The drive to standardize created a tension between Homer's story and his "meaning," albeit a tension which does not exist in the *Aeneid,* an epic written under the influence of Homeric criticism. Juno means the same things everywhere in the poem. Virgil then made such scenes polyvalent, in a sophistication of allegorical method which allowed him to "condense" complex processes into short episodes, one of the principal techniques he used to "reduce" the *Iliad* and the *Odyssey* into one epic.

I will discuss these matters first through Hera's scenes in the *Iliad* and then through those of her counterpart, Juno, in the *Aeneid*. Three passages from the *Iliad* are of particular concern. The first is a brief reference to a conspiracy against Zeus in which Hera took part (1.396–406). The second two compose the Διὸς ἀπάτη, the Deception of Zeus, where Hera seduces him on Mount Ida (14.153–355; 15.1–84).[1] The interpreters applied these passages to meteorological phenomena, thunderstorms and changes of season, topics which Virgil took over for his own epic. My main sources will be Heraclitus's *Homeric Problems*, an allegorical analysis of Homer's divine scenes which scholars generally date to the first century A.D.,[2] and the scholia to the *Iliad*, which go back to the same period.[3] The identifications are, however, much older. Hera was already air in the fifth century B.C., and the Stoics had maintained this interpretation.[4] I will begin with the Deception of Zeus.

We would not normally identify Hera with air in this episode, yet the equation has considerable support. Four classes of reference connect Hera to the air: her mode of travel, her persecution of Heracles, the clouds and mist with which Zeus associates her, and most important, her name. First of all, Hera never touches the ground when she travels. By herself she twice darts through the sky, from Olympus to Lemnos, gliding over mountain peaks (ἀΐξασα 14.225–30), and from Ida back to Olympus, as quickly as we change places in our thinking (ἀΐξη 15.79–83). With Hypnos she flies swiftly to Ida, ἠέρα ἐσσαμένω (14.282, "wrapped in mist").[5] Air is her medium of travel, and she moves as fast as the wind.

Second, she sends cyclones (θυέλλας, 15.26). On two occasions others recall an incident in which she and Boreas blew Heracles in the wrong direction (14.253–56; 15.26–28).[6] This is the story which Virgil later converted into his opening scene, where Juno tries to destroy Aeneas with a hurricane. In the *Iliad* the phrasing and the action anticipate the last battle, when the goddess spreads out ἠέρα . . . βαθεῖαν (21.6–7, "a thick mist") to slow the Trojan flight and orders the south and west winds to blow a whirlwind (θύελλαν) from the sea and thus propel a fire into the faces of the Trojans (21.334–37). Hera behaves like air and commands wind storms.

Three other things, two of which concern Zeus, suggest that Hera is air in the episode. Zeus conceals their love making with a golden cloud,[7] and later he reminds her that he once hung her in midair: ἐν αἰθέρι καὶ νεφέλῃσιν (15.20, "in the ether and among the clouds").[8]

Finally, there is her name. In Greek it is an anagram for air: Ἥρα / ἀήρ.[9] For many an ancient critic this "etymology" would have been the most convincing evidence.

The Deception of Zeus diagrams a physical process, as inevitable as that in a laboratory experiment. Its interpretation depends upon a conventional analysis of the four elements: dry versus wet, hot versus cold, light versus heavy. Each element has two qualities, the first of which unites it to another element, the second of which repels. In this scene it is Hera and Zeus, air and fire or ether. Air is hot and wet, while fire is hot and dry.[10] The heat in the two elements draws them together, while the opposition of wet and dry explains their mutual repulsion. Their interaction causes a thunderstorm. Philosophers gave different technical explanations for the phenomena of an electric storm, but they all assumed this interaction.[11] The commentators accordingly read Homer's episode as a diagram for a hidden physical process.[12] Through the episode they thought that Homer analyzed a thunderstorm. The event was a symbolic study removed from the plot of the *Iliad*. No rain or lightning disturbed the warriors in the story; the Trojans and Achaeans would have seen only a gold cloud on one of Ida's three peaks.

Heraclitus has a more elaborate reading of this episode and turns the electric storm into an allegory of spring (chap. 39). The lovers signify the thunderstorms which fertilize the earth and warm the atmosphere so that flowers can grow. At home Hera first washes, anoints herself richly with a fragrant oil, and combs out her hair. For Heraclitus the air is dark and sad after winter, and in the toilet the anointing with oil represents the odors of spring flowers, her hair the growth of leaves on trees. The girdle she borrows from Venus indicates the pleasant nature of the season, tempered as it is between extremes of hot and cold. The love making with her husband signifies the mixing of air and ether, which causes the new season. The golden cloud with which Zeus veils their love likewise carries a meteorological lesson, for in spring the dense, compact clouds of winter give way to thinner formations which brighten with golden flashes from the sun.[13]

The interpreters read this scene dynamically. Homer intimates through symbols not a static set of relations but a physical interaction, a process as it occurs. He tells us why and how thunderstorms arise and spring comes. The event in the story, Hera's deception of Zeus, occurred only once, long ago, like the war at Troy. It significance, however, applies to events which recur constantly. The symbols are necessary because they reveal causes, what we cannot see. The elements normally exist in a mixed state, and we call something dry or wet according to the quality which predominates in the mixture.[14] In its pure state no one sees air, much less an elemental interaction. Hence we need a symbolic vocabulary, a way to analyze the invisible. For Homer it is the gods.

We see these same qualities in the exegesis of the divine conspiracy. Achilles refers to it cryptically in *Iliad* 1:

πολλάκι γάρ σεο πατρὸς ἐνὶ μεγάροισιν ἄκουσα
εὐχομένης ὅτ' ἔφησθα κελαινεφέϊ Κρονίωνι
οἴη ἐν ἀθανάτοισιν ἀεικέα λοιγὸν ἀμῦναι,
ὁππότε μιν ξυνδῆσαι Ὀλύμπιοι ἤθελον ἄλλοι
Ἥρη τ' ἠδὲ Ποσειδάων καὶ Παλλὰς Ἀθήνη·
ἀλλὰ σὺ τόν γ' ἐλθοῦσα θεὰ ὑπελύσαο δεσμῶν,
ὦχ' ἑκατόγχειρον καλέσασ' ἐς μακρὸν Ὄλυμπον,
ὃν Βριάρεων καλέουσι θεοί, ἄνδρες δέ τε πάντες
Αἰγαίων', ὃ γὰρ αὖτε βίην οὗ πατρὸς ἀμείνων·
ὅς ῥα παρὰ Κρονίωνι καθέζετο κύδεϊ γαίων·
τὸν καὶ ὑπέδεισαν μάκαρες θεοὶ οὐδ' ἔτ' ἔδησαν.

Since it is many times in my father's halls I have heard you
making claims, when you said you only among the immortals
beat aside shameful destruction from Kronos' son the dark-
    misted,
that time when all the other Olympians sought to bind him,
Hera and Poseidon and Pallas Athene. Then you,
goddess, went and set him free from his shackles, summoning
in speed the creature of the hundred hands to tall Olympos,
that creature the gods name Briareus, but all men
Aigaios' son, but he is far greater in strength than his father.
He rejoicing in the glory of it sat down by Kronion,
and the rest of the blessed gods were frightened and gave up
    binding him.

                                                    [396–406]

The interpretations of this scene vary, but all assume process. For Heraclitus (chap. 25) this story allegorizes the danger of imbalance among the elements. Zeus, Hera, and Poseidon have their standard meanings: ether, air, and water. Athena functions uncharacteristically as earth. Three of the four threaten cosmic confusion, but Thetis/ Πρόνοια (providence) settles matters, not without great effort (the hundred hands of the giant). One scholiast sees, rather, a mixing of the elements. Homer separates Zeus from the other three because fire alone of the elements exists in a pure and unmixed state (ex. to *Il.* 1.400[bT]). The scholiast also records an allegory of the seasons, a reading closer to Virgil's concern with Hera/Juno (ex. to *Il*. 1.399–406[bT]). The conspirators and Thetis keep the same meanings, while Zeus is rather unmixed heat (θερμασία), the origin of being and of life or breathing, while Briareus becomes the sun. The binding signifies winter, when the sun goes south and our area cools. Air converts to water, and we have the rainy season. The period of heat is at its shortest, as the nights are long and the days brief. Zeus is therefore bound by air, water, and earth. Thetis, however, brings north Briareus of the hundred hands, the sun whose rays, shot everywhere, nourish plants and help them grow. And so summer comes.

Interpretations proliferate, but in all of them the critic does an elemental analysis. He finds processes which the poet makes visible to us but which in nature we never see. We perceive the changes of the season but do not see the causes for this change, the interaction of three of the four elements and their dependence on solar movement in the zodiac. Moreover, Homer presents this change in eleven lines, though in fact it takes months, from summer to winter and again from winter to summer. Symbolic analysis allows him to condense a protracted event the way a physicist expresses a complex interaction through a mathematical formula. A reference, a brief conversation between symbolic figures, can compress years and months into a few lines. In the *Aeneid* we shall see that the conversation of Juno and Aeolus has the same function. By it Virgil intimates the coming of winter.

This scene also illustrates a problem, one not evident in the Deception of Zeus. There is nothing in Achilles' words to support the equation of Hera with air.[15] The critic assumes this interpretation, and his assumption indicates another aspect of Homeric "allegory." Where possible, a divinity maintains the same signification: if Hera is air in the Deception of Zeus, she must be air here and in her other scenes.[16] Clouds, wind, and mist mark many of her appearances, but not all; and the allegorist wants even the smallest reference to fit his interpretation. In Heraclitus Hera is air everywhere.

There is a mechanical explanation for this uniformity of meaning, depending partially on the mythographic dictionaries. Heraclitus, for example, tries to explain the Homeric epithets of the divinities and in the case of Apollo indicates his source: the Περὶ θεῶν of Apollodorus of Athens (7.1). We may presume that he used a similar source when he analyzes the epithets for Proteus and Hermes (67.1–4; 72.9–13), probably also for the occasional etymologies scattered liberally through his arguments.[17] When Theodore Meliteniotes added his scholia to the Geneva text of the *Iliad*, he likewise used a dictionary to allegorize the divine names.[18] Such mythographic treatises present standard meanings and are not designed for the fluctuations of signification and tone which, in a long and complex poem, a divine figure may have from one episode to another. Critics who depend on such dictionaries will therefore tend to make uniform the significations of particular deities, whatever the particular context.

We can find a more adequate explanation once we consider the form of this allegorical criticism. It concerns itself solely with Homer's gods. Heraclitus presents interpretations not of the whole *Iliad* or *Odyssey* but, rather, of the divine scenes, which are often widely separated from each other. The scholia reflect this practice, for they normally list allegorical interpretations when the gods enter the action. This concentration on the gods reflects the origins of Homeric allegory and helps us to see its purpose. The philosophers had attacked Homer's representation of the Olympians, and Xenophanes had begun the argument when he said,

> πάντα θεοῖσ' ἀνέθηκαν "Ομηρός θ' Ἡσίοδός τε,
> ὅσσα παρ' ἀνθρώποισιν ὀνείδεα καὶ ψόγος ἐστίν,
> κλέπτειν μοιχεύειν τε καὶ ἀλλήλους ἀπατεύειν.

Homer and Hesiod have imputed to the gods all that is blame and shame for men, for they steal, commit adultery, and deceive each other. [B11][19]

The defenders of Homer could not deny the charge, as Hera does in fact deceive Zeus and the deities fight with each other on the plains of Troy. They could, however, deny that Homer's gods were gods, and in their response to the polemic they found their way to a notion of symbolism. Hera was air, not the goddess of the cult. Severed from religion, Homer's gods function rather as a technical vocabulary, ways in which the poet can discuss physics and psychology. The divine scenes make the *Iliad* and the *Odyssey* philosophical poems.

This defense in turn rested on rationalizing developments in the language. Prodicus of Ceos remarked that the ancients divinized what was useful to human life: earth as Demeter, wine as Dionysus, water as Poseidon, fire as Hephaestus.[20] That is, there was a tendency to use the names of certain deities as personifications for material substances or artifacts. Iris is an example, for among the Presocratics she is simply the rainbow.[21] Heraclitus cites for this practice some lines from Empedocles which name the four elements:

> Ζεὺς ἀργὴς Ἥρη τε φερέσβιος ἠδ' Ἀιδωνεύς
> Νῆστίς θ', ἣ δακρύοις τέγγει κρούνωμα βρότειον.

Zeus bright and Hera life [food] giving and Hades,
Nestis too, who with her tears moistens the mortal spring.

[24.6]

In the critic's interpretation we have Zeus-ether, Hera-earth, Hades-air, and Nestis-water.[22] The subject is one with which we are familiar, the four elements, and the Sicilian uses a symbolic vocabulary parallel to that which Heraclitus finds in Homer. Thus the *Iliad* represents for him an earlier mode of philosophic discourse, in which the poet talks of Athena and Hera rather than of prudence and air. Homer's vocabulary is nonetheless clear and rigorous, for a philosopher must keep his terms reasonably consistent. Hence the drive to standardize the divine names.

This apology had a polemic side. Heraclitus argues that those philosophers who attack Homer borrowed their ideas from him. They are ungrateful sons of a wise father. Heraclitus and the scholiasts all remark that Xenophanes, who began the attack on Homer, derived his theory of earth and water from a remark by Menelaus (*Il.* 7.99);[23] and Heraclitus similarly proves that Plato derived his psychology, and Epicurus his hedonism, from Homer. The technique is clever and elastic, as it has the potential to adjust to any development in philosophy but is open to logical attack. Seneca argued that Homer could not have maintained the positions of so many warring schools without contradiction and that the existence of such contradiction refuted the hypothesis (*Ad Lucilium* 11.88.5).

In their practical criticism the allegorists avoided Seneca's charge, because they found in Homer not detailed and specialized conceptions but, rather, what I will call "centrist" readings. For cosmology Heraclitus talks of the four elements, notions which could fit any number of philosophical systems. Specialized variations, such as the distinction between fire and ether, do not appear; and brilliant but peculiar readings such as the astrological are ignored. The allegorized Homer could fit any philosophy finally because his "ideas" are the basic sort of lumber everyone had to use.

Such an argument befits the time when allegory began, the sixth and fifth centuries, when philosophy and poetry had not been separated completely from each other. Many of the Presocratics wrote in verse, and, if they at times used a symbolic vocabulary, it was reasonable to argue that Homer did likewise. Moreover, it followed that the early philosophers learned more than a set of ideas from Homer. Some of them imitated his symbolic method, and Heraclitus in his little history of philosophical allegory cites examples from Empedocles and the other Heraclitus. Macrobius adds Parmenides and Pythagoras to the list (*Commentarii* 1.2.21).

In later periods there were sufficient borderline writers to make this archaic defense continue to seem plausible. Plato composed dialogues; Cleanthes and Lucretius wrote in verse. The Stoics in particular adapted the old defense of Homer to their own polemics. They found the standard allegory of the elements both in Homer and in Hesiod. Hera-air, for example, is both sister and wife to Zeus, sister because the air and ether are related to each other by their thinness, wife because air as the lower element is subject to fire.[24] The Stoics thus harmonized the ancient poetry with their own thought and could assert that their philosophy corresponded historically with the oldest thinking in Greece.

The defense of Homer then had sufficient plausibility. The boundaries between philosophy and poetry were often blurred, and many writers could be classed in this twilight zone. Consider, for example, the other Heraclitus, who fits the allegorist's criteria much better than Homer. He placed his book in the Temple of Artemis and in two famous fragments (B92–93) talked of oracles, which later critics have seen as descriptions of his own manner of discourse, riddles from the temple.[25] He stated that Nature loves to hide itself: φύσις κρύπτεσθαι φιλεῖ (B123); that the hidden harmony is stronger than the visible: ἁρμονίη ἀφανὴς φανερῆς κρείττων (B54); and that normal men, therefore, could not understand, either before or *after* they had heard an explanation. They fail to notice what they do after they wake up, just as they forget what they do when asleep.[26] These remarks express perfectly the typical allegorist's conception of a hidden truth which by its nature excludes the majority of men from its understanding. An oracular style follows as a logical consequence, a form of writing which the common people could not read, and his later followers argued by riddles.[27]

Heraclitus of Ephesus fits the apologist's polemic and also helps us to understand how Virgil transformed Homeric allegory, how Hera became Juno. The art of the two writers suggests the oracular, by style in Heraclitus, by both style and story in Virgil. We shall see in the next chapter how Virgil based his plot on oracles. Here I shall demonstrate that he wrote allegorically and now wish to show that allegorical and oracular speech are often the same thing. Consider this fragment from Heraclitus: ὁ ἄναξ οὗ τὸ μαντεῖόν ἐστι τὸ ἐν Δελφοῖς οὔτε λέγει οὔτε κρύπτει ἀλλὰ σημαίνει (B93, "The lord whose oracle is in Delphi neither speaks out nor conceals but gives a sign"). That is, the god allegorizes. An oracle normally applied to a historical event, envisioned in the immediate or remote future. Hence there existed in theory at least a key, and the exegete through history would discover a single meaning. Heraclitus' riddles, however, are ahistorical and have *multiple* application. They are therefore polyvalent and so resemble the allegorical discourse we associate with Virgil and later poets. The context of Heraclitus' argument may have controlled or prevented this proliferation of meanings, but we cannot recover his context with any certainty, and his followers certainly did not let context control their own use of the master's oracles. Two examples will illustrate this characteristic of his style: ποταμοῖς τοῖς αὐτοῖς ἐμβαίνομέν τε καὶ οὐκ ἐμβαίνομεν, εἶμέν τε καὶ οὐκ εἶμεν (B49a, "We step and do not step into the same rivers; we are and are not"); ὁδὸς ἄνω κάτω μία καὶ ὡυτή (B60, "The way up and the way down is one and the same"). Both violate the law of contradiction,[28] that is, make no sense on the literal level and allow for a double truth: a dissonance between the literal and the noetic. The first in conjunction with B12 + 91 would lead to the notion of constant if invisible flux, the theory attributed to Heraclitus by Plato and Aristotle.[29] Kirk, who denies the theory, must throw out the fragment as dubious.[30] Heraclitus the allegorist cites it as an example of allegory. The second fragment Kirk interprets simply: the road which is "down" to the villagers at the top of a hill is "up" to those who live at the bottom. Theophrastus and other ancients saw in it, rather, the interchange of world masses, and they have been followed by Burnet and Diels.[31] Eliot used it mystically, as the epigraph for *Burnt Norton*. In their present form these riddles do not yield single meanings, whatever they may have done originally, and as a result the modern interpreters of Heraclitus have been forced to argue their sense of his whole book. Here they need not agree either, for Kirk reads him cosmologically and Owens politically,[32] and both cite classical authorities for their positions. Critics project different systems and interpretations on his riddles because they are polyvalent. Turn the riddle into narrative, and we have Virgil.

Juno in the *Aeneid*

What we know of Virgil personally indicates that he wished to write a philosophical poem. We draw our evidence from the old biographies and from a topic which the poet raises in all his principal works. The *Vitae* are explicit, but their objective value is disputed by critics, who argue over the antiquity of the *testimonia* and the possibilities of honorific fabrication. We learn from them that Virgil studied under Siro the Epicurean, that he spent years in that circle of friends, and that he intended to devote the rest of his life to philosophy, once he finished his corrections to the *Aeneid*.[33] The parallels to Lucretius are strong: the poet-philosopher in the Garden of Epicurus, and in the poems he regularly presents his interest in cosmological topics.

Virgil outlines the kind of poetry he would like to write in one of his
more personal statements (*Georgics* 2.475–82). The list concerns astronomy and physics: (1) the ways of the sun and the stars, solar
eclipses and the various labors of the moon; (2) earthquakes and tides;
(3) the variation of the solar day from summer to winter. At Dido's
banquet Iopas sings about the same kind of topics (*Ae*. 1.740–76): (1)
the wandering moon and labors of the sun; (2) the origins of man,
beasts, storms, and fires; (3) certain constellations; (4) the variation of
the solar day from winter to summer. The addition of creation finds its
parallel in the sixth eclogue, where Silenus sings,

> ... uti magnum per inane coacta
> semina terrarumque animaeque marisque fuissent
> et liquidi simul ignis, ut his exordia primis
> omnia et ipse tener mundi concreverit orbis.

> ... that through the great void
> the seeds of earth, air, sea, and liquid fire
> were gathered together, that from these first things
> were all beginnings and this soft ball of the cosmos hardened.
>
> [6.31–34]

The atomistic description fits the four elements we know from Homeric
criticism: the seeds of the lands, of air, of sea, and of fire.

We might gather from these remarks that Virgil wished to write a
cosmological poem, modeled on but much more ambitious than the
Phaenomena of Aratus, the poet whom he imitated in *Georgics* 1. The
topic would be identical, astronomy and weather, but the presentation
would be philosophical rather than descriptive and include discussions
of the origins of storms, of fires, of the cosmos itself. Such a poem
would parallel the *De rerum natura*, but the difference in form and
expressed content between Lucretius' epic and the *Aeneid* have dis-
couraged critical attempts to read Virgil's epic philosophically. We,
however, would not be surprised to discover philosophy in a Homeric
imitation like the *Aeneid*, and in fact the topics which Virgil lists had all
been discovered in the *Iliad* and *Odyssey*. Here are those in the *Iliad*
which concern Hera/Juno:

the variation in the solar day	the conspiracy of Hera, Poseidon, and Athena against Zeus (1.399–406)
the origins of storms	the Διὸς ἀπάτη, where Hera seduces Zeus (14.153–355, 15.1–83)

elemental creation   Hera in chains (15.18–24)
the origins of fires[34]   Hera and Hephaestus versus
                              the River Xanthus
                              (21.328–84)

We might expect Virgil, therefore, to make the divine scenes of his epic into philosophical allegories, and the whole poem would thus in some sense complement the *De rerum natura,* the indirect, symbolic mode answering to Lucretius' direct presentation. Virgil would most probably stress the four elements, concepts common to any philosophical system, and presumably he would obviate the difficulties we have seen when Heraclitus and others looked for allegory in Homer. The meanings and symbols of the Roman poet would be consistent, and no strain would appear between the literal and allegorical levels. And, if we look once more at Hera/Juno, we find standard Homeric allegory: the goddess of air and an analysis of the origin of storms and the weather, subjects which Virgil included in his lists.

The Proem to the *Aeneid* indicates that Virgil had already made his Juno into a meteorological symbol. He makes the goddess responsible for all Aeneas' sufferings, on land and water, and at its close prepares us more especially for the Odyssean *Aeneid,* when he says that the goddess kept the Trojans away from Italy, wandering at sea (1.29–32). We anticipate, therefore, the goddess of air and storms, and we instantly see Juno stir up a great cyclone. She likewise sends the cloudburst which brings Dido and Aeneas together in a cave, and we assume her power behind the other storms, where we lack a privileged perspective and see no causes, as we experience the event through its human participants.[35] Virgil, however, identifies his Juno with the Hera of the Homeric critics much more completely than these episodes would indicate. Richard Heinze suggested that Juno is air *wherever* she appears in the *Aeneid.*[36] Her actions and the phrases which define her movements make her literally so in the text, and the dissonance between surface and interpretation disappears. Even in the Iliadic *Aeneid,* where weather has less importance, these telltale phrases continue to appear. She comes to Sicily *auras invecta tenebat* (7.287, "embarked upon the air") and later is met by Allecto, who comes *caeli convexa per auras* (7.543, "carried through the air").[37] In book 10 Juno descends to the battlefield *agens hiemem nimbo succincta per auras* (634, "cloaked in a cloud / and driving storms") and decoys Turnus from the fight by a cloud shape. In book 12 she watches the battle with her husband from an ether cloud *fulva . . . de nube* (792), and Jove asks her, *aut qua spe gelidis in nubibus haeres?* (796), "What is / the hope that keeps you lingering in these / chill clouds?"). We could extend the list.[38] The goddess has therefore a consistent signification, and, unlike the Hera of Homeric criticism, this signification fits all her appearances in the poem.

We can assess Virgil's purpose or "physical" allegory when we compare the tempests which his goddess creates with their originals in the *Odyssey*. With one exception, that off Cape Malea (*Od.* 9.80–84), all the storms which trouble Odysseus are cyclonic, whirlwinds which make the hero wander.[39] Virgil recalls this pattern in his first storm, which he describes carefully and makes paradigmatic for all the others. He changes the Odyssean formula, however, and regularly makes his tempests into thunderstorms.[40] By this change he indicates his interpretive source, which comes not from the *Odyssey* but from *Iliad* 14–15, the Διὸς ἀπάτη, which I have already discussed. Virgil found in the episode both the plot for *Aeneid* 1 and its interpretation.

He derived his plot from the references made by Hypnos and Zeus to an earlier intrigue of Hera's. I cite the first description, that by Hypnos:

> ἤδη γάρ με καὶ ἄλλο τεὴ ἐπίνυσσεν ἐφετμὴ
> ἤματι τῷ ὅτε κεῖνος ὑπέρθυμος Διὸς υἱὸς
> ἔπλεεν Ἰλιόθεν Τρώων πόλιν ἐξαλαπάξας.
> ἤτοι ἐγὼ μὲν ἔλεξα Διὸς νόον αἰγιόχοιο
> νήδυμος ἀμφιχυθείς· σὺ δέ οἱ κακὰ μήσαο θυμῷ
> ὄρσασ' ἀργαλέων ἀνέμων ἐπὶ πόντον ἀήτας,
> καί μιν ἔπειτα Κόωνδ' δ' εὖ ναιομένην ἀπένεικας
> νόσφι φίλων πάντων.

> Before now, it was a favour to you that taught me wisdom,
> on the day Herakles, the high-hearted son of Zeus, was sailing
> from Ilion, when he had utterly sacked the city of the Trojans.
> That time I laid to sleep the brain in Zeus of the aegis
> and drifted upon him still and soft, but your mind was devising
> evil, and you raised along the sea the blasts of the racking
> winds, and on these swept him away to Kos, the
>   strong-founded,
> far from all his friends.

> [*Il.* 14.249–56]

Zeus adds that she worked together with Boreas, the north wind, and that the storm was cyclonic (15.26). Virgil took over these particulars but rationalized the characters according to the standard meteorological interpretation. Juno attacks Jove's hero, again sailing from Troy, and sends a great whirling cyclone, which smashes the Trojan fleet and drives Aeneas south to Africa. She once more acts through a subordinate and must arrange a marriage. Only now her interlocutor corresponds to the goddess' meteorological significance: it is Aeolus, god of the winds, and not Hypnos. The other characters, Jove and Neptune, likewise fit a physical interpretation. Together they account for all the particulars of a thunderstorm: Juno (air), Aeolus (wind), Neptune (water), and Jove (fire).[41]

The interpretation of the love making of Zeus and Hera had been double. The scholiasts saw in it a thunderstorm, and Heraclitus the allegorist found there the coming of spring. Virgil combines the two interpretations. Servius remarks that the time of storms is when contraries meet, the time in between seasons, late autumn or spring.[42] Thus they signify either the approach of winter, the sterile time when Zeus is bound by the other elements,[43] or the approach of the warm season, when the earth greens and the days grow long. It is this double significance which governs Virgil's use of thunderstorms in the *Aeneid*, his obsession with the way the solar day varies from winter to summer.

The logic of this interpretation reflects the plot of the poem. Conflict in the story shadows forth meteorological wars. In the *Iliad* Hera and Zeus favor different sides in the battles before Troy, and earlier Hera conspired with other deities against her husband. By interpretation these conflicts indicate the storms which begin and end winter, the times when one element encroaches on another, air and cold on fire and then the reverse. Virgil similarly uses the clash of Jove and Juno to indicate seasonal change. The first storm, arranged by Juno, begins the winter season. The last, which comes after Aeneas prays to Jove and which extinguishes the fire in the Trojan ships, preludes the coming of spring.

In the *Aeneid* we know from the human characters that the initial storm occurs in autumn and introduces the season when Juno has most power. Here is how Ilioneus narrates the first storm to Dido:

> cum subito adsurgens fluctu nimbosus Orion
> in vada caeca tulit penitusque procacibus Austris
> perque undas superante salo perque invia saxa
> dispulit; huc pauci vestris adnavimus oris.

> when suddenly,
> rising upon the surge, stormy Orion
> drove us against blind shoals; and insolent
> south winds then scattered us, undone by brine,
> across the crushing sea, the pathless rocks.
> A few of us have drifted to your shores.

> [1.535–38]

The storm came suddenly upon them, from the direction of Orion, a constellation normally associated with storms and with the uncertain weather which characterizes the beginning of winter.[44] Anna later will suggest that Dido use the inclement weather to detain the Trojans:

> indulge hospitio causasque innecte morandi
> dum pelago desaevit hiems et aquosus Orion,
> quassataeque rates, dum non tractabile caelum.

> be lavish with your Trojan guests and weave
> excuses for delay while frenzied winter
> storms out across the sea and shatters ships,
> while wet Orion blows his tempest squalls
> beneath a sky that is intractable.

> [4.51–53]

And when the Trojans leave anyway, they are immediately struck by another storm.[45]

The dialogue of Juno and Aeolus symbolizes the meteorological causes for the storm and the season. Virgil locates the interview at Stromboli in the Liparic Isles, the traditional home of Homer's Aeolus.[46] This setting likewise illustrates the ancient theory that wind action explains earthquakes as well as the weather. Aristotle, for example, classed both volcanic eruptions and earthquakes under winds and cited Lipari as an example (*Meteor.* 2.8.366b31–367a20). Noise in the volcanic rifts foretells the coming of the south wind. Underground winds at their most violent cause earthquakes[47] and volcanic flames. The air breaks up into small particles, and the percussion causes fire. These explosions and shakings occur most frequently in the interim seasons, the time of the ἐκνεφίας ἄνεμος (2.7.365a2–6), which is Aristotle's technical name for the cyclonic storm which scatters the Trojan fleet (3.1.370b5–18).[48] All these phenomena—volcanic eruptions, earthquakes, whirlwinds, lightning—are varieties of the same thing: wind. Virgil catches the theory in a single image, the great volcano with the winds rumbling underneath, striving to escape:

> hic vasto rex Aeolus antro
> luctantis ventos tempestatesque sonoras
> imperio premit ac vinclis et carcere fremat.
> illi indignantes magno cum murmure montis
> circum claustra fremunt.

> In his enormous cave King Aeolus
> restrains the wrestling winds, loud hurricanes;
> he tames and sways them with his chains and prison.

They rage in indignation at their cages;
the mountain answers with a mighty roar.

[1.52–56]

Juno's offer and Aeolus' reply sketch the evaporation cycle which is the basis for all storms and precipitation.[49] In his commentary Servius notes the relevant equations (to 1.78), Aeolus (wind) replies to Juno (air) as servant to mistress (1.76–80); i.e., winds result from air movements. Wind in turn condenses air into clouds: *consurgunt venti, atque in nubem cogitur aër* (5.20, "Winds rise, and the air thickens into cloud").[50] Air, a wet element and now contracted, becomes water drops, which by their weight fall downward.[51] Juno accordingly promises Aeolus one of her nymphs in marriage, i.e., rainwater from clouds.[52] The marriage suggests the dependence of wind on watery movement, as water will become air and start the exhalation cycle over again. So the interchange represents process, the way a storm arises, and at the same time represents the modus operandi peculiar to air; for, as Servius explains at 7.311, Juno normally works through intermediaries:

> Quod autem Iuno ubique alieno uti introducitur auxilio, physicum est: natura enim aeris per se nihil facit, nisi aliena coniunctione, ventorum scilicet, qui creant nubes et pluvias.

> That Juno, however, is everywhere brought in using the aid of another is "physical." For air naturally by itself does nothing, except by conjunction with another, as with the winds, which make clouds and showers.

Hence her principal servant is Iris, who consistently trails a rainbow behind her, as she never does in Homer.[53]

The other mythological figures fit this meteorological scheme. The great storm in *Odyssey* 5 which gave Virgil the technical details for his description had ended awkwardly for the allegorists. Athena puts all the winds to sleep except Boreas, who blows Odysseus to Phaiakia (5.382–87). Athena's intervention fits her role as Odysseus' protectress but not her allegorical significance, as she is a psychological symbol and should not function in a physical reading of the scene.[54] Virgil instead has Neptune stop the storm; i.e., it ends when the clouds, cooled into rain, have returned to the sea. Thus the god brings back the sun (*Ae.* 1.143). Jupiter sits high above and does not interfere. With the cold season beginning, his power declines. The ether is nevertheless mental (Stoic fashion), and Jove can see through to the end and calm a disturbed Venus. The favorable conjunction of two such planets itself signifies a good end for the Trojans.[55] Hidden by clouds, the ethereal mind still operates through its messenger, Mercury, and its designs will be fulfilled. A parallel myth in Hesiod explains the situation "physically" as the concealment of Zeus from Kronos or Time. Rain falls endlessly to the ground in winter, but the water is absorbed, and the seed hidden in the ground prevails, the fiery principle which defeats the season and grows up as plants and trees.[56]

This scene shows how a poet reduces a complex development to a single incident or, in the case of Homer, what the interpreters assumed the poet did. The dialogue between Juno and Aeolus symbolizes both how a storm begins and a change of season.[57] Virgil needed such scenes because he had integrated the literal and symbolic levels of his epic. In Homer thunderstorms and seasonal change do not affect the warfare before Troy. They are fundamental, however, to the action of the Odyssean *Aeneid*. Virgil begins his epic with this condensed, symbolic method, because he must establish the season of the year, the winter which continues into book 5 and explains why the Trojans cannot reach Italy. After this initial scene brief descriptions and references are enough. Storms constantly frustrate Aeneas. Two thunderstorms drive him off course; another brings him to the cave with Dido; and a wind storm forces the Trojans to return to Sicily (5.10–34). We can attribute all these storms to the aerial goddess, though she is not always named or presented.[58] The first scene suffices.

Through her agents Aeolus and Iris Juno maintains winter at sea, and her power breaks only in the Iliadic *Aeneid*, when spring comes and the poet symbolizes this change by similar means: a dialogue which involves a supernatural power. A river god talks to Aeneas and the Tiber spread out into a lake (8.66–67). That is, Aeneas sails to Pallanteum on a river swollen with spring floods, and the change of season now favors the Trojans. The flood eliminates the difficulty of rowing against the current (8.66–67, 86–89), and the Trojans can land directly on the Palatine Hill.[59] These symbolic scenes allow Virgil to do what Homer never tried in the *Iliad:* to show the time of year and the change of season.[60]

We have seen the philosophical uses of this condensed, symbolic mode. We have yet to note its artistic advantages. Virgilian critics have long been aware of this technique, but they have seen it rather in psychological contexts. Heinze noted that Allecto makes visible a psychological development in Amata and functions as a kind of shorthand. Virgil abbreviates Amata's mental breakdown to a short scene of sixty lines (7.341–405). Both Heinze and Quinn have pointed to the episode of Eros and Dido, where Virgil similarly condenses into one scene the stages by which Dido falls in love (1.712–22).[61] In these judgments the latter critic tacitly employs modern criteria and assumes a contrast with the nineteenth-century novel, where we learn in detail what Virgil presents in a few lines. An ancient critic would have said the same thing in different words. He would have argued that allegory by its very nature condenses, presents much in little.[62]

The method likewise fits the requirements of epic. And here we must recall that such allegories symbolized invisible processes, what the epic poet could not represent because of his commitment to ἐνάργεια, his need "to represent phenomena in a fully externalized form, visible and palpable in all their parts, and completely fixed in their spatial and temporal relations."[63] We see Achilles and Aeneas in battle; we also see, with the same degree of clarity, Hera bathing and dressing in her bedroom. The epic poet had to visualize everything, even the invisible. Ares may cover seven acres when he falls in the theomachy, but, because the whole divine war was invisible, no human being saw him.[64] In the *Aeneid* we see Juno rage and bargain with Aeolus, the storm come, and Neptune intervene; but Ilioneus saw only the storm. The divine personae symbolize the invisible causes of the event and at the same time preserve the mimetic surface of the epic, as they interact as living beings. Virgil's innovation was to use such allegory for a seasonal change which he made fundamental to his plot. In the *Aeneid* mimesis and symbol merge.

Virgil's most unusual use of process allegory and condensation, however, was to achieve multiple meanings simultaneously, a usage which separates him from the traditions of Homeric criticism. He inherited condensation and the visible presentation of the invisible, but he seems to have invented polyvalency, at least for the epic. The riddles of Heraclitus the philosopher may be polyvalent, but the kind inherited by the Middle Ages and the Renaissance comes, rather, from the epic variety which Virgil devised for the *Aeneid*. Another storm scene exemplifies this innovation, the downpour which saves the Trojan fleet:

> vix haec ediderat cum effusis imbribus atra
> tempestas sine more furit tonitruque tremescunt
> ardua terrarum et campi; ruit aethere toto
> turbidus imber aqua densisque nigerrimus Austris,
> implenturque super puppes, semusta madescunt
> robora, restinctus donec vapor omnis et omnes
> quattuor amissis servatae a peste carinae.

> He had just said this
> when pouring rains, a lawless, furious
> dark tempest, rage across the hills and plains
> that tremble with the thunder; all the heavens
> let fall a murky storm of water, black
> with heavy south winds. From above the ships
> are filled, charred timbers soaked, until the heat
> and smoke are spent and all the hulls—except
> four lost—are rescued from that pestilence.
>
> [5.693–99]

This storm comes when Aeneas prays to Jove and thus indicates the breaking of the winter season, the turn toward spring. The warm ethereal element returns with the sun, and now all natural things, where they had previously hindered the Trojans, assist them. Their passage from Sicily to Italy is calm, and a light breeze wafts them from Cumae to the Tiber mouth. The river flood enables Aeneas to sail rapidly to Pallanteum, and sea nymphs push the relief fleet back to the beleaguered fort.

In another sense the rain signifies a confusion in Juno's actions. She sends Iris to stir the women to burn the ships, but the messenger goddess cannot come without a storm. We normally think of a rainbow appearing after a storm, but for the ancients it could be otherwise. She regularly precedes storms in the *Aeneid,* on this occasion and earlier, when she trails her colors over Dido's funeral pyre. Aeneas, who meanwhile watches the flames from mid-sea, immediately encounters a storm. Both events are described by the same phrase: *supra caput astitit* (4.702; 5.10, "she [it] stood over her [his] head").[65] So we can say that through the same agent Juno sets the ships on fire and extinguishes the conflagration.

This confusion in the goddess manifests her polyvalency. She operates here not only as the Queen of Air but as the deity who punishes her enemies by madness.[66] The scene combines perfectly both levels, the cosmological and the psychological. As air, the goddess blows Iris to the ships (5.606–7), and her servant comes and goes appropriately by a rainbow path. Among the women, however, she stirs up mutiny, tossing a burning firebrand into the Trojan vessels. Here, as Servius remarks (to 5.606), she brings discord (an etymological pun: Iris / ἔρις, strife), and her torch belongs later to Allecto, when the fiend stirs up wrath in Turnus' breast:

> sic effata facem iuveni coniecit et atro
> lumine fumantis fixit sub pectore taedas.

And saying this, she cast a torch at Turnus,
fixing the firebrand within his breast,
and there it smoked with murky light. . . .

[7.456–57]

At the close the two levels, psychological and physical, converge in one line. Iris suddenly departs, cutting a great rainbow under the clouds, and the women, *vero attonitae monstris actaeque furore*, ("truly stunned by the marvels and driven by madness," 5.659), burn the ships.

Virgil came to polyvalency by artistic necessity. His model for the divine scenes was the *Odyssey*, with its small cast of deities, rather than the *Iliad*. Single figures had to fulfill more varied artistic demands, and Juno acquired the characteristics which Heraclitus assigned to her son Ares, *furor* or rage.[67] She thus becomes polyvalent with applications to both cosmology and psychology, and so the goddess who brings in the winter storms for the Odyssean *Aeneid* stirs up war frenzy at the beginning of the Iliadic half. We move from what Brooks Otis calls the outer to the inner storm, from Aeolus to Allecto.[68] This shift, however, is a matter of degree. Following the trend toward consistency that he found in Homeric criticism, Virgil makes Juno both air and fury throughout the poem. We have seen that the appropriate epithets follow the aerial goddess through the war as well as through Aeneas' voyage, so she can decoy Turnus from the battle by a cloud shape (10.634 ff).[69] The converse also applies, for she is wrath consistently in the Odyssean *Aeneid*. The descriptive phrases once more indicate this persistent psychological dimension: *saevus, furor, dolor*. Virgil repeats the phrase *saevae memorem Iunois ob iram* (1.4, "because of the wrath of fierce, unforgetting Juno") almost immediately, as the memory of Paris and Ganymede stimulates *saevi dolores* (1.25, "fierce sorrows"). On the Scaean Gates she marshals the armies and is both *saevissima* and *furens*:

> . . . hic Iuno Scaeas saevissima portas
> prima tenet sociumque furens a navibus agmen
> ferro accincta vocat.

> and here the first to hold the Scaean gates
> is fiercest Juno; girt with iron, she
> calls furiously to the fleet for more
> Greek troops.

[2.612–14]

The same terms, of course, cluster about her in the Iliadic *Aeneid*. It is the *saeva Iovis coniunx* ("the fierce wife of Jove") who stands, *acri fixa dolore* ("fixed with cutting sorrow"), at the sight of the Trojans arrived in Latium (7.287, 291). In the Olympian council she replies to Venus *acta furore gravi* (10.63, "driven by oppressive wrath"). She is always both *aër* and *furor*.

This double reference allows Virgil to move between seemingly disparate topics, to pass from one analogy to another. Simile and metaphor unexpectedly juxtapose or equate different sciences and subject matters. Pöschl notes the first storm, where weather suddenly becomes politics: "In the Neptune episode, for example, a natural event explained by means of a political event serves to show that nature is a symbol of political organization."[70] I would add the brilliant simile Virgil uses to characterize war frenzy, for there we pass directly from *furor* to *aër,* the wind blowing up a storm at sea:[71]

> fluctus uti primo coepit cum albescere vento
> paulatim sese tollit mare et altius undas
> erigit, inde imo consurgit ad aethera fundo.

> as when a wave, beneath the wind's first breath,
> begins to whiten; slow by slow, the sea
> will lift its combers higher until, at last,
> it climbs to heaven from its lowest depths.

[7.527–30]

Such switching back and forth characterizes developed allegory, and I have noted elsewhere an example of it in the *Divina commedia*.[72] The author does not allow his reader to find a single rationale for a figure or scene but forces him to consider it on many levels.

The poet can change topics or talk about several simultaneously because he assumes that different sciences can have the same *form*. Analogies in one are then valid in another. Consider two examples in which meteorology and psychology meet. Amata feigns a Bacchic frenzy, drives the women out into the country, and so gets her daughter away from the Trojans (7.373–405). She feigns madness, but we know that she is clinically insane.[73] Allecto beats her with the goads of Bacchus, and the epic simile clearly expresses her hopeless case (7.378–83). It also crosses patterns. Boys whip a *turbo* (here a "top") and watch fascinated as it spins round and round and is borne through curved spaces. The analogy and the term could characterize a hurricane as well. Latinus provides the second example, when the *furor* for war spreads to all the people and leaves him isolated. Amata and her women, Turnus and his soldiers come to the city, and the king cries, *ferimurque procella!* (7.594, "We are carried by the storm"). By metaphor we return to the weather goddess, who now intervenes directly and breaks open the Temple of Janus. With such figures these scenes acquire depth, and the symbols are multilayered.[74]

Through Juno the poet diagrams a double reality and more than that. We have not begun to consider her political applications, the military goddess of the enemy, be it Greece or Carthage, who must be persuaded to settle in Rome, where she will bear shield and lance and protect the city from the foreigner.[75] Enough has been said to prove that Virgil made his divine scenes polysemous. He learned from the critics of Homer the necessary symbolic language and the need for consistency in the use of terms and for harmony between literal and figurative levels. They did not, however, teach him to make his symbols double or triple leveled. Heraclitus did not decode the *Iliad* and the *Odyssey* in this fashion. Polyvalency in Homeric criticism is rather a matter of historical accident. It comes from the bewildering variety of exegeses done by different people over a long period of time. The *Aeneid* is thus a unique achievement, and Virgil by his genius transformed a whole tradition and established the great model for creative allegory in the West.

Virgil did another thing with Juno which stimulated experiments one stage beyond his own. When he made the goddess central to his plot and at the same time polyvalent, he encouraged an allegorical reading of the *whole* epic. Juno focuses a set of related meanings which apply to many people and scenes. Dido, Amata, Turnus, the entire Latin people, all fall into *furor*. Juno expresses a psychological state which these very diverse people share. The same symbol and the same word apply, whatever the situation. Love, war frenzy, avarice[76] are all varieties of *furor*, and the same models apply as well to various stages of *furor*. Once they are possessed by this passion, for example, the two women become maenads. Dido goes through Carthage like a bacchant (4.301), and mad Amata feigns a Dionysiac ecstasy (7.385–405). Virgil's use of analogical patterns is so systematic, so thorough, that his medieval commentators allegorized the whole epic. We need not read the human characters symbolically, but we can understand why a Fulgentius or a Landino did so. Moreover, among creative writers Virgil's treatment of Juno led to experiments in continuous allegory, something which the *Aeneid* itself is not.[77] Dante calls him master, and the *Aeneid* stands behind the great examples of continuous allegory by medieval and Renaissance writers.

Technically, however, the allegory in the *Aeneid* remains discontinuous. We treat the gods, and not Aeneas, as symbols. This limitation likewise had its effect, for the examples of continuous allegory are few. The norm reflects, rather, the origins of allegory in Homeric criticism. The gods, with their enormous power and splendid accoutrements, signal allegory. Later it would be the fays and witches of romance: the evil Falerina of Boiardo's poem, with her garden of wondrous deceptions, Alcina on her island. These scenes also gave to epic and romance their marvels, and an interpretative procedure became identified with an aesthetic principle.

Consider this simile with which Homer describes the movement of Hera's chariot:

῍Ως ἔφατ', οὐδ' ἀπίθησε θεὰ λευκώλενος ῞Ηρη,
μάστιξεν δ' ἵππους· τὼ δ' οὐκ ἀέκοντε πετέσθην
μεσσηγὺς γαίης τε καὶ οὐρανοῦ ἀστερόεντος.
ὅσσον δ' ἠεροειδὲς ἀνὴρ ἴδεν ὀφθαλμοῖσιν
ἥμενος ἐν σκοπιῇ, λεύσσων ἐπὶ οἴνοπα πόντον,
τόσσον ἐπιθρῴσκουσι θεῶν ὑψηχέες ἵπποι.

So he spoke, nor did the goddess of the white arms, Hera,
disobey, but lashed on the horses, and they winged their way
   unreluctant
through the space between the earth and the starry heaven.
As far as into the hazing distance a man can see with
his eyes, who sits in his eyrie gazing on the wine-blue water,
as far as this is the stride of the gods' proud neighing horses.

[Il 5.767–72]

When the horses leap, they cover as much space as the mist or ἀήρ, seen by a lookout when nothing impedes his view (e.g., bT to Il. 5.770–72). Longinus adds that with another leap the horses will be out of the world (9.5). The comparison is sublime in the technical sense. Hera measures the cosmos with her horses, and the descent of her flaming chariot makes the scene fantastic. Such wonder had a clear artistic function. Aristotle said that the epic poet could have more of the marvelous in his plot than the tragedian, who had to represent his actions onstage (Poetics 24.1460a8). The supreme marvelous, however, were the gods: Hera in her chariot; a wrathful Apollo, his arrows clattering, as he descends angrily from Olympus; the daughter of the sun, singing alone in a wood and turning human beings into animals; Allecto blowing a shepherd's horn heard as far south as the Lake of Nemi and as far north as Umbria. And these scenes symbolized the unseen: air, the causes of a plague, a process of moral change, the spread of fear.[78] They were allegories. By the late Renaissance the two notions, Aristotelian and allegorical, had coalesced. Both Tasso and Boileau assumed that the marvelous was fundamental to epic, what raised it above history, and they both interpreted this marvelous allegorically.[79]

The medieval and Renaissance writers inherited from Virgil and the Homeric critics a tradition of allegory. They assumed that marvelous scenes symbolized and condensed complex and unseen processes, that such polyvalent figures and actions made epic and romance philosophical. This assumption is the classical basis for Falerina's Garden, the enchanted wood of *Gerusalemme liberata,* the kinds of scene which will be studied through much of this book.

2   Landino's Virgil

Not the least in that brilliant circle we call the Florentine Platonists, Landino devoted his major energies to the two chief poems which he knew: the *Aeneid* and the *Divina commedia*. He did for literature what Ficino, by his work on Plato and Plotinus, accomplished for philosophy and what Pico began to do for the Bible with the *Heptaplus*.[1] The *Camaldulensian Dialogues,* which Landino finished in 1473–74 and published in 1480, received during the period many printings[2] and together with his rhetorical and grammatical commentary to Virgil's text formed a lens through which his contemporaries could view Aeneas' adventures. The nature of Landino's influence befits the learned circle of his friends, for in the *Camaldulensian Dialogues* he included as much direct philosophizing as exegesis. In fact, he so intermingled the two that they are virtually inextricable. Landino's Virgil is a philosopher and his poem a representation of the contemplative life. Aeneas' many voyages, his battles, his love, all figure forth an inward reality, the psychic drama of a man's growth *out* of this world.

This allegory differs from that which has been discussed in two respects: it is continued and it is Platonic. Continuity was a medieval development from tendencies in Virgil's own allegory, tendencies which were briefly analyzed in the last chapter. The second difference concerns us now. In Virgil's Juno we have seen that an interpreter could have found either moral or physical allegory.[3] Landino chose the moral, and this choice bespeaks the influence of Plato.

Landino inherited this Platonized Virgil at the end of a thousand-year tradition which goes back to the Homeric critics, Numenius and Porphyry.[4] In this respect he complements Ficino, for the two Florentines carried into the Renaissance the exegetical methods and much of the outlook which characterized the last stages of pagan culture in the Empire. In their literary studies the writers of the Late Empire had concerned themselves mostly with the adventures of the soul, here or in the other world; and, while they did not reject the old physical readings, they either ignored or thoroughly transformed them. I will attempt through Landino to understand this Platonic Virgil, to see that such an interpretation has a basis in the *Aeneid* and a clear method. My discussion consequently will have a double focus, on the poem as well as on the dialogue. As the latter is unfamiliar to most readers, I have included an outline of Landino's interpretation in an appendix.[5]

I must, however, first remove a possible misconception. The tradition of Virgilian criticism would seem to indicate a syncretic, not Platonic, philosophy in the poet. From his biographers we know that Virgil studied under Siro the Epicurean. Later critics, however, assumed that the *Aeneid* was Platonic: Macrobius, Landino, and we might add "Bernardus Silvestris" and Petrarch.[6] Today we stress more often the Stoic in the *Aeneid*, something Landino reluctantly had to admit:

> Virgilius igitur quamvis in reliquis a Platone suo nunquam discedat: tamen cum vidisset Chrysippum in eo quem de natura deorum scripsit libro Orphei / Musei / Hesiodi / atque Homeri fabellas ita interpretari: ut idem priscos olim poetas sensise conetur ostendere: quod multis postea annis stoici senserunt statuit hac in re / ne ab iis poetis / quorum similis esse cupiebat dissimilis putaretur: et ipse porticum fulcire ac stoicis adherere.

> In other matters Vergil never departs from his Plato; but seeing that Chrysippus (in his book on the nature of the gods) had interpreted the myths of Orpheus, Musaeus, Hesiod, and Homer in such a way as to show that these ancient poets thought the same thing that the Stoics thought many years afterwards in this regard, and not wanting to be thought different from the poets he desired to emulate, he sticks with the Stoics and supports their philosophy. [LviR]

There are two ways in which Virgil could generate these differing interpretations without contradiction. He may have held a syncretic position, and therefore the contradictions may be apparent rather than real. We have long known that terms such as "Stoic" and "Platonic" could be misleading, that thinkers in the Empire often did not maintain "purist" systems, any more than the "Neoplatonists" later. The Academy by Cicero's day had borrowed much from the Stoics,[7] and Philip Merlan has shown that the common distinction among Plato, Aristotle, and the Neoplatonists in the Empire cannot be maintained historically. Plato's first generation of pupils resembles in many ideas the school of Plotinus, Aristotle's version of Plato reads like a Neoplatonic system, and Platonism marks much of Aristotle's own metaphysical thought.[8] In the Empire Porphyry was an Aristotelian in Plotinus' school and wrote an introduction to the *Categories*.[9] The school terms are a convenience for us, ways to indicate quickly a philosophical background and the general cast of a person's thought. Thus, when we say that X, a Platonist, followed the Stoics on a particular issue and the Peripatetics on something else, the statement does not necessarily indicate contradiction in X's thinking. Servius talks of Epicurean, Platonic, and Stoic elements in Virgil, but the critics must still go on to debate whether these elements coalesce in a consistent system or not.

This caveat applies a fortiori to the Florentines. Ficino and Pico both were trained Aristotelians,[10] and on ethics, which was the topic of the *Camaldulensian Dialogues,* Landino is explicitly syncretic. He derives from Cicero the notion that of the four principal schools in antiquity all but the Epicureans agreed on the moral end of man. He argues this point on the second day and is careful to refute the Epicureans.[11] His essential definition, man is his mind, and its corollary, virtue alone suffices, were shared by both Platonists and Stoics.[12] Landino's Platonism shows more clearly in his historical claim that in ethics Plato and Socrates provide the essential basis for all later thought.[13] Thus his discovery of a Platonic Virgil is not necessarily so far removed from the Stoic Virgil of modern criticism. Both assume a syncretist position, and Landino himself speaks from an "impure" one. The argument involves the overall cast of Virgil's thought, and here we are talking about degrees. I will, however, make the following argument for a Platonic Virgil as strongly as possible, as at present we do not make this assumption, and it is the principal thesis which separates Landino and his medieval predecessors from us.

My discussion will have three parts, all derived from statements made by Anchises in his Elysium lecture. In this, the sole passage of direct philosophy in the epic, the poet expressed three theories normally recognized as Platonic. Augustine, for example, cites the speech regularly in *The City of God,* when he analyzes or refutes Platonic opinions.[14] I will discuss the two which relate closely to each other, the assumptions that man is a soul imprisoned in a body (or in hell) and that he has a consequent need to escape through a process of purgation.[15] I will first sketch what the Platonic critics did with these two theories. Next I will consider how the poem itself supports the first proposition and finally how Landino's dialectic develops the second.

Anchises expresses the two propositions seriatim:

730   igneus est ollis vigor et caelestis origo
        seminibus, quantum non corpora noxia tardant
        terrenique hebetant artus moribundaque membra.
        hinc metuunt cupiuntque, dolent gaudentque, neque auras
        dispiciunt clausae tenebris et carcere caeco.
735   quin et supremo cum lumine vita reliquit,
        non tamen omne malum miseris nec funditus omnes
        corporeae excedunt pestes, penitusque necesse est
        multa diu concreta modis inolescere miris.
        ergo exercentur poenis veterumque malorum
740   supplicia expendunt: aliae panduntur inanes
        suspensae ad ventos, aliis sub gurgite vasto
        infectum eluitur scelus aut exuritur igni—
        quisque suos patimur manis; exinde per amplum
        mittimur Elysium et pauci laeta arva tenemus—
745   donec longa dies perfecto temporis orbe
        concretam exemit labem, purumque relinquit
        aetherium sensum atque aurai simplicis ignem.

                        Fiery energy
        is in these seeds, their source is heavenly;
        but they are dulled by harmful bodies, blunted
        by their own earthly limbs, their mortal members.
        Because of these, they fear and long, and sorrow
        and joy, they do not see the light of heaven;
        they are dungeoned in their darkness and blind prison.
        And when the final day of life deserts them,
        then, even then, not every ill, not all
        the plagues of body quit them utterly;
        and this must be, for taints so long congealed
        cling fast and deep in extraordinary
        ways. Therefore they are schooled by punishment
        and pay with torments for their old misdeeds:
        some there are purified by air, suspended
        and stretched before the empty winds; for some
        the stain of guilt is washed away beneath
        a mighty whirlpool or consumed by fire.
        First each of us must suffer his own Shade;
        then we are sent through wide Elysium—
        a few of us will gain the Fields of Gladness—
        until the finished cycle of the ages,

with lapse of days, annuls the ancient stain
and leaves the power of ether pure in us,
the fire of spirit simple and unsoiled.

[*Ae*. 6.730–47]

Servius (on *Ae*. 6.703) points to the influence of the *Phaedo* myth, and this dialogue parallels Anchises' speech in three respects. First, there is the comparison of the body and a prison, a familiar Platonic analogy given special relevance in this dialogue, as the discussion takes place in jail (62B, also 82E–83D).[16] Virgil translates φρουρά as *carcer*, which Cicero, another Platonist, used for the same Greek word.[17] The body poisons the soul, which must therefore go through a purification in the other world, great sinners in the streams of Phlegethon (fire) and Cocytus (water). Virgil makes the punishment general and adds a third element, air. Finally, the *Phaedo* helps to explain Anchises' remark that each soul must suffer its own shade. Our genius or guardian daemon leads us to the place of judgment (107D–E), and Plutarch in *De genio Socratis* developed this notion and argued that each soul after death is punished by this daemon. Servius records a further elaboration of this conception. The *manes* are the double angels we have from birth, who persuade us to good and evil.[18]

Later Platonists identified these two propositions, and this identification explains much in Landino's dialogue. The other world, the place of punishment, is this world. Numenius, whom we know through Porphyry and Proclus, brought about this change in his explication of the *Odyssey*.[19] The identification in turn involves a set of further assumptions, all of which Landino inherited:

1. The soul, imprisoned or entombed in the body, has its true home elsewhere, among the stars.[20]
2. This situation is explained cosmologically by the notion that the soul descends to this world through the constellation of Cancer and leaves again through Capricorn.[21]
3. A corollary is that Hades is in the space below the sphere of fixed stars, and narratives about hell must therefore apply to our earthly existence.
4. The rivers of hell, which ring Hades, then symbolize the soul's fall (Porphyry).[22]
5. And Troy symbolizes man's sensual condition, what he must leave (Proclus).[23]
6. The horizontal journey of the epic hero consequently diagrams a vertical movement, that of the soul out of matter and upward.

Individual applications vary considerably, both between Landino and his predecessors and among the earlier Neoplatonists, but the broad outline is the same, as are the philosophical assumptions.[24]

Landino found this material indirectly. He did not read *The Cave of the Nymphs*[25] but learned the ideas of the Greek critics from Macrobius, who may have suggested to him the exact identification of hell with the human body.[26] Landino cites Macrobius with the greatest respect,[27] and he probably received from the *Commentary on Scipio's Dream* the inspiration for his whole project. Throughout, Macrobius assumed tacitly that a Platonic exegesis would explain Virgil as well as his own subject, Cicero, and that the two greatest Latin writers shared the same philosophy. Porphyry, whom he imitated, had similarly brought together Homer and Plato. Thus Landino would complete the scheme, and his *Camaldulensian Dialogues* would prove Macrobius' argument and do for Virgil what the earlier critic had done for Cicero.

He found some of these ideas already applied to Virgil by Macrobius' younger contemporary, Servius Grammaticus, whose commentary followed the *Aeneid* like a shadow[28] and which Landino himself reprinted in 1488. Servius assumes that the *Aeneid* is full of *scientia*, book 6 especially. While Virgil says some things simply and others for historical reasons, much of the *Aeneid* concerns the deep *scientia* of the philosophers, theologians, and Egyptians (proem to *Ae.* 6). This philosophy includes much of the syncretic and Neoplatonic thought current in Servius' circle: the descent of the soul through the spheres and the location of Hades here on earth (to *Ae.* 6.127, 578). Servius concludes his analysis of book 6 with a long paraphrase of the *Phaedo* myth, which he argues Virgil adumbrated in the *Georgics*. Here we have many of the specifics of Landino's interpretation. The soul descends into the body, forgets its nature, and must go through a series of purgations to return. The body obstructs this action, and Servius explains the situation by an analogy, that of the lamp shut up (to *Ae.* 6.724). The power of its light remains the same, but the impediment must be removed in order for its rays to shine forth. So the soul, though its face be beautiful, must cleanse itself of the mud of material contagion.[29] This purgative conception of the human condition provides the essential basis of Landino's dialectic.

Landino draws the logical inference from this set of assumptions. If hell is the human body or this world, then a trip to hell actually signifies a contemplation of man here. Aeneas' descent into Hades is the mind's careful investigation, with learning for a guide, of the vices incident to the sensual condition of man (KiiV). The process, though intellectual, is not without danger. Aeneas needs the Golden Bough or wisdom because

> est enim Proserpina ipsa animi pars: quae nihil praeter sensus continet: ad quam si sine sapientia accederemus / nullum praeterea remedium daretur: quo minus de nobis actum esset. Illa enim irretiti / nulla unquam esset spes redeundi.

> Proserpina is that very part of the soul which embraces nothing but the senses; and if we were to approach her without wisdom, there would be no help afterwards for what would be done to us. For those who are trapped by her there is never any hope of returning. [KivR]

Tartarus or deep hell, the final vision of evil, is the concrete realization of this warning. Its triple walls, which even the gods cannot penetrate, show how a man damns himself while still alive. The three walls symbolize the stages of sin: the conception, the act, and finally the habit. With traditional Scholastic subtlety Landino has his speaker, Leon Battista Alberti, explain how people in fixed habits of action cannot be helped, even by God (LiiiV–ivR). His interlocutor, Lorenzo de' Medici, summarizes the position of such people aptly: "Erit igitur ... amissum in illis liberum mentis arbitrium ut et si velint ad virtutem redire nequeant" (LivR "In them the free will of the mind has been lost, and even if they want to return to virtue, they cannot"). Aeneas, of course, does not enter Tartarus, as "qui vitia speculantur/ non versantur inter vitia" ("those who contemplate vices do not become involved in them").

Purification or damnation in the other world now occurs here, and this conception enabled Numenius, Landino, and other critics to allegorize entire poems. The *Aeneid* provides a clear example, for the hero's career parallels the adventures of a soul in the other world, as Anchises describes them. Aeneas wishes to find his true home, where he has never been; goes through a series of trials, of suffering and renunciation; but at the end comes to Italy and Elysium. His story reflects the mythic tales traditionally allegorized by critics and therefore can be interpreted in the same way as the monsters and powers of the other world. Landino reads the *whole* poem allegorically.[30]

The equation inherited from Numenius likewise explains the emphasis in such criticism. Aeneas' visit to hell takes up more than half of Landino's exegesis. The author carefully explains everything here, quite unlike his earlier procedure. Nor was he the first: the sixth book of the *Aeneid* likewise received the most attention in the major medieval commentaries, the *De continentia Virgiliana* of Fulgentius and the commentary commonly attributed to Bernardus Silvestris. Because this world and the other mirrored each other, a katabasis could contain the whole poem in concentrated form.[31]

So far I have sketched the development of a critical outlook and its locus classicus in the *Aeneid*. Now I must show that the *Aeneid* elsewhere supports the notion that we are imprisoned in bodies and that the philosophical unraveling of Anchises' speech has its own inner logic. I will begin with the poem and its relation to an ancient philosophical dispute.

Epistemology was one of the principal issues which divided philosophers of the late Hellenistic period. It turned on the objections made by the Platonist Arcesilas and his followers, Carneades, Clitomachus, and Philo, who had carried the negative dialectic of Socrates and Plato so far that they had in effect founded another school, the so-called New Academy, which maintained a complete epistemological skepticism. By the time of Virgil, however, a reaction had set in; and Antiochus, leaning heavily on the Stoics, had revived what was called the "Old Academy," turning back to principles in Plato and Socrates which he thought his teachers had lost. Cicero in the *Academica* followed the skepticism of Arcesilas and provides much of the evidence concerning the school.[32]

The other schools had to account for this Platonic skepticism, and we will see that the *Aeneid*, as a philosophical poem, carefully reproduces the relevant data. This procedure does not commit Virgil to a Platonic theory, He merely renders the problems common to all the schools, which a Stoic would have answered differently from an Academician. Later critics, of course, would have found their own syncretic Platonism reinforced by Virgil's fidelity to a critique, which earlier Platonists had originated; and we can begin to understand why Macrobius or Landino would see Cicero and Virgil together as exponents of the same school. The Cicero of the *Academica* defends a Platonist position, and the *Aeneid* reflects the same polemic.

My argument will have two parts. First, I will discuss perception in the *Aeneid* and show that Virgil presents us with the kind of experiences, especially those in the vague region between sleep and waking, that generated Academic skepticism. I will then show that such scenes are crucial to the epic, that they concern the oracles and prophecies which guide Aeneas, particularly his descent to Hades and interview with Anchises.

I will begin my analysis with the evidence of the senses. Critics both ancient and modern have stressed how impressionistic yet visually accurate Virgil made the brief descriptions allowed him by epic convention. In the *Saturnalia* Macrobius has Caecina Albinus observe that in the following description the phrase *tremulo sub lumine* is *de imagine rei ipsius expressum* ("taken from the appearance of what is actually seen"):[33]

> ...postquam alta quierunt
> aequora, tendit iter velis portumque relinquit.
> aspirant aurae in noctem nec candida cursus
> luna negat, splendet tremulo sub lumine pontus.

> Aeneas, when the high waves have stilled,
> sets out his sails to voyage, quits the harbor.
> Night falls; the winds breathe fair; the brilliant moon
> does not deny his way; the waters gleam
> beneath the quivering light.
>
> [*Ae.* 7.6–9]

The waves, stirred by the breeze, make a wavering mirror for the moon so that its *reflected* light seems to tremble. Precise impressionism of this kind extends as well to Virgil's rare uses of color. Consider the following description:

> ut pelagus tenuere rates nec iam amplius ulla
> occurrit tellus, maria undique et undique caelum,
> olli caeruleus supra caput astitit imber
> noctem hiememque ferens et inhorruit unda tenebris.

> But when the fleet had reached the open waters,
> with land no longer to be seen—the sky
> was everywhere and everywhere the sea—
> a blue-black cloud ran overhead; it brought
> the night and storm and breakers rough in darkness.
>
> [5.8–11]

Kenneth Quinn argues that this picture is correct even to the time of day, the blue rain which comes at sunset time.[34] We might add the precise mention of the season and the perception of the waves "shaking with darkness." We apprehend the storm emotionally, as if we were on the ship.

Servius sees in this subjectivism an explanation for Virgil's hyperbole. In the first storm the following phrase characterizes as much the frightened sailors as the objective reality:

eripiunt subito nubes caelumque diemque
Teucrorum ex oculis.

Then, suddenly, the cloud banks snatch away
the sky and daylight from the Trojans' eyes.

[1.88–89]

The sudden winds blew clouds into one sector of the sky, the direction in which the sailors were anxiously looking, so Virgil could say that the clouds took away the day. That is, Virgil's descriptions reflect not just the observed object but that object viewed from a particular, emotional viewpoint. So Aeneas is *pulcherrimus* on the hunt (Servius to 4.141) because Dido is in love. Brooks Otis, perhaps inspired by Servius' remarks, says that we experience the whole of book 1, the first storm, Venus, Carthage, *through* Aeneas and therefore apprehend everything subjectively.[35]

To express these observations more precisely, Virgil carefully presents not just shapes viewed from a particular point but the way objects seem to move and look when *seen* from that subjective standpoint. Servius makes this attention to motion particularly clear in his observations on the epic formulas which Virgil uses several times in book 3, as Aeneas sails from one place to another. Let us consider the phrases involving *appareo* first. When the Trojans leave Crete, "nec iam amplius ullae / apparent terrae" (192–93, "nor do any more lands appear"). The movement, however, is that of the Trojans, sailing away. Soon after, an island appears in the water: "iam medio apparet fluctu nemorosa Zacynthos" (270, "now in the middle of the waves appears wooded Zacynthos"). Camarina in Sicily gets the same term (701). A variant concerns Mount Etna: "tum procul e fluctu Trinacria cernitur Aetna" (554, "then, far from the flood, Sicilian Etna is seen"). The Trojans see the top of the mountain long before they perceive the Sicilian coast. To the Trojans things simply appear, though we know that they are the ones in motion. The first sight of Italy is even more interesting. The Temple of Minerva first appears in the standard phrase: "templumque apparet in arce Minervae" (531), but then it flees back from the shore, as the Trojans sail closer: "refugitque ab litore templum" (536). Servius explains that either the temple, seen from far out at sea, seems to move away as the Trojans get nearer, or its hill seems to grow taller (to *Ae*. 3.536). Either way the phrase is remarkable for its economy and precision, and the second explanation also has its

standard expression: "se . . . attolere." Islands seem to raise themselves up out of the water.[36] We need not be surprised that, according
to the *Vita Focae* (102–4), Virgil set out on his fatal voyage to see
things in Greece at first hand, *oculo dictante,* a gesture certainly appropriate for a poet so concerned to intimate how things appear and
move in relation to an observer.

Such visual experiences are misleading. Virgil presents cases in
which mountains seem to move and temples to run, perfect illustrations
of deceptive sense impressions. And in fact his epic formulas fit easily
into the negative list Cicero uses to undermine the validity of all sense
impressions. In the *Academica* he points out to one of his companions a
ship in the Gulf of Cumae and says, "Videsne navem illam? stare nobis
videtur, at iis qui in navi sunt moveri haec villa" (2.25.81, "Do you see
yonder ship? To us she appears to be at anchor, whereas to those on
board her this house appears in motion"). Little separates this example
from Virgil's epic formulas. They correspond perfectly to the central
proposition of the New Academicians, "qui omnia non tam esse quam
videri volunt" (*Academica* 2.14.44, "who hold that everything does
not so much exist as seem to exist").

To support their skeptical epistemology, the philosophers of the
New Academy stressed dreams and borderline cases, situations in
which deception, illusion, and uncertainty bedevil the senses. And here
they would have in the *Aeneid* an encyclopedia of such borderline
cases. In a typical scene characters blunder about in the dark or guess
uncertainly at objects by the light of the moon: Nisus and Euryalus in
the dark wood, in book 3 the Trojans sailing blind before the storm, the
dark dust cloud which veils Camilla's cavalry battle, Aeneas hardly
able to discern the features of Palinurus and Dido in the Hades murk,
and the uncertain visions which shimmer in the moonlight: the Penates,
Father Tiber,[37] the ship nymphs. Perhaps the best example is that of
the priest of Albunea, who in the silent night sees images flying in
strange ways and hears voices (7.82–91). Now these visions, particularly, inhabit the vague area between sleep and waking and would
provide the Academician with his strongest evidence. Aeneas is awake
at the tiller when he sees the nymphs, asleep by Tiber bank for his
conversation with the river god, and stretched on his bed when the
Penates appear by window light and where he claims he was awake.[38]
The list could be lengthened.

Cicero's *Lucullus* complained bitterly that the New Academy ignored healthy, normal experience and drew its evidence from prophetic dreams and oracles, in which the mind could be stimulated by
itself (*Academica* 2.15.47–48). And in the dialogue he forced Cicero to

defend the sensations of the sleeper, the mad, and the drunk (2.27.88).
In this respect an Academician could make a devastating case out of
Virgil's hero, ghost haunted, dream obsessed, who makes all his im-
portant decisions on the basis of spectral evidence.

The following quotation from the *Academica* is pertinent here. Arcesilas is engaged with Zeno, the founder of the Stoics, in an imaginary
argument about sensation:

> Tum illum [Zeno] ita definisse, ex eo quod esset, sicut esset,
> impressum et signatum et effictum. Post requisitum, etiamne
> si euisdem modi esset visum verum quale et falsum. Hic
> Zenonem vidisse acute nullum esse visum quod percipi posset,
> si id tale esset ab eo quod est ut eiusdem modi ab eo quod non
> est posset esse. Recte consensit Arcesilas ad definitionem ad-
> ditum, neque enim falsum percipi posse neque verum si esset
> tale quale vel falsum.

> Hereupon no doubt Zeno defined it as follows, a presentation
> impressed and sealed and moulded from a real object, in con-
> formity with its reality. There followed the further question,
> did this hold good even if a true presentation was of exactly the
> same form as a false one? At this time I imagine Zeno was
> sharp enough to see that if a presentation proceeding from a
> real thing was of such a nature that one proceeding from a
> non-existent thing could be of the same form, there was no
> presentation that could be perceived. Arcesilas agreed that this
> addition to the definition was correct, for it was impossible to
> perceive either a false presentation or a true one if a true one
> had such a character as even a false one might have. [2.24.77]

If a false impression resembles a true, or a true a false one, or if a false
impression hypothetically *could* resemble a true impression, then such
an impression at best must be classed as probable. But all true impressions could have false simulacra; therefore all sense evidence is
merely probable, can never be trusted completely, and objective certainty becomes impossible. This is the principal contention of the New
Academy and once more finds ample support in the *Aeneid*.

Consider Aeneas' frustration before his mother in the first book. He
asks why she deceives her child with false appearances (407–8), and
she responds characteristically by cloaking the two Trojans in a dark
cloud. Venus has practical reasons for this action, but philosophically
the scene is paradigmatic. Think of the Trojans disguised in Greek
armor, killing enemies and slaughtered by their own countrymen. Better yet are the dream visions, that in-between area of perception which

the Academy stressed in its polemic. Servius reads a number of them in such a way that they exactly fit Arcesilas' argument. Here is a typical example:

> huic se *forma* dei vultu redeuntis eodem
> obtulit in somnis rursusque ita *visa* monere est,
> omnia Mercurio similis, vocemque coloremque
> et crinis flavos et membra decora iuventae....

> And in his sleep the form of the god
> returned to him with that same countenance—
> resembling Mercury in everything:
> his voice and coloring and yellow hair
> and all his handsome body, a young man's....
>
> [4.556–59; emphasis mine]

Something in the form of the god, something just like Mercury, something which *seems*. *Visus* in its various forms is one of the most frequent terms in the Virgilian vocabulary.[39] Servius argues plausibly that, as man rarely sees the gods, the dream takes a shape which Aeneas could recognize (to 4.556).[40] Afterward Aeneas is quite convinced that he has seen a god (574–76). Philosophically, he thinks he has seen a god when he has probably only seen a dream shape. A false representation may well have replaced the true. The dream vision of Anchises creates similar problems. It is another affair of seeming:

> visa dehinc caelo facies delapsa parentis
> Anchisae subito talis effundere voces....

> down from the sky the image of his father
> Anchises seemed to glide. His sudden words....
>
> [5.722–23]

For Servius this might not be Anchises at all but a power sent by Jove which adopts the countenance of Anchises: "nam et 'visa' ait: aut certe intellegamus a Iove missam potestatem aliquam, quae se in Anchisae converteret vultum"[41] ("For he says 'seemed,' and certainly we should understand some power sent by Jove, which changes itself into the likeness of Anchises"). This something then asks Aeneas to seek him in hell.

We would expect from the old tradition of Virgilian criticism that the katabasis would present the same epistemological problem, in a purer form, and we are not disappointed. It is doubtful that Aeneas ever went there at all. The medieval critics quite correctly refused to take the episode literally, and among moderns Otis cautiously suggests that

Aeneas' "experience is not waking reality or literal truth." James Nohrnberg has assembled the relevant evidence.[42] Overarching the vestibule of Hades is a great elm tree:

> In medio ramos annosaque bracchia pandit
> ulmus opaca, ingens, quam sedem Somnia vulgo
> vana tenere ferunt, foliisque sub omnibus haerent.

> Among them stands a giant shaded elm,
> a tree with spreading boughs and aged arms;
> they say that is the home of empty Dreams
> that cling, below, to every leaf.

[6.282–84]

To enter hell Aeneas must pass a tree filled with empty dreams, a tree which encompasses the whole entryway; to leave hell, he exits by the Ivory Gates of false dreams. Servius, talking of the tree, suggests that the two can be identified: "Et intellegimus hanc esse eburneam portam, per quam exiturus *Aeneas* est. Quae res haec omnia indicat esse simulata, si et ingressus et exitus simulatus est et falsus"[43] ("And we understand this to be the ivory gate, through which Aeneas will leave. Which indicates that all this is feigned, since both the entrance and the exit are counterfeit and false"). If both doors are dreams, then the whole is fiction. Charon's definition of Hades, where he mentions sleep explicitly, reinforces Servius' suggestion (390): "umbrarum hic locus est, somni noctisque soporae" ("This is the land of shadows, / of Sleep and drowsy Night"). Moreover, it is by dreams that Eustathius explains the images which Odysseus sees in the Nekyia, the episode which gave Virgil his model (to *Od.* 11.41).[44] Odysseus perceives the dead not as the dead but as they were at the end of their lives, and so does Aeneas. Ajax is still wrathful; warriors slain in battle wear their stained armor; hunters appear in hunting costume; Aeneas sees Deiphobus mangled as he died, much as the hero saw Hector in a dream, when Troy fell (*Ae.* 2.270–73). That is, what both heroes perceive are phantasms, which bear the resemblance of living beings with all their passions. The dead do not wear armor, nor can a shadow be wounded. These are the phenomena of life. Eustathius observes that these shades have the characteristics of dream images. When we dream of the dead, we see them as we knew them when they were alive. In the *Aeneid* these phantasms appear as the result of a religious sacrifice. The dream is part of a mystery ritual.

Servius points to sciomancy when he describes the ritual which Aeneas performs (to *Ae.* 6.149). The grammarian argues that there are two ways to perform the rites of Proserpine: necromancy and sciomancy, the levitation of a cadaver by blood or the evocation of *umbrae*. Lucan imagined a scene of necromancy, while Homer and Virgil preferred the more civilized experience with shadows. We should add to the latter category Apollonius (*Argonautica* 3.1026–41, 1191–1224) and Statius (*Thebaid* 4.443–645). Sciomancy in fact was the normal way for the epic poet to describe a visit to hell.[45]

The notion that Aeneas undergoes some kind of mystery ritual makes more sense than an actual visit to Hades, which even on the literal level would be difficult to present. Cicero had the Stoic Balbus remark, "quaeve anus tam excors inveniri potest quae illa quae quondam credebantur apud inferos portenta extimescat?" (*De natura deorum* 2.2.5, "where can you find an old wife senseless enough to be afraid of the monsters of the lower world that were once believed in?").[46] It is more probable to assume that the Sibyl's solemn and frightening ritual puts Aeneas into a kind of trance similar to her own, without the violence of divine possession,[47] in which he perceives a procession of dream images and through which he gains the vision necessary to carry on his task. It is Virgil's subjective style which makes us feel as if we were actually in Hades. We experience the *umbrae* in the same way as Aeneas: we participate in his trance.

In the *Tusculan Disputations* (1.16.36–37) Cicero explains the need for *umbrae*. People cannot see souls, so they think in visual images and have shadows speak, though these lack the proper organs. Servius shows that *umbrae* as a term could describe the *nature* of the images which Aeneas perceives as well as the familiar shades of the departed. They are phantasms similar to the nocturnal figures of Mercury, Anchises, and Tiber which visit Aeneas in other parts of the poem (4.554–59, 5.721–23, 8.29–67). In his commentary on the Nekyia (to *Od.* 11.41), Eustathius again gives us the most detailed analysis. Odysseus looks at aerial images, dark and feeble like those which a skiagraphic painter impresses upon the imagination. Skiagraphy for the ancients was a technique of shading by which a painter made surface illusions for distant viewers. Plato and Aristotle both stress its lack of clarity and the deception fundamental to it.[48] Aristotle classed skiagraphy with dream visions, things which appear as things which themselves do not exist (*Meta.* 1024b23). The Virgilian equivalent is the uncertain dark in which Aeneas visits the underworld and guesses at the features of Palinurus and Dido (6.269–72, 340, 451–54).

All this makes the final and most convincing case for a skeptical epistemology. Even the visit to Elysium, brilliantly lit, fits the New Academic criteria. When Aeneas tries to embrace his father, the *imago* escapes his hands like breezes or sleep (6.700–702). Similarly, Odysseus cannot grasp the psyche of his mother, which flees from his hands: σκιῇ εἴκελον ἢ καὶ ὀνείρῳ (11.207, "like a shadow or a dream"). Eustathius contends that Odysseus perceives this psyche in the *same* way he would perceive a shadow or dream (to 212).[49] In Academic terms there is no way to distinguish the true from the false image.

This explanation creates other difficulties. Are we to believe that the people whom we see in hell—people like Palinurus and Dido, whom we already know and who speak and act according to character—are delusions, false images resembling the true?[50] The case is particularly tricky, for if the real *umbrae* of the dead existed, they would also in some sense be classed as images, this time true images.[51] Here, unfortunately, we cannot tell whether they are true or false.

At this stage we can begin to understand why later critics said that hell was this world. Aeneas finds hell here, and the experience exhibits the same epistemological problems which trouble a person living in this world. Awake or dreaming, sailing from island to island or visiting hell, Aeneas lives in an environment where everything *seems*. We have only to define Hades as faulty perception to identify the two realms. That is, we must understand *why* the Platonists developed their skeptical phenomenology.

The philosophers of the New Academy attacked perception not because they wished to deny knowledge or call all things into doubt but because they wished to discredit the body and the sensible world. True knowledge cannot be found here. Plato compares the body to a prison or cage through which the soul must perceive being indirectly (*Phaedo* 82E). As Anchises says in his Elysium lecture, we cannot see the sky, because we are shut up in darkness and a blind prison (*Ae.* 6.733–34).[52] The goal is the same among the Platonists, though the means may differ. Other members of the school did not thus attack perception, yet they *valued* the sense world in the same way.[53] Ficino, a trained Aristotelian, accepted the validity of sensation, but here is how he judged it:

> During the whole time the sublime Soul lives in this base body, our mind, as though it were ill, is thrown into a continual disquiet—here and there, up and down—and is always asleep and delirious; and the individual movements, actions, passions of men are nothing but vertigos of the sick, dreams of the sleeping, delirums of the insane, so that Euripides rightly called this life the dream of a shadow. But while all are deceived, usually those are less deceived who at some time, as

happens occasionally during sleep, become suspicious and say to themselves: "Perhaps those things are not true which now appear to us; perhaps we are now dreaming."[54]

If Cicero's *Lucullus* had complained that the New Academy based its evidence on the insane and the dreamer (*Academica* 2.15.47–48), what would he say of Ficino? Or what is the worth of accurate shadow vision? In fact, both the New Academy and the Florentine go back to a crucial Platonic distinction. In the *Academica* Cicero remarks, "Plato autem omne iudicium veritatis veritatemque ipsam abductam ab opinionibus et a sensibus cogitationis ipsius et mentis esse voluit" (2.46.142, "Plato, however, held that the entire criterion of truth and truth itself is detached from opinions and from the senses and belongs to the mere activity of thought and to the mind"). Hence the Platonic preference for mathematics.

Man is his mind, the rest is superfluity. These are cardinal concepts in the Platonic tradition, which forever separate it from that other school derivative from Aristotle which held to the fundamental union of body and soul.[55] Landino could have found this idea in Plato, in any of the Neoplatonists, in Cicero; for it is one of the major lessons which Scipio learns in his dream,[56] one which Macrobius need only elaborate. Man is an immortal mind ruling a mortal body, as God rules a cosmos which contains perishable parts. The proof comes from the *Phaedo:* self-moving things are eternal and have mind. In the *Tusculan Disputations* Cicero compares the body to a vase or receptacle (1.22.52) and considers it an alien home, as the soul's true home is in the sky. The body, unfortunately, drags this immortal being into mortality. It is the prison of the soul, and what we call life is death. Plotinus sophisticates the division but keeps the same moral. Our first soul is simple and sinless. Its psychic εἴδωλον (1.1.8) or image belongs to the synthetic being which we call man, and it is this image which has terrible passions and sins. When the first soul looks up to νοῦς (mind), however, the image ceases to exist. Homer expresses this situation in the Nekyia through Heracles. His εἴδωλον is in Hades, but his true self lives in heaven (1.1.12). Porphyry condensed the argument into an epigram, which others quoted and elaborated: "Omne corpus esse fugiendum, ut anima possit beata permanere cum Deo" ("We must flee every body, so that the soul can remain blessed with God"). His translator draws the logical inference, that mind and body exist in perpetual war: "Est ergo incorporeum quiddam in nobis, cui adversa corporis universi contagio est, et quid istud erit, nisi imago Dei, et quid imago Dei, nisi humanus animus?" ("There is, therefore, something incorporeal in us, to which contact with all body is a contagion, and what could that be, except the image of God, and what is the image of God, but the human mind?'').[57] It is at this point, with this set of assumptions, that Landino has his lecturer begin his arguments.

The conflict of body and soul and a psychic inwardness underlie Landino's whole philosophical interpretation. Early in the dialogue Landino has Alberti establish a mental definition of man on which all his later arguments depend. While he reluctantly admits the soul-body union, Alberti nevertheless claims that man is essentially mind.[58] Man shares his corporeal powers with the animals, the powers of movement and of sensation. He does not share his mind with the angels, whose mentalities differ in kind from man's discursive intellect.[59] The mind is therefore unique to man, while the body, relegated to the animal sphere, tends to be regarded as a hindrance and the body-soul split an active war. Alberti compares the body successively to a chain soon to be loosed, an earthen vessel to be broken, a garment soon old. He frequently calls it a prison, a *carcer*, the term which Anchises uses in his Elysium lecture (6.734).

From this initial definition Landino has Alberti derive two primary arguments. In the first he rejects the whole Epicurean sect because they did not observe the mind-body distinction and could conceive of nothing above the senses (CvV).[60] He likewise makes virtue and the active life generally subservient to the mind. Before man can act virtuously, he must know what are true goods, what to pursue and what to flee (DiV). In politics, for example, a blind prince will lead his followers into an abyss (BvV–viR). As a painter or sculptor must understand his art before he can express what he has conceived mentally, so the politician must first know truth, have a proper goal, before he can lead anyone. Accordingly, the politician will generally be a lesser person than the contemplative because his very immersion in the tangled world of human affairs will distract him from the inward vision. Landino illustrates this by a biblical analogy, the familiar distinction between Martha and Mary (BvR–V). Martha is distracted by *hyle*, by the material world with its storms and perturbations: "in qua omnia tumultuantur et variis perturbationum fluctibus aestuant." Mary, on the other hand, sits at a feast. In the words of the psalm (Ps. 26.4 Vulgate; Ps. 27 Authorized): "unam . . . petii a domino: hanc requiram, . . . ut inhabitem in domo domini: omnibus diebus vitae meae" ("she will dwell in the House of the Lord all the days of her life").[61]

This definition of man likewise determines the Platonic understanding of purgation. It is simultaneously an intellectual and a moral process and could not be otherwise, as man is mind. Landino's form, the dialogue, directly expresses this purgative process. Alberti and his friends debate philosophically the ends proper to man, and at the same time Alberti presents Aeneas to them as the moral hero of the way, painfully detaching himself from false moral and intellectual commitments. As Alberti puns (AviV), "Putare enim purgare est." *Putare* means both a process of thought and a cleansing. The analogies drawn are to pruning[62] and to the refining of gold. Later the method is defined by a battle analogy (DvV). One set of philosophers defeats another, but the contest is hot and draws in the *triarii,* the veteran reserve troops kept for extreme emergencies.

The purpose of this dialectic is withdrawal. Plotinus expresses the general conception behind such purgation (2.3.9).[63] Evil resides in the mixture which we call man, that combination of first soul, psychic εἴδωλον, and body. Goodness comes when the first soul has detached itself from the rest. Escape, however, is difficult. Immersed in sensations, the mind must choose the true out of many false alternatives: "Cum enim plurima se undique offerant/quae quoniam vero similia sunt/animum in diversas partes trahunt..." (AviV). Things deceptively like the truth draw the mind in various directions; therefore the mind must examine its alternatives rigorously and proceed by elimination. It can only accept as true what it cannot confute. That is, for Landino the mind must engage in dialogue, a literary form common in Virgilian criticism, the one used by Fulgentius and Macrobius as well as by Landino himself.

Cicero defines the dialogue method succinctly when he says, in his personal introduction to the *Academica,* "neque nostrae disputationes quidquam aliud agunt nisi ut in utramque partem dicendo eliciant et tamquam exprimant aliquid quod aut verum sit aut id quam proxime accedat" (2.3.7, "the sole object of our discussions is by arguing on both sides to draw out and give shape to some result that may be either true or the nearest possible approximation to the truth").[64] The speakers proceed by disjunctive logic, choosing between alternatives after exhaustive examination of either position. Landino constantly works by such bifurcation. He pits the active against the contemplative life, the mental against the sensual conceptions of man. And he goes over this material not once but several times. Alberti refutes the political alternative twice in book 1 and again in the Virgil commentary, when he comes to Dido and Aeneas. In the first two books alone he rejects Epicurean conceptions of the good three times: first because pleasure is common to cattle and other animals as well as to men (AvR), second through a survey of philosophical opinions on the ultimate good (CivV–vR), and finally for strictly Platonic reasons (DivV–vV). By the end of the *Camaldulensian Dialogues,* we feel that two or three points have been argued over and over again, from numerous different perspectives. And in this sense the Virgil commentary is part of the ongoing argument.

Landino's Aeneas is a hero constantly at the crossroads, choosing between opposed alternatives, often deceptive. The symbol for his situation and for the whole procedure recurs constantly in the *Camaldulensian Dialogues:* the Pythagorean Y, man choosing morally as well as intellectually.[65] Aeneas' response to the Delian oracle exemplifies this bifurcation perfectly. Apollo orders him to seek out his origins, which Aeneas on the advice of his father decides must be Crete, where Teucer was born. Here he has replaced Italy with a false alternative, the Dardanus of immortal parentage with the Teucer of mortal origins, the soul with the body (GiiV). Consequently his mistake is simultaneously moral and intellectual, as he cannot act properly if he has the wrong goal. That is, the Platonic identification of Truth and Goodness follows directly from the location of all values, of all significant choice, within the mind.

This disjunctive methodology necessitates a complicated dialectic. What follows is a diagram of the choices or distinctions as they present themselves:

1. Troy (FivR)	Heavenly Venus (journey into spirit)	
	Earthly Venus (begetting in the flesh)	
2. The sea (FviV)	*Voluntas* (appetite subordinate to reason)	
	Libido (appetite subordinate to sense)	
3. Delos (GiiV)	Italy	immortal origins
	Crete	mortal origins
4. Sicily (HiR)	Italy	superior reason
	Sicily	inferior reason (concerned with appetite)
5. Storm (HiV–iiR) (this is essentially the Sicilian schema with different symbols)	Neptune	wisdom (upward directed)
	Aeolus	prudence
6. Africa (HivR)	Italy	contemplation
	Carthage	action

The most complicated series, however, involves the theoretical preliminaries which Alberti makes for the Hades trip (KiV–iiR):

Soul		*Cosmos*	*Myth*	*Symbol*
infused, divine light	two wings of the soul (Venus' doves, (KvR)	fixed stars (*aplane*)	Elysium	nectar
innate, natural light		planets + earth	hell	Lethe

For his crucial distinctions, moreover, Landino goes beyond simple disjunctions. He defines moral action with a four-part classification (GiR):

temperance	habit
continence	intermediate state
incontinence	intermediate state
intemperance	habit

The distinction is a Scholastic one, between habitual and nonhabitual action:

> Hoc igitur interest/inter temperantiam et continentiam. Nam quamvis utraque idem praestet continens tamen eo deterior est: quia cum dolore abstinet: nec est satis firmus adversus voluptates: temperans vero bene volens letusque / abstinet.

> This therefore is the difference between temperance and continence; although each may be responsible for the same thing, nevertheless the continent man is weaker insofar as he abstains with sorrow and is not firm enough against pleasures; the temperate man, however, abstains joyfully and with a good will. [GiR]

Dido illustrates the process. She passes from continence to incontinence through the persuasions of Anna (GiR) and then to intemperance (HviiV). The virtuous, considered by themselves, return a triple classification and set up the structure of the *Aeneid:*

> Horum trium inferior/est eorum qui in sociali ac civili vita degentes rerum publicarum administrationem suscipiunt. His proximi (sed tamen erectiori gradu constituti) ii sunt: qui a publicis actionibus veluti tempestuosis/ac percellosis et in quibus fortunae temeritas omnino dominetur: se in portum tranquillitatis transferunt: et a turba in ocium se recipientes/ quietam vitam degunt: non ita tamen: ut non aliquid adhuc restet/adversus quid luctandum sit. Supremo autem loco eos cernes/qui penitus a rerum humanarum concursatione: ac tumultu remoti: nihil cuius poenitendum sit committunt.

> The lowest order of these three is composed of those who live a social and civic life and who undertake the administration of public affairs. Next to them (in a higher grade) are those who withdraw themselves from public life as something dangerous, stormy, and completely dominated by the chances of fortune; they find some haven of tranquillity, withdraw themselves from the crowd into a kind of retreat, and lead a quiet life—not

in such a way, however, that there is not something against which they must still struggle. And in the highest rank you will see those who are completely removed from the concourse, the tumult, of human affairs; they do nothing that is worthy of blame. [GvV]

When Aeneas leaves Troy, he begins the purgative way.[66] In Italy he is just beginning at the third and highest level, the drama of the contemplative life which Landino only hints at.[67]

The purpose of this elaborate dialectic is negative. To return to the original definition, the mind can accept as true only what it cannot confute. It must therefore eliminate a whole series of alternatives, particularly those involving pleasure and political action, which are rejected again and again. This vigorous negative method operates both in Landino's dialogue form and in his exegesis.

By the end we might wonder if anything is left. Scorn has been cast on pleasure of all sorts, on useful political action, on the whole visible cosmos; and the positive alternatives, though strongly affirmed, are hardly presented. Hints about the Beatific Vision and references to Mary and Martha hardly offset this massive negative dialectic and the repeated rejection of the same set of values. We want to know, therefore, why Landino limited himself to negative argumentation and why he was so reticent about the object of his dialectic, the contemplation of God or supreme being.

For this question we can present three different answers: literary, moral, and metaphysical. As a literary critic, Landino remains faithful to his text, for the *Aeneid* dramatizes an ascetic quite as rigorous as that of the Florentine. Value loci in the poem are always internal, and anyone who turns to outside objects dies. The glitter of a helmet kills Euryalus, a gilded belt is enough for Turnus (described at *Ae.* 10.499), and Camilla, momentarily distracted by the finery of Chloreus, dies in her hour of glory. All external things are finally either rejected or lost in the *Aeneid,* and Virgil's setting perfectly mirrors this dynamism of negation.

I spoke in the last chapter about the winter season, which established the negative mood for Aeneas' wanderings. It mirrors Aeneas' purgative way, for as Otis says, "his fate is to sacrifice every present enjoyment or satisfaction to an end he cannot hope to witness himself" (p. 222). He loses his home, his wife, his father and Pallas, and he sacrifices to Dido. What could be more austere? As he says at the end to Ascanius, "disce, puer, virtutem ex me verumque laborem / fortunam ex aliis" (12. 435–36, "From me my son, learn valor and true labor; / from others learn of fortune"). Landino is hardly more ascetic and would have seen in Virgil confirmation of his Platonic reading.

Morally, Landino is explicit on the virtues of negative argumentation and says so in his first lecture as a professor, that devoted to the *Tusculan Disputations*. There he argues that Cicero frees us from fear of death and other possible dangers and so brings us tranquility of mind, which is the goal of the arts generally.[68] Landino considers philosophy in this respect a kind of medicine, which helps us bear misery and redirects our aims, so that we do not pursue inappropriate ends. It is the viaticum of our mortal journey which keeps us safe from bodily contagion in order that we might return to our pure and simple nature ("Pref. Tusc." 302–4). Landino expresses this conception with quotations from Anchises' Elysium lecture. Thus the *Camaldulensian Dialogues*, by shattering our false conceptions of human ends, prepares us to see clearly and shelters us from the ills of life.

Metaphysically, this negativism is necessitated by Landino's topic. He wishes to portray the highest ideal, the contemplative man, but in a Neoplatonic system there is no way in which he can express directly the object of philosophical contemplation. God, the One above or identical with supreme being, cannot accept predication, since to say he is this or that would limit his essence. "For this type of thinking it is quite natural to face the problem: in what way can this 'unrestricted' being become object of our knowledge? Ordinary knowledge seems to be precisely predicative knowledge, but how can anything the essence of which is to have no predicates (any predicate being the expression of determinateness) be known?" The Neoplatonist decided that "it can be 'known' only in a negative way, i.e., by first positing and then negating all possible predicates. *Agnoscendo cognoscitur.*"[69] This is what Alberti does in the dialogue, and it is the prose equivalent to allegorical poetry in that both assume a truth which can be expressed only by indirection.[70]

Not all is dark, however, either in Virgil or in Landino. Amidst the turmoil of war Aeneas can recall the transcendental vision of Elysium and the pastoral quiet of Pallaneum. And in the *Camaldulensian Dialogues* Landino has an implicit positive focus which we can see in its structure. The dialogue consists of a series of rising curves, each broken off, until it ends with Aeneas in Elysium. Alberti begins the discussion with Plato's ladder, stretching from earth to heaven.[71] This is parried by Lorenzo with a long rebuttal. The second day consists of a steady ascent, from Epicurean sensuality to the Beatific Vision, only to conclude with an analysis of evil. The upward direction finally dominates the remainder of the dialogue. Aeneas leaves Troy in flames and finds at the end of the fourth day a kind of paradise. The physical symbol of this ascending movement is the setting itself. Each day the interlocutors climb to the top of the mountain overlooking Camaldoli. Alberti remarks on the first day that peace and vision come only after such toil (AviR): "Non datur igitur quies: nisi prius laboraveris." They had to climb the mountain before they saw the view from the top.

The immediate surroundings on the mountain reinforce this positive feeling. It is a *locus amoenus:* a meadow through which a stream runs murmuring, for coolness a large beech tree, a breeze, and the harmonious song of different birds (AivR–V). To Alberti it recalls the setting of the *Phaedrus* with its little stream and plane tree. To us its "patula fagus" suggests as well Virgil's first eclogue with its praise of the quiet, pastoral life.

The monastic buildings lend depth to this traditional locale. The Camaldolese monks practiced a version of the contemplative life stricter than the normal contemplative orders and included eremites.[72] Their abbot acts as host for the discussion, and the monuments of this ancient sanctity please the minds of the talkers (CivR). Landino tacitly juxtaposes the philosopher and the monk, as did another Virgilian critic nearly a thousand years before: "Prima igitur contemplativa est quae ad sapientiam et ad veritatis inquisitionem pertinet, quam apud nos episcopi, sacerdotes ac monachi, apud illos philosophi gesserunt" (Fulgentius *Mitologiae* 2.1.66, "For the first or contemplative life is that which has to do with the search for knowledge and truth, the life led in our days by bishops, priests, and monks, in olden days by philosophers").[73] In this quiet scene, behind and above the monastic buildings with their rigorous ascetics, we might discern the positive glow amid all this negation. The monk had to learn through discipline to open his eyes so that he might see (Benedict *Regula* prologue 8–9).[74] So in the epic. After years of travel, a descent to hell, and a blundering about among shadows dimly seen, Aeneas at last came to broader fields, clothed with the light of another sun and other stars.

Italian

3   Falerina's Garden

Nihil enim prohibet intellectum nostrum intelligere multa, et multipliciter referri ad id quod est in se simplex, ut sic ipsum simplex sub multiplici relatione consideret. Et quanto aliquid est magis simplex, tanto est maioris virtutis et plurium principium, ac per hoc multiplicius relatum intelligitur: sicut punctum plurium est principium quam linea, et linea quam superficies.

Nothing prevents our intellect from understanding many things and referring these in multiple fashion to that which is in itself simple, so that we might consider the simple itself by a set of multiple relations. The simpler a thing, the greater its power, and it is the beginning of more things. And it is understood through this set of multiple relations: as a point is the beginning of more things than a line, and a line than a surface.[1]

The great creative allegorist of the early Renaissance was Landino's contemporary, Matteo Maria Boiardo, and his *Orlando innamorato* (1483, 1495) returns us to the tradition of discontinuous allegory, which was discussed in the first chapter. Boiardo does not invent a complete allegorical plot, as Spenser and Tasso do a century later, but alternates scenes of symbolic adventure with episodes of chivalric duels and the clash of armies, the stuff of chronicle and history. Similarly, Homer's critics found allegory most often not in the battles before Troy but in the wondrous descents and ascents of the Olympian deities. Boiardo emphasizes this discreteness by his literary method. Unlike Virgil or Tasso, he does not present a single antagonist, a Juno or Armida, who remains active throughout the poem and creates a series of wonders. Instead, he follows the precedent of the *Odyssey* and multiplies his enchantresses, who, while they resemble each other, are normally contained within discrete episodes. He thus invites the minute consideration of single adventures, a familiar appeal throughout the two millennia of allegorical interpretation. Heraclitus the allegorist interpreted single scenes in the *Iliad;* Porphyry in the late Empire wrote a whole treatise on eleven lines of the *Odyssey;* and the Renaissance allegorizers of Ariosto dwelt long on Ruggiero's visit to Alcina's isle. This format reflects the origins and basis of secular allegory, which was an explanation not of whole poems but of the supernatural and fabulous where they occurred in poems.

We can see this notion of allegory in the poet's response to Virgil. Critics generally recognize how much the Roman affected Boiardo, from his early pastorals to the epic. They point to his imitation of Virgilian battle scenes in the *Innamorato* and more particularly to the poet's pastorals.[2] The implications of this influence, however, require some comment, for the Virgil of Boiardo's day was still an allegorist. Three years before Ercole d'Este had the *Innamorato* printed, Landino had published his commentary on the *Aeneid,* the latest in a long tradition of such allegorical readings, and the *Eclogues* had been allegorized long ago by Servius: symbolic and allusive poems which set up paradigms for the complex politics of the Rome of the triumvirs and for Virgil's personal relationships with his friends and his loves. Boiardo does much the same in his *Pastoralia.* The characters are allegorical, for under personae Boiardo figures forth himself, his patron Ercole, and his uncle T. V. Strozzi.[3] The symbolic method cuts across the division between recreational and political, and in fact it is the amatory and private which normally eludes the critic, whether of Virgil or of Boiardo. The sixth Italian eclogue with its enigmatic allegory provides an extreme example, where Boiardo says in the argument that both the personae and the matter are hidden. And he uses the method in his lyrics as well. The two named allegories (82, 179) in his great lyric sequence, the *Amorum libri,* approach more closely the methods of the *Innamorato* than do any of the pastorals: in 82 the enchanted fountain, the bait of the food, and the hidden snake; in 179 another enchanted fountain, Narcissus, and the Siren. All these have direct parallels in his romance epic and establish the continuity of his symbolic method.[4]

In the *Innamorato* we would then expect allegory of love and of politics. It would be intermittent (as in the *Amorum libri* and in the pastorals), because not all the eclogues are allegorical, rather than continued (as in Dante or Spenser). In this respect Boiardo follows Virgil's actual practice rather than that of the Virgil of the medieval expositors. We would accordingly assume that, as in Virgil, the fabulous episodes should yield the allegorical readings: the monsters and the fays with their enchanted gardens, those modern equivalents of the classical marvelous. Boiardo, however, changed the literal presentation of these wonders in two respects: he made them mostly evil, and he made them fantastic in the way we refer to dream sequences. These changes affect our interpretation.

In his *Dei romanzi* (1554), Giraldi Cinthio argued that when romance writers wished to equal the *meraviglie* wrought by the ancient gods of Virgil and Homer, they turned to fays and sorcerers with their troops of demons rather than to saints, because such good characters did not fit well in episodes of chivalric adventure, where the story demanded military virtues rather than martyrdom, patience, or silence.[5] In romances the fabulous is therefore often demonic and disruptive and its interpretation a moral exorcism of what we must avoid. This principle applies as well to the *Gerusalemme liberata*, in which the visit to the wizard of Ascalon hardly balances the long episodes which concern the enchanted wood or Armida.

Second, these scenes resemble dream fantasies, and such a comparison is constantly made by critics of the *Orlando innamorato*.[6] Certainly within the tradition of epic and romance few writers more closely approach the fairy tale. Boiardo's phantasmagoria of enchanted gardens and knights who battle monsters and rout whole armies resembles, rather, the allegorical wonders of the Grail stories or of Edmund Spenser. And yet we might say that the *Innamorato* is a logical result of the epic tradition. Virgil had already connected his wonders to dreams, and, though he balanced carefully the demands of myth and of mimetic representation, medieval commentators stressed almost exclusively the symbolic side of the *Aeneid*. A highly creative poet, responding to this way of reading the epic, would normally produce a fiction much more fantastic and symbolic than his original. The paradigm applies to the *Innamorato*.

In this chapter I will examine one such dream, Orlando's adventures in Falerina's Garden. The story itself is simple, like those in German fairy tales, but the analysis will be detailed and complex. I will proceed by different topics and cover the text exhaustively, point by point. During the discussion, the wondrous adventure will dissolve into rational arabesques, everything rearranged, turned around, according to the question asked. If critics compared the *Innamorato* with dreams, it helps to remember that similarly, Freud would state the story of an actual dream in a brief paragraph and spin an analysis over many pages.

Dreams are unique and individual in their symbolism, not generic and communal, and this metaphor of dreaming points to another problem, partly historical, partly artistic. Historically, the *Orlando innamorato* was overshadowed by its great continuation the *Orlando furioso* and did not generate a tradition of interpretation. We have no

documents which register interpretations of Boiardo's text historically
as we have for Homer and Virgil in the *Homeric Problems* and the
Camaldulensian Dialogues. Nor is this problem peculiar to Boiardo.
While Spenser has a long and respectable tradition of criticism, he did
not produce a series of *allegorical* interpretations. His *Faerie Queene*
came at the end of the Renaissance, when critics were turning away
from symbolism to questions of mimesis, and this shift affected their
responses to his poem. Spenser's allegorizers are mostly modern. For
both poets we must be content with the next best thing, probable
hypothesis based on a historical and literary study of their symbols in
context and in comparison with earlier uses of such symbols. And here
I will confine myself to as few texts as possible. Private libraries in the
Renaissance were usually small, and Boiardo did not reside at Ferrara
for most of his career, though through the Este lending library he would
have had easier access to books than did Spenser, isolated in Ireland.
Our first guides, however, will be those who wrote on the *Teseida,* as
the allegorical houses of Mars and Venus in Boccaccio's book 7 influenced Boiardo's presentation of Falerina. Two critics closely annotated these scenes: Boccaccio himself, in his autograph manuscript of
the *Teseida,* and Piero Andrea dei Bassi. Boiardo probably knew dei
Bassi's commentary as well as Boccaccio's text, as it was written for
Niccolo d'Este III and its *editio princeps* was printed with the *Teseida*
at Ferrara in 1475.[7] Beyond these two texts we may confine ourselves
to sources which Boiardo probably used or which were in the Este
library. For the Falerina episode, the texts which we know he read
are the *Aeneid*, Ovid's *Metamorphoses,* and Herodotus. He may
also have read the *History of the Mongols* of Friar Giovanni da
Pian del Carpine. Of the texts which he could find in Ercole's library, I stress Marco Polo and Boccaccio's *Genealogie deorum gentilium*. The latter is particularly important: the Este family had more
than one copy of it, and for a time Duke Ercole kept one in his study.[8]
Boccaccio's encyclopedia would make available to Boiardo the entire
wealth of late classical and much medieval mythographic analysis.
More specifically, Boccaccio consistently presented the historical as
well as the moral sense of a myth, and this euhemerizing may have
suggested to Boiardo his most original symbolism, the use of Falerina
for political and historical analysis.

Even such a cautious selection has dangers, and here we come to the
artistic implications of the dream metaphor for the *Innamorato*. There
are no keys to the poem. We know that Boiardo took sources for the
plot from many places and combined them in original ways.[9] There is
therefore no reason to assume anything less when we discuss traditions

of interpretation. A mythographer will not necessarily explain a particular scene, and in this independence Boiardo, like Spenser, differs from the practitioners of orthodox imitation. Jonson and Chapman, for example, write what we might call an archaeological allegory in that, when they imitate a Roman wedding, they simultaneously revive the classical explication of the rite. They may suggest a new context for the ceremony or their own meanings beyond the classical explication, but the originals are necessary and carry the reader very far into the new text. With Boiardo and Spenser, however, at times this method fails. Such poets might invent a new myth out of old materials, reduce a polysemous story to its literal meaning, or read into another story meanings not mentioned or developed by the mythographers. Furthermore, we can do no justice here to the French romancers and their Italian imitators, though we know that Boiardo borrowed episodes from them and imitated their interlace structure in his plot. The romances lacked academic commentary in the Quattrocento, and an attempt to ferret out such meanings would require a separate book.

One last warning: Falerina's Garden is one among a number of false Elysia which the poet explores in the *Innamorato*. They relate to each other and contain more or less the same themes, but Boiardo's emphasis differs markedly. If the critic reads mechanically, he will blur essential distinctions and reduce the poet's variety to monotones. The gardens of Dragontina, Falerina, and Morgana are all forms of Hades and have the appropriate symbolism; but in Dragontina's Boiardo stresses the psychological condition of the victim, of those lost while yet alive; in Falerina's, the deranged psychology of the victimizer and her political state, which murders instead of protecting its citizens; and in Morgana's, the kingdom of metals and of Death itself. The emphasis is all-important and determines the choice of symbols and their arrangement. For the present analysis I will go from the simple to the complex, from the unstressed meanings to the psychological dimension, which the allegorical tradition would lead us to expect; and I will conclude with the historical and political levels, which as the most original are also the most difficult to discuss. At many stages the discussion will veer off into other levels, and I will have to anticipate later arguments or recall earlier ones. The garment of allegory being seamless, any attempt to cut it automatically tears more than one pattern.

The Minor Levels

At Albracca Angelica interrupts Orlando's duel with Rinaldo and sends him to Orcagna, officially to destroy the garden of the evil Falerina but really to save Rinaldo's life, the enemy whom she loves. As she admits

afterward, she has sent Orlando to certain death, for Falerina has constructed a game of lethal mathematics, in which victory entails further
risk of life. She ensnares all travelers and has them fed to a dragon
which guards the entrance to her garden. If a hero should manage to
overcome this monster, he would find himself locked *inside* the garden
and condemned to repeat the same experience with different monsters
at three other gates. To get out he must kill the monster guard, but the
portal automatically closes once the monster dies. If he wins, he loses.
Further, on the road to each gate are monster women waiting in ambush, and finally, Falerina expects Orlando. She has prepared a special
sword to kill him, designed to cut through all enchantments and thus to
penetrate his skin. The giants at the North Gate best symbolize the
situation, for they double in number each time one is killed.

The witch queen constructed this elaborate system for two people,
the faithless Origille and her lover, Ariante. The dragnet almost
worked, for a mob held Origille two miles from the dragon gate when
Orlando rescued her. Extravagant means for accomplishing personal
vendettas characterize many of Boiardo's women. Alcina is willing to
destroy Rinaldo's entire party because they disturbed her fishing;
Marfisa, angered at the interruption of a duel, slaughters the army of
her liege lord; and Morgana, to capture Orlando, arranges a dragnet
more fantastic than Falerina's.[10] Their actions parallel those of men
like Gradasso and Agricane, who move huge armies to capture a
woman or devastate kingdoms to acquire a horse or sword. The burning cities of Spain and the death of millions around Albracca, though
situations which the narrator does not stress, darken the grand gestures
of many a Boiardo hero and suggest for this colorful epic what Reichenbach called a pessimistic and bitter undertone.[11]

Outside the garden Orlando encounters two women: Origille, who
steals his horse and sword; and one of Falerina's servants, who gives
him advice and a guidebook containing the information he needs to
succeed in his adventure. The advantage is Orlando's, as he clubs the
dragon to death with a makeshift weapon and enters the garden.
Catching Falerina unaware, he replaces his sword with a better one,
her blade designed to cut through all enchantments. Throughout, Orlando acts like a practical soldier: first he breaks into the fortress garden; then he gains possession of the weapon designed to kill him; next
he finds a way out; and only then does he return to destroy the place.
The queen's enchantments, on the other hand, are directed against
each other, for Orlando uses her special sword to kill the monsters.
Again, when captured, the enchantress refuses to tell Orlando how to
escape, knowing that he has barely begun the game; but her silence

serves to remind Orlando of his guidebook. Later, the automatically closing gates force him to kill more of her monsters.

With his escape route clear, Orlando returns to demolish the garden. He learns that he must cut a branch from the top of a tall tree; dangerous to approach and impossible to climb. The branches grow high up; the bark is slippery; and the trunk, which is an arm's breadth at the bottom, tapers to the size of a finger above. Quivering at every footstep, the tree drops gold fruit as large as a man's head, which falls thick as snowflakes. Orlando makes a shield of beech and earth-grass, runs through the murderous rain, and with a single blow cuts down the whole tree. The earth trembles and smoke covers the place, a fire in its midst, the demon destroying the garden.[12] Everything vanishes but a sobbing Falerina, who offers her remaining prisoners in exchange for her life.[13]

The plot itself suggests a philosophical reading, the familiar drama of fate and fortune. By *chance* Orlando meets a woman who by *chance* is willing to betray her mistress' secrets and by *chance* has a book which accurately describes all of Falerina's snares. She also says that the witch discovered by *destiny* that Orlando would wreck her enchantments, and that the queen is convinced that her efforts at defense will fail (2.4.7–8). In fact, Falerina is caught unprepared by Orlando, mirroring herself in her sword. We could fairly say that Boiardo uses fate rhetorically, to make the chance meetings of romance plausible, but he develops the theme through the entire episode. When Orlando captures Falerina, he seizes a fleeing fortune by the hair, a gesture which he repeats immediately afterward with the Siren and which is defined iconographically later when he encounters the Fata Morgana. Finally, Iroldo, one of Falerina's earlier victims, blames bad fortune for his misadventure and explains that the two prisoners sent daily to the dragon are chosen by lot (1.17.6–10). The theme recurs frequently in the *Innamorato*. For example, Boiardo assumes the reliability of astrology. By examining the heavens, the king of Garamanta, priest of Apollo, foresees the disaster which Agramante and Rodamonte are arranging for the Africans, has accurate knowledge of a siege occurring several thousands of miles away, and predicts his own death.[14] The narrator locates his epic astrologically when he requests grace and strength for his endeavor from the celestial bodies of Mars and Venus (2.12.1). We can assume that these references are more than fictional devices, as Borso and Ercole d'Este regularly followed the advice of their astrologers and collected many relevant texts in their library.[15] The famous Schifanoia frescoes of the months memorialize their belief in the powers of the stars.

Games of murder, fortune-tellers, and the stars might suggest a detailed astrological reading of the adventure, but I have not found anything beyond what the incidents of the plot dictate. The monsters and symbols of the garden do not render, as far as I can determine, a consistent astrological interpretation. Boiardo carefully analyzes the moral side of fortune soon after the episode, when Orlando visits Morgana's kingdom of riches, so he need only suggest the matter here. The publisher of the 1576 edition, however, who saw fortune in many places, found her in other events of this episode. When Orlando kills the dragon and acquires a sword, he shows us how much fortune can do when she wishes to make someone happy, and his rescue of Origille, Griffone, and Aquilante from the execution squad demonstrates unexpected good luck.[16]

If we turn from the plot to a consideration of the four garden gates, we find a cosmological reading. Each faces a different point of the compass, and they open in a set order, beginning with sunrise in the east (the dragon gate). Together they describe the course of the sun through a day. Here is the sequence (I have added Fiordelisa's directional terms, which already imply the interpretation):[17] We begin "dove il sol nasce," proceed to the South Gate ("mezo giorno"), then west ("occidente"), and end at the north portal, "tramontana." The gate materials make the symbolism concrete: gleaming bronze for midday, jewels for sunset, silver for the light of moon and stars. If we consider the monster guardians together with their gates, the cycle suggests likewise the course of human life. The giants at the gate of night, for example, effectively signify death, the one battle man cannot win. Though Orlando binds the giants, he cannot harm them, because death multiplies their number. More specifically, the sequence signifies human life negatively, by the major vices and failings incident to its various stages. In his *rifacimento* Berni added a moral reading of the monsters which supports this interpretation:[18]

> Considerate un poco in conscientia
> Se quella donna che'l libretto porse
> Al Conte, potesse esser la prudentia,
> Che salvo pel giardin sempre lo scorse,
> Ciò è pel mondo, & se con riverentia
> Quell' asino, & quel toro, e drago, forse,
> Et quel Gigante, esser potessin mai
> I varii vitii, e le fatiche, e' guai
>
> Che vi son dentro. . . .

Consider a little in your mind
if that lady who gave the booklet
to the Count could be Prudence,
which took him everywhere safe through the garden,
that is, through the world; and reflect
if that ass, and that bull and dragon, perhaps,
and that giant could possibly be
the different vices, the labors and difficulties

which are there within it. . . .

[2.4.4–5]

The lady with the book is prudence; the garden, the world; the animals, our various vices. Much of what I argue below will flesh out this brief description at the profounder level of the human soul. But first, before the readings become totally complicated, some diagrams are useful. Here is a spatial outline of the garden, with arrows indicating the order in which the gates open:

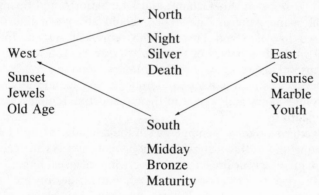

Then one for all the items and their significations (there is of course no vice representative of death):

	Direction	East	South	West	North
Gates	Material	Marble	Bronze	Jewels	Silver
	Signification	Sunrise	Midday	Sunset	Night
Gates and	Monsters	Dragon	Bull	Asinel	Giant(s)
Guardians	Stages of Life	Youth	Maturity	Old Age	Death
Together	Signification	Lust	Wrath	Avarice	
Monstrous	Senses	Origille	Siren	"Peacock"	Fauna
Women		Touch	Hearing	Sight	Taste and Smell

The Psychological Level

We can organize the temptations most clearly if we classify them as appeals to either the concupiscible or the irascible appetites, to Venus or Mars, the planets which the poet invokes and his basic division both of his subject matter and of his audience:

> Però diversamente il mio verziero
> De amore e de battaglia ho già piantato:
> Piace la guerra a l'animo più fiero,
> Lo amore al cor gentile e delicato.

> But I have already planted my garden
> diversely with love and battles.
> War pleases the more fiery mind;
> love, the gentle and refined heart.

[3.5.2]

The division and the deities are of course conventional. Boccaccio began his *Teseida* in this fashion, and later Ariosto and Spenser followed the same pattern. The *Aeneid* could also yield this reading, symbolized by Dido and Turnus, who represent Aeneas' principal problems in the two halves of the epic.[19] Boccaccio, however, is particularly useful, as we know that Boiardo imitated the *Teseida,* and we have Boccaccio's own glosses to the poem. The section in which the lovers invoke Mars and Venus in their respective temples will especially concern us.

The two terms signify the appetites of the animal soul, and I will use them throughout in this technical, Scholastic sense. As Boccaccio explains, man either desires to possess what pleases him (the concupiscible appetite) or becomes angry when these desires are impeded (the irascible).[20] Physiologically, the two relate by blood, as love is within the heart and wrath is an inflammation of the blood around the heart.[21] The distinction likewise describes character types determined by the planets Mars and Venus. The categories fit Orlando in particular, the warrior in the service of love.[22] The emphasis is on the concupiscible, as we would expect from the *Innamorato.*

These drives ought to serve our human will, what Aquinas calls the *appetitus rationalis* or *intellectualis.*[23] When out of control, they degrade the individual below the human level; he becomes worse than an animal, because he exists in the realm of moral choice and has inverted the powers of his soul. This is the condition of Falerina, and it is this situation which the garden figures, the animal drives out of control and breeding monsters. The appetites each have two gates. The East and

West signify the concupiscible; the North and South, the irascible.

Out of rational control, the concupiscible appetite shows itself either as false love or as avarice, the vices conventionally associated with youth and old age, the gates of morning and sunset. Boiardo symbolizes the first with a dragon or serpent,[24] and the sequence of events makes this identification clear. Orlando approaches the gate in the company of Origille, the lady whom he earlier wanted to seduce (1.29.46–48) and has now isolated from her young friends Griffone and Aquilante.[25] He has to postpone the project that night, because Falerina's servant warns him that the dragon slayer must be chaste for three days. After the battle he wanders through a *locus amoenus,* which Boiardo borrowed from Venus' garden in the *Teseida.* Here are the two passages:

> ... vide quello
> ad ogni vista soave e ameno,
> in guisa d'un giardin fronzuto e bello
> e di piante verdissime ripieno,
> d'erbette fresche e d'ogni fior novello,
> e fonti vide chiare vi surgeno,
> e intra l'altre piante onde abondava,
> mortine più che altro le sembiava.
>
> Quivi sentì pe' rami dolcemente
> quasi d'ogni maniera uccei cantare,
> e sovra quelli ancor similemente
> li vide con diletto i nidi fare;
> poscia fra l'erbe fresche prestamente
> vide conigli in qua e'n là andare,
> e timidetti cervi e cavriuoli
> e altri molti varii bestiuoli.

> ... she saw that which is sweet and pleasant to every sight, in the guise of a leafy and beautiful garden full of very green plants, of fresh grasses, and of every new flower, and she saw clear fountains springing there, and it seemed to her that among the other shrubs the myrtle flourished most.
>
> She heard birds of almost every kind singing through the branches. She watched them with delight, too, as they made their nests. She also saw rabbits darting about here and there through the young grass, and timid little stags, and roebuck and a great variety of many other little animals. [*Teseida* 7.51–52][26]

E caminando sopra del rivaggio
Mirava il bel paese sbigotito.
Egli era aponto del mese di maggio,
Sì che per tutto intorno era fiorito,
E rendeva quel loco un tanto odore,
Che sol di questo se allegrava il core.

Dolce pianure e lieti monticelli
Con bei boschetti de pini e d'abeti,
E sopr'a verdi rami erano occelli,
Cantando in voce viva e versi queti.
Conigli e caprioli e cervi isnelli,
Piacevoli a guardare e mansueti,
Lepore e daini correndo d'intorno
Pieno avean tutto quel giardino adorno.

And walking along the bank of the stream, he wondered, amazed, at the lovely landscape. It was the month of May, so everything was in flower, and the place exuded such a scent that this alone cheered the heart.

The level fields pleased, and the hills charmed with their lovely groves of pine and fir, and birds in the green branches soothed one with song. This beautiful garden had everything: rabbits and roebuck and swift stags, gentle and pleasant to see. Hare and fallow deer darted here and there. [*Innamorato* 2.4.22–23]

The authors list the same classes of objects because they incite to love, the fir rather than palm trees, for example. In his long note Boccaccio explains how bird song chases away melancholy, a frigid humor; that pine fruit is an aphrodisiac; and so on. Each detail has significance, even the smallest—a flower's perfume rather than its color or form.[27] And the spring setting and the timid but fecund animals communicate the meaning without a gloss to the most casual reader. In Boiardo's allegorical lyrics such a setting normally symbolizes the onset of love,[28] the situation in which the lover first met his lady. As we saw in Homer or Virgil, allegory normally signifies a process rather than a static condition, and this particular process allegory was familiar as far back as Guillaume de Lorris.

This serpent sequence sets the mood for the whole garden. The ass (Asinel), the other manifestation of desire, has a snake's tail, as do the women at the East and West Gates (the Siren and Fauna). The plethora of snakes connects Falerina to the fays or *fate*, that special race of beings endowed with supernatural powers. When Brandimarte saves Febosilla, we learn that fays live in their own forms for a millennium or much longer but then change into serpents, a form they must keep until they have been kissed (2.26.15). The general idea was widespread, and noble houses like the Angevins and the Lusignans counted snake women among their progenitors.[29] Falerina, however, is never called a fay, and with her the snake has darker qualities. She is a *cantatrice,* and like Malagigi she operates by witchcraft, through the agency of demons.[30]

Berni explains this allegory morally. The monstrous women, human above, snake or fish below, symbolize the pleasures which begin delightfully and end in revulsion. Boccaccio's gloss on the sirens connects them, rather, with the hypocrisy involved in seduction.[31] Where Boccaccio sees prostitution, Boiardo dramatizes murder, the literal level of the myth. Boccaccio had said that the sirens sang men to sleep, then murdered and ate their victims, the Siren's method in Boiardo (which Orlando thwarts by filling his ears and helmet with roses, blocking the sound of her voice). In fact the monstrous women are all cannibals, and the other women plan murder. With sword raised Origille stands over the sleeping Orlando, wondering how to kill him, in a tableau repeated immediately afterward partly by Falerina, who sits with the sword Balisarda, and partly by the Siren, whom Orlando decoys by a pretence of sleep. In this sense the garden symbolizes the way a woman uses sex to fight men successfully, those who abuse chivalry to devour knights.

Boiardo distinguishes his women according to the five senses, and Orlando must encounter an assault upon one or more of these before he fights each monster at its gate. With Origille it is touch or sex, the siren by its song involves voice and hearing, the birdwoman blinds her victims, and Fauna with her banquet engages taste and smell.[32] So we have gone through the circuit of the day, the stages of human life, and the senses.

These scenes have a further, private application, because they recapitulate the allegorical lyrics of the *Amorum libri.* The original for the Siren appears in 179, a "moralis allegoria," and kills by the same methods. The poem itself itemizes love's different sensual appeals: sight, smell, hearing. More generally, the lover of the lyrics symbolizes his mistress by a snake or another wild animal. The lady either runs away or devours the unwary. So in 179 the animal waits to kill the man, who sleeps in the meadow, charmed by the colors of the roses. Or his mistress is the animal of 130 (a sonnet), which captures everyone who enters its *locus amoenus.*[33] The lyric lover has escaped but still drags with him the chain of his captivity. The *Innamorato* literalizes the metaphors and conceits of the lyric cycle.

The Fauna episode most clearly demonstrates this transformation. Orlando comes to a flowered valley with tables set with gold cups and steaming food, arranged by a fountain. Whoever enters the circle, drawn by hunger and the smell of food, is netted and dragged off into the bower, where Fauna eats her victim. She herself is a serpent lady, female above, reptilian below the breasts. Forewarned by his guidebook, Orlando walks around the net, pursues and decapitates the monster, as he had done to the Siren earlier. He separates the human from the monstrous. This adventure reworks the "Allegoria" of *Amorum libri* 82, where the lover walked knowingly into the trap and found he could not escape from the snake, which dispelled all his joys. The snake reappears in 179, once more part of an ambush. Fauna's net or lasso likewise appears in several other lyrics (130, 151, 179) and symbolizes variously the yoke of a relationship, once love has cooled (151), the lady's hair, and her falsity (179).[34] All these metaphors—the ambush, the monsters, the net, the cannibalism—reveal the male's vision of an unhappy courtship. Love at first sight has gone sour, the lover wasted much time and now feels trapped and devoured, an unwilling victim.

Orlando succeeds where the lyric Boiardo failed. Undeceived, he cuts through the ambushes, on his way to the open foes which he fights at the garden gates. The epic poet corrects his personal history, or we might say that, if Orlando repeats with Angelica Boiardo's frustrated love for Antonia Caprara, this very love shields him from Falerina's wiles.

The other corruption of the concupiscible appetite is avarice, our desires directed toward objects rather than persons. As such it relates directly to love, and Boiardo makes it a recurring theme. He touches on the matter lightly here, as he explores the question much more fundamentally with the Fata Morgana. The poet stresses its comic aspects: a gold-plated ass with a serpent's tail and a loud voice, guarding a gate made of jewels. Orlando has little trouble killing the monster, not being susceptible to the vice. He gave up Morgana's tests earlier when found that he had to pursue the white hart with the gold antlers. His moral there appears several times in the epic: the avaricious never cease wanting more, and therefore they lead a life deprived of both honor and pleasure (1.25.14–15). The gold king who sits at dinner in Morgana's underworld, a sword suspended over his head, bears a similar moral (2.8.26), and the novella of Prasildo and Iroldo illustrates the theme graphically. Prasildo, having plucked a golden bough from the Treasure Tree, must give half of it to Lady Ricchezza at the gate. Avarice sits by her, and those who have want more (1.12.36). The vice affects a surprising number of Boiardo's heroes, including Brandimarte, who pursues the white hart which Orlando ignores (1.22.59). In this fashion Boiardo brings into his romance the realities of court life and the scramble for patronage and property by literary men and nobles. He himself nearly suffered assassination over his estate, and he fought losing legal battles with his relatives over similar questions. The career of a courtier made occasions for avarice more or less inevitable. And Boiardo discusses the matter explicitly during the Morgana episode, where he advises the courtier to follow whatever lord gives him favor: "Servendo sempre, e non guardare a cui" (2.9.1, "Serving always and not considering whom you serve"). Here, appropriate to the decorum of aristocratic epic and to the nature of the vice, he keeps the episode humorous.[35]

Normally Boiardo connects avarice to the Argonaut myth, the great treasure hunt which provided a model for many episodes in the *Innamorato*. Here we find Jason's monsters at the other gates: the serpent, the bull, and the armed men. The emphasis is not on the private vice, however, but on the political dimensions of wealth. Falerina is a queen and needs revenue. Juno, the goddess who patronized Jason's expedition and who bestows wealth and royal power, symbolizes this side of avarice; and Boiardo uses her peacocks, her rainbow colors, and her golden apples both here and at the center of the garden: the great tree on which all the enchantments depend. At the West Gate it is the monster bird which waits in ambush. She is a grotesque Juno, a bird woman who wears a crown and has the colored tail of a peacock.

The mythographers liked to point out that when the peacock struts about and raises its huge colored tail for display, it simultaneously shows its backside. They went on humorlessly to draw the conventional distinction between appearance and reality, the splendid appearance which conceals the anxiety and evils of a wealthy man.[36] Boiardo crossed this bird with Virgil's Harpy and made it a cannibal. Where the Harpies fouled the food which they ate, this bird excretes a boiling fluid which blinds its victims. Again the moral is the same. Servius considers Virgil's Harpies figures of avarice, as they are famished despite the rich flocks on their island.[37] More specifically, we might see in this bird of prey what Fulgentius found, wealth acquired by armed extortion or robbery, which, as we shall see, symbolizes Falerina's methods.[38]

The scene is quite effective in its violence and filth; and at the same time Boiardo demonstrates through the fictional action fine psychological perception. To defend himself against the bird's boiling fluid, Orlando first takes off his crest and laces his shield over the front of his helmet. In this way the poison will run over a flat surface and down the rest of his armor rather than trickle through the openings of his helmet. Simultaneously, this defense requires him to walk with his eyes on the ground, as he cannot look forward or upward. During its attack the bird flies around Orlando and harasses him, trying to force him to look out for danger and thus become blinded. The attack is subtle, as it uses our normal defense reactions to kill us.

The man without a crest, walking with eyes on the ground, iconographically signifies humility and can be glossed from St. Bernard's treatise on the subject. In one place the Cistercian contrasts the man of pride who looks up and the man of humility who looks down: "Ut quid audes oculos levare ad caelum, qui peccasti in caelum? Terram intuere, ut cognoscans te ipsum. Ipsa te tibi repraesentabit, quia terra es et in terram ibis" (*De gradibus humilitatis* 10.28: "How dare you, who sinned against heaven, raise your eyes to heaven? To know yourself, look at the earth. It will show you what you are, for dust you are and to dust you shall return").[39] The man who looks around and upward will be caught by the serpent at the tree. He forgets his earthly nature and thus is blind. In the context of the poem, we could say that wealth and political power are likewise blinding: the royal lord surrounded by flatterers and yes-men, the wealthy man who hears what he wants to hear about a given situation and not the reality. Hence he acts ignorantly, shut up in the darkened mind which is his inheritance from the Forbidden Tree. On the other hand, Boiardo gives the scene an unexpected twist. Bernard allows his monks to look around for two reasons: to help themselves, when necessity demands, and to help others. It is precisely the first that the bird tries to make Orlando do, to look up when danger threatens, the area of the morally permissible. And here is the subtlety of the temptation.

The varicolored plumage of the peacock associated it with Juno, and this bird has a similar array of colors. The many colors suggested the rainbow, and Juno, as goddess of the air who sends storms and showers, kept Iris as her special servant. The mythographers glossed Iris both morally and politically. The many colors suggested the splendor of riches but at the same time their evanescence, the bow in the clouds which shines momentarily and then vanishes. The political reading is more complex and depends on an etymological pun, the identification of Iris with Eris, goddess of strife, who with her golden apple started the Trojan War.[40] And of course the apples are on this tall tree, as they are on the other, which Orlando cuts down, when he destroys the garden. The two trees in turn are paralleled: by their height and by the makeshift shields with which Orlando defends himself against the perils of the air. They both mirror Juno, and we do not need Boccaccio's gloss on golden apples to know that they mean wealth.[41] Leodilla's tale makes this meaning explicit, for she is the rich king's daughter who loses her marriage race chasing after golden apples.[42] She returns us to the famine of the rich, the tendency of wealth to acquire more.

In his reading of the myth Boiardo does not represent civil strife or war, what the mythographers found in Iris and Eris. If there is conflict, it is that between ruler and ruled, the monarch who enriches himself and impoverishes his people. There is no civil war in Orcagna but, rather, a government which destroys its subjects. Fulgentius provides a better parallel in his discussion of Juno, when he refers to the political tyrants of old, Dionysius of Syracuse and the illegal despots of classical history.[43] As we shall see in a moment, Boiardo wrenches the myth of the serpent and the armed men in exactly the same way: from political strife to repressive government. The reasons for this change are complicated and must wait for my analysis of the political level. Now it is sufficient to suggest that Boiardo here treats wealth and avarice politically, for their connection with government; and that when Orlando cuts down the tree and causes the garden to vanish, he simultaneously images the man who destroys an unjust political system.

At the other two gates Boiardo explores the corruptions of the irascible appetite. The wild bull and the giants symbolize the problems of the warrior, who must learn to restrain his sanguine temperament. Orlando has more difficulty with the giants than with any of the other monsters, and he must bind rather than kill them.

In the *Innamorato* the normal indication of wrath is the reddened face of the sanguine humor, a frequent characteristic of Boiardo's heroes during a battle or tournament. In more extreme cases, their eyes flash fire and their breath flames.[44] Falerina's giants, however, are literally born of blood and fire:

> Quella era morto, e 'l sangue fuora usciva,
> Tanto che ne era pien tutto quel loco;
> Ma, come fuor del ponte in terra ariva,
> Intorno ad esso s'accendeva un foco.
> Crescendo ad alto quella fiamma viva
> Formava un gran gigante a poco a poco;
> Questo era armato e in vista furibondo,
> E dopo il primo ancor nascìa il secondo.
>
> Figli parean di 'l foco veramente,

Tanto era ciascun presto e furioso,
Con vista accesa e con la faccia ardente.

That one was dead, and his blood poured out so much that
the whole place was filled with it. But as the blood came from
the bridge to land, it caught fire. The living flame shot up high
and formed, little by little, a great giant, who was armed and
had an angry expression. After the first yet another was born.

They really seemed children of the fire, each one was so
sudden and furious, with a fiery look and a reddened face.
[2.4.74–75]

The giants personify wrath and so guard the North Gate, for the sanguine and choleric types thrive in cold northern climates. Dei Bassi
parallels Thrace, where the Mars of the *Teseida* has his house, to
Germany. In the north fierce, warlike people strive with each other for
the least causes and occasion the greatest evils.[45] As foremost warrior
of Charlemagne's court, Orlando likewise rages violently on occasion.[46] Consider the description when he falls into a battle frenzy at
Albracca:

Nel core e nella faccia viene un foco,
Fuor de l'elmo la vampa sfavillava;
Batteva e dente e non trovava loco,
E le genocchie sì forte serrava,
Che Brigliadoro, quel forte corsiero,
Della gran stretta cade nel sentiero.

A fire came into his heart and face, the flame sparkled outside
his helmet. He ground his teeth and did not find place, and he
locked his knees so strongly that Brigliadoro, that strong
horse, fell on the path because of his movement. [1.15.19]

Orlando cannot kill the giants because on one level they reflect the
problems of his own temperament. Boccaccio defines the dilemma precisely when he glosses his Temple of Mars:[47]

Questo appetito irascibile si truova prontissimo negli uomini
ne' quali è molto sangue, perciò che il sangue di sua natura è
caldo, e le cose calde per ogni picciolo movimento leggier-
mente s'accendono; e così avviene che gli uomini molto san-
guinei subitamente s'adirino, come che alcuni con grandissima
forza di ragione raffrenino e ricuoprano la loro ira.

You find this irascible appetite very ready to manifest itself in men who have much blood, because blood by its nature is hot, and warm things easily catch fire by the smallest movements, and so it happens that sanguine types quickly become angry, so that some only with great effort of reason restrain and cover up their anger.

Dei Bassi makes the same point with a different terminology. The sanguine person loses his temper less easily than the choleric because he has a gentler spirit, which by the greatest rational effort can restrain outbreaks of wrath.[48] It is this quality of rational composure which Boiardo associates especially with Orlando. He is the hero who gets the soliloquies, who reflects on his situation, moralizes episodes, lectures Agricane, and instructs Brandimarte. And here he wins by his own ingenuity, since his guidebook has no advice to offer about the giants.

In his novella of Fiello (1.8.16–9.35) Boiardo diagrams what happens when the sanguine temperament gets out of control. In one brief narrative he has collected all of Herodotus' exotic horrors.[49] Out of love for Stella, Marchino de Aronda murders Griffone, her husband and his host. In retaliation his own wife murders their children. One begs for pity, but she grabs it by the foot and dashes its head on the stones. She then cooks the two children and betrays the castle to her old suitor, the king of Orcagna, while Stella, the mistress, serves the boys to Marchino for dinner. In a rage he binds Stella to the putrid corpse of her husband and, when he sees the enemy troops coming, first murders her and then sexually violates her corpse. The victorious king of Orcagna has Marchino put to death by red hot pincers and buries Stella and Griffone together. He leaves Marchino's wife alone in the castle, guarded by three giants. Eight months later, she hears a terrible cry from the tomb. One of her giants opens it up and is devoured, bones and all, by Fiello, the monster born of sexual union with the dead, who henceforth requires daily human victims. Rinaldo, the last prospective victim, sees the castle from a distance, red as blood or fire, its walls hung with corpses, heads, and other parts of bodies still quivering. His own remedy is drastic but necessary, for he kills *everyone*. This story is particularly important because it introduces us to Orcagna, and I will return to it later.

The giants in this perspective diagram a process, how violence spreads and grows, something which Piero Andrea dei Bassi once more discusses in his *Teseida* commentary. He divides the order of Mars into three stages: wrath, discord, wars. Wrath moves a man to harm others, an act which provokes a reaction and hence discord, which in turn generates battles, where now many wraths drive men to great and irrational evils.[50] The violence multiplies by mutual response, as the giants multiply by murder, while in contrast a single one can be contained.

The giants also symbolize pride, the warriors who fought against heaven. In the manner of heathens they fight with scimitars, and their mode of birth indicates the peculiar character of their resistance, for their blood does not catch fire before it touches soil. In the *Genealogie* Boccaccio explains that the giants were born of Titan blood and of the Earth; hence they spring from an impious race which denied the gods. They have the pride of the Titans and inherited from their mother a downward tendency, never thinking of higher things.[51] That is, they resist heaven by turning earthward. They have strength and force without chivalry. On this level, then, Orlando overcomes pride in two forms: as royal power and wealth and as self-reliant force, the strong man armed, guarding his gate. Rodamonte is the supreme example of this tendency, the agnostic giant who fights unchivalrously and who relies solely on himself.[52] Orlando's giants are personifications, but in Rodamonte Boiardo discovered how to represent the psychology of a giant, how he thinks, which is one reason why Rodamonte is such a successful invention.

At the second gate Orlando encounters a wild bull, which comes up out of the ground and attacks him with a horn of iron and one of fire. It is the second which troubles Orlando, and the animal scorches him from head to foot. Orlando, however, has prepared himself. When he killed the Siren on his way to this gate, he smeared himself all over with her blood, and it protects him from death. Orlando kills the animal, which once more disappears beneath the ground. Boiardo here imitates the scene in Ovid in which Jason, protected by Medea's herbs, yokes the fiery bulls and plows the field of Mars (*Metamorphoses* 7.100–119). There are still more parallels in Apollonius' version, where the bulls issue from the ground and where all the tests involve Mars. The fleece hangs on an oak in the Grove of Mars and is guarded by an enormous serpent, born of Earth when Zeus smote the giant Typhon.[53] And in Boiardo the bull, earth-born and wild, fittingly balances the giants as a symbol of the irascible appetite. We can most conveniently analyze Orlando's duel, however, if we return to Ovid, whom we know Boiardo read, and consider the fight together with the other tests which Jason faces, the dragon and the warriors born armed from the earth. In Ovid they appear twice, associated with Cadmus and with Jason. As Boccaccio glosses only the first in the *Genealogie deorum gentilium*, we will have to consider both versions to understand Boiardo's variation.

In Ovid Cadmus loses his followers when they are destroyed by a serpent ("Martius anguis") which guards a grove.[54] He replaces them with the dragon's offspring, after he kills the animal and sows its teeth in a field. They shoot up armed men, and a fearful Cadmus seizes his arms, but one of them warns him not to interfere in civil strife. The soldiers battle each other to the death, and those who survive form the original Thebes.

On one level the myth explains the tragic history of Thebes, which culminated in the civil war sung by Aeschylus and Statius. Ovid wrote the moral into his text, and Boccaccio's historical gloss develops the idea. The Tuscan interprets the serpent as an old warrior who stirs up civil discord when he brings in outside forces (Cadmus' men). This action provokes a further intervention, this time by the Spartans, who were at that time a neighboring tribe. They appear suddenly, as if burst from the ground.[55]

The Jason story relates to the Theban dialectically. If one explained how civil strife came to Thebes, the other shows how it is avoided. When Jason accepts the challenge of the fleece, he saves his city from civil war, as he is the rightful heir to the crown and Pelias is a usurper. And he controls rather than kills the monsters. With Medea's help he charms the serpent to sleep and yokes the fiery bulls. The rest of the story runs parallel to Cadmus'. Jason plants the dragon's teeth and then watches as the armed men destroy each other. This time, however, it is discord in Colchis, not in Thessaly, abroad and not at home.

That Boiardo intended a political reading of this episode seems probable both from his sources and from his verses for the Tarot series. The face cards included a bull, the emblem of which represented Brutus and Cassius dressed in red, killing Julius Caesar. In his commentary Pier Antonio Viti stressed the unpredictable violence which such an assassination represents, for a bull strikes randomly with its horns.[56] The politician cannot defend himself adequately against such a danger, and the successful assassin often causes worse evil than he hopes to cure. In his verses for the card Boiardo connects the murder of Caesar to the massacres which immediately followed, modeled on the proscriptions first practiced by Marius and Sulla. The class of senators and knights suffered severely in these quasi-legal procedures, in which an informer on flimsy evidence could attack a creditor, a political opponent, or a private enemy.

> *Pericol* de gran foco una favilla
>   Porta: ecco Caesar morto nel Senato
> Da duo; e fuggì già el furor di Scilla.

> Danger takes a spark from a great fire. Two kill Caesar in the
> senate, and the madness of Scylla has already escaped.

And the red-robed Brutus and Cassius lead us back again to the giants,
born of fire.

On the other hand, these parallels do not establish the specific
meaning behind Orlando's duel with the bull. Where Jason charms, he
kills, and the armed men fight him rather than each other. Boiardo has
twisted the meaning. He has not, however, made it obscure. We can
plausibly argue that the bull has the root meaning assigned it in the
Tarot series: random violence, which Orlando removes. This was a
principal concern for Boiardo when he became captain at Modena. The
citizens carried arms, and homicide was frequent.[57] Vendettas, street
murders, and chronic urban violence plagued most of the Italian city-
states during the late Middle Ages and the early Renaissance. Sometimes the violence reached the level of real war, sometimes it did not.
Dante's Florence and Perugia under the Baglioni are good examples.
We have already seen that the giants represent the basis for this disorder, the sanguine humor out of control. These Orlando binds. Politically we could say that he rationalizes the use of power in the state or
destroys a system in which the passions express themselves in such a
corrupt or lethal fashion. For Italy the allegory could not be more
pertinent. Many city-states, torn by private feuds and disorders which
the government could not restrain, finally lapsed under the control of a
condottiere or illegal strong man, a situation closer to that in Orcagna,
where instead of a violence which the government cannot control we
see a government-sponsored misrule by violence. But I am sliding over
into political allegory and need some preliminary considerations before
I develop this, the most difficult part of my analysis.

The Historical and Political Levels

In the *Genealogie deorum gentilium* euhemerism is one of Boccaccio's
fundamental analytic methods. It explains his attempt to straighten out
the various divine families, to rationalize their interrelationships, and
to establish a chronology. Whether he discusses the *Aeneid* or a myth,
Boccaccio always takes care to state the historical sense of an event,
what other critics then called the "literal" level of an allegory. At that
time this insistence made much more sense, for the forms of history
and fiction were often close. In the first part of the Vulgate *Lancelot*,
for example, Pharien's tortuous politics—as he is caught between the
assertion of the usurper King Claudas, the rights of the infant heirs,
Lionel and Bors, and the demands of his own knights and of the

townspeople of Gannes—differ little from the actual dilemmas and choices of many barons when the Plantagenet system collapsed in France. Pharien's situation seems more "historical" than many a chronicle.

If romances often resemble history, we should not be surprised to find in military dispatches, chronicles, or travelers' reports the literary methods of romance. Ludovico Gonzaga writes home of an important battle as if it were a tournament.[58] Or consider Marco Polo: when he describes the battles of Chinggis and Qubilay Khan, he uses the inflated numbers and the formulaic superlatives and transitional sentences familiar to any readers of Boiardo or of Arthurian romance: "E fu la maggiore battaglia che mai fosse veduta. . . . Or lasciamo di Cinghys Cane, e diremo del Preste Giovanni e di sua gente . . . poteva ben fare quattrocentomilia uomini a cavallo" ("And it was the greatest battle that was ever seen. . . . Now we leave Chinggis Khan, and we will speak about Prester John, and of his people . . . he could well field 400,000 horse").[59] The Venetian (or his amanuensis) tries to give a sober account of his travels, but people read it for fantasy. Or we might turn to the *Istoria imperiale,* the narrative which Boiardo expanded out of Ricobaldo's bare chronicle. Giovanni Ponte has already shown that the grotesques and infernal hordes which confront Charles Martel resemble the Saracens of the *Innamorato;* and at Acre Saladin fields 600,000 horse.[60] The transformation of fact into fiction creates little strain when their literary forms are so close. This merging of history and romance applies particularly well to Boiardo, since in the *Innamorato* he uses a pseudo history for his authority and consistently calls his material a "storia."

Furthermore, in his pose as historian he is careful with his geography and places his wonders on the map. Boiardo locates his eastern marvels very precisely. They are all in Turkestan, the region north and east of Iran, between the Oxus and Jaxartes, the modern Amu Darya and Syr Darya. Ponte identifies "Orcagna" with "Organca" or "Organza," two of the many spellings for Urgench, the capital of Khawrazm, the area of the Oxus delta. He further equates Albracca (al-Bracca) with Bukhara, the next major city to the east, and argues that the siege of that city by Agricane (Agri Khan) recalls Chinggis Khan's celebrated capture of Bukhara (and Urgench as well) in 1220/21.[61] The vast empires and armies which fight around Albracca would therefore suggest the importance of a war which brought the Tatars pouring into the Muslim world and as far west as central Europe.

The merging of forms again helps to explain Ponte's argument. Marco Polo had already transformed Chinggis Khan into a typical

Boiardo hero. Like Agricane, the Tatar lord in the poem, he wars with large armies for a king's daughter and holds "la signoria bene e francamente" (*Il milione* 53: "he rules well, without deceit"). Like other Boiardo heroes, he wants to conquer the world and wins victories by courtesy.[62] Furthermore, Boiardo would have seen on Duke Ercole's *mappamondo* a Tatar empire roughly corresponding to that of Agricane and including specifically Orcagna.[63] In the poem the lord of Orcagna, Polifermo, serves the Tatar khan at Albracca.

The internal evidence of the poem supports these identifications. Angelica says initially that her father's realm of Cathay is 200 days' journey beyond the Tana or Don, a location on the Northern Silk Route which the Mongol armies constantly used and which Charlemagne's knights follow back and forth from Albracca.[64] This road was open only while the Mongols controlled the steppe and had been closed in Boiardo's lifetime.[65] The specific itineraries of the paladins place Orcagna east of Media and Iran, and casual references assume this location.[66] We know that Orcagna is nearer Nineveh than Babylon[67] and that Origille comes from Bactra or Balkh in Khurasan (1.29.6), and finally we learn that Orcagna has a seacoast, the Ponte Rose where Falerina traps Griffone, Aquilante, and Origille. This Boiardo calls the Sea of Baccù or the Caspian (2.2.39), into which the Oxus then flowed.[68] The internal evidence therefore confirms Ponte's equation of Orcagna with Urgench.

When Boiardo located Orcagna, his realm of wonders, in central Asia, he was following standard practice. I discuss elsewhere fairyland's drift eastward.[69] Here I will only say that in a romance like *Huon of Bordeaux,* the fairy king Oberon already lives in the Middle East. This area, removed from direct contact with the West, allowed the poet freedom of invention. Crusaders and merchants might frequent the coasts of Syria and Palestine; they seldom saw Iran or the Caspian. The poet could therefore create various marvels for these places, which none need question too closely. For the crusaders and for their readers, the Old Man of the Mountain had already made the general area fabulous when he built near the Caspian his fortress paradise and from there sent out his assassins. Modern romancers follow a similar practice when they set their stories in little known areas of the globe or on other planets.[70]

In the Quattrocento Tamerlane, his son Shahrukh, and grandson Ulugh Beg, had made Turkestan in particular the center for the fabulous. Cities like Samarkand, Bukhara, and Urgench suddenly rose anew, constructed with Asian plunder. Artisans, conscripted from everywhere, erected giant mosques and palaces, models for later imitation. Clavijo, who visited Tamerlane's court, wrote an account of it which reads like a fairy tale.[71] These cities, rather than those of India or Iran which Tamerlane had destroyed, were the places "where the gorgeous East with richest hand / Showrs on her Kings *Barbaric* Pearl & Gold" (*Paradise Lost* 2.3–4).

Boiardo did not strain reality, therefore, when he put his enchantments in Orcagna.[72] The garden palaces of his enchantresses, with their walls and gates studded with gems, suggest as much the pavilions of Middle Eastern *harem* as Western villas. The visitor to an Italian palace, for example, normally can see its monumental facade from the road and passes through the building to the large gardens at the back. Orlando, on the other hand, once inside the gate needs directions even to find Falerina's palace, and, as he approaches, he mistakes what he sees:

> A piè d'un monticello alla costera
> Vide un palagio a marmori intagliato;
> Ma non puotea veder ben quel che gli era,
> Perché de arbori intorno e circondato.
> Ma poi, quando li fu gionto dapresso,
> Per meraviglia uscì for di se stesso.
>
> Perché non era marmoro il lavoro
> Ch'egli avea visto tra quella verdura,
> Ma smalti coloriti in lame d'oro
> Che coprian del palagio l'alte mura.
> Quivi è una porta di tanto tesoro,
> Quanto non vede al mondo creatura,
> Alta da dieci e larga cinque passi,
> Coperta de smiraldi e de balassi.

At the foot of a hill he saw on its flank a palace carved from marble, but he could not see well what it was because it was encircled by surrounding woods. But when he came closer to the palace, he was beside himself with wonder, because the workmanship which he had glimpsed through the foliage was not marble but enamels colored with gold leaf, which covered the high walls of the palace. Here is a portal of a worth such as no creature ever sees on this earth, ten feet high and five wide, covered with emeralds and balas rubies. [2.4.24–25][73]

Here is a richness so buried in a park that Orlando cannot see it clearly through the trees. The palace does not exist for public display, and the many flowers and trees of the garden indicate Falerina's wealth as much as the emeralds and gold. The oasis or orchard in the East needs a strong wall for more than privacy. And Falerina uses balas rubies from neighboring Badakhshan, an area which could also have supplied Morgana with the *carbone* which lights up her treasure chamber.[74] Marco Polo has a description of Qubilay's winter palace which parallels Falerina's or Dragontina's in many particulars: the different kinds of trees, the varied landscape, the palace with its sculptured walls, covered with precious metals which gleam from afar, the fortress enclosure and security system, even the animals in the park: "cirvi bianchi, cavriuoli e dani" (*Il milione* 71, p. 86: white stags, roebuck, and fallow deer). These details have literary sources, of course, and we have already talked about the connections between the gardens of Falerina and Venus. Which is my point: the literary tradition and the oriental fact accurately reflect each other. At Orcagna reality is fantasy.

Boiardo provided his own best gloss when he inserted into the Ricobaldo a long passage from Bernardo Tesoriere which concerns the Old Man of the Mountain. The myth has a remarkable consistency wherever it appears, and it combines politics and fantasy in a way which might have stimulated Boiardo to invent Falerina's Garden: the Old Man lives in a remote mountain fortress and there makes a *locus amoenus* adapted to the requirements of the Qur'an, so that besides the pavilions of gold and marble, the timid animals, decorative birds, green trees, and odorous flowers, there are *huris* and fountains from which flow milk, wine, and honey. These items in themselves would not create a convincing parallel, but when we remember that the narrator treats his authority with the same irony that Boiardo directs at Turpin in the *Innamorato*,[75] that the garden is secret, strongly fortified, and closed to everyone but the Old Man's servants, the two gardens draw closer to each other. And the politics make the parallel striking, for both gardens serve lethal political and social ends. In Ricobaldo the Old Man is a dispossessed monarch, descended from the Parthian royal line and driven for refuge to the Caspian mountains. In retaliation he trains assassins, willing to risk anything, even death, to see the Old Man's garden once more, a brilliant inversion, appropriate to a revolutionary, of the Muslim paradise and the holy war—salvation by death in battle. His opponents are naturally those who drove his family from their throne, the new rulers and their administrators; and we shall see that when Queen Falerina in turn adapts paradise for murder, she chooses similar victims. Right now we must answer a preliminary question. Why should our poet have chosen Turkestan for his lethal paradises? Is it only the example of the Old Man of the Mountain?

If Boiardo found in these *harem* fitting symbols for Mongol splendor, be it of the first khans or of Tamerlane, their dark shadows, their hellish aspect reflected quite as accurately the other tradition, which Denis Sinor summarizes. Europeans, shocked at the violence of Mongol warfare, connected them to hell. The *Tatars* became the *Tartars* from the River Tartarus, beasts rather than men which ate human beings and drank blood. For such a sedentary people nomadic government was no better. High taxation and the "rapacity" of government officials made their rule intolerable. Giorgio Pullé thinks that the oppressions of the peacetime government outweighed all the massacres of war.[76] This fact may have suggested to Boiardo the way to read the bull at the South Gate and Orlando's final test, in which he does not battle a monster but cuts down Juno's Tree with the golden apples: the wealth at the basis of royal power, the taxation and system of administration. We can gloss both Boiardo's symbols and Pullé's analysis out of Friar Giovanni da Pian del Carpine, papal envoy to the grand khan, sent to examine their system and to understand their intentions. His report is one of the fullest, and there is evidence that Boiardo may have read it.[77]

Friar Giovanni relates that the Mongols tried to eliminate the governing classes in the countries which they ruled directly: "Intendunt etiam delere omnes principes, omnes nobiles, omnes milites et honestos viros de terra." (8.3: "They intend to destroy every prince, every nobleman, every soldier, and every man of worth on the earth"). The best a noble could expect was perpetual prison.[78] The Mongols further used hostages to control people and constantly demanded "gifts," which even the friar himself had to pay, though he was an ambassador.[79] Or they might poison their servants: "Eorum enim intentio est, ut ipsi soli dominentur in terra. Iccirco querunt occasiones contra nobiles, ut illos occidant." (7.5: "For it is their intention to rule the earth alone. Therefore they seek occasions against the nobles for the purpose of murdering them"). The artisans, however, and those designated as slaves were normally spared, though deported, once the Mongols had conquered a country (chap. 6.16). At his death Tamerlane had collected 100,000 such foreigners in Transoxiana, and he guarded the borders carefully lest any escape.[80] According to Friar Giovanni all aristocrats and artisans, old men, women, and children, paid taxes; and failure to pay meant slavery. The Mongols generally took one-tenth of both the people and their goods.[81] We might summarize the Friar's report by saying that the Mongols destroyed the governing class, deported the skilled labor, and taxed everything as much as possible.[82]

The Old Man of the Mountain and the khans, the heretic assassin and the lords who destroyed his castles and themselves misruled vast realms—these figures throw shadows across Boiardo's romance. In Orcagna he presents vivid images of misgovernment, of the abuse of political power, which Rinaldo and Orlando then shatter. The analysis is classical and therefore appropriate for an Italian Humanist: an exploration through a romance plot of tyranny in the polis. Iroldo, in fact, who gives us our first description of Falerina, may be hinting that her rule is illegitimate and therefore tyrannical in the old legal sense of the term. The Italian is ambiguous: "Quella incantatrice / Che ora de Orgagna se appella regina" (1.17.8, "That enchantress who now calls herself queen of Orcagna").

Boiardo creates this dimension through the myth of the Minotaur: the people served to the beast. He emphasizes this point through two earlier episodes, both involving Rinaldo. We have already discussed the Rocca Crudele, the red castle whose mistress serves wayfarers daily to Fiello, the beast so horrible that none dare view it (see 8.16– 9.35). This novella introduces Rinaldo to Orcagna, and Boiardo makes the whole into a harrowing of hell. The horned beast lives in a tomb and, Cerberus-like, is caught with a waxen cake. Moreover, astral time establishes the positive pattern, that of the Resurrection. When Angelica appears in midair, bringing aid, the night sky clears and the moon comes out. The morning star rises on the death scene, and Rinaldo breaks out of the tomb at sunrise. The horror of the place and the theological imagery effectively define Orcagna.

Shortly after, Rinaldo witnesses another such scene, which is our introduction to Falerina. A crowd leads Prasildo off to feed the dragon. The vignette is almost unique in the *Innamorato:*

> Chi senza usbergo, chi senza gambiera,
> Chi senza maglia si vedea venire,
> Tutti ribaldi e gente da taverna;
> E peggio in ponto è quel che li governa.
>
> Era colui chiamato Rubicone,
> Che avia ogni gamba più d'un trave grossa;
> Seicento libre pesa quel poltrone,
> Superbo, bestïale e di gran possa;
> Nera la barba avea come un carbone
> Ed a traverso al naso una percossa;
> Gli occhi avia rossi, e vedea sol con uno:
> Mai sol nascente nol trovò digiuno.

> One came without hauberk, another without greaves, another without mail: all of them coarse, tavern types, and worse in degree their captain.

His name was Rubicone. His legs were thicker than logs.
Proud, bestial, and of great strength, the lazy man weighed 600
pounds. His beard was black as coal, and his nose broken. He
had red eyes but saw only with one. The rising sun never found
him fasting. [1.17.23–24]

Boiardo translates the attack on the ruling classes into a romance setting and presents us with an image of an inverted social order. Now
aristocratic myth rarely represents the lower classes, and these are
dismissed comically. Rinaldo chases them two miles, leaving Prasildo
and Iroldo to wonder at the 600-pound man cut in half at a blow. The
rustics do not forget the incident, for when Orlando repeats the exploit,
the captain flees instantly, muttering about Rinaldo and Rubicone.[83]
The point is clear, however comical, and important enough to merit
almost exact repetition. Falerina kills knights and rules through the
mob.

Herodotus outlined the logic for this kind of politics when he staged
the debate over tyranny (5.92). Sosicles of Corinth reports the
following anecdote of a man who cut down the best of his own harvest.
I give it in Boiardo's version:

Ma dapoi che egli hebbe l'affinità e l'amistanza con
Thrasybulo Signore di Mileto divenne assai del padre peggiore,
e dicesi che havendolo gia dimandato per uno suo messo come
benissimo potesse lo stato governare. Thrasybulo menò l'imbasciadore fuore della terra à uno campo di biada, e parlando
tutta fiata con seco di cose fuor di proposito, a quello ch'era
dimandato percotea con una verga tutte le belle spiche che
l'altre sopra avanzavano, e sanza darli altra riposta rimesse
l'imbasciadore adietro, il quale ritornato a Periandro espose
non havere riposta alcuna, e che uno pazzo a lui parea Thrasybulo che le sue cose in tale forma guastava, ma Periandro intese essere consigliato di levare via gli houmini più
eminenti tra il populo, & in tale modo seguì questo consiglio
che redusse Coryntho quasi a ultima consumatione.

But then because he [Periander] had affinity and friend-
ship with Thrasybulus, lord of Miletus, he became even worse
than his father. It is said that he had already asked Thrasybulus through a messenger how he might best rule the state.
Thrasybulus led the ambassador outside the area to a field
of corn. Speaking all the time of matters irrelevant to the man's
question, he struck with a stick all the lovely corn ears that

overtopped the others. Without giving another answer, he sent the ambassador back. When this man returned to Periander, he explained that he had no reply and that Thrasybulus seemed a mad man to him, who was destroying his own property in such a fashion. Periander, however, understood that he was advised to remove all the most eminent men among the people, and he followed the advice in such a way that he reduced Corinth as if to its final destruction.[84]

If the tyrant kills the able, he maintains his power. His good is the ruin of the polis, and it is this symbiotic relationship which Angelica stresses in her concise summary of Falerina's system:

> ... Una regina piena di magagna
> (Così Dio ne la faccia dolorosa!)
> Ha fabricato un giardin per incanto,
> Per cui destrutto è il regno tutto quanto.
>
>   Perché alla guarda del falso giardino
> Dimora un gran dragone in su la porta,
> Qual ha deserto intorno a quel confino
> Tutta la gente del paese, e morta;
> Né passa per quel regno peregrino,
> Né dama o cavalliero alla sua scorta,
> Che non sian presi per quelle contrate,
> E dati al drago con gran crudeltate.

> ... A queen full of malice (so may God make her suffer for it) has built by enchantment a garden for which an entire kingdom has been destroyed.
>   Because as guard for the false garden lives a great dragon above the door, which has emptied the land round about of all its inhabitants, now dead. No traveler passes into that kingdom, no lady, no knight-escort, who is not captured in that district and given with great cruelty to the dragon. [1.28.30–31]

The monster daily requires more knights and ladies; i.e., the garden depends on continual, organized murder. It requires a wasteland or, rather, makes and extends one. And it is this political sense which distinguishes Boiardo's symbol. Through their Alcinas and Acrasias, other writers had explored, or would, moral and psychological problems closer to what I discussed earlier. Boiardo sets his garden in a tangle of historical and political circumstances and there demonstrates why Orlando must destroy it.

First of all, this paradise deserves ruin because it is literally demonic. Falerina creates her marvels through witchcraft. By night she works on the magic sword with charms, with the juice of herbs and roots, and the garden itself depends on demons. When Orlando cuts down Juno's Tree, he sees one in the fire destroying the garden. Witches normally work through devils, and in this case the spirits construct for Falerina a demonic parody of Eden: the *locus amoenus,* the dragon, the serpent women, the tree with its precious fruit, and the reward of death. It functions traditionally according to theories of demonic action. It manifests a drive to nothingness, the paradise that kills.

The demonic also suggests Falerina's weakness, for though witches had access to enormous power, they normally used it trivially. Despite the fact that they could control weather, raise storms and call down the moon, witches normally directed these awesome powers against single individuals, most often for revenge or in matters of love. We know how Faustus acted, and anyone who reads through the *Malleus maleficarum* and the witchcraft manuals will find cases similar in their logic to that of Falerina. The queen constructed this gigantic system of death solely to get at Origille and her lover. In this sense Falerina is a traditional witch with all the limitations inherent in privation, the technical definition of evil, a power based on absense or lack. Politically, she abuses power for private ends, a normal charge against a tyrant. In his speech Sosicles of Corinth exemplfies tyranny through Periander's abuse of the city's women, and we can easily recall the long list of sexual crimes which the Roman historians attributed to Tiberius and Nero. This misuse of power leaves the tyrant insecure and his government fragile, unable to survive a serious crisis. The ruler who acts for private ends loses public support, and no one has an interest in saving his government. Falerina, who rules by fear and kills her warriors, has in her hour of need no human defenders.

Boiardo demonstrates this peculiar weakness in the scene in which Orlando captures the queen. He finds her alone, unprepared and with the door open. Falerina is one among a number of powerful women who live in great fortress gardens, designed to keep everyone out, and are thus caught defenseless by the single soldier who manages to enter. Falerina's case has its particular irony, as we learn that she came to the palace the day before specifically to work on the sword (2.4.6–7), the weapon designed to kill Orlando, and she may be at present trying to discover his whereabouts. Kittredge observes that witches practiced sword gazing in order to detect a thief.[85] Several women in the *Innamorato* are captured while mirror gazing, and the differences clarify Falerina's particular weakness. Alexander the Great and Prasildo in his novella use their shields as mirrors to turn the weapons of their enemies against them: the basilisk, which kills with a look, and Medusa, who traps men by her beauty but who sees in the polished shield her own face crowned with serpents and flees in terror, forgetting everything.[86] Now Orlando afterward certainly uses Falerina's weapon against her monsters, but the scene of her capture differes markedly from these cases. Falerina looks at her own offenses, her sword, not another's shield. Her mechanism of death is finally her fragility, the demonic abuse which destroys its own instruments.

Politically, her system makes her servants unreliable. Her lower-class guards, who do not have proper armor, run away at the first attack, and her lady-in-waiting betrays her. The damsel speaks only very briefly to Orlando. Terrified by the queen, whom she hates,[87] she hurries off on a royal message, but she has time enough to reveal everything: the plans and defenses of the secret garden, even the thoughts of her mistress. Falerina can constrain obedience but not loyalty, and her system encourages treason. She rules by fraud, a fact suggested by her Latin name: *fallere,* to deceive.[88] Her garden is all ambushes and deceptions, and she has the Old Man trap travelers at the bridge. To rule by deceit befits the witch, since most demonic marvels are such, but on the political level fraud destroys trust. She who betrays will herself suffer betrayal. And her government, weak and corrupt, cannot survive the determined warrior who suddenly appears.

The happy ending of a romance? Perhaps, but a situation familiar to classical historians and political philosophers. We could cite proverbial examples such as Dionysius and the sword of Damocles, but the career of Nero is more suggestive, and the accounts of his reign by Tacitus and Suetonius were in the Este library. The aristocracy literally could not live under his regime. Whatever one's position, a man perished: Petronius, who directed his master's revels; Seneca, who withdrew; Lucan, who defended in poetry republican values; Thrasea Paetus, who fought for them in the senate. Neither family nor marriage could protect Agrippina, Octavia, and Poppaea Sabina. By night the emperor and his guards assaulted citizens on the city streets. And yet, with all his informers, Nero almost did not find out about the Pisos' conspiracy, though they planned ineptly and told a remarkable number of people about it; and when Galba marched south with an army, no one tried to defend the emperor. Nero is a particularly useful parallel in this case because, after the great fire which many thought he had commanded, he constructed his Domus Aurea and created a huge park in an area where people once had houses:

Ceterum Nero usus est patriae ruinis extruxitque domum in qua haud proinde gemmae et aurum miraculo essent, solita pridem et luxu vulgata, quam arva et stagna et in modum solitudinum hinc silvae inde aperta spatia et prospectus. . . .

Nero meanwhile availed himself of his country's desolation, and erected a mansion in which the jewels and gold, long familiar objects, quite vulgarized by our extravagance, were not so marvellous as the fields and lakes, with woods on one side to resemble a wilderness, and, on the other, open spaces and extensive views.[89]

He lived there barely three years.

Conclusion

I have tried to give an exhaustive analysis of Falerina's Garden. For each level I have isolated something different, a group of persons or objects, another part of the plot, and by asking a new set of questions, I have spun out the various allegorical senses. The plot yields philosophical and political readings; the gates, a cosmological one; the monsters, a psychological. I have shown that the fairy tale demands many explanations and relates to many different concerns, practical and profound. Yet we must recall that in itself the tale remains simple and is expressed in uncomplicated language. The chaste lover in the garden of the witch, the magical gates, the beautiful enchantress with the sword mirror: the whole could fit easily into Grimm's collection. Most people who love fairy tales have felt that they somehow say more than they appear to, and many have tried to express this *more* by theories or by interpretations. This chapter is one such.

4   Tasso's Enchanted Wood

Nam veluti pueri trepidant atque omnia caecis
in tenebris metuunt, sic nos in luce timemus
interdum, nilo quae sunt metuenda magis quam
quae pueri in tenebris pavitant finguntque futura.

As children in blank darkness tremble and start at everything,
so we in broad daylight are oppressed at times by fears as
baseless as those horrors which children imagine coming upon
them in the dark.[1]

For his *Gerusalemme liberata* Tasso claimed an allegory more complete and detailed than any since the *Divina commedia,* and at the same
time the process by which he came to that allegory shows the strain of
any such attempt in the late Renaissance. He and his friends were
neoclassicists by education, and the unified plot of the *Liberata* manifests the poet's commitment to Aristotelian principles. I have argued
elsewhere that such principles discourage the writing of allegory,[2] and
Tasso's experience illustrates my point. A century earlier Landino and
Boiardo had written allegory without apologies. Tasso had to argue for
his, and he came to the theory late. His early aesthetic, elaborated in
the *Discorsi dell'arte poetica,* has nothing to say about allegory, and
the continued caution and half-apologies with which he later brought
up the matter with his friends and which we read in his letters indicate
an attitude in his milieu either contemptuous of or hostile to the whole
endeavor. These comments of Tasso have in turn allowed modern
critics to ignore his allegory. One letter is frequently cited, that of 15
June 1576, in which Tasso tells his friend Scipione Gonzaga that he
devised the allegory as a shield against the censors. That is, there has
been a sense, encouraged by the poet's own remarks, that the allegory
is an afterthought imposed upon the text, a bluff for the Inquisition but

not serious matter for literary criticism. And yet we can cull from Tasso's letters statements to the contrary, assertions that the whole poem is allegorical and was allegorical from the very beginning. The wavering, the caution, the double statements manifest his strain.

The "Allegoria del poema," or what we call the Prose Allegory, shows the other side, the radical nature of Tasso's experiment. It introduced the epic in the early printed texts and presents the *entire plot* as allegorical. By this claim Tasso aligns his poem with works like the *Divina commedia* and the Vulgate *Queste del saint graal,* which demanded from their readers a symbolic interpretation throughout. Tasso thus returns us to the problem of continuous allegory, which I first discussed in connection with the *Camaldulensian Dialogues* and will speak of again with regard to *The Faerie Queene.* Emphases, however, will differ. For Landino I analyzed the whole interpretation, which applied to half of the *Aeneid.* Here I will develop, rather, the methods of the last chapter and explain a single, magical place: the wood near Jerusalem possessed by demons. My choice illustrates the differences between continuous and discontinuous allegory. In Boiardo Orlando visits Falerina's Garden, destroys her enchantments, and never returns. The episode can be interpreted in isolation, detached from its context in the *Innamorato.* Not so Tasso's wood: his characters return there again and again, and its signification grows over thirteen cantos.

We will begin with the poet's own explanation in the Prose Allegory:[3]

> Gli incanti di Ismeno ne la selva che ingannano con delusioni, altro non significano che la falsità de le ragioni e de le persuasioni, la qual si genera ne la selva, cioè ne la moltitudine, e varietà de' pareri e de' discorsi umani: e però che l'uomo segue il vizio e fugge la virtù, o stimando che le fatiche ed i pericoli siano mali gravissimi e insopportabili, o giudicando (come giudicò Epicuro, ed i suoi seguaci) che ne' piaceri e ne l'ozio si ritrovi la felicità: per questo, doppio è l'incanto e la delusione. Il fuoco, il turbine, le tenebre, i mostri e l'altre sì fatte apparenze, sono gl'ingannevoli argomenti che ci dimostrano le oneste fatiche, gli onorati pericoli sotto imagine di male. I fiori, i fonti, i ruscelli, gl' instrumenti musici, le ninfe sono i fallaci sillogismi che ci mettono dinanzi gli agi e i diletti del senso sotto apparenza di bene.

> The enchantments of Ismen in the wood, deceiving with illusions, signify no other thing than the falsity of the reasons and

persuasions which are engendered in the wood; that is, in the variety and multitude of opinions and discourses of men. And since that Man followeth vice and flieth virtue, either thinking that travels and dangers are evils most grievous and insupportable, or judging, as did the Epicure and his followers, that in pleasure and idleness consisted chiefest felicity; by this, double is the enchantment and illusion. The fire, the whirlwind, the darkness, the monsters, and other feigned semblances, are the deceiving allurements which do show us honest travails and honourable danger under the shape of evil. The flowers, the fountains, the rivers, the musical instruments, the nymphs, are the false syllogisms, which do here set down before us the pleasures and delights of the Sense, under the show of good.

The schematic and abstract nature of this passage initially might seem to justify its neglect by current critics. We do not normally think of dancing nymphs as false syllogisms. The remainder of this chapter, however, is designed to prove the contrary, to show that Tasso is a good guide to his own poem.

My argument has three parts. In the first section I will consider the genesis of the allegory and its relation to the manuscripts and early printed editions of the *Liberata*. Here I contend that the essential basis for Tasso's allegorization existed in the original draft of the whole poem. In the second I will analyze the various adventures of Tancredi, Rinaldo, and other knights in the enchanted forest and argue that the Prose Allegory gives a proper explication of these scenes. At the end I will discuss Tasso's Platonism, compare his allegory with that of the *Republic,* and try to place it within a critical tradition.

The evidence for the preliminary discussion is complicated. The so-called Poetic Letters document the genesis of the Prose Allegory. Tasso wrote them mostly to his Roman friends during the year 1575–76, when he revised his epic, and they indicate the kinds of arguments which occasioned a rethinking of his own poetic.[4] For the poem itself, we must consider more than one stage of its composition, though I will confine myself to citing a few relevant manuscripts and texts and will use the standard abbreviations established by Solerti.[5] Tasso began years earlier with a draft of the beginning, the *Gierusalemme* (1559–60); and by 1566 he had written a considerable portion of the epic, mostly that which concerned the historical preliminaries to the siege and perhaps the Tancredi-Clorinda story.[6] He returned to it in the early 1570s, and the manuscripts indicate two stages of composition, probably dated at 1572–73 and 1574–75. It is here, when Tasso is also writing the *Aminta,* that the wonders of the woods and gardens are introduced in the *Liberata.* By 1573 he had completed most of the poem through canto 16 (1–10, 12, 14–16) and so had practically completed Rinaldo's idyll with Armida. The following manuscripts represent this second stage, listed in probable order of execution: Cv (Cavalieri) and Mc (Marciana) together, Bm (British Library), Br₁ (Barberiniana).[7] The scenes in the wood are partially worked out: canto 7, in which Tancredi and Erminia lose themselves, and a prose sketch for canto 13, in which the demons possess a wood. He introduces this enchanted forest only in the 1574–75 stage of composition. The manuscripts for this period have the complete poem, including later revisions—essentially what he read before Duke Alfonso by June of 1575 (Letter 32, 2 June 1575, p. 81). I list them again in probable chronological order: Fr (Ferrara), Au (the manuscript of Sir John Soane) together with Es₁ (Este), and Es₂. To the period of revision belong Es₃, Br₂, and N (Naples).[8] Finally, there are the printed texts which editors at various times have considered authoritative: the two which Febo Bonnà edited at Ferrara in 1581 (B₁, B₂ and that done by Tasso's close friend and critic Scipione Gonzaga, which Francesco Osanna published at Mantua in 1584 (O).[9] We must remember, however, that the situation is much more confused than this schema suggests, for later corrections appear in earlier copies, creating the kind of inconsistency which naturally occurs when a poet sends various drafts off in the mail and gets them back at different times, while he is still writing and revising.[10] Finally, I append here a chronology for those of the Poetic Letters which document the stages by which Tasso made his Prose Allegory:

Date	Letter	Topic
15 April 1575	25	T. first mentions allegory in the poem: Goffredo as the head, Rinaldo as the right hand.
2 June	32	T. reads the last canto to the duke; the whole poem is now complete.
22 June	36	The Roman critics object to parts of the plot.
27 June	37	T. wants Tancredi overcome by fear in the enchanted wood.
17 September	46	Allegory is in the poem, though the literal is sufficient for the reader.

1 October	47	T. begins to repent of the wonders in the wood.
4 October	48	Allegory will defend the marvelous. It is already in the poem, but T. wants others to know it. Not every detail is allegorical, and the readers can make multiple readings.
5 March 1576	56	T. likes allegory better than he used to.
30 March	60	T. lists marvels that can be dropped. Rinaldo is the hand and Tancredi an incontinent youth.
14 April	63	T. provides a longer list of marvels to be dropped.
22 May	75	T. has written to Flaminio Nobili for help on the allegory.
15 June	79	The Prose Allegory which will introduce the poem has been written. T. did not think of allegory at first, as it is open to various readings and not in the *Poetics*. Not all of the literal level has allegorical meaning. T. has developed a new poetic: poetry through allegory serves the state.
June	76	The Prose Allegory explains everything in the poem. T. may have thought of it when he began the poem. He has left blank spaces in the draft of the Prose Allegory for Flaminio Nobili to fill in.
29 July	84	T. has received Flaminio's discourse on allegory and disagrees with him in that T. applies allegory to the nonfabulous portions of his poem as well.

Meraviglie and Allegory

Tasso turned to allegory for the same reason that motivated Homer's defenders in antiquity. They rationalized the marvelous episodes which involved the Olympian divinities and which Xenophanes and early philosophers found scandalous. Tasso in turn wished to protect his demonic and magical marvels from an anticipated similar kind of theological and critical attack. He was conscious of the parallel and said as much to Scipione Gonzaga, recapitulating *in nuce* the logic which led to allegory in the first place.[11]

Tasso had not thought of allegory earlier for two reasons: it invited multiple and capricious readings by others, and because Aristotle ignored it, he did not consider allegory part of the poetic art.[12] The first reason befits a man who was worried about censors and had seen all the allegories read into Ariosto. The second is borne out by other remarks in his letters and notes[13] and by his silence in the *Discorsi dell'arte poetica,* with which he intended to introduce *Gerusalemme liberata* to the public and which B. T. Sozzi considers the appropriate manifesto for the poem, rather than the later *Discorsi del poema eroico.*[14]

The marvelous, on the other hand, Tasso considered essential to epic poetry, as distinguishing it from other genres, and we must review his theory briefly, in order to understand how he later fits allegory into his ideas. I shall refer mostly to his earlier *Discorsi.* Tasso required the epic poet to be both verisimilar and marvelous in the *same* action, verisimilar because imitation was essential to the very definition of poetry,[15] marvelous because such effects were intrinsic to the genre of epic. As he later said to Scipione Gonzaga, "In questo sono ostinatissimo, e perseverò in credere che i poemi epici sian tanto migliori, quanto son men privi di così fatti mostri" ("In this I am most obstinate, and I will persevere in the belief that epic poems are so much the better, the less they are deprived of such marvels").[16] The poet made possible this union of seeming contraries by an appeal to the double level or viewpoint from which the Christian could analyze a particular event. He could consider it from either a natural or a supernatural perspective, and so the epic poet could describe marvels which would be miracles on the natural level but probable and verisimilar on the supernatural:

> Può esser dunque una medesima azione e maravigliosa e ver-
> isimile: maravigliosa, riguardandola in se stessa e circonscritta
> dentro a i termini naturali; verisimile, considerandola divisa da
> questi termini nella sua cagione, la quale è una virtù sopra-
> naturale, potente ed avvezza ad operar simili maraviglie.

An action, then, can be at the same time marvelous and verisimilitudinous: marvelous, when looked at in itself, and referred to natural limits; verisimilitudinous, when viewed apart
from these limits in its cause, which is a supernatural virtue,
powerful and accustomed to perform similar marvels. [*Discorsi dell'arte poetica* 1.356]

So far the theory. Here we find the poet already viewing the marvels
of epic on a double level, the natural world of visible facts and the
supernatural world of invisible agents. He is not talking about allegory,
but we can see how easily his theory could accommodate such thinking. Allegory had traditionally explained the invisible behind the visible,
and the marvelous episode had become its signal in the Renaissance.[17] Moreover, Tasso was thoroughly familiar with the theory and
principles of *allegoresis* and had already provided a practical example
in his lectures on Pigna's *Tre sorelle*. This demonstration occurred
before the second stage in the composition of the *Liberata* (1572–73).[18]

It was hardly surprising, then, that when Tasso's Roman friends
attacked the marvelous episodes in *Gerusalemme liberata,* he should
eventually turn to allegory for its defense. The dispute involved much
more than the Roman Inquisition: it concerned the deepest principles
of Tasso's art. Already in June of 1575, shortly after he had read the
first draft to Duke Alfonso, Tasso remarked to Pinelli, a Paduan friend,
that the Roman critics, while favorable to the style of the poem, objected to parts of the plot.[19] These parts were mostly the *meraviglie,*
and Tasso's normal line of defense was either to appeal to history or to
give way on nonessentials. And he could give way to a remarkable
degree. By 14 April of the following year he told Scipione Gonzaga that
he was willing to eliminate a long list of marvels, including the miracle
of Sveno's tomb, the fish metamorphosis, the magical entrance to the
mago's underground kingdom, the ship of fortune, and the parrot's
song (Letter 63, p. 161). At almost the same time, to Silvio Antoniano
he defended as matters of historical report the demonic storm, the
magical healing of Carlo, the attempt by magicians to enchant a siege
machine, and the apparition of the blessed souls as Jerusalem falls
(Letter 60, pp. 144–45). Beyond this point he did not go, and none of
these proposed changes was made for the *Liberata* as we have it. Tasso
went so far as to mark passages in manuscript which required deletion,
but they all remained in the poem.[20] Less than a month earlier he had
told Scipione that he liked allegory much more than he had before
(Letter 56, p. 134). And with allegory, of course, he could defend *all* his
marvels.

Tasso would have had to turn to allegory or some other such defense because the historical arguments he was using could never defend his principal episodes, the wood and the garden: neither had historical support. He argued with his friends over the garden in lively fashion and, though flexible on details, never suggested dropping the episode. With respect to the wood, he sensed trouble even before he received his readers' response and wondered whether its wonders really suited this particular history of Goffredo.[21] Three days later he had already worked out his allegorical defense, to which I now turn.

Tasso's turn to allegory took place in two stages: in the autumn of 1575 and in the spring and summer of 1576. In the first he talked of the poem; during the second he wrote the Prose Allegory. The evidence for the first stage comes from two letters to Scipione Gonzaga, written on 17 September and 4 October, respectively. The latter document is the important one. Here he first states that he will use allegory as a shield against censors, a point he will return to often in the letters. He is talking about Silvio Antoniano, a strict friend of Cardinal Borromeo and Tasso's most feared critic. The irony applies as much to Antoniano as to the notion of allegory: "Giudicai c'allora il maraviglioso sarebbe tenuto più comportabile, che fosse giudicato c'ascondesse sotto alcuna buona e santa allegoria" (Letter 48, p. 117, "I judged then that the marvelous would be held more tolerable because it would be thought to hide under some good and holy allegory"). He next states explicitly that, though he does not consider allegory part of the art of poetry, he has labored to put it into his epic:

> Se dunque i miracoli miei del bosco e di Rinaldo convengono a la poesia per sé, com' io credo, ma forse sono soverchi per la qualità de' tempi in questa istoria; può in alcun modo questa soprabondanza di miracoli esser da' severi comportata più facilmente, se sarà creduto che vi sia allegoria. *V'è ella veramente....* E sì come v'è, così avrei caro c'altri credesse che vi fosse.

> If, therefore, the miracles of the wood and of Rinaldo are appropriate to the poetic art in itself, as I believe, but are perhaps excessive for the quality of the times in this history, the severe [critics] are more likely to tolerate this superabundance of miracles if it is believed that there is allegory in them. *There really is* ... and since there is, I dearly wish others to believe that there is. [Ibid., p. 118; italics mine]

If we accept his words as straightforward, the allegory already existed in the text, long before the poet wrote his prose explication of the symbolism.

The manuscripts and printed texts of the *Liberata* support his statement. Tasso wrote the episodes of the wood late (cantos 7, 13, 18): the manuscripts of 1572–73 contain only canto 7 and an outline for 13; the rest do not appear until the final stage of 1574–75. As we shall see later, he wrote them at the same time as he developed his basic allegorical conception, the metaphor of the body politic. We would accordingly expect allegory in these fabulous episodes, and we are not disappointed. The lacunae which separate these original but late versions from the printed texts are few[22] and do not include the moral which closes Tancredi's and Rinaldo's adventures in the enchanted wood. The basis for this moral existed first in Tasso's preliminary sketch for canto 13, where the poet stated that all the enchantments of the wood were illusions.[23] The moral itself was in his first draft and is the same as the interpretation which he made for the Prose Allegory, namely, that the wood represents intellectual error. In the first episode, as Tancredi fails before the speaking tree, the narrator carefully says,

> Così quel contra morte audace core
> nulla forma turbò d'alto spavento,
> ma lui che solo è fievole in amore
> falsa imago deluse e van lamento.

> Thus no form of profound terror troubled his heart, courageous against death; but a false image and vain lament deluded him, who was weak only in love. [13.46]

In his revision Tasso strengthened his moral by prefacing it with a simile in which he compared Tancredi's reactions with those of a sleeper during a nightmare.[24] Tancredi fears the chimera in a dream and yet suspects "che'l simulacro sia non forma vera" (13.44, "that it is a phantom and not a true form"). Rinaldo, after he disenchants the wood, makes the point himself: "Oh vane / sembianze! e folle chi per voi rimane" (18.38, "O shadows vain! O fools, of shades afraid!"). The text thus bears out Tasso's claim to this extent, that each episode contains an official allegory. His later Prose Allegory would therefore be a legitimate reading of the poem, even though the poet wrote it posterior to his composition of the *Liberata*. It would not have been difficult, of course, to add such moral tags, but as we shall see in the second section of this chapter, the episodes themselves demand this interpretation.

At this time Tasso's attitude to allegory remains cautious. He still does not consider allegory a part of the poetic art, nor does he require more of the reader than a literal understanding:

> ch'io crederei che potesse bastare l'esaminare il senso litterale, ché l'allegorico non è sottoposto a censura; né fu mai biasmata in poeta l'allegoria, né può esser biasmata cosa che può esser intesa in molti modi.

> I believe that it is enough to examine the literal sense, that the allegorical is not put underneath it for censure; nor was allegory ever blamed in a poet, nor could something which can be understood in many ways be blamed. [Letter 46, p. 112]

The reader may rest content at the fictive level of the poem, but if he wishes to allegorize, he may draw what he can or wishes to from the *Liberata*.[25] That is, Tasso no longer objects to the freedom of allegorical interpretation which upset him originally, a temporary concession which he will soon cancel. Similarly, he does not claim allegorical valence for all the details of an episode and in a later letter quotes Ficino's *Banquet* for support, where the philosopher in turn refers to a practical comment of Augustine:

> Non omnia quae in figuris finguntur, significare aliquid putanda sunt; multa enim praeter illa, quae significant, ordinis et connexionis gratis adiuncta sunt. Solo vomere terra proscinditur; sed ut hoc fieri possit, caetera quoque huic aratri membra iunguntur.

> Not everything which is feigned in figures must signify something, for many things besides those which have symbolic meaning are added for order and connection. The earth is cut only by the plowshare, but other parts are also joined to this plow so this can take place. [Letter 79, p. 195]

The farmer needs more than a plowshare to dig the earth, and the artist has to put some things into his poem not for their possible meanings but for the organization and connection of events.

After a summer's argument with his friends, Tasso found his way to one of the classic theoretical positions over allegory. Some details, perhaps sections, of a poem have allegorical significance. The reader may stick with the literal meaning, or he may proceed further and discover other meanings as well. The readings of several people need not correspond. What we still miss was later suggested to Tasso by Flaminio Nobili: the equation of allegory with the fabulous or nonhistorical parts of a poem,[26] that is, with those portions of *Gerusalemme liberata* which Scipione Gonzaga and the Romans had been attacking. Tasso's later position, however, would be much more extreme.

Half a year afterward Tasso wrote the Prose Allegory for his poem. Four letters supply the evidence, two to Scipione Gonzaga (22 May and 15 June 1576) and two to Luca Scalabrino (an undated June letter and one of 29 July). It begins when he tells Scipione on 22 May that he sent his allegorical conceit to the philosopher, Flaminio, asking for advice. It closes on 29 July, when Tasso communicates to Scalabrino his re-actions to the *discorsetto* on allegory which Flaminio sent him.

Tasso turned to Flaminio Nobili for aid because, as he admits in the two June letters, he wished to work out a moral and psychological allegory for his poem but had read recently neither Plato nor Aristotle, the thinkers whom he tried to harmonize. He drew on his own memory and on various notes he had made earlier; but he left blank spaces in which Flaminio could write the original draft. The poet's dilemma once more involved the censors. Errors in philosophy or a philosophical position not strictly consistent with Christian theology could create difficulties at the press; and he intended the Prose Allegory to introduce the poem.[27]

This was not the first time Tasso had turned to Flaminio for help. Six years before he had heavily annotated the philosopher's treatise on love and had used it for his *Conclusioni amorose*.[28] Flaminio also had a manuscript of *Gerusalemme liberata* (Es₂) and marked passages in it for revision.[29] The two would naturally have known each other, as they both served the Este family and they had mutual friends.[30] Flaminio had studied philosophy in Ferrara, set his dialogue *De vera et falsa voluptate* in that city, and made one of the interlocutors Tasso's Inquisitorial correspondent, Silvio Antoniano.[31] My concern will be to gauge his influence on the Prose Allegory, as Tasso invited his collaboration, and later I will use his technical language, where necessary, when I turn to a practical analysis of the wood. I draw my evidence from a group of three treatises which Flaminio published in 1563 and Tasso annotated like a school text. The group comprises *De hominis felicitate, De vera et falsa voluptate,* and *De honore.*

Tasso would have found Flaminio's cast of mind congenial—an Aristotelian who liked to quote Platonists[32]—one willing to allegorize poetical myths.[33] His exegeses, while brief, fit the moral and psychological range which Tasso wanted and in themselves can be quite interesting. So in Hercules, the son of Jove, who nevertheless served Eurystheus, Flaminio finds an Aristotelian allegory of human life; for though the soul may shine amidst the highest glories of the universe, it serves the humble needs of the body. Tasso's *postilla* (to *De voluptate*,

p. 312) sums it up succinctly: "Hercules Jovis filius qui servit Euristheo animus qui corporis commodis servire cogitur" ("Hercules, the son of Jove, who serves Eurystheus: the mind which is constrained to serve the needs of the body"). Flaminio's philosophical thinking, however, was traditional, as he remarks in *De voluptate:* "Multa vero cognoscet ille, qui aliorum inventa quasi in unum locum conduxerit, animoque, et memoria comprehenderit" (p. 324, "That man indeed knows many things who has put together, as in one place, the discoveries of others and has apprehended them in his mind and memory"). He therefore designed *De felicitate* as a compendium of all moral philosophy (p. 82). Tasso found in him exactly what he needed: a contemporary and syncretic presentation of moral and psychological theory, derived principally from Platonic and Peripatetic sources. For Flaminio's influence on the Prose Allegory, however, we must first assess Tasso's general position.

The two June letters give us Tasso's ideas before he received Flaminio's *discorsetto*. They document a significant change in the poet's thinking. He now tells Scipione that he will combine Plato with his original Aristotelian position and produce a new poetic (Letter 79, pp. 194–95). He goes on to state the nucleus of the position he will later elaborate in the revised *Discorsi*. Allegory is the mode in which the poet serves the state. That is, allegory pertains to poetry insofar as the poet himself forms part of a larger community, the state, which can legitimately make certain demands upon its subjects. The poet delights by his art; as a citizen, he teaches and provides moral instruction.[34] Tasso assumes this distinction in the Prose Allegory: the poet delights his audience by imitation and instructs them by allegory. In this perspective we can see that Tasso intended the Prose Allegory to complement his earlier *Discorsi dell' arte poetica*. Both were intended to introduce his epic and together presented an artistic and political defense of the *Liberata*.

Flaminio had already suggested a theoretical basis for this new mixture when he recommended that Tasso read Maximus of Tyre. An orator and professed Platonist, Maximus lectured in Rome under Commodus and would have connected the poet directly to the traditions of Homeric apology and allegory. Tasso made use of him both for his general theory and for the Prose Allegory. He particularly developed notions from three lectures: 16(26), "Homer's Intention"; 17(27), "Whether Virtue Itself Is an Art"; and 29(4), "Whether Poets or Philosophers Discussed the Gods More Effectively."[35]

First of all, Tasso derived from Maximus his argument that poetry serves two ends, one proper to the art, one outside it. This second end concerns *virtus,* the use of an art, and in Sermo 17 Maximus gives some examples. While artisans have the skill to make plows or armor, other people and other considerations determine their use. The same distinction applies on a higher level. The end of medicine is not medicine but health and right habit (xlixV–lR). Tasso sums up the argument by his *postilla:* "Usus artis non est ut arte efficiat" (lR, "The use of an art is not that it makes [something] by art"). With this distinction Tasso was able to add allegory to his Aristotelian poetics. Allegory concerns the use of poetry, the end outside the art. Though he did not make this specific application, Maximus nevertheless provided its theoretical basis in Sermo 29, where he tacitly equated poetry with allegory.

In that lecture Maximus first identified philosophy and poetry, as Tasso's note indicates: "philosophia et poetices res nomine duplex simplex substantia" ("Philosophy and poetry are two names but one substance").[36] The two are distinguished like verse and prose, old and young, and veiled or fabulous and naked discourse. The advantage of poetry is its accuracy in the investigation of truth; its disadvantage, that it cuts off its practitioners from a broad audience. The old poet-philosophers responded to the basic need of the human mind, which does not honor things present but, rather, admires things remote. The poet appeals to this side of the mind, darkening truth with fable and making its understanding difficult. On the other hand, this cloak pleases the multitude, like the gilded clothes which priests put upon statues to induce greater reverence for them. Maximus' analogy is that of the poet-philosopher Lucretius: physicians put their bitter medicines in a sweet drink (lxviiiR–V). Tasso picked up the simile and put it into the proem of his epic:

> Così a l'egro fanciul progiamo aspersi
> di soavi licor gli orli del vaso:
> succhi amari ingannato intanto ei beve,
> e da l'inganno suo vita riceve.

> So we, if children young diseas'd we find,
>   Anoint with sweets the vessel's foremost parts,
> To make them taste the potions sharp we give;
> They drink deceived; and so deceiv'd they live.

[1.3]

This comparison probably came into the poem very late, and Maximus' argument could have inspired it.[37]

Poetry thus serves an educational and ethical purpose in society,[38] and Homer provides the model in his epic poems. In Sermo 16

Maximus approaches this question by his distinction between *ars* and *virtus*. In painting *ars* is the true imitation of shapes and bodies. *Virtus* is the appropriate arrangement of lines which gives an imitation of the beautiful: "linearum decora dispositio imitationem pulchritudinis reddat." In poetry, however, *virtus* becomes a philosophical category, and the philosophy involved is half ethical: "Id namque quod poeticem spectat—fabulae effigiem intendit: quod philosophiam respicit: id ad amorem virtutis ac veritatis cognitionem—penitus fertur"[39] ("For that which concerns the poetic art applies to the shape of the story; that which concerns philosophy—that directed toward the love of virtue and the knowledge of truth—is carried deep within"). By Maximus' analysis, Homer's philosophy is all ethical and political.[40] Both epics teach by example: ethics in the *Iliad,* politics in the *Odyssey.* That is, the philosophical spectrum corresponds exactly to what Tasso will sketch out in his Prose Allegory, as well as to the concerns of his friend Flaminio Nobili: a philosophy for human beings in action, shorn of metaphysics, epistemology, and physics.

Tasso likewise found in Sermo 16 an analytical model which he in turn transformed. Maximus argued that the characters of the *Iliad* exemplify different passions: fortitude in Ajax, shrewdness in Odysseus, confidence in Diomedes (xlviiiV). Instruction could be effected through negative exempla, as when the two young leaders, Agamemnon and Achilles, come through wrath into conflict (xlviiiR). For Maximus the individual personae in a poem reflect different internal passions. Tasso applied this notion not to the passions themselves but to the dispositions of the soul from which passions and thoughts proceed. So Rinaldo signifies the irascible and Tancredi the concupiscible appetites. Tasso thus made the ethical categories of Maximus more profound and thereby moved closer to Plato's *Republic,* in which whole classes of people correspond to similar appetites, the warriors, for example, to the irascible, the plebs to the concupiscible.

This experience likewise changed the poet's mind about what might or might not be allegorical. In June 1576 he still maintained a conservative position and told Scipione Gonzaga that he did not find allegory in every part of *Gerusalemme liberata* (Letter 79, p. 195). Maximus, however, made no distinction between the marvelous and the mimetic but read the entire *Iliad* and *Odyssey* from a single ethical and philosophical position. Tasso does the same to the *Liberata,* and in the other June letter, to Luca Scalabrino, he now claims that his allegorical reading applies to *every* part of the poem:

> Stanco di poetare, mi son volto a filosofare, ed ho disteso minutissimamente l'Allegoria non d'una parte ma di tutto il poema; di maniera che in tutto il poema non v'è né azione né persona principale che, secondo questo nuovo trovato, non contenga maravigliosi misteri.

> Tired of poetizing, I have turned to philosophizing and have extended most minutely the allegory not of a part but of the whole poem, in such a manner that in the entire poem there is neither action nor principal character that, according to this new finding, does not contain marvelous mysteries. [Letter 76, p. 185]

He then says that Luca probably will laugh but defends himself by an appeal once more to the censors. And we can hypothesize his thinking here with some probability. Tasso had originally objected to the open-endedness of allegory, to the fact that every reader made of it what he wanted. By a particularization of the allegory and its application to every episode in the poem, the poet could successfully delimit this freedom, if not close it off altogether. In this way no censorship could ever occur. And the Prose Allegory supports this hypothesis. Few people or incidents escape explicit mention, and the general theory is flexible enough to apply anywhere.[41] A month later, when he received Flaminio's letter, he reaffirmed this new position and at the same time distinguished his own thinking from that of the philosopher. Flaminio equated allegory with the fabulous parts of poetry, the standard notion which Tasso may have shared until June of 1576. Now he extends his exegesis to the other parts of the poem and defends himself by reference to the critics of Homer and Virgil.[42] And in the Prose Allegory he makes no distinction between historical and fabulous events and is willing to read them both symbolically. Everything has become allegorical. We might hypothesize that while Flaminio helped the poet toward a new art theory, particularly when he recommended that Tasso read Maximus of Tyre, he himself merely suggested a vocabulary for the Prose Allegory and perhaps sharpened some of the poet's distinctions. His thought supplements that of the poet, but his letter arrived too late. The Prose Allegory in its essentials was probably already complete.

In his two letters of June Tasso reviewed this whole development in what seems contradictory terms. Modern critics normally quote his skeptical remark to Scipione Gonzaga: "quando cominciai il mio poema non ebbi pensiero alcuno d'allegoria, parendomi soverchia e vana fatica" (Letter 79, p. 192, "When I began my poem, I had no idea of allegory, for it seemed to me an excessive and empty labor"). To Scalabrino, in contrast, he implies that he thought allegorically from the start:

> Ma certo, o l'affezione m'inganna, tutte le parti de l'allegoria son in guisa legate fra loro, ed in maniera corrispondono al senso litterale del poema, ed anco a' miei principii poetici, che nulla più; ond' io dubito talora che non sia vero, che quando cominciai il mio poema avessi questo pensiero.

> But certainly, or affection deceives me, all the parts of the allegory could not be more internally consistent and correspond in a manner to the literal sense of the poem and also to my poetic principles, whence I wonder sometimes if it were not true that, when I began my poem, I did not have this idea. [Letter 76, p. 185]

Both statements point to truths. Certainly the historical sections of the *Liberata* which Tasso wrote in the 1560s contain nothing that suggests the Prose Allegory. When he returned to the poem in the early 1570s, however, we find right away the metaphor of the body politic, the basic conception behind the Prose Allegory. It thus comes into the poem along with the marvelous episodes of the woods and gardens, the kind of scenes which Flaminio identified with allegory. The metaphor first appears in the revision of canto 1 which Tasso did in 1572–73. At the initial conference Peter the Hermit uses it to climax his argument that the crusaders should elect a monarch:

> Ove un sol non impera, onde i guidìci
> pendano poi de' premi e de le pene,
> onde sian compartite opre ed uffici,
> ivi errante il governo esser conviene.
> Deh! fate un corpo sol de' membri amici,
> fate un capo che gli altri indrizzi e frene,
> date ad un sol lo scettro e la possanza,
> e sostenga di re vece e sembianza.

> Where divers Lords divided empire hold,
>   Where causes be by gifts, not justice, tried,
> Where offices be falsely bought and sold,
>   Needs must the lordship there from virtue slide.
> Of friendly parts one body then uphold,
>   Create one head the rest to rule and guide,

To one the regal power and sceptre give,
That henceforth may your king and sovereign live.

[1.31]⁴³

In 1574–75 Tasso elaborated the metaphor. It appears in the scene in
which Guelfo and Ugone plead for Rinaldo's recall:

Perché se l'alta Providenza elesse
te de l'impresa sommo capitano,
destinò insieme ch'egli esser dovesse
de' tuoi consigli essecutor soprano.
A te le prime parti, a lui concesse
son le seconde: tu sei capo, ei mano
di questo campo.

For as the Lord of hosts, the King of bliss,
    Hath chosen thee to rule the faithful band,
So he thy stratagems appointed is
    to execute, so both shall win this land;
The first is thine, the second place is his,
    Thou art this army's head, and he the hand:
No other champion can his place supply,
And that thou do it doth thy state deny.

[14.13]

Rendi il nipote a me, sì valoroso
E pronto essecutor rendi a te stesso.

To me my nephew, to thyself restore
a valorous and prompt executor.

[14.24]⁴⁴

Goffredo is the head; Rinaldo, his right hand. It is to this notion that
Tasso later refers in a letter to Scipione Gonzaga, written more than a
month *before* the poet finished reading the first full draft of the poem to
the duke and long before he adopted an allegorical theory. He is defending Rinaldo's wanderings:

io so molto bene d'essermi dilatato assai più di Virgilio e
d'Omero, procurando di dilettare; ma che stimo però che
questa latitudine, per così dirla, sia restretta dentro a i termini
d'unità d'azione almeno, se non d'uomo, benché i molti
cavalieri sono considerati nel mio poema come membra d'un
corpo, del quale è capo Goffredo, Rinaldo destra; sì che in un
certo modo si può dire anco unità d'agente, non che d'azione.

I know well that I have gone much further than Virgil or
Homer in trying to delight. However, I consider that this so-
called latitude is restricted at least within the bonds of unity of
action, if not of the hero, because the many knights in my
poem are considered as members of a single body, of which
Goffredo is the head, Rinaldo, the right hand, so that in a
certain manner one could speak also of unity of agent, not just
of action. [Letter 25, p. 65]

That is, if we consider the various heroes as parts of a single human
being, then there is unity of agent as well as action in *Gerusalemme
liberata*. This is exactly the interpretation of the poem which Tasso
wrote a year later for the Prose Allegory:

L'esercito composto di varii principi e d'altri soldati cristiani, significa l'uomo virile, il quale è composto d'anima e di
corpo, e d'anima non semplice, ma distinta in molte e varie
potenze.

The army compounded of divers princes, and of other
Christian soldiers signifieth Man, compounded of soul and
body, and of a soul not simple, but divided into many and
diverse powers.

He supports the interpretation by two quotations, taken from those
sections of the epic which he wrote in the early 1570s:

Tu il senno sol, lo scettro adopra;
ponga altri poi l'ardire e 'l ferro in opra.

Rule with thy sceptre, conquer with thy word,
Let others combat make with spear and sword.

[7.62]

L'anima tua, mente del campo e vita
cautamente per Dio sia custodita.

Your happy life is spirit, soul, and breath,
Of all this camp, preserve it then from death.

[11.22][45]

Goffredo is the mind of the body, its life principle or soul.[46]

It is this allegory, moreover, which explains what could have been an
embarrassing crux in the plot. After his warriors have failed to dis-
enchant the wood, Goffredo considers braving its marvels by himself

(13.50–51). The situation demands urgent action, because the army needs siege towers to capture Jerusalem and can find wood nowhere else. Besides his reputation for piety, Goffredo has proved himself in many chivalric exploits, both in open battle and in single combat,[47] and seems the right person to battle demonic miracles. Peter dissuades him, and drought afflicts the stalled army. In his vision Peter alludes indirectly to Rinaldo, the proper hero for this enterprise, and Goffredo learns later that Rinaldo is indeed the appropriate person because of the allegory. Ugone in a dream reverts again to the metaphor of the head and the right hand (14.13), which I just quoted. Here the literal level of the plot depends upon the allegorical conception.

The evidence indicates that Tasso was thinking allegorically when he returned to finish the poem in the early 1570s. In the *Discorsi dell'arte poetica* he had defined the marvelous as essential to epic, and it was in this last period of writing that he put most of his marvels into the *Liberata*. Such scenes had conventionally been read as allegory in the Renaissance, and in his *Considerazione sopra tre canzoni di . . . Pigna* Tasso had shown a thorough command of allegorical theory and practice. The demand for the marvelous and familiarization with allegorical technique existed before he returned to the poem in 1572. In that last push which finished the poem, Tasso not only developed the fabulous episodes in woods and gardens but worked out a central metaphor, that of the body politic, which he introduced to the historical sections of the epic. That is, he was seeing the entire epic allegorically, including scenes originally written ten years before. Then in response to friendly criticism he saw how allegory related to his already established theory of poetry and wrote out a prose introduction to the symbolism of the *Liberata* and a defense against the neoclassical critique which he had received during his year of revision. The Prose Allegory thus reinforces and clarifies earlier ideas and accurately reflects the content of *Gerusalemme liberata*.

The poet found these ideas and his allegorical model ultimately in Plato's *Republic*. When Tasso lectured on Pigna's *Tre sorelle*, he had already used its psychological map of the soul with which we have become familiar through Boccaccio, and he later applied these categories to the *Liberata*. We will look briefly at the Platonic original now, to clarify the kind of thought which Tasso demanded from his readers. Though we know the psychological theory, we have had little experience with the literary method. We do not normally reduce characters in a mimesis to psychological categories per se or turn a plot into a chess game of the *anima*.

Much of the *Republic* is an exercise in analogical thought. Socrates introduces his utopia to clarify another problem (2.368–69). He wishes to contrast the just man with the successful tyrant and decides that it is easier first to understand justice in the state and then to apply this understanding to individuals. The analogy of *B* (the state) diagrams *A* (the individual). Socrates explains this method by another analogy. Suppose we are asked to read small letters at a distance but find ourselves unable to see clearly. If able, we would go elsewhere and read the same letters writ large and then, of course, come back and check to see whether the small letters were indeed the same. Thus the description of utopia becomes one term in an analogy, and the argument applies simultaneously on two levels: that of the state and that of the individual. In books 8 and 9, for example, Socrates constantly veers between the two. He is describing the decline of the polis and normally illustrates the process by the development of typical individuals in a family situation. So in a tyrannical state the lawless desires which sleep reveals, both sexual and homicidal, are liberated and rule over a young man. First he spends his inheritance, then steals from his parents, and finally revolts against both parents and state. His degeneration diagrams a political process, the movement from street violence to revolution and a tyrannical takeover (9.571A–576C). Thus Socrates moves between terms in his analogy, and his metaphor allows him to explain psychological traits and political behavior simultaneously.

Tasso saw that Maximus in Sermo 21(37) applied to Socrates' fable the terms he reserved elsewhere for poetry (KvR).[48] Socrates uses a dream method for the ruder sort, a speech which resembles that of oracles because it depends upon analogy. Platonic myth is thus polyvalent speech, a fable which explains more than one topic. It does so because the interlocutors in a Platonic dialogue seek explanations which apply to several questions at once. In Sermo 22(38) Maximus has Plato say that he seeks the *virtus* by which a person can best govern either his family or the state (lxiiiR). Such pursuits naturally invite polyvalent analogies. The poets later adapted this Platonic method, and it characterizes developed allegory. We have seen, for example, how Virgil used Juno to explore both meteorological and psychological phenomena. The same model applies in diverse sciences and explains why critics could discover many "levels" of meaning in a scene or poem. The poet does not imagine simultaneously disparate problems and studies. He thinks in paradigms which he can direct to different questions and which the critics can then extrapolate. The formula is simple and the poetry polyvalent.

Tasso thinks in the same way. The Christian army, paralyzed before

Jerusalem, signifies the disintegration of the individual. Reason loses control over the passions, as Rinaldo (the irascible) rejects its rule and the other soldiers desert camp, pursuing women (the revolt of the concupiscible appetite). By canto 8 reason is confined to camp, where mutiny occurs. A countermovement then begins as Goffredo (reason) first quells the mutiny, receives the defectors back in camp, and with them repels a guerrilla attack. Rinaldo, however, remains abroad, and only with his submission can the whole man act in harmony and achieve civil felicity (capture Jerusalem). The general or group dilemma mirrors that of the individual, or, rather, as in Plato the two reflect each other. The poem is both the mimesis of a historical event, in which characters have complete and individualized personalities, and a symbolic paradigm for the psychological growth of Everyman.

It is also evident that both Plato and Tasso use the process allegory which I have discussed. Socrates presents the origins of justice and injustice in the state and later sketches the decline of a typical polis, while Tasso similarly dramatizes the disintegration and reintegration of the individual. The symbolism applies not to static objects or conceptions but to change and growth. In Plato a lion, man, or many-headed beast can represent the interaction of θυμός (the irascible), reason, and ἐπιθυμία or the concupiscible (9.580–89); and Tasso does the same with his warrior heroes: Rinaldo, Goffredo, and Tancredi. The method is simple in its assumptions but complex in its application, as it depicts a series of fluid situations. We shall see how complex as we turn now to the adventures of Tancredi and Rinaldo in the enchanted wood and see how Tasso's allegory was more than an elaborate theory or a series of moral tags or metaphors scattered through his story.

The Wood of Error

The analysis here has three parts. I will first sketch the significance of the wood itself and show that Tasso developed a traditional conception. Second, I will examine the fear which the wood evokes and demonstrate how this emotion fits into Tasso's psychological allegory. Third, I will analyze the way in which the wood causes lovers to wander and try to explain how the poet could convert nymphs into syllogisms. Throughout I will refer to two sources which clarify Tasso's presentation: the dark wood of *Inferno* 1 and 2 and an episode from Boiardo's *Orlando innamorato,* in which the nymphs of Riso possess a wood and enchant knights (2.31.33–36, 43–48; 3.6.40–7.41).

Tasso presents his wood primarily in three cantos. Tancredi and Erminia lose themselves in a wood (7) which Ismeno then enchants (13) and Rinaldo exorcises (18).[49] This forest is fundamental to Tasso's plot. Without timber the Christians cannot make siege towers to assault Jerusalem. They cannot cut wood anywhere else, but demons protect the trees of this wood and frighten away the crusaders. Its exorcism is thus the necessary preliminary to the capture of Jerusalem, which falls immediately after. We would accordingly expect the wood to focus a problem crucial to Tasso's allegory, and that problem concerns the mind.

Tasso tells us in the Prose Allegory that Ismeno's enchantments signify false reasoning and the forest itself the circumstances which generate it: the variety of appearances and of human discourse. His presentation of the possessed wood in canto 13 exactly corresponds to this interpretation. Those who visit it shrink before different illusory phenomena and explain what they experience in conflicting interpretations. These explanations in turn illustrate a pattern of circular reasoning.

The enchantment of the wood itself proceeds from a confused mind, for though Ismeno may order demons about like servants, he himself exists in mental contradictions:

> Questi or Macone adora, e fu cristiano,
> ma i primi riti anco lasciar non pote;
> anzi sovente in uso empio e profano
> confonde le due leggi a sé mal note.

> A Christian once, Macon he now adores,
>   Nor could he quite his wonted faith forsake,
> But in his wicked arts both oft implores
>   Help from the Lord, and aid from Pluto blake.

[2.2]

Clorinda, the orthodox Muslim, indicates this confusion later, when she censures a man who pollutes mosques with Christian statues (2.50–51). The demons in their turn develop local fantasies about the wood, the kind of popular opinion which Peter the Hermit condemns as inherently misleading and untrustworthy:

> ... O cavalier, seguendo il grido
> de la fallace opinion vulgare,
> duce seguite temerario e infido
> che vi fa gire indarno e traviare.

> Sir kinghts (quoth he), if you intend to ride
>   And follow each report fond people say,

You follow but a rash and trothless guide,
      That makes men circle about in vain and wander.

[14.30]

Circular motion indicates false reasoning, and Tasso develops this metaphor in two ways. The explanations of Ismeno's wood make a circular argument, and characters literally wander in circles.

Common opinion in this instance connects the wood to witchcraft. The natives of the region believed that witches celebrated their Sabbat in this wood. The shepherds generally avoided the place and if there would not even pluck a branch from a tree. The basis for this belief was fear of the dark:

Ma quando parte il sol, qui tosto adombra
notte, nube, caligine ed orrore
che rassembra infernal, che gli occhi ingombra
di cecità, ch'empie di tema il core;
né qui gregge od armenti a' paschi, a l'ombra
guida bifolco mai, guida pastore,
né v'entra peregrin, se non smarrito,
ma lunge passa e la dimostra a dito.

But when the sun his chair in seas doth steep,
      Night, horror, darkness thick, the place invade,
Which veil the mortal eyes with blindness deep,
      And with sad terror make weak hearts afraid.
Thither no groom drives forth his tender sheep
      To browse, or ease their faint in cooling shade;
Nor traveller nor pilgrim there to enter
      (So awful seems that forest old) dare venture.

[13.3]

That is, the common opinion lacks any sort of verification, though it reflects a familiar psychological reaction. Boccaccio describes the mentality when he explains how the Arcadian peasants from an analogous experience invented a god:

Cui errori auxit fidem apud rusticos antra ac profundissimos terrarum abditus intrasse non numquam in quibus cum in processu languescente luce silentium augeri videatur, subintrare mentes cum nativo locorum horrore religio consuevit et ignaris presentie alicuius divinitatis suspicio quam a talibus suspicatam divinitatem, non alterius quam Demogorgonis existimabant, eo quod eius mansio in terre visceribus crederetur ut dictum est.

What added faith to error among the country people was that they never entered caves and deep secret places but that, along with the native horror of such places, a religious sense normally entered their minds, as they advanced inside, and the light failed and the silence grew. Such experiences made the ignorant people suspect the presence of some god, whom, though his divinity was for some suspect, others thought to be no other than Demogorgon, because they believed his house to be in the bowels of the earth. [*GDG* 1, p. 14]

The rustics projected their fantasies of Demogorgon on the dark, and the Syrian shepherds do likewise. They dream, Renaissance-fashion, of witches who fly to the wood and perform impious rites, "che fallace imago / suol allettar di desiato bene" (13.4, "allured by the false image of a desired good"). Fittingly, they fantasize others deceived, and error turns on error.[50]

We can gauge the extent of their mistake because the narrator allows us another view of the wood. Though dark, it has old and lovely trees, which we see through a decorative catalog as the crusaders cut them down the first time (3.75–76). The wood is neutral, a natural object which the euhemerist imagination turns into a bad dream.[51]

By delusive images and sounds the demons work variations on this original error.[52] Tasso dramatizes the process most effectively, and we can see the whole series of conjectures and reports leading the Christians back to a false belief not much different from that of the Syrian rustics. The dark suffices to frighten the first group of woodcutters, who, as they saw nothing, invent horrors (13.18–19). Each individual having a different imagination and projecting different monsters, they talk in contradictions. The soldiers rightly greet these statements with scorn and disbelief. The second expedition, though it returns in rout and disorder, nevertheless gives a clearer answer. One speaks for all:

> Signor, non è di noi chi più si vante
> troncar la selva, ch'ella è sì guardata
> ch'io credo (e 'l giurerei) che in quelle piante
> abbia la reggia sua Pluton traslata.

> My lord, not one of us there is, I grant,
>   That dares cut down one branch in yonder spring;

> I think there dwells a sprite in every plant,
>> There keeps his court great Dis, infernal king.

[13.23]

The theory here is largely correct, as we know the wood is possessed, and on its basis Goffredo later asks Alcasto whether the marvels are natural or the results of demonic magic ("prestigi," 13.30). The evidence, however, is flimsy: a terrifying sound. The Swiss leader, who next goes to the wood, by his silence and failure only increases the mystery and uncertainty. Tancredi finally brings Goffredo what he asked: a careful, accurate description of the marvels, accurate but for one crucial slip. The Tancredi who failed before the tree which spoke in Clorinda's voice still suspected deceit:

> tal il timido amante a pien non crede
> a i falsi inganni, a pur ne teme e cede.

> So the timid lover did not fully believe in the false deceptions but feared them and gave in. [13.44]

In his speech to Goffredo, however, he repeats without qualification what the demon says. Tancredi would have the Christians believe that human beings and not demons inhabit the trees. We have gone from one mistake to another, from dreams of witches' revels to fantasies of metamorphosis.[53] The true guess lacked evidence, while the false has the full panoply of inductive verification.

All here is traditional: the wood, the psychological effect of darkness, the circling, and the signification of these symbols. They existed already in the first canto of the *Divina commedia*.[54]

The commentators in two of Tasso's three editions of Dante agreed on the significance of his dark wood. Landino's gloss suffices:

> come disse a principio, perché sì come la selva oppressa da molti e spessi albori si rende oscura per non potervi penetrar il lume del Sole, così mente oppressa da molti e spessi errori si rende oscura per non poter usar del lume della ragione.

> As I said at the beginning, just as the wood, oppressed by many dense trees, becomes dark because the light of the sun cannot get through, so the mind, oppressed by many and dense errors, becomes dark because it cannot use the light of reason. [Landino-Vellutello 2Vb]

Darkness signifies a mind thinking irrationally. Daniello equates the wood with ignorance, blindness of mind.[55] Tasso in turn works out this interpretation dramatically, as we see the various soldiers devise fantastic explanations for the phenomena which they see. Fear stimulates their interpretations,[56] and this emotion signifies the moral basis for mental confusion.

In the *Inferno* Virgil tells Dante many times that his recurring fear indicates a soul weakened by cowardice.[57] When it considers an honorable enterprise, the soul imagines beasts in the dark. Tasso has the same explanation for the demonic marvels of canto 13:

> però che l'uomo segue il vitio, e fugge la virtù, o stimando, che le fatiche, e i pericoli siano mali gravissimi, e insopportabili, . . . Il fuoco, il turbine, le tenebre, i Mostri, e l'altre sì fatte apparenze, sono gl'ingannevoli argomenti, che ci dimostrano le honeste fatiche, e gli honorati pericoli, sotto imagine di male.

> And since that Man followeth vice and flieth virtue, either thinking that travels and dangers are evils most grievous and insupportable, . . . The fire, the whirlwind, the darkness, the monsters, and the other feigned semblances, are the deceiving allurements which do show us honest travails and honourable danger under the shape of evil.

Flaminio Nobili could explain with Aristotelian precision the situation imagined by both poets. Virtue and vice are not natural to man but are, rather, habits acquired through practice (*De felicitate*, pp. 83–84). In the state of virtue reason has imprinted itself upon the appetites so that they respond automatically to the dictates of the mind. Unfortunately, we grow up sensually, and the mind wakes late and is educated with difficulty.[58] If we are badly brought up, our minds serve the senses, which, because they naturally shrink from exertion, now have the rationale of false opinion.

In *Gerusalemme liberata,* accordingly, man achieves this virtuous state slowly. The army moves to Jerusalem and is stalled there for fourteen cantos (4–18). The dark wood objectifies this mental paralysis, man's inability to capture the city, to achieve felicity. In one scene Tasso turns the wood itself into another city, with a wall, towers, and defending soldiers:[59]

> Cresce il gran foco, e 'n forma d'alte mura
> stende le fiamme torbide e fumanti;
> e ne cinge quel bosco, e l'assecura
> ch'altri gli arbori suoi non tronchi e schianti.
> Le maggiore sue fiamme hanno figura

di castelli superbi e torreggianti,
e di tormenti bellici ha munite
le rocche sue questa novella Dite.

    Oh quanti appaion mostri armati in guarda
de gli alti merli e in che terribil faccia!
De'quai con occhi biechi altri il riguarda,
e dibattendo l'arme altri il minaccia.
Fugge egli al fine, e ben la fuga è tarda,
qual di leon che si ritiri in caccia,
ma pure è fuga; e pur gli scote il petto
timor, sin a quel punto ignoto affetto.

The fire increas'd, and built a stately wall
    Of burning coals, quick sparks, and embers hot;
And with bright flames the wood environ'd all,
    That there no tree nor twist Alcasto got:
The higher stretched flames seem'd bulwarks tall,
    Castles and turrets full of fiery shot,
With slings and engines strong of every sort;
What mortal wight durst scale so strange a fort?

O what strange monsters on the battlement
    In loathsome forms stood to defend the place!
Their frowning looks upon the knight they bent,
    And threaten'd death with shot, with sword, and mace.
At last he fled, and though but slow he went,
    As lions do whom jolly hunters chase,
Yet fled the man, and with sad fear withdrew,
Though fear till then he never felt nor knew.

[13.27–28]

The hitherto fearless Alcasto fails here, and his failure is that of the
Christians before Saracen Jerusalem.

    Psychological harmony, the appetites cooperating with each other
under reason, precedes correct thinking. The Christians cut down the
trees of the wood once all the soldiers have come back, in particular
Rinaldo, the last to submit to Goffredo and the symbol of the irascible
appetite. As Tasso remarks, this appetite actually verges on reason:

Irascibile è quella la quale fra tutte l'altre potenze de l'anima
men s'allontana da la nobiltà de la mente, intanto che par che
Platone cerchi dubitando s'ella sia diversa da la ragione o no.

The Ireful Virtue is that, which amongst all the powers of the mind, is less estranged from the nobility of the mind, insomuch that Plato, doubting, seeketh whether it differeth from reason or no. [Prose Allegory]

Plato in fact distinguished them by a special argument in the *Republic* (4.439–44). Odysseus smites himself and says to his heart, "Endure!" That is, his reason and his irascible appetite in this instance clash. By the law of contraries, the irascible power must be a different psychic faculty, for opposites cannot be in the same thing at the same time in the same respect and relation (4.437). Normally, however, the irascible collaborates with reason, and the two together control the concupiscible. In the poem this cooperation begins with Rinaldo's return to the Christian camp.[60]

Fear cannot affect the irascible virtue, so the demons cross patterns. They appeal to Rinaldo's desires, to his love for Armida. The temptation is so far successful that the demons are able to surprise their opponent (18.19). Rinaldo expected nightmare phantasms, but instead the demons welcome him to a paradise. They have won the first round, often the crucial one. In *Paradise Lost,* for example, Eve, though fully warned about Satan, came disarmed to the Tree. She had expected an angel and found instead a curious talking reptile.

The demons operate by contraries. They confront the acquisitive or concupiscible types with terrors, the irascible with pleasures. And for Rinaldo their method has a special application. He has already demonstrated his susceptibility to love, something which Tasso explains in his lectures on Pigna's *canzoni.* The irascible is located in the region of the heart, and warriors are especially prone to love—Mars to Venus or, we might add, Aeneas to Dido and Antony to Cleopatra.[61] The demons instantly appeal to Rinaldo's most obvious weakness. The hero, however, has already overcome this temptation, and Tasso has just shown us his departure from Armida's garden. He thus easily breaks the demonic enchantments, and Jerusalem falls in the same canto.

Rinaldo's victory clarifies another aspect of Tasso's allegory, again one which he inherited. The wood of fear exists properly not for the martial hero but for the victims of love. In Scholastic terminology it corresponds to the concupiscible appetites. Dante had standardized this symbolism and included the interpretation in his text. His commentators repeated his explanation and confined themselves to citations of outside sources like the *Convivio* or a satire of Horace.[62] The interpretation occurs in the *Purgatorio,* when the pilgrim stands before his mistress and confesses his sins. In the passage which Tasso bracketed, Beatrice claims and Dante agrees that after her death he turned:

... per via non vera
imagini di ben seguendo false,
che nulla promission rendono intera.

And he did turn his steps by a way not true, pursuing false
images of good, that pay back no promise entire. [30.130–32][63]

In the same scene Dante gave the metaphor a twist which later writers
imitated. Beatrice later talks of this intellectual wandering as a treason
in love, a turning to other women (*Purgatorio* 31.58–63). She understands Dante's love story simultaneously on an intellectual and philosophical level, just as Spenser later will have his knight turn from Una
to Duessa, from truth to falsehood. The heroes of the *Liberata* accordingly meet in the wood false images of their loves: demonic imitations of Clorinda and Armida. Their love stories similarly are susceptible to a philosophical reading.

Tancredi is the hero whom Tasso particularly associates with these
scenes. He found in the historical Tancredi a young man troubled with
incontinence. He says of him to Silvio Antoniano, "Fu nondimeno
molto incontinente ed oltramodo vago de gli abbracciamenti de le
saracine" (Letter 60, p. 145, "He was nonetheless very incontinent
and beyond measure eager for the embraces of Saracen women").
Tasso muted this vice for his epic. The women become a single lady, the
visionary Clorinda, and the hero another Lancelot, abstracted and in
another world, whenever his mistress appears. In this fashion Tasso
accommodated the historical Tancredi to the elevation of character and
style he required for epic. The change also fit the notion of heroic virtue
which he learned from Flaminio Nobili. He tells Scipione Gonzaga that
Flaminio considers an *excess* of love and ire proper to heroes. Flaminio
discusses this conception in *De felicitate*, where he contrasts it with
feritas, the subhuman status of people who rejoice in evil (pp. 121–22,
172).[64] Only heroic virtue can eliminate this condition, as illustrated by
the myths of Hercules and the monsters. This virtue, however, is ambiguous and prone to violent excess:

> Non caret autem haec virtus affectionibus, quinimò, ut inquit
> Proclus in commentariis suis in Politiam, finguntur heroes à
> poetis maximè obnoxii amori, et irae, et huiusmodi aliis per-
> turbationibus; quoniam sine quadam animi concitatione, res
> magnae, et praeclarae geri non possunt.

> This virtue does not lack affections; rather, as Proclus remarks
> in his commentaries on the *Republic*, heroes are feigned by

poets to be especially liable to love, wrath, and other disorders of this sort, because, without a certain passion of soul, they cannot carry out great and splendid deeds. [*De felicitate*, p. 122]

Hercules at times may resemble his monsters. Thus we should not be surprised if Tasso's heroes in the *Liberata* at times seem to exist in excess, and the mere presence of Clorinda induces psychological paralysis in Tancredi.

Through this hero Tasso dramatizes the wandering traditionally associated with the confused mind. In canto 7 Tancredi pursues a frightened Erminia, who lets her horse run so that "per tante strade si raggira" (7.1, "it circles through many paths"). Tancredi himself cannot see in the dark; he circles about (7.22), reacting to sounds (7.24), and is finally led by a false messenger to the Dead Sea, where he is made a prisoner.

The episode suggests its own interpretation clearly enough. For a parallel and less idealized case, we could consider Eustazio, whom the narrator explicitly moralizes:

> Segue Eustazio il primiero, e pote a pena
> aspettar l'ombre che la notte adduce;
> vassene frettoloso ove ne 'l mena
> per le tenebre cieche un cieco duce.

> First Eustazio followed and could hardly wait for the shadows which night led in. He goes quickly where a blind leader leads him through blind darkness. [5.80]

Though Daniello is explaining Dante's dark wood, he nevertheless provides the best allegorization of this scene:

> selva oscura, rassomigliando l'humana vita ad una oscura e folta selva d'ignoranza, e d'errori piena; nella quale chi qua, e chi là, chi su, e chi giù senza mai scorgere il vero e diritto sentiero a guisa di forsennati si vanno gli huomini continuamente avolgendo e aggirando. Onde Horatio nel 2. lib. de' Sermoni nella 3. Satira;—velut sylvis, ubi passim Palanteis[65] error certo de tramite pellit: ille sinistrorsum, hic dextrorsum abit: unus utrique Error: sed variis illudit partibus.

> The dark wood—comparing human life to a wood, dark and thick with ignorance and full of error, in which men go, one here, one there, one up, one down, continually winding around

and circling like madmen, without ever perceiving the true and direct path. Whence Horace in the third satire of book 2: "As in woods, when error drives men wandering at random, far from the right path, this one goes off to the left, that one to the right. The same error applies to both but deceives them by different equivalents." [Daniello, p. 2]

Literally Tancredi pursues the wrong woman, Erminia in Clorinda's armor. In this sense Horace's comment applies exactly, for it makes no difference which direction Tancredi takes or whether he finds Erminia or not. In his next visit to the wood he falters before another false image, the demonic voice which mimics Clorinda's and speaks out of a tree. Wandering indicates false goals or a psychological misconception of a goal.

This confusion applies to Tancredi on the literal level of the poem as well. He appears initially as the brilliant bumbler, the man whose distraction in love adversely affects his otherwise successful chivalric enterprises. In the first skirmish he chases after one of the Christians and returns barely in time to succor his troops, surrounded by Saracens. At the duel his distraction allows Ottone to intervene and fall captive, and Tancredi misses the second appointment with Argante.

Tasso described this frustration much earlier, when he lectured on the *Tre sorelle*. Pigna had argued that the sensual lover can never achieve true union because he lives in internal discord. Pigna compared such a lover with a man blown here and there by winds:[66]

> E chi da se medesmo ognor discorda,
> E raggirato è da contrari venti,
> Come con altri mai stretto s'accorda?

> How can he who is divided in his heart and whirled about by contrary winds ever come to a close union of hearts with another?

Tasso here remarks that the concupiscible opposes union, because it exists in internal discord and one desire fights another.[67] It concerns different ends—food and drink, sex, possessions, money—and so one desire can cancel out another. Such a person makes no direct progress and is well shown circling about, traveling nowhere, like Tancredi and Erminia in canto 7. They, however, are caught in a war of the soul's faculties, as they want both honor and love, ends proper to different appetites. They attain neither. Erminia risks her honor when she leaves Jerusalem for Tancredi and then, in an attempt to save that honor, flees from her beloved. Tancredi would both duel with Argante and find Clorinda. He ends instead at the Dead Sea, trapped by these contrary impulses.

Boiardo helps us understand this psychological dilemma more precisely. The episode of the nymphs of Riso parallels Tasso's wood on a literal level and contains the same moral. Boiardo's water spirits create and possess a wood in which they ensnare knights. They mirror psychological drives. Each knight finds a false image of his goal: a horse for Gradasso, women for the others.[68] Similarly, Tasso's demons invent false mistresses for Tancredi and Rinaldo. Boiardo repeats his moral several times. The initial vision which Orlando follows vanishes in smoke like an empty thing: "Tutto andò in fumo; come cosa vana" (2.31.44). Next two warriors fight for what they will never have, and Gradasso mounts a phantom horse. In Tasso, when Rinaldo disenchants the wood, he draws the same moral, which I have cited: "Oh vane / sembianze! e folle chi per voi rimane!" (18.38, "O shadows vain! O fools, of shades afraid!").

Both authors liken the situation to dreaming. Tasso makes the dream a nightmare, as the spirits who possess the wood are not natural powers, like Boiardo's water nymphs, but fallen angels. He compares Tancredi's failure with our fears of dream chimeras, and the woodcutters at the beginning experience similar fears:

> Qual semplice bambin mirar non osa
> dove insolite larve abbia presenti,
> o come pave ne la notte ombrosa,
> imaginando pur mostri e portenti,
> così temean, senza saper qual cosa
> siasi quella però che gli sgomenti,
> se non che 'l timor forse a i sensi finge
> maggior prodigi di Chimera o Sfinge.

> As seely children dare not bend their eye
>   Where they are told strange bugbears haunt the place;
> Or as new monsters, while in bed they lie,
>   Their fearful thoughts present before their face;
> So feared they and fled, yet wist not why,
>   Nor what pursu'd them in that fearful chace;
> Except their fear perchance, while thus they fled,
> New chimeres, sphinxes, or like monsters bred.

[13.18]

Fear and wandering have the same meaning. The former stresses the psychological condition which creates error. The second demonstrates how we go from one error to another.

The second metaphor perhaps assumes but does not indicate how error *generates* further error, another fact which both poets stress. In Boiardo the knight Ruggiero starts to cut down a tree. A nymph comes out of the bark and claims that she has been imprisoned there by enchantment. The deceiver represents herself as the victim of deception, and the error multiplies. Tasso does the same with Tancredi in canto 13. A demon masquerades as Clorinda and tells Tancredi that all those who died in battle at Jerusalem have been imprisoned in trees. It thus suggests metempsychosis, a heretical belief.

The last stage in such a process would be sophistics, a train of false reasoning. This is what the demons try with Rinaldo in canto 18. They argue Epicurean philosophy, the one form of thought habitually condemned by everyone, false syllogisms to create a double delusion:

> o giudicando (come giudicò Epicuro, ed i suoi seguaci) che ne' piaceri e ne l'ozio si ritrovi la felicità, per questo, doppio è l'incanto e la delusione.

> Or judging, as did the Epicure and his followers, that in pleasure and idleness consisted chiefest felicity; by this, double is the enchantment and illusion. [Prose Allegory]

The delusion is double because reason itself would have been corrupted. Fear can induce false belief, but it will not prevent the rational process itself. If Rinaldo had failed, he would not have suspected delusion, as does Tancredi. He would have thought sophistically like the incontinent man, whom Flaminio compares with one drunk or asleep, quoting lines memorized from Homer (*De felicitate* 131).[69] Though in themselves logical, the words do not express a rational mentality. And in an Epicurean system all thought must err, as its premises are totally false. For Rinaldo no partial defeat is possible, only total surrender or the complete victory which he in fact wins.

So far I have stressed what was traditional in Tasso's allegory. It is clear that many an educated reader would have assumed that the wood signified erroneous opinion, and the poet developed his symbols accordingly. Other writers, however, had not stressed this symbol so strongly. Tasso dramatizes it, returns to it again and again, makes it crucial to his plot. He also adds a further dimension, one implicit in his conception of the epic.

Tasso required that the epic be marvelous, and we saw in the last chapter that the Renaissance marvelous was normally demonic. In standard theory such marvels were illusions, and Tasso carefully notes the insubstantial character of the marvels of the wood. This thinking directly suggests his allegory of error and in turn relates to the issues which he debated with his Roman friends. They wanted fact in his plot and knew that the wood and the garden lacked historical verification. They were fictions which contrasted with the objective material with which Tasso began and ended his poem. Tasso agreed with his friends insofar as he presented these fictions as illusions *within* his plot, illusions which vanish before the historical climax of the poem. Thus a critic might argue that Tasso creates a clash of fiction and history, in which the latter wins. More fundamentally, the demonic surrenders to the divine, falsehood to truth. Tasso required the marvelous *throughout* his epic, and we see it in the beginning when God rouses Goffredo through an angel. The divine operates through history, arranging the campaign against Jerusalem; and Tasso symbolizes this difference by the contrast of the named and the unnamed, the true and the false, the light and the dark.

Nameless places, which we slowly define, occur in special sections of the *Liberata*. Tasso normally does not identify the nonhistorical places and persons of his epic; he might locate them geographically or allow them some slight historical basis, but he develops them in a fabulous manner. Namelessness thus signals allegory, the fabulous episode which the reader would expect to define himself. We have long known that, *grosso modo,* Tasso enclosed his unknown *meraviglie* in a historical frame. It has not been observed, however, that his geography is also both historical and fabulous. Jerusalem is the area of clear historical action, of normal chivalric encounter, where knights duel and skirmish and armies fight beneath walls and in siege towers. Beyond this small circle stretches the nameless, an area where knights wander alone and in peril, where magicians and sorcerers set traps and have magical castles. It includes the mago's underground palace, Armida's fortified garden on the Dead Sea, the enchanted forest. It is the area of psychological exploration, of the inner self. Tasso explains in the Prose Allegory that epic has scenes both of action and contemplation. The former have multiple personae; the latter, the solitary knight, a pilgrim figure like Dante or Ulysses, an Aeneas in hell. The wood fits this contemplative side of the epic, for in it the heroes wander alone. We might schematize this mythic geography and say that the *Liberata* has at Jerusalem a narrow circle of the rational and the communal in which human beings interact with one another, but that beyond exists an indefinite area of the psychological unknown, with nameless powers, some good, more evil.

This contrast likewise appears as light and darkness. The wood creates its own night, but darkness characterizes the fabulous center of *Gerusalemme liberata*, a fact which scholars have often discussed. Guerrillas assault the Danes by night, and Sveno is glorified in darkness. Tancredi has most of his adventures by night. And the dark can extend temporarily to the circle of the rational and historical, as when Solimano attacks the Christian camp and when lone knights encounter each other outside the city walls. This fabulous dark contrasts directly with the clarity and repeated sunrises which mark the historical frame of the poem and climax on the last day:[70]

> Non fu mai l'aria sì serena e bella
> come a l'uscir del memorabil giorno:
> l'alba lieta rideva, e parea ch'ella
> tutti i raggi del sole avesse intorno;
> e 'l lume usato accrebbe, e senza velo
> volse mirar l'opere grandi il cielo.

> The skies were never half so fair and clear
>   As in the breaking of that blessed day;
> The merry morning smil'd, and seem'd to wear,
>   Upon her silver crown, sun's golden ray;
> And, without veil, heav'n his redoubled light
> Bent down to see this field, this fray, this fight.

[20.5]

Tasso makes this series of oppositions dialectical. Each generalization, for example, includes an exception. Darkness and the nameless are normally evil but for the miracle of Sveno's tomb and the mago of Ascalon. Demons operate by delusion but also send a real storm in canto 7. Morning visions come from God, but in canto 8 Argillano sees one from Aletto. Tasso forces us to distinguish, to recognize that these oppositions interact and develop. In this way he creates a dialectic and reveals the Platonic bases of his allegory. In fact the myth of the cave could well describe the progress of his action, and that myth concerned education. The Christians, immobilized before the dark wood, finally return to the war and win their battle under the brightness of a summer sun. They leave the cave and its shadow figures for the truth.

Tasso and Plato

Tasso's allegory grew out of his Platonism. As noted, the *Republic* in particular provided models for his central metaphor, the body politic, for his use of an extended analogy between the individual and the state, and finally for the psychological categories with which he interpreted his poem. Critics have long recognized the importance of Plato for Tasso,[71] and we have seen his influence earlier. Landino used the dialogue method for literary analysis and read the *Aeneid* Platonically. A millennium earlier the Neoplatonists had interpreted Homer in a similar fashion.[72] Plato's effect on allegorical criticism perhaps equals that of the Homeric poems, and his myth making will help us to understand how Tasso fits into that tradition. Both writers tried desperately to clarify their symbolism, to control their audience response. They did not completely succeed because they both shared in the aesthetics of mystery.

I will begin with the problem of audience. Plato objected for moral reasons to the indirection assumed in Homeric allegory (*Republic* 2.378). Theomachies, divine duels, and conspiracies might all be symbolic presentations of ethical and physical truths, but the literal stories would encourage factionalism in the polis and make bad pedagogy. A child could not distinguish an allegorical from a nonallegorical story, a superficially immoral symbolic narrative from another simply so, with no further meanings. At first Tasso likewise worried about this opacity in allegory and told Scipione Gonzaga that the interpreters projected meanings upon the text at their own caprice and that, for any good poem, the exegeses varied, were inconsistent among themselves (Letter 79, pp. 192–93). Plato and Tasso emphasized different aspects of the same situation. Opaque or dark allegory does not help the reader enough and therefore allows for capricious readings and cannot guarantee moral instruction. Accordingly, both writers took extraordinary measures to control audience response. We have seen how Tasso achieved this end, both by explicit statements in his narrative and by the Prose Allegory, a critical guide to the overall poem. Plato likewise wrote his meanings into his story and worked out separate interpretations. We can see this fact most easily in a familiar myth like that of the cave.

Socrates interprets his story three times and applies it to different but related problems: epistemology and education. His explications are so detailed that we could proceed to make a point-by-point analysis and account for everything in the myth. Proclus in fact made such an analysis later in his *Commentary on the "Republic."*[73] Nor could we disagree with Socrates or with each other, on the meanings of Socrates' myths, as we might argue over our understanding of a complex tale. The only serious disagreements would concern the whole dialogue, not this particular scene. Socrates does not allow the plot independent status and so avoids opacity. The myth of the cave remains an analogy and becomes absurd once we ask the questions appropriate to an ordinary narrative: Why are the people in the cave? What is the attitude of the peculiar people who carry the images past the fire? Who unties the hero? Deprived of a literal level, the myth of the cave exists only in its meaning. No disjunction, therefore, can exist between literal and figurative, and hence there can be no misreadings.

This is allegory without the veil. The form is there, the extended metaphor or comparison, but all is explained and we have nothing to interpret. Such allegory is at best borderline, if it is allegory at all, as the word presupposes obscurity, a veil over truth, the darkness which leads us inward. And yet such a statement would not be adequate, would account solely for the pressures of moral persuasion which affected Platonic dialectic. The truth which the participants of the dialogue seek cannot be expressed directly; it demands complicated and often inconclusive debate, at times dark myth. This very myth of the cave outlines the epistemological situation which requires indirection.

Having glimpsed the sun, the hero returns to his friends, who are still chained underground. He cannot convince them that his education was either useful or true. Coming from daylight, he cannot see properly in the dark and so performs laughably in the old competition which is the sole occupation of the prisoners. He cannot guess the shadow figures correctly and has lost his emotional commitment to the attempt. The others naturally conclude that his trip upstairs ruined his eyes and would kill the man who released him if they could. That is, the truth which the philosopher learns through dialectic remains essentially incommunicable to others; nor can he apply his wisdom. In the law courts, for example, he would have to work within the mistaken assumptions of the blind and strive over shadows of justice and the images of shadows. He cannot talk with sleepwalkers, in the analogy which Socrates uses earlier (5.476–80). The lover of objects, who has no true knowledge, confuses resemblances with identities, sees a dream monster and thinks it real. So he lives a dream, whether asleep or awake. No dialogue can exist between the philosopher and such a man. The situation demands opaque allegory or some other literary equivalent, for the truth involved is too remote and its communication almost impossible.

The myth of the cave represents in vision what Socrates and his friends achieve through discussion. It is an allegory of dialectic, of which the *Republic* is a particular example. Thus its signification is basic to the whole Platonic procedure and explains why the dialogue ends with unmediated vision: the myth of Er, for which Socrates provides no commentary. It is a plot, not merely an analogy, and while the morality is always clear, the cosmology passes unexplained. Plato's myth making thus displays two aspects or, rather, it ranges from the clear exemplary to the opaque and symbolical. Tasso's allegory varies in similar fashion and proceeds from parallel assumptions.

In the *Minturno* Tasso places the beautiful beyond definition.[74] Most things suffer change, including the celestial bodies and the divisible part of the soul, so they cannot make a definition; while for the angels or the indivisible part of the soul, any definition becomes an impudence. Tasso's conception of the beautiful is presented in a Platonic dialogue and parallels the philosopher's notion of the Good, the sun which we can only glimpse but, once seen, we recognize to be the intelligible cause of beauty in objects. Plato uses an extended comparison to express this idea, and Tasso employs a biblical analogy. To see the beautiful is like going through the veil into the Holy of Holies. Inside we might contemplate and know, but outside, *where we are,* we wonder at the columns, the arches, the cypress wood. We call beautiful externals, what appear so or most nearly so or what enchant our sentiments. Tasso's notion of the beautiful accordingly requires indirection, and we find this same veiled mystery at special places in the *Liberata*.

The dreaming Goffredo apprehends the situation. Rapt above the heavens, he sees the earth far below as a single point and wonders how humanity can fix its interests on shadows and smoke: earthly fame and power. Ugone expresses the philosophical dilemma:

> Quanto è vil la cagion ch'a la virtude
> umana è colà giù premio e contrasto!
> in che picciolo cerchio e fra che nude
> solitudini è stretto il vostro fasto!
> Lei come isola il mare intorno chiude,
> e lui, ch'or ocean chiamat'è or vasto,
> nulla eguale a tai nomi ha in sé di magno,
> ma è bassa palude e breve stagno.

> How vile, how small, and of how slender price,
>   Is there reward of goodness, virtue's gain;
> A narrow room our glory vain up-ties,
>   A little circle doth our pride contain;
> Earth like an isle amid the water lies,
>   Which sea sometime is call'd, sometime the main;
> Yet naught therein responds a name so great,
> It's but a lake, a pond, a marish strait.

[14.10]

We are familiar with the situation and with the moral. They derive from Macrobius and the Dream of Scipio and were often imitated during the Middle Ages and the Renaissance. In *Gerusalemme liberata* they have a very particular function and finally explain Tasso's erring heroes. The normal realm of human activity is incredibly, almost comically, small and limited, when compared with the true nature of reality, a reality too great for names or words. We apprehend this situation rather through spatial metaphors: islands in an ocean, whether we think of our continents or of the earth itself within the universe. This metaphor recurs in the next canto, when the two messengers pass the Straits of Gibraltar. They move from the Mediterranean, the sea within the lands, to the sea which contains all lands:

> Or entra en lo stretto e passa il corto
> varco, e s'ingolfa in pelago infinito.
> Se'l mar qui è tanto ove il terreno il serra,
> che fia colà dov'egli la in sen la terra?

> Now through the strait her jolly ship made way,
>   And boldly sail'd upon the ocean large;
> But if the sea in midst of earth was great,
> O what was this wherein earth hath her seat!

[15.23]

The moral is complex. Hercules, seeing the Atlantic, withdrew and tried to circumscribe man within fixed limits:

> non usò di tentar l'alto oceano:
> segnò le mète, e 'n troppo brevi chiostri
> l'ardir ristrinse de l'ingegno umano.

> Yet durst he not assay the ocean main;
> He marked the turning posts, and restrained
> The venturesomeness of human wit in over-narrow cloisters.

[15.25]

In contrast, Magellan and Columbus liberated the human mind, for they equaled the old myths and opened up new worlds. No terror will be so formidable for Columbus,

> ... che 'l generoso entro a i divieti
> d'Abila angusti l'alta mente accheti.

> [That] within Albila's strait shall keep and hold
> The noble spirit of this sailor bold.

[15.31]

Tasso has here combined the new sense of discovery, of widening man's talent and mind, with the old *contemptus mundi* inherited from the Neoplatonists, a formula which itself suggests how complicated intellectual history can be. For the poem we can express Tasso's conception by an epistemological question: If we live in the sea within the lands but must understand that the lands are really islands in an infinite sea, if the whole earth in turn is merely a speck in the universe, how do we apprehend this nameless reality, which is infinite and seems even to reverse our normal postulates?

This epistemology requires opaque allegory. The situation parallels the mythic geography we have already discussed. Historical man exists in a small circle surrounded by a vast darkness, which he experiences in peril and for which he has no proper names. Only here the reality is vertical and supernal, an excess of light beyond vision, which man must apprehend obliquely. Goffredo, for example, dreams his vision, and a simile emphasizes the necessary indirection in such an experience: "sì come entro uno speglio, ei scerse / ciò che là suso è veramente in elle" (14.4, "As in a mirror, he saw that which above is really there"). At such moments *Gerusalemme liberata* must become opaque allegory, for the poet has no other means to intimate this reality.

In the Prose Allegory Tasso does not discuss this mysterious side to his epic, for the *Liberata* normally concerns not the other world beyond, the heaven which Goffredo sees momentarily, but the narrow circle of this life. In the Prose Allegory Tasso classes his poem with the *Iliad* and the *Aeneid,* epics which represent the active life, not with the *Odyssey* and the *Divina commedia,* visionary poems which shadow forth the contemplative. Similarly, he says to Scipione Gonzaga that, while he wanted advice from Flaminio on the active life, he did not want theological ideas inserted into the *Liberata* (Letter 79, p. 195). Jerusalem for Tasso is the civil felicity possible here, not the mystical city of Revelation. And in fact he worked carefully to eliminate biblical allusions from a story which constantly invited them. At the beginning and at the turning point, when the rain falls at Goffredo's prayer, we see biblical analogies. Elsewhere we look for them in vain. A poet who neglects to tell us that Jerusalem fell on a Friday at the ninth hour is not encouraging a theological perspective.[75] Hence the Prose Allegory describes the true problematic of the epic, its ethical and psychological concerns, and ignores metaphysics.

This choice forced Tasso to an allegory of negatives. He wished to depict this world and the psychological warfare within Everyman but believed that reality was infinitely removed from this visible sphere.

Hence he had to image half-truths, and his characters necessarily became involved in delusion. The problematic of error therefore dominates the poem, expressed through the technique of negative exempla. All the places which the poet stresses imaginatively are evil: Armida's garden, the wood, even Jerusalem. We learn about Saracen Jerusalem, see the massacre of its inhabitants, and never experience the Christian city. Positive visions like Goffredo's dream or a wondrous place like the mago's underground palace pass by in a few stanzas. Tasso had to stress delusion and error because his epistemology here allowed for nothing else.

Such dwelling on evil was a logical development from tradition. Boiardo had made most of his marvels evil, and the practice originated with Virgil. We have seen how the Roman epic could generate a Platonic dialogue and reading. Aeneas never approches the city which he seeks. Lost in a faraway future, Rome haunts his dreams, and he finds instead a false alternative like Carthage or sees his own city destroyed and his future land in civil war.

It is this combination of negative dialectic and allegorical method which accounts for the peculiar effect of *Gerusalemme liberata*. Our sense of the mysterious extends far beyond occasional scenes of ecstasy and vision. The poet presents and destroys so many possible alternatives, constantly says more than he means but hardly represents this more. We end sensing it everywhere.[76]

English

5   Spenser's Fairyland

> You will take especial note of the marvellous independence
> and true imaginative absence of all particular space or time in
> the Faery Queene. It is in the domains neither of history or
> geography; it is truly in land of Faery, that is, of mental space.[1]

Coleridge's remark has been one of the most influential in Spenser
criticism, and it is directed to what is most distinctive in *The Faerie
Queene*. At least in the epics and romances which I know, nothing
resembles Spenser's use of fairyland. In this chapter I would like to
examine it with the allegorical methodology which historical research
has recovered for us, to redo and modify Coleridge's evaluation, in
some ways fundamentally. Particularly in book 2 of *The Faerie
Queene*, Spenser asks us to define the nature of his fairyland and deliberately instigates a search which leads us into strange realms. The
search does not produce an interpretation of the Legend of Temperance but, rather, reveals the radical nature of Spenser's art. On the
literal or historical level of the poem, we find a complex euhemeristic
amalgam, which in turn forces us to reconsider our own relation to the
poem. Out of this reconsideration arise the allegorical levels, which
finally concern not the poem but certain fundamental human problems.
Spenser manipulates us in such a way that he moves us from wonder at
his art to wonder at ourselves.

For this investigation I must adopt methods which I used for the
Orlando innamorato rather than for *Gerusalemme liberata*. The cul-

An earlier version of this chapter appeared under the title, "The Rhetoric of
Fairyland," in *The Rhetoric of Renaissance Poetry: From Wyatt to Milton*,
edited by Thomas O. Sloan and Raymond B. Waddington (Berkeley, Los
Angeles, and London: University of California Press), © 1974, by The Regents
of the University of California.

tural situations of Tasso and Spenser are so different that they discount
the obvious similarities of the poets: the fact that they were exact
contemporaries, that they both wrote continued allegory, that they
frequently used the same tropes and descriptions. An example will help
to clarify this difference. On its publication (1580), *Gerusalemme
liberata* was an international event. Editions multiplied, critics argued
over it, and outside Italy it was printed at Lyons as early as 1581,
Spenser borrowed passages for *The Faerie Queene* (1590), and Fairfax
had it translated by 1600. We have, as a result, a mass of critical
documentation relative to the *Liberata*. We know which episodes
Tasso wanted to change and why. We can reconstruct his literary
problems and understand how the poem was read. Spenser's case
differs completely. *The Faerie Queene* provoked no elaborate controversy, nor did it introduce a new aesthetic to England. In its first
eighty-nine years it had five printings, while the *Liberata* went through
eight in one year (1581). Yet for England the number was respectable.
The large reading public, the educated circles, the numerous academies
and universities—none of these existed in Spenser's time. We even
lack book lists, as the poet spent his mature life away from London and
the universities. We cannot therefore base our reading of Spenser on
objective documentation of this sort. It does not exist.

In this situation the scholar has two alternatives. As he does not
know what books Spenser may have used, he can enlarge or narrow his
frame of reference. The Variorum editors opted for the first and regularly cite multiple texts for the same point. This alternative has the
advantage of all-inclusiveness but encourages an indiscriminate use of
texts. Too many influences and "sources" have been adduced for *The
Faerie Queene,* and the procedure does not correspond to historical
probability. Spenser would not have had a large personal library in
Ireland. I have therefore chosen the other alternative, what I used for
Boiardo. I will confine myself in the first place to texts commonly
available, school authors like Horace and Terence/Donatus or a popular religious writer like Augustine. Second, I will use as far as possible
texts which Spenser cites directly or uses in an obvious fashion, such
as *Huon of Bordeaux* and *Melusine*. On the other hand, I will work out
all the levels which I outlined in *The Veil of Allegory*. Scholars have
normally stressed one or two levels, the moral and psychological,
but have recognized that in certain scenes, like the Garden of Adonis,
more was required. Fairyland similarly demands this more elaborate
consideration. More than an episode or scene, it is the precondition
for the whole poem, its general setting.

My analysis will differ from the others I have made in one other respect. I will stress the rhetorical dimension of allegorical interpretation, how the critic moves from level to level and how the poet encourages these changes. This requires an attention to details on the literal level and a set of "unimaginative" questions which most critics, perhaps inspired by Coleridge's remark, normally ignore. Once a critic decides that *The Faerie Queene* lacks a "particular space or time," he will not listen when Spenser gives it a particular location and a set of historical personae and will miss the puzzle which the poet creates by his radical anachronism. He will therefore not observe a unique and profound side to Spenser's art, its philosophical and perhaps theological dimension.[2] The poet starts encouraging these questions right away, in the prologue to book 2.

Classical epic provides no precedent for Spenser's prologues, nor do Ariosto and Boiardo, despite the direct address to the audience with which they begin their cantos. In the Italian epic the speaker's address is not formally separated from the rest of the text but merges with the story. The narrator's comments usually have an informal, personal character to them. Spenser, on the other hand, uses a public voice and a formal address. Here in book 2 he defends himself against hostile critics, and his audience is the queen herself. The only real parallels for this are the prologues of Roman comedy, where, as Trissino remarks, "the poet said what he wanted in his own voice."[3] Not through the intermediary of a narrator, whether naive or ironic, but directly, in propria persona, Spenser discusses a number of different questions, and in this practice he follows Donatus' description of the prologue form. The poet may explain something about the story, praise his own poem, or raise more complicated questions about his art. For book 2 Spenser does the third, a method particularly favored by Terence, who used prologues "only in order to defend himself from the criticism of his old rivals and mean poets. So in his prologues he didn't say anything relative to the development of the action...."[4] It is typical of Spenser to turn comic forms, whether Terence's or Chaucer's, to serious purposes. The prologue speaker, screaming to get attention from the noisy, milling crowds of the Roman festivals, would have been astonished to find himself elegantly introducing the high epic.

In this particular prologue Spenser claims objective status for his fairyland, an argument sufficiently outrageous to draw anyone's attention. To say that fairyland really exists, outside *The Faerie Queene*, should disconcert the most obliging audience, and yet Spenser asserts that we can find it ourselves:

> Of Faerie lond yet if he more inquire,
>   By certaine signes here set in sundry place
>   He may it find. . . .

[2.Pro.4]

The negative corollary of this position should in turn upset the critics. In contemptuous language Spenser flatly denies *any* imaginative status for his poem. *The Faerie Queene* is not "th'aboundance of an idle braine" or a "painted forgery."[5] He would reverse Coleridge's statement. What are we to make of a poet who vehemently denies that this most imaginative poem is imaginative?

We can at least understand why he is suspicious of the human imagination. In the House of Alma Spenser associates Phantastes with folly and madness (2.9.52). The flies which buzz about his chamber are idle thoughts and fantasies, and his walls are painted with a confused array of images:

> Infernall Hags, *Centaurs,* feendes, *Hippodames,*
>   Apes, Lions, Ægles, Owles, fooles, louers, children, Dames.

[2.9.50]

Reason and discrimination are absent here, and one can see the inherent dangers of solipsism and madness. Dependent on such an imagination, a mind, however healthy, could lose all contact with reality and believe in centaurs as well as apes. And it is this failing which in book 2 gives Acrasia her power. The Genius who presides over her bower deceives men by false phantoms, much as Archimago deceived the Red Cross Knight (see 2.12.48, 1.1.45–2.6). Of a threatening horde of sea beasts, the Palmer says,

> . . . these same Monsters are not these in deed,
>   But are into these fearefull shapes disguiz'd
>   By that same wicked witch, to worke vs dreed.

[2.12.26]

In his fear and suspicion of the imagination, Spenser expresses a standard Renaissance attitude. One need only read Gianfrancesco Pico's treatise on the subject or look at the manuals on witchcraft.[6] The devil controlled people through their imaginations, since he had no power over their intellects. Witches, who flew to Sabbats, actually spent the nights at home in bed. One can understand why Spenser would wish to dissociate his poem from such a dubious power, but his stance creates serious problems. He cannot glory in his poem as an

imaginative triumph, the way Giraldi Cinthio can in *Orlando furioso;*
he has to defend it in some other fashion.[7] He must claim objective
status for what we would consider fantasy.

Spenser models his argument on one used by Ariosto in similar circumstances. In canto 7 of the *Furioso* Ariosto introduces Alcina's
wondrous island with a contrast between what travelers see and what
others believe (7.1–2). His conclusion is Spenser's main point:

> Why then should witlesse man so much misweene
> That nothing is, but that which he hath seene?
>
> [*FQ* 2.Pro.3]

Englishmen should not doubt the existence of marvelous places like
Peru merely because they have not been there. But an important difference separates Ariosto's argument from that of Spenser. Ariosto is
urging his audience to read this particular tale of emotional experience
allegorically. He is not arguing that Alcina's island really exists in the
East Indies. Unfortunately, Spenser is: fairyland is a definite place,
one which we can find. Spenser found the true exemplar for his argument where he found Guyon, the hero of book 2—in the *Melusine* of
Jean of Arras (1394). This was a romance chronicle of the House of
Lusignan, which described many adventures in the Near East, where
that family had ruled Cyprus and where Christian battled Saracen. Jean
begins and ends his romance chronicle with a logical defense of faery,
parallel to Spenser's.[8] He establishes possibility for faery by evidence
of similar marvels, something he must do since his central character is
a half-fay. And Jean carries the defense of faery to its furthest extremes. To deny faery is to ascribe limits to the divine omnipotence.
Universal negatives are blasphemy.

As logic this argument falls apart, and Jean's exaggeration manifests
its basic absurdity. If Spenser claims that a wondrous land exists, we
can fairly demand some evidence. If he can adduce none, we certainly
may reject his claims, however many undiscovered lands there may be.
By this negative logic Spenser really begs the question. But if the
argument collapses logically, it more than succeeds rhetorically. A
scene in *Colin Clouts Come Home Again* provides an exact paradigm
for this kind of rhetoric. Colin Clout has been describing his trip to
England, and Cuddie is surprised that another land exists besides the
island on which he lives (290–91). Colin answers him gently but
amusedly with the same argument that Spenser uses in this prologue:

> Ah *Cuddy* (then quoth *Colin*) thous a fon,
> That hast not seene least part of natures worke:

Much more there is vnkend, then thou doest kon,
And much more that does from mens knowledge lurke.

[292–95]

We can laugh at Cuddie's naiveté and ignorance but may not realize
that Spenser has put his critics in the same position. Whatever the
quality of the logic, no one wishes to assume Cuddie's role.

Having developed this unusual argument and aroused the expecta-
tions of his audience, Spenser ends the prologue in very mundane
fashion and seems to close off discussion. Elizabeth can see her own
realms *mirrored* in faery. So the wondrous lands reflect England, and
any further search seems unnecessary. But first of all, this identification would not apply to the narrative, in which the characters are either
natives of faery or British visitors from abroad. The poet does not
identify the two. Moreover, such an identification would ignore
Spenser's image and therefore collapse the distinction between the
mirror and the object which it reflects. The substance of a mirror differs
markedly from the diverse objects which it may image, and its shadow
reflection *reverses* the position of the original object. We should not be
surprised to find the mirror of England wonderful and splendid in a way
that England could not be. And the relationship between the two is
odd. In the Renaissance a person might argue that England mirrors an
ideal order. He normally would not claim that the ideal mirrors the real,
which is what Spenser asserts. This inversion of relations upsets a
traditional, hierarchic structure, assumed for an aeon. So Spenser has
not answered the questions of his critics, though he purports to do so.
With his negative argument he seems to say much about fairyland and
at the same time gives us as little information about it as possible.
The poet tantalizes his audience. He wants us to wonder about faery,
to search for its traces. And he provides some remarkable clues.

The first of these occurs in the prologue itself. Spenser hints at a
possibility which dazzles. In his discussion of new worlds he includes,
besides America, the moon and stars, twenty years before Galileo
turned his telescope in that direction. Then the poet implies that when
Francisco de Orellana sailed the wrong way down a Brazilian river, he
proved the reality of the old Amazon myth. Do other classical myths
mirror realities not yet discovered by man? The euhemerist critic saw
these stories as reflections of a dim past. Spenser seems to be turning
the mirror in the other direction:

What if in euery other starre vnseene
Of other worlds he [any man] happily should heare?
He wonder would much more: yet such to *some* appeare.

[*FQ* 2.Pro.3; italics mine]

Augustine once had wondered "utrum similis sit causa etiam praedicendorum futurorum, ut rerum, quae nondum sunt, iam exsistentes praesentiantur imagines." (*Confessions* 11.18, "whether a similar process enables the future to be seen, some process by which events which have not yet occurred become present to us by means of already existing images of them")[9] Is Spenser making just such a claim? He has listed places in America, unknown until they were discovered, places intimated in classical myth but found ages later, and places no one could as yet visit: the stars and planets. To which category does his fairyland belong? Spenser does not clarify the matter any further, nor need he. By his hints and negative argument he has already accomplished his purpose. We are off on a hunt for faery.

The first stage of the search leads us out of the specifically rhetorical situation of the prologue and back within the text. The poet ceases to address us and turns to his tale, while we look for clues, most of which are clustered at the beginning of book 2 and in the House of Alma. The preliminary explanation which this evidence warrants forms the literal and political levels of fairyland. We are concerned, in other words, with the relations of fairyland to history and contemporary politics.

The first and most obvious question which we put to the Legend of Temperance has already been determined by the prologue. We want to know where Spenser locates fairyland and what evidence he presents for its existence. I will take the question of location first, which Spenser answers quite succinctly. In the House of Alma Guyon reads of the faery beginnings:

> The first and eldest, which that scepter swayd,
> Was *Elfin;* him all *India* obayd,
> And all that now *America* men call.

> [2.10.72]

Fairyland is India and America. And here Spenser faithfully follows his sources, the Charlemagne romances. Since Spenser generally ignored Malory and imitated the Italian epics about Orlando and Rinaldo, he found faery in the Near and Middle East. Boiardo strews the area with enchanted gardens, dragons, and fays, while with the episodes of Prester John and Alcina, Ariosto takes in the whole Indian Ocean. Boiardo even moves Fata Morgana to the East.[10] There is one medieval Charlemagne romance which is of particular interest in this respect, as Spenser refers to it specifically in book 2. *Huon of Bordeaux* clearly shows how faery drifts even further east. This was a thirteenth-century *chanson de geste,* later much expanded and turned into prose in 1454.[11] It was popular and had gone into an eleventh edition by 1586; Lord Berners had translated it into English (1534); and its other main character, the fairy king Oberon, reappears in Shakespeare's *Mid-summer Night's Dream*. In the original *chanson de geste* Huon meets Oberon on the way from Jerusalem to Babylon (Cairo), but in the continuations of the romance the marvels have receded beyond the Euphrates. When Huon finally arrives in Momure, the faery capital, he is in Hyrcania, or the Elburz Mountains of north Iran. Arthur's new realms, which he receives from the dying Oberon, are further east, for they include Tatary or central Asia. So Spenser follows this eastward drift and locates faery in India and finally in America.

The inclusion of America resolves another potential dilemma. In contrast to the Charlemagne romances, Arthurian tradition locates the wonders of faery in the west of Europe, in the Arthurian realm itself or still further west on the hidden isle of Avalon, where Morgan the Fay lives. Boiardo, however, put her realm in Asia. As both Arthur and his sister Morgan rule lands which are both west and east, we can infer that fairyland itself can be found in opposite directions. Columbus sailed west to go east, and Orellana discovered the Amazon sailing east to go west. With a round world contradictory directions can be reconciled. Spenser includes both Indies in fairyland and so reflects the contemporary opinion that the American Indians migrated to the New World from Asia.[12] We can see that this equation of the newly discovered lands with fairyland is not farfetched if we look at Bernal Díaz del Castillo's reactions, when with Cortez' troops he first beheld Mexico City:

> Y otro día por la mañana llegamos a la calzada ancha y vamos camino de Estapalapa. Y desque vimos tantas ciudades y villas pobladas en el agua, y en tierra firme otras grandes poblazones, y aquella calzada tan derecha y por nivel cómo iba a Méjico, nos quedamos admirados, y decíamos que parescía a las cosas de encantamiento que cuentan en el libro de Amadís, por las grandes torres y cues y edificios que tenían dentro en el agua, y todos de calicanto, y aun algunos de nuestros soldados decían que si aquello que vían, si era entre sueños, y no es de maravillar que yo lo escriba aquí desta manera, porque hay mucho que ponderar en ello que no sé como lo cuente: ver cosas nunca oídas, ni vistas, ni aun soñadas, como víamos.

> During the morning, we arrived at a broad Causeway and continued our march towards Iztapalapa, and when we saw so many cities and villages built in the water and other great towns on dry land and that straight and level Causeway going towards Mexico, we were amazed and said that it was like the

enchantments they tell of in the legend of Amadis, on account of the great towers and cues and buildings rising from the water, and all built of masonry. And some of our soldiers even asked whether the things that we saw were not a dream. It is not to be wondered at that I here write it down in this manner, for there is so much to think over that I do not know how to describe it, seeing things as we did that had never been heard of or seen before, not even dreamed about.[13]

No quotation could better illustrate the discovery of fairyland.

The equation of faery with the Indies and America likewise establishes the political level of the allegory. Since 1580 both India and America had been ruled by Philip of Habsburg and formed the first true world empire. To the Habsburgs with their immense power and Roman mystique of universal dominion, Spenser opposes a crusader's myth. The Spaniards and Portuguese are interlopers in territories previously visited by various ancient English heroes. The mirror of Elizabeth's realm itself should belong to Elizabeth. We know that Spenser strongly supported the Virginia settlement and those like Ralegh who advocated imperial expansion.[14] Faery is thus a dream of empire.

On this level fairyland becomes wish fulfillment. Harry Berger has shown how the chronicle of fairyland presents an ideal order, in striking contrast to the relative chaos of English history.[15] Similarly, in *Huon of Bordeaux*, where the earthly rulers are mostly weak and foolish, Oberon rules his faery realm justly and compassionately, and his commands are instantly obeyed.[16] In the Charlemagne romances this wish fulfillment more frequently takes the form of military victory over the infidel. In both the *Innamorato* and the *Furioso* Orlando battles the forces of Agramante, and Spenser's Guyon has for enemies the paynim brethren Pyrochles and Cymochles.[17] Huon of Bordeaux likewise spends most of his time fighting Saracens. With Oberon's aid and a few French knights, he captures Cairo and makes it into a Christian fief. In the Huon Continuations the Egyptians get beaten again, this time by a newly Christianized Persian army. In this respect fairyland responds to the Christian sense of frustration after the Third Crusade and to their hopes in Prester John. For Spenser this function of faery would have a renewed application. Ariosto had already depicted an ideal victory over the Saracens by a gigantic Christian alliance, and Spenser looked forward to the battle of the Faerie Queene and Arthur with the paynim invaders of Britain. Englishmen were just recovering from the shock of the Armada and could well appreciate the general situation. Ariosto emphasized the fantasy involved in his details: an Ethiopian army crosses the Sahara; stones become horses; leaves, ships (*Furioso* 38.33–34; 39.26–28). The myth contradicts the reality. In Ariosto's time the Turks moved from victory to victory, conquering Syria, Egypt, Rhodes, and Hungary. They seemed invincible. In Spenser's time reality had changed very little. Despite Turkish preoccupation with Persia and Christian victories at Malta and Lepanto, the Christians did not win back a single foot of territory, and Cyprus fell to the Turks.

In this manner the political level of the allegory differs from the literal. While both relate to historical reality, from one level to another the relation of myth to fact reverses itself. On the literal level fairyland reflects reality, the Asia of the crusades. On the political level it contradicts reality. The grandiose vision of world empire compensates for political weakness. The Englishman fears for the survival of his nation, the Protestant worries for his faith, and the Christian perpetually loses to the Turk.[18] For the Christian especially the war had gone badly for hundreds of years, and an appeal to faery remained viable, whether made in the time of Emperor Frederick II or in that of Queen Elizabeth.

Faery's continued existence over so long a period eventually gave it a status peculiarly its own, partially independent of any single literary text. This tendency appears first of all in the habit of cross-reference. The Huon Continuations include references to two other romances. We learn that Reinold of Montalban captured Angora twenty years earlier and that Ogier the Dane destroyed Colanders en route to India. Spenser's remark about Huon and Guyon is the last in a series of such cross-references:[19]

> Well could he [Guyon] tourney and in lists debate,
> And knighthood tooke of good Sir *Huons* hand,
> When with king *Oberon* he came to Faerie land.
>
> [*FQ* 2.1.6]

By such a method fairyland becomes an entity unto itself, a general place which draws together many different romances and chronicles and unites the matter of Britain with that of France. In *Huon,* when Arthur and Morgan the Fay arrive at Momure, we learn that Morgan has newly married Ogier the Dane, who is now acting as Arthur's regent.[20] Spenser's choice of fairyland, then, has considerable artistic significance. In the other romances fairyland is a place visited amidst a number of adventures set in more mundane lands. In *Orlando innamorato,* the most fantastic of the Italian romances, by the end the heroes are all drifting back to France. Spenser alone staged all his action in fairyland, the place where all other romances cross over, one into another. This choice allows Spenser to practice his basic *con-taminatio*, to transfer situations and stories from the Charlemagne romances (of which that of Ariosto and Boiardo is the last) to his Arthurian plot. Boiardo began the practice when he brought into the Charlemagne cycle, with its crusade settings and clash of Christian and Saracen, the courtesy and love longing associated with Arthur's knights. Spenser reverses his invention and moves Arthur to central Asia.[21]

We have defined the where of faery. It is India and America, the new lands which by his circumnavigation of the world Drake had opened up to the English and which friends of Spenser, like Ralegh, were trying to colonize. At the same time Spenser's faery has certain peculiar characteristics which require a reformulation of this definition. The mirror of future empire is itself old, and the principals of Spenser's romance lived long ago. Why is faery in the dim past, remote in time as well as place? We already know from book 1 that the "antiquities, which no body can know" (2.Pro.1) are in Calliope's keeping, for she has the ancient rolls of fairyland put away in an "euerlasting scryne" or box (1.Pro.2). So we also know that Spenser is not talking of historical evidence in the normal sense of this term. The Muses do not preside over the Public Record Office. Guyon's experience at Alma's Castle further clarifies this assumption. In the Chamber of Memory he reads the "*Antiquitie* of *Faerie* lond" (2.9.60). Another answer, then, to the where of faery is anywhere that human beings exist. Fairyland is not a place per se but a memory in the mind of man, something preserved in books. Literary memory has this advantage over imagination, in that its images and data have already been filtered through reason. In Augustine's metaphor, memory is the stomach of the mind (*Confessions* 10.14). Books and chronicles express this difference clearly, for they result from a rational ordering of experiential phenomena. Now Spenser normally indicates what texts are specially connected with each book of *The Faerie Queene:* the Legend of Saint George for book 1, e.g., or the *Canterbury Tales* for book 4. For the Legend of Temperance the relevant books are three: *Melusine, Huon of Bordeaux,* and the traditional English chronicle history derived from Geoffrey of Monmouth.[22] Only the first two treat of faery and need concern us here. Unfortunately, if we turn to these romances, we find another puzzle. *Melusine* and *Huon* (in its final form) are both romance chronicles of particular families in Aquitaine. Neither has any demonstrable influence on the narrative of *The Faerie Queene*.[23] Spenser did not borrow any episodes, magical devices, or palaces from these sources. His appeal to them must have a different purpose.

A more likely explanation would be that Spenser wishes us to see in these sources euhemerist analogues for his own poem. He had already used *Melusine* for his theoretical argument in the prologue. We can find out something about this if we look again at the episode in *Colin Clout*. Colin has been telling his friends about his little voyage to England:

> So to the sea we came; the sea? that is
> A world of waters heaped vp on hie,
> Rolling like mountaines in wide wildernesse,
> Horrible, hideous, roaring with hoarse crie.

[196–99]

What for an experienced person would be an uneventful trip Colin transforms into high heroics. We realize that the sea amazes and terrifies the shepherd because he has not seen it before. Therefore, while in our terms he exaggerates matters and wanders in hyperbole, he nevertheless conveys to us a genuine, authentic experience: his first view of the sea. One could argue that a similar process occurs in *Huon of Bordeaux* and explains its presentation of faery. At the battle of Rames Huon's valor stuns his Persian allies, and the narrator remarks, "He that had sene Huon howe he slewe and bet downe the Sarasyns and paynymes, wolde haue sayde that he was no mortall man / but rather a man of the fayrey, for the great prowes and maruayles that he dyd. . . ." (p. 598). In fact Huon wears powerful gems which make him invincible, so the judgment is appropriate. But the process of judgment is curious. Because Huon displays unusual abilities, he must be of "faery," despite the fact that he is of mortal birth and has not yet journeyed to Momure. Now invincibility need not warrant exaggeration but probably will. Following such logic, the author of the text could himself *invent* marvels to convey the quality of superior human achievement. If the history represents some such logic, then Oberon's faery wonders could be demythologized, and the chronicle would become another kind of euhemeristic narrative. And, whether the medieval authors of *Huon* and its continuations ever intend such distortions, familiar as Spenser was with Renaissance modes of exegesis, he would probably have read *Huon* in this fashion. He could easily have seen that *Huon* conformed to a euhemeristic pattern. One of the most marvelous episodes occurs at the Castle of Adamant, where adherents to King Ptolemy besieged Julius Caesar after he had set up Cleopatra in Egypt. Spenser could tell from Plutarch and other classical sources that this event never happened. Caesar did not sleep with the Lady of the Privy Isle, command a troop of faery beings, and pass away his time in a castle whose "walles and toures were of fyne alabaster clere shynyng, and the towres rychely coueryd with fyne golde of Arabe" (*Huon*, p. 380). If he wished to, Spenser could gauge with some precision the way *Huon* distorts reality into myth.

Spenser's own form of euhemerism is more complicated. He manufactures endless wonders but disengages them from his faery heroes. As Isabel Rathborne says, "His good fairies are thoroughly humanized and rationalized. They possess, or at least exhibit, no supernatural powers that are not also possessed by the human characters. In fact the principal enchanted weapons in the poem belong to Britomart and Arthur, neither of whom is a fairy."[24] Spenser manages to suggest simultaneously the original mundane hero (Guyon) and the effect of his career on others (the wonders with which the poet surrounds the hero). The process dramatizes the bases of euhemerism and explains the nature of Spenser's "evidence."

We have now come to a preliminary judgment on Spenser's faery. It is the literary expression of a complex mental experience. It begins with a person's response to an unfamiliar reality, the way Colin felt about the sea, the Persians about Huon's prowess, and the explorers about the two Indies. Therefore in its very origins faery involves more than an external reality; it includes both perceiver and the thing perceived. This perceptual act is unique, for Colin's second or third experience of the sea will not have for him the same wonder and surprise as the first. The poet expresses the unity of this perceptual event by a restructuring of this whole process, which in turn stimulates a set of special reactions in us. We participate not in a firsthand experience, as in a romantic poem, but in its symbolic rearrangement, where the whole landscape can look different and impossible images rest next to everyday horses. To take one example, consider the great bridge of Cleopolis:

> ... *Elfinor,* who was in magick skild;
> He built by art vpon the glassy See
> A bridge of bras, whose sound heauens thunder seem'd to bee.
> [*FQ* 2.10.73]

One first imagines a shining bridge stretched over a calm or "glassy" sea, but then the syntax creates problems. Spenser identifies the bridge with thunder, which does not fit a calm day. Or, if we take the other syntactic possibility, how can a calm sea make thunderous noises? But if the bridge is really thunder and lightning, then the glassy sea suggests the apocalyptic sea of heaven. The description is already half stellified.

We cannot simply distinguish truth from hyperbole here or in many other scenes of *The Faerie Queene* because the formal vision does not represent an external reality; rather, it mediates a perceptual process.

The blending of truth and hyperbole creates a peculiar rhetorical situation. Our response to Spenser's faery differs more than a little from Colin's wonder at the sea, and it is in this area that we come upon the allegorical levels of fairyland. We observe in book 2 certain phenomena which are ignored by the characters and the narrator of the poem. We move, therefore, away from the literal level, where we dealt mostly with formal questions, matters of geography and sources. Now we must try to sift truth from hyperbole and enter the realm of psychology.[25] The questions which we will ask, the *whys* for which we will devise answers, provide the mechanism of transition. What we find at first is that Spenser systematically violates our notions of probability in an ever increasing degree. What we make of these violations takes us out of the poem altogether.

To begin with, though Spenser has located fairyland in a definite place and furthermore given it a coherent time scheme, our predominant reaction to faery is quite different.[26] No one seriously wonders what road Arthur took from Orgoglio's Castle to the area by Mammon's vale or what happened at Medina's after Guyon left.[27] We feel that Medina with as much probability could cease to exist once Guyon has departed. Images and personifications appear and disappear in a largely deserted landscape. This dreamy sense contrasts markedly with the Italian romance epic. Tasso and Ariosto both present coherent societies with a real geography and history. We know exactly how to go from Paris to Arles or from Palestine to Armida's Garden in the Canaries. Likewise, we know that Jerusalem has its own history, both before and after the events narrated in Tasso's poem. Solimano's descendant will be Saladin (*Gerusalemme liberata* 10.22–23). Ariosto can leave Marsilio unpunished in Spain, confident that we will draw our own conclusions about Roncesvalles. The typical scene in *The Faerie Queene* generates no such probable illusions. It resembles more the vague, unending forest of adventures in which Malory's heroes wander. And Malory finally does not apply either, for two reasons. In a story like that of the Knight of the Cart, Malory can locate his events specifically and familiarly, near London. He can create a probable and real world when he wants to. The other reason is more fundamental. Spenser makes his landscape in places deliberately incoherent.

The hag Occasion gives a fine example of what I have called elsewhere the Absurdity Principle.[28] When she instigates battle between Furor and Pyrochles, she uses a weird torch:

His mother eke, more to augment his spight,
Now brought to him a flaming fire brond,
Which she in *Stygian* lake, ay burning bright,
Had kindled. . . .

[2.5.22]

Where could she get this prop all at once? It is ridiculous to assume that
she kept it hidden and *burning* while Guyon tied her up. But the other
possibility is equally unacceptable. Who could imagine her suddenly
running off to Hades and back again, all in an instant, unnoticed either
by the other characters or by the narrator? The scene violates probability. Then there is the episode in which Guyon literally padlocks
her tongue (2.4.12). Or take another, less obvious example: Who can
seriously imagine Guyon sailing for two days over the open sea—in a
rowboat? (2.12.2). But these are minor "lapses" compared with the
systematic violation of all probability which Spenser achieves with his
major characters. If he is so concerned over the objective truth of
faery, why does he have characters interact who could never have
met? Arthur is a fifth- or sixth-century personage, Huon lived in the
eighth and Guyon in the twelfth century. Arthur's "contemporaries"
are backward projections from the distant future. And all these dates
are assumed in the chronicles, not invented by modern historical research. What would we make of a play or film with a fourteenth-
century setting whose major characters were Edward II, Henry VIII,
and Sir Winston Churchill?

There was precedent for such anachronism in classical and Renaissance epic. Dido and Aeneas made love despite the 400 years separat-
ing their lives, and Ariosto could move a twelfth-century ruler of
Damascus back to the time of Charlemagne (or at least use the same
name: I refer to Norandino—Nur ed-Din, the father of Saladin). But
both of these were isolated incidents, while Spenser has made his
central and continued action anachronistic. Perhaps no epic or romance poet ever grounded his plot on such a radical principle. Spenser
made poetic license the focus of his epic.

Isabel Rathborne tried to explain this phenomenon in *The Meaning
of Spenser's Fairyland*. She associated fairyland with the classical
Elysium, the residence of the famous dead (pp. 143–44). Thus she
could explain with precision how renowned heroes from different
periods could meet one another. The Christian version would be
heaven and hell and would have an additional value, for it would rationalize our psychological apprehension of faery. Aquinas had argued
that man in the Beatific Vision apprehends many things at once, while

now we think successively and by means of many ideas (*Summa theologica* 1.12.10). This was a conventional notion, not one peculiar to Aquinas, and could help to explain why in *The Faerie Queene* we perceive several different times at once.

Unfortunately, Rathborne's theory, though attractive, does not really apply to Spenser, or at least not in the manner in which she formulates it. Such a hypothesis cannot explain the everyday activities of faery. Guyon lives a life of chivalric action, by which he acquires fame. Heaven and Elysium, on the other hand, are not places in which one makes oneself a hero: they are *rewards* for such virtuous action. Therefore moral choice does not exist in these afterworlds, and good and evil are separated from each other. In fairyland the condition is just the opposite. Guyon and Arthur are constantly making moral choices, and the bad mingle with the good.[29]

We can still keep much of Rathborne's theory, however, if we give it a different basis. We must look not to the *meaning* of fairyland but to a rhetorical set of relationships, namely, those between ourselves and the poem. While reading *The Faerie Queene* we experience the interaction of Guyon and Arthur with perfect ease, while on reflection all the difficulties appear. When we try to rationalize what we have experienced in Spenser's poem, we stumble and talk inaccurately.[30] Somehow we can understand the coexistence of times in a literary form but not in philosophical discourse—or theological discourse, for that matter. If we can sense how Guyon and Arthur interact, we approach dimly divine comprehension of history, the interaction of Abraham and Christ. Unlike a romantic poet who might image in his poetry *how* his mind grapples with the primary data of experience, Spenser transforms this perceptual process. He makes us think of the conditions for perception, the *whatever* which underlies our mental processes. It is one thing for the mind to understand a mathematical theorem or a perceived object like a cat. It is quite another for the mind to understand why it understands, to comprehend its own form, particularly when the problem turns on the contrast between mental and external time.

Here I must make a short digression to clarify the next point. By the Renaissance philosophic discourse on time had become extremely subtle and complicated. A few examples will suggest some of the dimensions of the problem. With his Alexandrian love of hierarchy, Plotinus had insisted that eternity must be defined first, since it is the precondition for the temporal order (*Enneads* 3.7.1). The caveat is logical but makes an already difficult question almost impossible. Who can talk about not-time? Augustine perhaps did it better than anyone else, when he tried to explain how the mind can comprehend past, present, and future simultaneously (see *Confessions* 11.14–31). By the Middle Ages Aquinas, drawing on such late classical speculation, could weave a set of truly fine distinctions. One could argue that the term "eternity" applied to God alone and then find a new term for various intermediary beings. So "aeviternity" was applied to changeless beings which nevertheless approach change in limited ways. Thus one could distinguish immortal beings from an eternal being, those which had a beginning but will never end from the One who was, is, and ever shall be.[31] For a complex set of abstruse problems Aquinas used a clear and precise terminology, of the sort possible only when there has been sustained disputation over a long period. But for us this discourse remains unsatisfactory for a number of reasons. Aquinas inherits the Alexandrian love of endless intermediaries, none of which are part of normal experience, and today we have different assumptions and philosophies. Perhaps any rational explanation will be inadequate. Augustine says, "quid est ergo tempus? si nemo ex me quaerat, scio; si quaerenti explicare velim, nescio" (*Confessions* 11.14, "What, then, is time? I know well enough what it is, provided that nobody asks me; but if I am asked what it is and try to explain, I am baffled").[32] And yet the problem is very much our problem. Somehow we exist in two worlds at once, an eternal and a temporal one.[33] The second world we understand, not the first, which we define negatively (not-time) as unlike the second and yet somehow its precondition. Through a specialized literary form, Spenser has demonstrated the reality of this second world. To perceive the coexistence of times in his poem is to have the viewpoint of eternity on time. Spenser has thrown us out of the temporal flux and into that area of our mind which we cannot define but can experience: a nontemporal perspective on the temporal.

We are now in a position to recall Coleridge's famous remark and develop further his notion of mental space. Spenser reorganizes primary mental experience symbolically for rhetorical purposes. In response to faery, we move outside the poem and try to know ourselves. Later we attempt to formulate this understanding philosophically. And for Spenser or anyone else in the Renaissance our reaction should also involve cosmic speculation. We apprehend the eternal of which this temporal order, this universe of earth, stars, and planets, is but a moving image.

There may also be a theological level to fairyland, for Spenser's characters create more than temporal problems. So far I have examined fairyland literally as a place and its characters rhetorically. On the philosophical level I have devised theories to explain our response to the characters in the poem. I will assume the same rhetorical situation on the theological level as on the philosophical, but my attention will be directed to another set of discrepancies, quite as notorious as Spenser's anachronisms.

Horace's rules about characterization delineate the problem most clearly. In the *Ars poetica* he demands complete consistency of characterization:

> Aut famam sequere, aut sibi convenientia finge.
> Scriptor honoratum si forte reponis Achillem,
> impiger, iracundus, inexorabilis, acer
> iura neget sibi nata, nihil non arroget armis.
> Sit Medea ferox invictaque, flebilis Ino,
> perfidus Ixion, Io vaga, tristis Orestes.
> Si quid inexpertum scaenae committis et audes
> personam formare novam, servetur ad imum
> qualis ab incepto processerit, et sibi constet.

>   You should either stick to tradition
> Or invent a consistent plot. If you bring back Achilles,
> Have him say how laws don't apply to him, have prowess
> Prevail over status, make him ruthless, impatient and fierce,
> And ANGRY! Let Medea be wild, inconquerably so,
> Ino tearful, Io "lost"; let Ixion
> Go back on his word; let Orestes be sadly depressed.
> If it's something as yet untried you put on the stage
> And you dare construct a new character, you must keep
> To the end the same sort of person you started out with,
> And make your portrayal consistent.[34]

Now one could argue plausibly that Spenser follows the latter part of this advice. Within his poem he keeps his characters reasonably consistent.[35] The problem comes with the first part of Horace's advice. The Roman poet wants the dramatist to keep famous characters consistent to the preconceptions of the audience. A timid and quiet Achilles would empty the theater very quickly.[36] This is sound rhetorical advice and recognizes the fact that for many works of art there exists what the French call a *prétexte*. If an author wishes to depict a famous hero, he must conform to the traditional type of that hero. Spenser put some famous heroes into his poem, heroes like Arthur and Saint George, but they might as well be new characters like Britomart—despite their names. The change is deliberate, for it is more difficult to establish inconsistency in romances, and yet Spenser does so. Unlike the characters of tragedy, the heroes of romance have far less developed personalities. They lack the necessary monologues and dramatic speeches. Physical oddities and repeated actions normally define them. In *Melusine,* for example, Guyon has one eye higher than the other (p. 103), and in his tale Huon frequently disobeys Oberon. Even so, Spenser has managed to disengage his heroes completely from their literary tradition.

Consider the case of Arthur. In the romantic lover of Gloriana (whom he saw only once) or the experienced knight perpetually out on quest, with his horse Spumador and his sword Morddure,[37] who would recognize the adolescent who pulled the sword from the stone and married Guinevere? Or who could find the Arthur of Geoffrey's *Historia regum Britanniae,* who spent money so fast that he had to attack the Saxons for plunder?[38] Spenser's Arthur supposedly precedes these youthful Arthurs, yet he more resembles accomplished knights. Orlando or Lancelot. Guyon presents the same problem. Where is the boy who followed his brother to Cyprus and became king of Armenia? The two Guyons relate to each other so little that scholars have wondered whether Spenser did use *Melusine,* and yet they relate as well as the two Arthurs. Why should Spenser insist on historical figures and then give them almost complete changes of personality?[39]

I do not think that we in the twentieth century would have any obvious response to this problem other than general dismay. Although modern writers have much concerned themselves with fluid personalities, by and large they have not worried about the theological dimensions of this problem. In the Renaissance, however, a theological conception of discontinuity did exist and was accepted by all, Protestant or Catholic. A Christian then would define a person as an identifiable individual who not only lives through a certain span of time here but after death lives a transformed existence in heaven and hell. This idea involves as radical a discontinuity as we find in Spenser's historical characters. I am not suggesting, of course, that Guyon and Arthur somehow signify the saints in heaven. Rather, the discontinuity which we observe in Spenser's characters logically parallels the discontinuity a Christian would perceive in his own existence. Paul's analogy for the risen body clearly demonstrates this. The glorified body of a human being relates to his earthly body as does the plant to its seed (1 Cor. 15:35–44). Now in form a seed does not remotely resemble a tree or flower, though we understand their hidden continuity and ordinarily give them the same name: we buy *aster* seeds and *tulip* bulbs. Similarly, a Christian would ascribe the same name to what appears drastically different. It is still Paul, whether on earth or in heaven.

Personal names would be the normal way to indicate such a continuity in discontinuity. We know that such words signify unique personalities, which we get to know gradually but never completely. Our initial judgment usually depends upon givens, the accidents of birth. Belphoebe is beautiful, and Arthur is strong. It takes years to guess the use of these gifts and so to approach the unique aspect of a person. Nevertheless, some kind of reasonable judgment on an individual can finally be made here, a judgment which is succinctly expressed by the old Greek proverb: "Call no man happy until death."[40] We cannot assess the value of a man's life or come to know it properly until we perceive it teleologically. We have to know the man's complete record, how his story ends. Only then can we say we know, as much as we are able to know any particular, what the name of that person really denotes. But in the Christian tradition we can never achieve such a perspective. If someone believes in resurrection, then the life of the individual literally has *no end,* and teleology becomes impossible.[41] It is as if we were limited to the prologue of a story. Time will fade before eternity, and each person will be transformed, will become like angel or demon. Augustine relates a conversation with his mother shortly before her death, and his narrative shows effectively the mystery of that future life which by its brilliance annihilates this present existence:

> Cumque ad eum finem sermo perduceretur, ut carnalium sensuum delectatio quantalibet, in quantalibet luce corporea, prae illius vitae iucunditate non conparatione, sed ne conmemoratione quidem digna videretur, erigentes nos ardentiore affectu in id ipsum, perambulavimus gradatim cuncta corporalia, et ipsum caelum, unde sol et luna et stellae lucent super terram. et adhuc ascendebamus, interius cogitando et loquendo et mirando opera tua, et venimus in mentes nostras et transcendimus eas, ut attingeremus regionem ubertatis indeficientis, unde pascis Israel in aeternum veritate pabulo, et ibi vita sapientia est, per quam fiunt omnia ista, et quae fuerunt et quae futura sunt. et ipsa non fit, sed sic est, ut fuit, et sic erit semper: quin potius fuisse et futurum esse non est in ea, sed esse solum, quoniam aeterna est: nam fuisse et futurum esse non est aeternum. et dum loquimur et inhiamus illi, attingimus eam modice toto ictu cordis.

> Our conversation led us to the conclusion that no bodily pleasure, however great it might be and whatever earthly light might shed lustre upon it, was worthy of comparison, or even of mention, beside the happiness of the life of the saints. As the flame of love burned stronger in us and raised us higher to-

wards the eternal God, our thoughts ranged over the whole compass of material things in their various degrees, up to the heavens themselves, from which the sun and the moon and the stars shine down upon the earth. Higher still we climbed, thinking and speaking all the while in wonder at all that you have made. At length we came to our own souls and passed beyond them to that place of everlasting plenty, where you feed Israel for ever with the food of truth. There life is that Wisdom by which all these things that we know are made, all things that ever have been and all that are yet to be. But that Wisdom is not made: it is as it has always been and as it will be for ever—or, rather, I should not say that it *has been* or *will be,* for it simply *is,* because eternity is not in the past or in the future. And while we spoke of the eternal Wisdom, longing for it and straining for it with all the strength of our hearts, for one fleeting instance we reached out and touched it. [*Confessions* 9.10]

In response to Spenser's poem, we have gone through a process similar to that described by Augustine. We went from things mundane to an eternal viewpoint on the temporal order in which we live, and theologically we got some intuition of what our personalities look like from the other world. But the vision does not last; it wavers and soon vanishes. As Augustine goes on to say,

> et suspiravimus, et reliquimus ibi religatas primitias spiritus, et remeavimus ad strepitum oris nostri, ubi verbum et incipitur et finitur. et quid simile verbo tuo, domino nostro, in se permanenti sine vetustate atque innovanti omnia?

> Then with a sigh, leaving our *spiritual harvest* bound to it, we returned to the sound of our own speech, in which each word has a beginning and an ending—far, far different from your Word, our Lord, who abides in himself for ever, yet never grows old and gives new life to all things.

Back in this mundane world, where we live and die and where works of art have finite limits, we nevertheless have left with us a new vision of ourselves and our daily life. The simplest and most insignificant acts throw long shadows into eternity. By his denigration of this world, the Christian simultaneously transvalues it. On one hand it is a brief prologue to eternity. On the other, human existence here assumes an importance so great that it is difficult to express in words. In allegory this vision reveals itself in two seemingly contradictory character types. There are the shadowy personifications and half-developed characters of *The Faerie Queene*, perfect emblems for the unfinished personalities which we have in this temporal life. There are likewise the realistic characters which Auerbach found in the *Divina commedia*, realistic because they are the essence of an individual's total life, its consummation in eternity.

If the heavens are so far away from earth, the gap which must be bridged by a name is too great, and the mind cannot comprehend it. Not so in some of the classical stories. When Odysseus crossed the Ocean Stream to Hades, he found there the same personalities which he had known at Troy. Though they were insubstantial shadows of themselves, Achilles could not refrain from making outrageous remarks, and Ajax still could not forgive Odysseus (*Od.* 11.465–67). But for the Christian the whole set of connections between here and there had become labyrinthine and yet fundamental to his whole vision. We do not see in the girl next door a glorified saint or a damned being, but the Christian had to call them by the same name. A familiar example from literature might help here (*Purgatorio* 30.22–48). When we read the *Divina commedia*, it is difficult to see any relation besides the name between Beatrice Portinari of Florence and the glorious creature Dante meets in the Earthly Paradise, clothed in living flame and riding a griffin-drawn chariot. But when they look at each other, the pilgrim recognizes his old love.

6 The Language of Milton's Heaven

What is the meaning of Sinai? The mountain from which *sinah* [hostility] toward idolatry descended. [Talmud]

Milton did not allegorize the war of the angels in *Paradise Lost,* and this choice signals the end of a tradition. Allegory had begun as a defense for just such scenes, the wrangling and fighting of Homer's gods which so offended Xenophanes and other philosophers, and in subsequent periods marvelous episodes of this sort had normally been written and read as allegory. Milton's refusal coincides historically with the triumph of neoclassicism in England, which itself did not encourage allegory. *Paradise Lost* was published in 1667, and Addison would later find in it the ideal exemplification of neoclassical principles. Yet Milton avoided allegory for another set of reasons, theological rather than artistic, ones not communicated to later writers, and it is this thinking which I will work out here.

Theologically, Milton had no choice but to describe heaven and the battle between the angels. He believed that Satan caused man's fall and that this angelic coresponsibility set up the possibility of man's return to grace.[1] Therefore Milton had to explain who Satan was and outline his history. He had to show the revolt in heaven. This requirement linked *Paradise Lost* to the *Iliad* and, to a lesser degree, *Gerusalemme liberata,* epics of military encounter in which gods as well as human beings came to the battlefield. These epics were mimetic, and such scenes required concrete and clear presentation. He could not narrate unimaginable clashes between god and monster, Marduk and Tiamat, Michael and the Ancient Serpent, but had to present divine combats visually. In the *Iliad* Athena picks up a large rock and hits Ares on the neck, and the war god falls, sprawling over seven acres, his air trailing in the dust, his armor ringing (21.403–8). With her left hand Hera seizes

An earlier version of this chapter appeared in *Modern Philology* 74:360–65, © 1977 by The University of Chicago.

Artemis by the wrists; with her right she takes away the bow and beats the virgin goddess over the ears, while Artemis twists around and her arrows scatter on the ground (21.489–92). Such scenes presuppose physical deities who inhabit a physical heaven. Zeus lives in a brazen house (14.173); the gods drink from gold cups and sit on a golden pavement (4.2–3); Hera's bedroom has a bar on the door (14.167–68); and her chariot has removable bronze wheels with gold rims, silver hubs, and bronze tires (5.722–26). Similarly, the heaven of *Gerusalemme liberata* has a castle where the angels store their weapons, which include the spear which Michael used to fight the Dragon, lightnings and plague "arrows," a trident for earthquakes, and a large diamond shield (7.79–82). Milton follows the same pattern. His angels keep their chariots in a stable between two brazen mountains (*PL* 7.199–203); they wear armor of diamond and gold (4.553–54) and drink nectar in cups of gold, diamond, and pearl (6.634). In battle Michael wounds Satan all down his right side (6.326–27), and the demons with cannon shot overturn ranks of angels (6.590–607).

This physicality in heaven has invariably drawn criticism. Xenophanes, the first person to attack Homer, argued that God is not made in the image of man. Giovanni Getto recently found Tasso's angel with the diamond shield too material, and the complaint is a familiar one to Milton students.[2] A standard answer to such a charge also existed. These deities were actually symbols, not to be taken literally, and the scenes in which they appeared were allegories. In his Prose Allegory Tasso said that the diamond shield symbolized divine protection and the angels generally either divine aid or divine inspiration. The poet could thus make his gods and angels as physical as he wished on the literal level, knowing that his audience would read them symbolically. Milton instead invented a special language for his heavenly scenes, one which he derived from the Bible and which protected them from literalist readings. It also made the allegory which we have been studying impossible.

My argument will have three parts. I will first look at Milton's biblical models, then the discourse he used for heaven; finally, I will suggest its theological rationale. I will return to the topic of allegory only at the end of the chapter.

Milton began with a theological dilemma. He thought that the angels probably fell before the creation of the world and that heaven may have existed considerably earlier.[3] He could not, therefore, depict man's sin accurately unless he devoted much of his narrative to relatively arcane matters, to events which preceded man's very existence. A casual remark in the *De doctrina Christiana* exemplifies this problem theologically. Milton begins his discussion of the creation with the general statement "Sed ante mundum conditum quid egerit Deus, insipiens nimis sit qui quaerat; nec qui respondeat multo sapientior" (1.7, "As to the actions of God before the foundation of the world, it would be the height of folly to inquire into them, and almost equally so to attempt a solution of the question"; p. 973b). This statement jars when we remember how much of *Paradise Lost* concerns just such foolish matters and that Satan makes a similar point in the epic.[4] In such a situation, where he had to write about what he could not know, Milton's natural recourse was to Scripture, to whatever representations of heaven and the angelic war he could find in the inspired Word. There alone could he find the necessary authority and objective truth.

In the Bible Milton found answers to his problem—answers, however, which contained their own puzzles. First of all, very few scriptural episodes occur in heaven. When they do, heaven functions more as a setting for a divine manifestation than for its own sake. It is the epiphanies that count, not the heavenly props. And here we run into Milton's doctrine of accommodation: "Ideoque tantum sui retexit Deus, quantum vel nostra mens capere, vel naturae debilitas ferre potest" (*De doctrina* 1.2, "God therefore has made as full a revelation of himself as our minds can conceive, or the weakness of our nature can bear"; p. 923b). Much has been said about this principle, but not enough about the severe limitations it imposed on Milton himself as a literary artist. For heaven and for all matters which precede the foundation of the world, Scripture becomes an *absolute* model, one which cannot be altered, as it represents the way God wants us to conceive of Him. We know how rigorously Milton pursued both this doctrine and his scripturalism. C. A. Patrides has shown that Milton's God is therefore anthropopathic. He expresses a range of emotions not because they are philosophically appropriate or conceivable but because God is so represented in the Bible. He reacts first with scorn, then with wrath when Satan revolts.[5] For the creative artist this doctrine means that practically all room for invention is eliminated. If Milton succeeded in his heaven scenes, and the matter is debatable, he did so in very difficult circumstances. To paraphrase an old proverb, the highest praise should be given not to the poet who ranges freely in the zodiac of his own wit but to him who, restricted by historical données, nevertheless transforms his intractable matter into great poetry.

As there are few heavenly scenes in Scripture, it should not surprise us that Milton chose for his principal model the most spectacular of God's earthly manifestations, the Sinai covenant. Raphael begins his narrative with the whole military contingent of heaven assembled together at the foot of God's holy mountain. They stand in circles around the mountain, before which spreads an immense plain, wider than the earth stretched flat (5.583–94, 648–50); and there they learn of a new decree which they are required to accept or reject. The situation and the topography strictly parallel those of Exodus, where on the large plain which borders Mount Sinai[6] the Israelites were asked to accept or reject the Mosaic Law. And once Raphael's hyperbole has been removed from the following description, we have a military camp in a desert oasis, with the tents set up among the trees:[7]

> . . . Th' Angelic throng
> Disperst in Bands and Files thir Camp extend
> By living Streams among the Trees of Life,
> Pavilions numberless, and sudden rear'd,
> Celestial Tabernacles, where they slept
> Fann'd with cool Winds. . . .
>
> [5.650–55]

The parallel extends as well to army rations. The angels enjoy wondrous food (mostly fruits and juices) automatically provided, much as the Israelites for forty years lived on the "Bread from Heaven" (Exod. 16:4). Raphael described the archetype for manna earlier, when he told Adam that in the morning the angels "find the ground / Cover'd with pearly grain" (*PL* 5.429–30).[9]

Most especially God's iconography (if it can be called that) comes from the Exodus situation. The angels hear the Father's voice "as from a flaming Mount, whose top / Brightness had made invisible" (*PL* 5.598–99). The parallel with Exodus becomes complete once the wrath of God is aroused by Satan's revolt:

> So spake the Sovran voice, and Clouds began
> To darken all the Hill, and smoke to roll
> In dusky wreaths, reluctant flames, the sign
> Of wrath awak't: nor with less dread the loud
> Ethereal Trumpet from on high gan blow.
>
> [6.56–60]

Similarly angered by man's sin, God speaks through cloud and thunder (10.31–33), and the trumpet sounds again for the Heavenly Council in book 11, where it is explicitly paralleled to the Sinai event (11.73–81). So whether within or outside of Raphael's narrative, Milton attributes to God the fixed particulars of the Sinai epiphany, a description which we would say combines features of a storm and of a volcanic eruption: lightning and thunder, a thick cloud, the trumpet sound, the whole

mountain smoking and trembling as God comes down to it in fire
(Exod. 19:16–19). It is a picture understood in Pauline fashion, the Law
proclaimed which convicts unto sin, the iconography of a wrath stirred
by the defection of men and angels.

Milton's other two models reflect different aspects of this same representation. One concerns the Messiah's chariot, which the poet found
in Ezekiel, and the other involves the ritual of heaven, which he imitated from Apocalypse.

We might call the Messiah and His chariot a thunderstorm pushed to
the limits of poetic hyperbole. The Messiah rides enthroned in rainbow
colors above the firmament, grasping 10,000 thunders (*PL* 6.758–60,
836), while beneath the cherubim and wheels shoot forth lightning (for
the whole, see 6.749–66, 824–55). In these details Milton follows
Ezekiel's vision of a large cloud filled with fire, within which he saw the
vision of the firmament and chariot. It was the storm of wrath come
upon Jerusalem from the north, and we can relate both versions to the
One who speaks from above the cherubim in the inner tent or to the
weather God who rides the clouds in Psalms. Ultimately they all relate to
the Sinai theophany in which Yahweh both thunders and lightens from
the mountain and appears to the Seventy Elders, standing on the blue
vault of the heavens (Exod. 19:16, 20:18, 24:10).[9] The numerous details
of the image need not disguise its inherent simplicity.

Like most other writers, Milton derived his notions of heavenly
ritual from the fourth chapter of Apocalypse. We might say that the
writer of Revelation turned Ezekiel's storm vision into a permanent
stage set, a comparison made in Milton's own time by David Pareus.[10]
As in *Paradise Lost,* it continues throughout the action with its props
essentially unchanged. Ezekiel's four cherubs are there, like the
firmament or glassy sea and the One seated upon a throne associated
with lightning, thunder, and rainbow colors. But to this has been added
the paraphernalia of the Jerusalem Temple: the seven-branched
candlestick, the altar, the incense, and the appropriate architecture.
These in turn reappear in *Paradise Lost:* lamps burn nightly before the
throne, an altar breathes forth odors and flowers (2.244–45), and the
Son offers incense prayers.[11]

Together these three models create apparent discrepancies in the
poem. People talk interchangeably of God's mountain and His temple,
and in places the two images blur. The lamps, for example, burn on the
mountain (5.712–13), and after the Messiah's victory the singing angels
circle the mountain as if it were a building (6.743–44). A choir circling a
whole mountain or a temple which itself *is* a mountain may seem awkward or a gigantic hyperbole, but Milton was scripturally sound in

merging the two images. In Psalms the worshiper ascends the hill or "mountain" of God's temple in Jerusalem,[12] and the temple ritual itself was instituted and first performed at Mount Sinai. Moreover, the connection explains Milton's use of Psalm 2 for the events of his narrative: the rebellion of the heathen, the laughter of the Lord, the proclamation of His Son on Mount Zion. The mere allusion by the psalmist to God's mountain suffices to generate the parallel, for the Exodus epiphany finally lies behind both images. However strange it might seem to model heaven on a desert mountain, the procedure reflects an accurate and careful reading of scriptural texts. No one had yet changed the dates for Exodus or separated the book into separate strands, so Milton would naturally have seen both Ezekiel and Revelation essentially as sophistications of the primary Mosaic vision. And as we shall see later, the connection is much more fundamental than a group of borrowed images.

Milton's debt to Scripture extended to method as well as images and scenes. Because this is a complex matter and one which affects my principal concern, the nature of the poet's language, I will discuss it in detail. A good example would be the initial description of heaven (bk. 3), a scene which does not involve a problem with narrators, as does the heavenly war. Moreover, it is the first and only full-length description of heaven given by the narrator:

> No sooner had th' Almighty ceas't, but all
> The multitude of Angels with a shout   345
> Loud as from numbers without number, sweet
> As from blest voices, uttering joy, Heav'n rung
> With Jubilee, and loud Hosannas fill'd
> Th' eternal Regions: lowly reverent
> Towards either Throne they bow, and to the ground   350
> With solemn adoration down they cast
> Thir Crowns inwove with Amarant and Gold,
> Immortal Amarant, a Flow'r which once
> In Paradise, fast by the Tree of Life
> Began to bloom, but soon for man's offense   355
> To Heav'n remov'd where first it grew, there grows,
> And flow'rs aloft shading the Fount of Life,
> And where the river of Bliss through midst of Heav'n
> Rolls o'er *Elysian* Flow'rs her Amber stream;
> With these that never fade the Spirits elect   360
> Bind thir resplendent locks inwreath'd with beams,
> Now in loose Garlands thick thrown off, the bright

Pavement that like a Sea of Jasper shone
Impurpl'd with Celestial Roses smil'd.
Then Crown'd again thir gold'n Harps they took,   365
Harps ever tun'd, that glittering by thir side
Like Quivers hung, and with Preamble sweet
Of charming symphony they introduce
Thir sacred Song, and waken raptures high;
No voice exempt, no voice but well could join   370
Melodious part, such concord is in Heav'n.

Milton creates a familiar picture of heaven. We expect the many terms for light and consider normal the singing angels derived from Revelation. And yet the scene is peculiar, partly because the traditional pictures of heaven depend on a specialized use of language, partly because Milton has developed this language intelligently. The short similes in the passage illustrate this problem. A simile should clarify; these finally do not.

Milton uses four similes which range from the correct to the unfamiliar. The shout of the angels is loud as from an infinite number, sweet as from blest voices. The pavement on which the angels stand resembles a sea of jasper, and the harps hang at their sides like quivers. Of the four the last is normal and describes the position of the harps by a familiar example. The first two, while biblical, are more difficult. We might dismiss the first as hyperbole, though it remains rather paradoxical to talk of numbers with no number. The second is more intractable: "sweet / As from blest voices." It could be read as a tautology, for we know the angels are blessed and we are talking of their shout. More likely, however, the *whatever* of the angels resembled *somehow* many happy voices. Otherwise why say that the shout was only *like* to the noise made by voices, except to remind us that angels are not human and do not have voices in the normal sense of the term? The simile asserts difference perhaps as much as similarity. The third comparison, while clear, functions in a similar retrograde manner. Why compare a familiar object like a pavement with a totally mysterious entity, a sea of jasper? If the color is meant, then Milton should have chosen a stone with less of a range of possible colors. I would gloss the term as blue-green, but D. C. Allen prefers yellow or brown.[13] The phrase itself probably refers to the Crystalline Ocean, the waters above the firmament, which Milton says are "a bright Sea / . . . Of Jasper, or of liquid Pearl" (3.518–19). That is, instead of illuminating the unknown by the familiar, Milton explains the familiar by the unknown, the pavement by the waters above the firmament which have aroused arcane speculation for millennia. The literary method seems backward. In this case, however, we must blame Milton's source, for his expression covers the heavenly ground which Revelation (4:6) describes as like "a glassy Sea, like crystal" (cf. Ezek. 1:22), an expression which provoked as much speculation as the waters above the firmament with which it was sometimes equated.[14] The more similes Milton uses, the stranger the scene becomes.

The angels' crowns "inwove with Amarant and Gold" provide further examples of this technique and indicate that the uncertainties in this scene extend beyond the similes. Let us consider the flower first. In a nonscriptural passage Milton defines it circumstantially. While in heaven it shadows the fountain of life and blooms by the river of bliss; we also learn that it once grew on earth. But the excursus, for all its specificity, actually does not tell us much about the flower. As it no longer grows here, we have no idea what amaranth looks like, except the purple color of celestial roses, and we do not know what these are, any more than elysian flowers.[15]

The gold in the angels' crowns is even less helpful. It seems later to describe the beams of light which wind through the angels' hair (3.361). In a similar sense Milton equates Uriel's golden tiara with the sun's rays (3.625–26). Here the expression may help to explicate the amber stream which flows over elysian flowers. As no flowers grow at the bottom of a river, the phrase may refer to shining light of some sort or to some entity indeterminate between water and light. The golden harps of line 365, however, suggest substance and seem to give a definite frame of reference, until we realize that *all* "material" artifacts in heaven are of gold and/or diamond, whether the "frontispiece" of the heavenly gates (3.506) or Lucifer's palace, whose pyramids and towers were hewn from diamond quarries and rocks of gold (5.756–60). Armor in particular invariably flames with diamond and gold.[16] Such terms are used consistently but convey nothing more certain than color and light. If they apply to a substance, which seems probable, we cannot in the least say what kind of substance. On a simpler level, for example, Milton mentions rivers of potable gold on the sun (3.607–8) and appears to say that the sun contains in a molten state precious metals, stones, and iron. But the persistent conditional should make us pause:

> *If* metal, part *seem'd* Gold, part Silver clear,
> *If* stone, Carbuncle most of Chrysolite,
> Ruby or Topaz. . . .

> What wonder then *if* fields and regions here
> Breathe forth *Elixir* pure, and Rivers run
> Potable Gold. . . .[17]

Is the flowing gold *like* or *of the same substance as* the gold which we mine?[18]

If we look back now at the passage in which Milton first describes heaven, we can risk a few generalizations. He works with simple, if hyperbolic, pictures: angels singing and throwing flower crowns on a pavement. At the same time through his use of similes, certain terms, and references to objects, he moves the scene quite out of any normal frame of reference. We might say that through his scriptural investigations Milton discovered a perfect formula for representing matters "invisible to mortal sight" (3.55). The objective invisible, that world of beings which man could not experience and whose history preceded his own creation, found fitting expression in these simple yet indecipherable pictures. For finally, the system is self-enclosed. Armor may always flash diamonds and gold, the terms may be used consistently, but we have no idea what these terms might mean outside their context. Heavenly terms refer to *each other* and build up a complete world, but one we cannot enter. If other artists created self-contained models, at least they allowed us to understand the vocabulary and did not shut us out. Here it is rather as if we were asked to interpret an unknown language. We have no means of gauging Milton's language, no point of comparison with our experience.

This same hermetic containment informs Raphael's method, as scholars have long recognized. The angel merely extends the narrator's technique and replaces simile with extended metaphor.[19] Raphael's statement of principle may be clear enough and has often been quoted:

> ... And what surmounts the reach
> Of human sense, I shall delineate so,
> By lik'ning spiritual to corporal forms,
> As may express them best, though what if Earth
> Be but the shadow of Heav'n, and things therein
> Each to other like, more than on Earth is thought?
>
> [5.571–76]

Unfortunately, we never know *when* Raphael must resort to analogy, when he must interpret the spiritual by the corporeal, so that we cannot distinguish tenor and vehicle in the narrative. The angel throws out contrary hints here and there. He may suggest, as here, that heaven is very much like earth, or he may state later that a particular episode is indescribable; but these remarks will not decipher the narrative. We may of course try to interpret the story of warring angels in many ways, but we will never break through the narrative to the reality which it images.[20] And this frustration in turn affects the criticism of Milton's central action, the heavenly war.

There are at least two contradictory understandings of the three-day battle, one sublime and serious, the other comic and ironical. Addison developed the former; the latter has been argued by many recent critics, most notably Arnold Stein.[21] Now with a normal text we should be able to assess either position, its strengths and limitations, and come to some kind of reasonable evaluation. If we cannot, we assume that the split manifests, rather, a peculiarity in the text itself, something which resists the efforts of the commentator. An example from the *Iliad* will help to clarify this point, for a similar division separates Pope and Lattimore when they translate the battle of the gods. Pope, like Addison, presents the divine war with seriousness and sublimity, while Lattimore and Stein reveal farce and comedy. But the parallel, however interesting for its cultural implications, does not quite apply because Homer allows us to decide between the two interpretations, whereas Milton does not.

Homer mixes men with gods and places the battle in the familiar surroundings of Troy. We can therefore assess his hyperboles with precision and argue much more plausibly whether they are too extreme, whether they pass from the sublime to the absurd. Fallen, Ares covers seven acres of ground. In Milton's war, however, there are no human beings, no earthscape, to give the necessary standards. How can we determine whether a particular passage is ironic or sublime when we do not understand the vocabulary? We cannot decide simply between Addison and Stein because the text does not respond to the normal questions of the literary critic.

A third approach, the biblical, applies more directly to Milton's literary mode and gives a clear answer. The war in heaven is for Milton typological as well as historical. Even the most literalist among Protestant interpreters had to allow for a typological dimension in certain biblical passages, because Paul and the Gospel writers had so explained certain prophecies and events in the Old Testament.[22] Milton accepts typology for the Old Testament[23] and also for the heavenly war, though its source is Revelation 12. We have seen that the descriptions of heaven in Revelation are extrapolations from Old Testament contexts and so might be susceptible to such an analysis, but the war itself had a specific typological dimension. In Luke Jesus sends before Him the seventy-two disciples who cast out demons in His name, and Christ explains that He saw Satan falling like lightning from heaven (10.18). Commentators traditionally applied this episode to Revelation 12. Andrew of Caesarea, who wrote the basic exegesis in Greek, saw in the heavenly war a type of Christ's victory over Satan when He died on the cross. Pareus applied it to Christ's whole life (pp. 267–70). The

Redeemer began His battle with Satan in the desert, won it by His death and the Resurrection, and celebrated His triumph in the Ascension. The accuser fell from heaven, and the Blood of the Lamb washed away the guilt of the saints (Rev. 12.10–11).[24] Milton assumes this reading at 4.1–5, where he refers simultaneously to Revelation 12 (the heavenly war) and Luke 10 (Satan's second fall). He develops the reading at 10.182–92 and still more explicitly at the end of *Paradise Regained,* where he anticipates Satan's second defeat and stresses the parallel between his two epics. Christ, especially by His exorcism of demons, will defeat Satan and drive him out of Satan's own aerial kingdom.[25]

By typology we understand how the heavenly war relates to another event. We do not, however, understand the war itself in a clearer fashion, nor will the method answer any of the problems which I have just been discussing. For Paul, the crossing of the Red Sea may have anticipated baptism (1 Cor. 10.1–2), but it had its own historical reality. The same applies to the events which occur in the heaven of Milton's epic. Typology will not explain them, though it does indicate that Milton's method is biblical and that an explanation for that method should likewise be biblical.

The Hebraic models for Milton's heaven were theophanies. He would have understood their language, therefore, by the doctrine of accommodation.[26] In *De doctrina Christiana* Milton argues that we should conceive of God as He appears in Scripture: "Quamvis enim hoc concedatur, Deum, non qualis in se est, sed qualem nos capere possumus, talem semper vel describi vel adumbrari" (1.2, "Granting that both in the literal and figurative descriptions of God, He is exhibited not as He really is, but in such a manner as may be within the scope of our comprehension"; p. 923b). That is, though we might distinguish between the literal and the metaphoric in a particular passage or literary work, in Scripture the distinction breaks down where God is concerned. From a rhetorical point of view, *all* of it is metaphoric and indirect, what we can bear, not what accurately reflects the divine reality.[27] This principle extends as well to the speeches delivered by the Father and Son, the discourses of heaven. If the Father argues a perfectly rational logic, for example, we should not understand this as a mirror of divinity or as Milton's conception of God; rather, it too fits a figure of accommodation. Reason is traditionally man's highest gift, that which places him above the animals, so naturally we would associate God with rational discourse. Not that He speaks or thinks in this fashion, as tradition had assigned to the angels more effective modes of thought; but we can best understand Him in this fashion. The rationalist deity balances the mysterious figure alluded to in the Invocations. Both are ways in which we can approach the divine, but neither mirrors it.

We can understand this whole matter more clearly if we look at another biblical theophany. Ezekiel's vision of the chariot (chap. 1) best serves our purposes. It gave Milton a spectacular episode and modeled heaven both for him and for the writer of Revelation. The passage therefore lies behind the heavenly war in a double sense and illustrates to an extreme degree the original for Milton's peculiar method. In the following quotation I have italicized all similes and words denoting appearances:

4. And I looked, and, behold, a whirlwind came out of the north, a great cloud, and a fire infolding itself, and a brightness was about it, and out of the midst thereof *as the colour of amber,* out of the midst of the fire.

5. Also out of the midst thereof came the *likeness of four living creatures.* And this was their appearance; they had *the likeness of a man.*

6. And every one had four faces, and every one had four wings.

7. And their feet were straight feet; and the sole of their feet was *like the sole of a calf's foot:* and they sparkled *like the colour of burnished brass.*

8. And they had the hands of a man under their wings on their four sides; and they four had their faces and their wings.

9. Their wings were joined one to another; they turned not when they went; they went every one straight forward.

simile explicated ⟨ 10. As for the *likeness of their faces,* they four had the face of a man, and the face of a lion, on the right side: and they four had the face of an ox on the left side; they four also had the face of an eagle.

11. Thus were their faces: and their wings were stretched upward; two wings of every one were joined one to another, and two covered their bodies.

12. And they went every one straight forward: whither the spirit was to go, they went; and they turned not when they went.

simile explicated ⟨ 13. As for the *likeness of the living creatures,* their appearance was *like burning coals of fire,* and *like the appearance of lamps:* it went up and down among the living creatures; and the fire was bright, and out of the fire went forth lightning.

14. And the living creatures ran and returned *as the appearance of a flash of lightning*.

15. Now as I beheld the living creatures, behold one wheel upon the earth by the living creatures, with his four faces.

16. The appearance of the wheels and their work was *like unto the colour of a beryl:* and they four had one *likeness:* and their appearance and their work was *as it were a wheel in the middle of a wheel*.

17. When they went, they went upon their four sides: and they turned not when they went.

18. As for their rings, they were so high that they were dreadful; and their rings were full of eyes round about them four.

19. And when the living creatures went, the wheels went by them: and when the living creatures were lifted up from the earth, the wheels were lifted up.

20. Whithersoever the spirit was to go, they went, thither was their spirit to go; and the wheels were lifted up over against them: for the spirit of the living creature was in the wheels.

21. When those went, these went; and when those stood, these stood; and when those were lifted up from the earth, the wheels were lifted up over against them: for the spirit of the living creature was in the wheels.

simile } 22. And the *likeness* of the firmament upon the heads of the
explicated } living creature was *as the colour of the terrible crystal,* stretched forth over their heads above.

23. And under the firmament were their wings straight, the one toward the other: every one had two, which covered on this side, and every one had two, which covered on that side, their bodies.

24. And when they went, I heard the noise of their wings, *like the noise of great waters* [*as the voice of the Almighty, the voice of speech,* [*as the noise of an host:* when they stood, they let down their wings.

25. And there was a voice from the firmament that was over their heads, when they stood, and had let down their wings.

26. And above the firmament that was over their heads was the *likeness of a throne,* [*as the appearance of a sapphire stone:* and upon the *likeness of the throne* was the *likeness as the appearance of a man above* upon it.

27. And I saw *as the colour of amber* [*as the appearance of*

fire round about within it, from the *appearance* of his loins even upward, and from the *appearance* of his loins even downward, I saw *as it were the appearance of fire,* and it had brightness round about.

28. *As the appearance of the bow that is in the cloud in the day of rain,* so was the *appearance* of the brightness round about. This was the *appearance* of the *likeness* of the glory of the LORD. And when I saw it, I fell upon my face, and I heard a voice of one that spake.

The accumulation of similes—nearly twenty of them—plus what concrete details we are given make the vision mysterious and finally resistant to analysis. We have experienced before the storm phenomena which structure this vision, but never anything like what Ezekiel actually sees. It is not only that we have never encountered four-headed beasts and wheels covered with eyes, but the assertion of similarity to so many different objects actually proclaims dissimilarity to anything. Alphonsus Mantuanus pointed to this peculiar use of the simile when he tried to explain one of the fabulous beasts in Revelation. Its seven heads, ten horns, and various anatomical parts which resembled successively a leopard, bear, and a lion made him conclude that it was a horrible beast unlike *any* known type.[28] So here, when Ezekiel uses the feet of oxen, shining brass, different animals, coals, turquoise, and lightning to explain his vision, we must say that what he saw resembles *nothing.* The prophetic use of simile reverses its normal use in classical rhetoric, the attempt to assert a form of identity and to explain the unknown by the known. Ezekiel accumulates the known to create the incomparable.[29]

As a consequence, we cannot imagine the Yahweh of Ezekiel's vision. We think of a thunderstorm but realize at the same time that this visualization does not fit. The rich proliferation of images makes impossible a single, clear image in our minds. The picture blurs, defies imaginative synthesis. And here we must recall that the Jews, many Protestants, and Milton in particular were iconoclasts, people who refused to have images made even of the true God. In his commentary of Ezekiel's vision, Calvin makes this point emphatically (Lecture 5 [Myers 1:96], on Ezek. 1:25–26). If the One on the throne is incomparable, then no images can be made to represent Him. And this, of course, is the First Commandment. Now we do not normally associate iconoclasm with language, the rejection of cultic statues and pictures with a concern for verbal images, but the two interrelate in that the prophet chooses a kind of discourse which prevents possible cultic abuse. No one who reads Ezekiel could on the basis of that vision carve a statue of Yahweh.

The iconoclast could either multiply images or dispense with them altogether, opposite verbal techniques which have the same preventive function. At Sinai, for example, there was only a voice from a fire; and Moses learned a similar lesson when he asked to know the name of the God who spoke from the burning bush. He had to identify this God somehow to the Jews and found disconcertingly that God will be what He will be (Exod. 3:13–14). Whether in the bush or on the mountain, all we have iconographically is a voice from the fire, a fact which forms the basis for the great iconoclastic sermon in Deuteronomy and which in turn molded Milton's theology. In chapter 4 the speaker "Moses" stresses as much as possible the fact that the Israelites saw no *shape* at Sinai, only the mountain covered with darkness and clouds, flaming to midheaven. They heard the voice from the fire and yet lived, a greater miracle for the Deuteronomist then anything which had happened since the Creation (v. 33). He constantly returns to this point (vv. 15, 23–24, 36) and includes (vv. 16–19) a catalog of forbidden sources for images much longer than the parallel one in Exodus. If Israel turned to images, she would deny her unique experience, the event which happened to no other people. Her God was close to her, but as a consuming fire, dangerous to others,[30] a fire with a voice. In this sense the Spirit which filled the Apostles at Pentecost and enabled them to spread the good news manifested itself iconoclastically. The Apostles saw tongues, as though of fire (Acts 2.3).

Milton quotes this sermon from Deuteronomy when he defends his own iconoclasm (Deut. 4.15–16): "Quamobrem cavebitis vobis ipsis valde; nam non animadvertistis ullam imaginem. quo die allocutus est vos Iehova in Chorebo e medio ignis illius, ut non corrumpatis vos, et faciatis vobis sculptile, similitudinem ullius simulachri, formam maris aut foeminae" (*De doctrina* 2.5, "Take ye therefore good heed unto yourselves, for ye saw no manner of similitude on the day that Jehovah spake unto you in Horeb, out of the midst of the fire; lest ye corrupt yourselves, and make you a graven image, the similitude of any figure, the likeness of male or female").[31] There shall be no likeness, not even of the true God.

Milton's choice of models for his heaven scenes probably reflects his iconoclastic theology. He avoided the weather deity of some psalms, easily visualized, whose voice is thunder and who splits the cedars of Lebanon and lightens in the wastes of Kadesh (Ps. 29). He imitated, rather, the Sinai epiphany and its variants, scenes which taught him a closed discourse and made visualization impossible. Ezekiel and his apocalyptic imitators, who multiply images, and the Exodus theophany, which has none, safeguard the reader both from a naive imaginative response and consequently from possible cultic abuse. I would add that they likewise have a positive psychological function. The Sinai command, though expressed negatively, functions positively. It is designed to liberate, to open man to divine action. Once Abraham hears God's call, he leaves his idols and wanders to an unknown land. That call draws the Jews from Egyptian slavery to the fiery mountain in the desert, and a star guides wise men to a child in a remote provincial town. All these men were taken out of themselves and lived stories beyond the possibilities of their own dreams. Protestant theologians point to the alternative, to what happens when we make images and close ourselves in self-made prisons. Idolaters walk in the imagination of their own hearts.[32] Calvin says succinctly, "Itaque non apprehendunt qualem se offert: sed qualem pro sua temeritate fabricati sunt, imaginantur" (*Inst.* 1.4.1, "They do not therefore apprehend God as he offers himself, but imagine him as they have fashioned him in their own presumption").[33] An idolater creates a delusive world, the product of his own imagination. On external signs and objects he bestows the holiness absent from his interior life. Zwingli describes the result:

> Ut lignum, lapides, terram, pulverem, soleas, vestes, annulos, galeas, gladios, cingula, ossa, dentes, pilos, lac, panem, quadras, tabulas, vinum, cultros, amphoras et quicquid unquam attrectarunt pii homines, adoraverimus amplectendo, osculando; et quod stultissimum erat, nos plane beatos existimabamus, si quid talium solummodo aspexissemus. Promittebamus nobis ipsis abolita esse peccata, propiciam fortunam ac mundum totum. Veram autem pietatem, quae nihil aliud est, quam ex amore timoreque dei servata innocentia, sic deseruimus, ut communem iusticiam, hoc est: humanam, ne apud infideles quidem sic frigere videamus, ut apud Christianos.

> We worship with embraces and kisses wood, stones, earth, dust, shoes, vestments, rings, hats, swords, belts, bones, teeth, hair, milk, bread, tables, tablets, wine, knives, jars, and anything that pious men have ever handled. And (most foolish thing of all) we think ourselves distinctly blessed if we have got just a look at any such thing; we promise ourselves the remission of our sins, prosperous fortune, and the whole world. But true piety, which is nothing else than blamelessness preserved

through love and fear of God, we have abandoned so completely that not even among infidels do we see ordinary, that is,
human, righteousness so utterly prostrate as among Christians.[34]

Such people, literal slaves to their imaginings, could never think objec-
tively and find God. To the idolatrous Jews who asked for an oracle,
Ezekiel had to deny its possibility: "Son of man, these men have set up
their idols in their heart, and put the stumbling block of their iniquity
before their face: should I be inquired of at all by them?" (14:3).[35]

Once established, idolatry brutalizes the human soul. The concrete
image removes fear of God and leads the mind to further error: "Hoc
enim facit et quodammodo extorquet illa figura membrorum, ut animus
in corpore vivens magis arbitretur sentire corpus, quod suo simillimum
videt" (Calvin, *Inst.* 11.13, "For the shape of the idols's bodily members makes and in a sense compels the mind dwelling in a body to
suppose that the idol's body too has feeling, because it looks very like
its own body").[36] Milton expresses this logic when he introduces his
catalog of demons:

> By falsities and lies the greatest part
> Of Mankind they corrupted to forsake
> God thir Creator, and th' invisible
> Glory of him that made them, to transform
> Oft to the Image of a Brute, adorn'd
> With gay Religions full of Pomp and Gold,
> And Devils to adore for Deities.
>
> [1.367–73]

All images are demonic, as they block off the invisible God.

Linguistically, iconoclasm cut Milton off from the traditional language of analogy. An older poet could have represented heaven
through allegory, a method rarely used in *Paradise Lost*. There are the
brief personification allegories with Sin and Death, the visit to Limbo,
allegorical passages which Anne Ferry[37] notes are confined to the
world of fallen experience and are associated with Satan. For heaven
the tradition of neither biblical nor secular allegory was available to
Milton. He was a literalist in his scriptural interpretation,[38] and the
typology which he did allow would not yield analogy in this context.
The Temple ritual which he found in heavenly scenes would not give a
clear meaning before the end of time. The poet could not go beyond the
type. This limit applied generally to phenomena beyond or on the edges
of human time. Pareus observed that the great hail which followed the

Seventh Vial (Rev. 16:21) could be a literal event: "And who knows, but that this very thing shall be literally accomplished: for touching the signs of the last days nothing must be thought incredible" (p. 401). The same dilemma troubled those who interpreted the Creation narratives in Genesis 1–2. What was literal, what was symbolic, for the events which began and ended time or for matters concerning the heavenly court which existed outside our time? Calvin classed all the phenomena of the Last Judgment as accommodation metaphors.[39]

For similar reasons Milton could not apply to Scripture the ancient pagan methods of allegory which we have studied in this book. When Giovanni Pico, for example, interpreted Genesis by classical principles, he had to maintain an absolute system of correspondences between worlds. His allegorical interpretation required such correspondences and grew out of them. Cosmologically, heat exists in our world as an element (fire), in the visible heavens as power (the sun), and in the invisible heaven as idea (the seraphic intellect). Image making thus has precise meanings and can be decoded, based as it is on the hidden affinities of nature.[40] With the same assumptions, Proclus had explained the heavenly war in the *Iliad,* where clashes in our world resolve themselves in the invisible. Hera and Artemis live in peace on Olympus, but they supervise separate categories of souls, the rational and the irrational, which oppose each other on earth.[41] Such an elaborate interpretative method presupposes that man can have genuine knowledge of heaven and in fact locates truth there rather than here. It presupposes too much knowledge, and Milton had to reject it. He allowed for its possibility and had Raphael suggest that earth is but the shadow of heaven, but as an iconoclast the poet could not assert such a correspondence pattern with certainty and therefore could not use allegory for his epic. A mode which began with heavenly powers, with the deities of Homer, here comes to an end.

In lieu of tradition Milton took over prophetic techniques and tried to convert vision literature directly into epic narrative. The strange scenes which I discussed earlier are the result of this attempt. Whatever our final feelings about his experiment—and long rational discourses proceeding from volcanoes do create difficulties—we must allow that Milton integrated them with his overall imaginative action, where, if handled less boldly, the heaven scenes could have wrecked his poem. The reader does not experience strain in these episodes, and they particularly moved a neoclassical critic like Addison. From a theoretical and ahistorical position, in fact, he considered them *imaginative* successes and classed book 6 as the Homeric sublime, that which moves the imagination by what is great rather than by beauty or magic (see *Spectator* no. 417).

Here, in summary, is Milton's solution. Like the prophet, he chose spectacular events for heaven, huge military assemblies and extreme natural phenomena, events which, however, a person theoretically could witness. He then transformed each representation verbally so as to suggest that no one actually could view it. The picture of singing angels exemplifies this method at its simplest. In more complicated scenes the poet might combine two very different objects and assert that what he described somehow resembled *both:* a war chariot and a thunderstorm, a temple and a volcano in eruption. The superimposition of unlikes by itself created a necessary strangeness. With either type of scene the language both represented and did not represent. In this way Milton could satisfy the imagination and draw attention simultaneously to the limits of his art and to human comprehension generally.[42] The heavenly scenes combine a pictorial simplicity with a mystery jealously guarded, quite appropriate for an iconoclast—the verbal signs of Israel's God.

When Pompey captured the temple in Jerusalem, he wished to see the God which the Jews worshiped.[43] None dared forbid the heathen, as he walked through the outer courts, past the great sacrificial altar, into the sanctuary with its ritual objects. But when he entered the Holy of Holies, all he found there were darkness and an empty room.

Epilogue
The Disappearance of Homer and
the End of Homeric Allegory:
Vico and Wolf

Allegory began with Homer, and in his work its death was slowest. Neoclassicism, which in England destroyed allegory, did not affect Homer, who fell, rather, to the historicism of the eighteenth century. An evolutionary model did not allow for anything in Homer's period so sophisticated as multilayered allegory, which became instead a by-product of later cultural development, as the *Iliad* and the *Odyssey* by hypothesis became composite pieces made over long periods of time, without a governing intention and therefore incapable of the ordered interchange between author and reader necessary for *allegoresis*.

Neoclassicism

I have discussed in *The Veil of Allegory* how different and inimical were the allegorical and neoclassical models of the poetic process (chap. 7, esp. pp. 168–73). Here a summary will suffice. The allegorist served a truth which he received under divine inspiration. This truth required a symbolic mode of utterance which split his audience into the few who understood the code and the many who contented themselves with poetic surfaces. The neoclassical poet, on the other hand, worked within the assumptions of his audience, did not conceive of himself as inspired with profound truth, and so had no need for veiled fictions. He was a craftsman, and Homer's epics provided him with standards for plot, character, and style, not with a paradigm for symbolic communication. Yet the neoclassical critics left Homer his allegory. The historical evidence required it and led Pope and Blackwell to strengthen the equation. They considered allegory inseparable from Homer's art. D'Aubignac, who found in history the basis for the disintegrationist hypothesis, nevertheless argued his case aesthetically rather than historically, on foreign grounds, and did not win an audience. The change had to wait for a revolution in the historical discipline itself, a revolu-

173

tion which simultaneously denied assumptions fundamental to neoclassicism.

D'Aubignac. François Hedelin, abbé d'Aubignac, whose *Pratique du théâtre* (1657) made him one of the most prominent neoclassical critics, later wrote *Conjectures académiques, ou dissertation sur "l'Iliade."* This essay appeared posthumously (1715) during a battle between the Ancients and Moderns, when Madame Dacier was defending Homer against the criticisms of Houdard de la Motte. The *Conjectures* had no effect on that controversy and, despite the reputation of its author, were ignored.[1]

D'Aubignac argued that the *Iliad* was a collection of poems composed by different poets or rhapsodes. He derived this hypothesis from a set of facts which he found in classical writers and which forms the nucleus of the disintegrationist position. Later critics make the same points with more scholarship. They are four. First, the Homeric lives state that Homer was a poor blind rhapsode, who went from door to door and made his living by song.[2] Second, Homer's poems were transmitted not by writing but by rhapsodes, some of whom by their specialization came to be called Homerids (pp. 8–9, 40). The source here is Josephus' *Against Apion.* Third, Plutarch relates in his *Life of Lycurgus* that the Spartan was the first to collect Homer's songs, finding them in Ionia and bringing them back to Greece (pp. 40, 42). Fourth, Pisistratus made the definitive compilation and first distinguished the *Iliad* from the *Odyssey.* Many writers narrate this incident, although Diogenes Laertius credits Solon with the collection and Plato, Hipparchus (p. 46). As proof, d'Aubignac and the others cite Aelian, who remarks that Homer's episodes were sung separately and known by separate titles: for the *Iliad,* the Catalog of Armies, the Valor of Agamemnon, the Combat by the Vessels, the Patrocleia, and the Ransoming of Hector; for the *Odyssey,* Calypso's Cave, the Discussions with Alcinous, the Cyclops, Circe's Bath, and the Death of the Suitors. The inference is clear. For hundreds of years there was no text for Homer's poems. Rhapsodes sang single episodes by memory. The present arrangement of the *Iliad* and *Odyssey* we owe to Pisistratus.

This is the historical evidence, which separates the poet from the arrangement of his poems,[3] and it directly contradicts the literary criticism of antiquity, in which Homer is praised for the unity and organization of his two epics. D'Aubignac tried to harmonize these two conflicting views and defended his historical thesis by aesthetic criteria. He wanted to show that Aristotle, Horace, and Longinus erred; that the *Iliad* is an aesthetic confusion. Here he failed because in this case aesthetics yields opinions and systems rather than facts, and his logic was not better than or even equal to that of the great classical critics. We believe Aristotle, not d'Aubignac, so the evidence remains irreconcilable—one reason, perhaps, why d'Aubignac had no success with the *Conjectures*. He needed more history for his thesis, a methodology (what Wolf later found) to counter the aesthetic formulations of an Aristotle.

For his aesthetic proof d'Aubignac collected and then amplified all the criticisms of Homer made by the ancients and some Renaissance judgments. He attacked everything in the *Iliad:* its plot, characters, style, and allegory.[4] He tried to make these criticisms prove his hypothesis of multiple authorship,[5] but they went beyond and obscured this argument. The *Conjectures* reads more like Renaissance polemic and satire. His analysis of allegory supplies a useful example.

D'Aubignac objected that allegorical interpretation violated good sense. It had no controls (pp. 84–85), and individual, brilliant readers twisted Homer in every direction. Heraclitus the allegorist followed his own ideas on the *Iliad,* and Porphyry was so subtle on the Nymphs' Cave that it is hard to imagine a poet able to conceive such reasoning for twelve lines.[6] Moreover, no fable was too ridiculous for an allegorical sense.[7]

D'Aubignac also rejected the basis for such readings, Homer's reputation for wisdom (p. 8). The *sententiae* of the *Iliad* are brief and not profound (p. 120). No other works of quality come from this period (p. 8), and we know that the arts developed gradually over the ages. Homer could not have been master of all the arts: the assumption is itself absurd, as the arts are scattered among many people (pp. 121–22). D'Aubignac's theory of multiple authorship, on the other hand, explains how this reputation developed. The various poets of the *Iliad* made references to the different arts which they knew so that the final poem contained material applicable to all the later arts and sciences. Hence Homer's reputation as an encyclopedist.

This sort of argument both depends upon neoclassical norms and anticipates later critics. D'Aubignac appeals to the common sense of every man, an oratorical requirement familiar to the neoclassicist, which excludes the special reader assumed by allegorical theory,[8] and for d'Aubignac excludes as well the poet with a special vision. Applied to culture, this emphasis on the general produces a developmental hypothesis and looks forward to the eighteenth century. No single person discovered the arts and sciences; they evolved through collective effort over hundreds of years. Sophistication is communal. And here we verge on Vico's primitivistic model for beginnings. If Homer comes from a rude, early period, what follows?

D'Aubignac "proves" that the *Iliad* is not allegorical by a witty, satiric catalog which reveals the inconsistencies of the standard allegorical readings. They all involve the gods, and all violate the norm of common sense. Juno (air) and Minerva (wisdom) are stopped from driving out of Olympus when Jupiter sends Iris (rainbow) to say that he will smash their chariot. D'Aubignac asks, Can air and wisdom, a natural and a moral thing, be wounded by the same blow? And the message brought by a rainbow? Why should air conduct wisdom? We know that a head full of wind is hardly wise (pp. 87–88). Here are some other examples (pp. 86–88):

1. Apollo (the sun) causes the plague in *Iliad* 1, but must the sun go down to a ship for this purpose?
2. Why must Jove go to Ida to shoot thunderbolts at the Greeks?
3. Aurora cannot bring light both to gods and to men, because the gods themselves are light.
4. When Mars is war, how can he withdraw from battle and the fighting continue?

To create this humor, d'Aubignac confounds the literal sense and its interpretation. A thunderbolt (the literal level) cannot injure wisdom (the allegorical level), and a personification like Mars must so function in the plot. This is effective polemic but inferior argument, as it proceeds from a deliberate misunderstanding of allegorical interpretation, in which the literal and hidden levels are kept distinct. Its strength consists in its bogus appeal to common sense. D'Aubignac does not wish to refute *allegoresis* directly; he wants us to feel that it is silly.

For his thesis, this kind of argument has a more serious deficiency. D'Aubignac argues a historical hypothesis ahistorically. He appeals to the eternal norm of common sense but is talking about growth and change through time. D'Aubignac would have the standards of common sense apply both to Homer's primitive age and to the court of Louis XIV. Such a deficiency affects his whole argument, and we can see this by another example. Homeric allegory explained the gods, whom d'Aubignac analyzes with the same satiric good sense. He judges them by three absolute categories and finds them wanting in each case:

1. Gods should never disguise themselves, but Homer's deities change shapes so often that the *Iliad* becomes a masque (p. 79).
2. The gods should intervene only *in extremis,* but Homer's divinities intervene incessantly and in trivial matters, such as the funeral games (p. 79) or the scene in which Iris plays maid and tells Helen about the duel of Paris and Menelaus (p. 80).
3. There should be no mingling of high and low, but Jove and Juno are introduced squabbling like a lower-class couple; the husband threatens violence, and his wife calms herself with a big drink (p. 132). And so generally for the Juno scenes.[9]

These incongruities require different poems, some comic, some serious, and d'Aubignac hypothesizes that two poets probably wrote the comic scenes. One did the burlesque stories involving Juno; another, the licentious episodes, in which Venus puts Helen to bed with Paris and Juno seduces her husband (pp. 132–33). Similarly, the "incessant" divine intervention "proves" that small poems, in which such interventions have a rationale (p. 90), were put together into a long poem, in which they do not have a rationale.

The three principles which justify this historical guess are absolute. No god may have lower-class manners. This requirement especially demonstrates d'Aubignac's ahistoricism. It was a Renaissance commonplace to remark that manners change, that Nausicaa could with propriety wash her clothes, while a contemporary princess could not.[10] Decorum therefore could not be codified, because it concerns social situations which change through time. D'Aubignac makes of it a fixed principle. He would talk of flux with standards which deny it.

Aesthetic analysis cannot prove a historical position; it can only demonstrate that a poem is bad or good. To prove his thesis, d'Aubignac had to show that the *Iliad* is aesthetically bad. He had against him the general admiration of antiquity and his contemporaries for Homer. It is not surprising that no one listened.

Pope. With the same evidence, Alexander Pope left Homer his poem[11] and strengthened the poet's allegory. He did so despite his wish to orient Homeric criticism to aesthetic questions and his half feeling that allegory did not concern art. He recommends, for example, that the reader avoid the physical interpretation of Homer's gods, where pos-

sible, as fables normally should ornament plain truth ("Essay," 7:78).
And the encyclopedic learning necessary to allegory does not properly
fit a poet's style ("Postscript," 10:390) and has ruined previous commentaries:[12]

> It is something strange that of all the Commentators upon
> *Homer,* there is hardly one whose principal Design is to illus-
> trate the Poetical Beauties of the Author. They are Voluminous
> in explaining those Sciences which he made but subservient
> to his Poetry, and sparing only upon that Art which con-
> stitutes his Character. This has been occasion'd by the Osten-
> tation of Men who had more Reading than Taste, and were
> fonder of showing their Variety of Learning in all Kinds, than
> their single Understanding of Poetry.

Despite these remarks, Pope carefully notes the traditional allegories
for the divine scenes[13] and even writes them into his translation. Consider Juno: by interpretation she was air, though never so named in the
Iliad. Pope makes air her epithet.

> Full on the Sire the Goddess of the Skies
> Roll'd the large Orbs of her majestic Eyes
>
> [1.712–13]

> Well-pleas'd the Thund'rer saw their earnest care,
> And prompt Obedience to the Queen of Air.
>
> [15.176–77]

And Iris trails her rainbow, as she does in Virgil but never in Homer:

> ...the God that gilds the Day,
> And various *Iris* wing their airy way.
>
> [15.168–69]

> The winged *Iris* heard the Hero's Call,
> And instant hasten'd to their airy Hall,
> Where, in old *Zephyr*'s open Courts on high,
> Sate all the blustering Brethren of the Sky.
> She shone amidst them, on her painted Bow;
> The rocky Pavement glitter'd with the Show.
>
> [23.244–49]

The old interpretation has become the text.

Pope allegorized Homer for three reasons, all historical, which he
discusses in his introductory essay to the *Iliad.* He believed that
allegory in Homer's day was the vehicle for moral and political in-

struction (7:68) and cites Maximus of Tyre for an explanation. People disdain the plain and admire the hidden, so the poets cloaked philosophy in allegory (7:70).[14] Second, the poet made his allegory out of episodes which involved the gods, and each of these had his province. Pope stresses the psychological deities: "We find he has turn'd the Virtues and Endowments of our Minds into *Persons,* to make the Springs of Action become visible; and because they are given by the Gods, he represents them as Gods themselves descending from Heaven."[15] Third, these allegorical divinities came to Homer from Egypt. On the evidence of the historians Herodotus and Diodorus Siculus, Pope believes that Homer studied in Egypt and was initiated into the Egyptian mysteries ("Essay," 7:33–34, 47–48).[16] This hypothesis Blackwell elaborates, and it is the reason why the neoclassical critics made Homer more allegorical than before. Whatever their artistic preferences, they had to accept what for them was historical fact, what the classical historians had themselves assumed.

The historical evidence taken together, then, could encourage two very different hypotheses. Scattered through various writers were the materials for the disintegrationist hypothesis, but the theory itself was not something transmitted to the Middle Ages and the Renaissance. D'Aubignac had to put the evidence together and then did not argue it historically. Pope, on the other hand, had the explicit judgments of the historians and biographers, connecting Homer to Egypt and to allegory. He did not accept all this evidence uncritically. He suspected that admiration and envy distorted our view of Homer's life, and he stressed in particular the dangers created by the historians who interested themselves in the unimportant ("Essay," 7:26–27) and who took low passages in the epics as fictionalized autobiography (7: 40–41). He demanded impartiality and an adherence to probability (7: 27), but while these criteria may guarantee discretion in the use of a given text, they will not help the reader assess an entire document or sift his sources. The ideals are too generalized, apply to numerous disciplines, and will not of themselves produce a historical methodology. In this case Pope accepted the Egyptian story, because it did not consist of low matter or seem exaggerated or malicious, and it fit the criterion of probability. He did not commit himself to the details of Diodorus' elaborate theory and rejected the story that Homer stole his tales from the lady Phantasy of Memphis ("Essay," 7:33–34). The caution makes his acceptance of the general hypothesis all the more persuasive.

Blackwell. In his *Enquiry into the Life and Writings of Homer* (1735), Thomas Blackwell amplified many of Pope's positions. He had the usual neoclassical assumptions about epic[17] and accordingly wrote his *Enquiry* to replace the notion of divine inspiration with a more plausible rationalistic explanation.[18] He discussed the commonplaces concerning rhapsodes in section 8 (pp. 102–28) and said that letters were little known in Smyrna when Homer grew up (p. 81),[19] but, like Pope, he assumed that Homer was an allegorist, despite his own principles, despite the evidence for an unlearned Homer, and despite the fact that Blackwell held a developmental notion of culture which would have suggested a primitive environment for the poet. He maintained Homer's unique wisdom because the many sources he examined all supported this hypothesis and led him to assume a milieu for the poet thoroughly under Egyptian influence.

I will examine Blackwell's notion of culture, wherein he resembles his contemporary Vico, and then proceed to his Egyptian hypothesis. Velleius Paterculus said that great men in special areas come in groups or not at all (p. 74), so there were tragedians in the fifth century, orators in the fourth. Blackwell converts this notion into a sequence of historical periods (p. 76).[20] Homer came after the first age of religious song, when heroes were becoming the subject of verse (p. 78). His period contrasts with that of contemporary Continental culture and leads Blackwell to argue that civilization and poetry do not go together (pp. 24–27), a position Vico will likewise assume.[21] We value Homer's descriptions of life and manners, for the natural and simple appeal to those suspicious of the sophisticated and double. To poetize on the higher levels, we must therefore unlearn the daily round. Blackwell explains these conclusions by two arguments. Epic requires the marvelous, which does not occur in a well-ordered state except in civil war (p. 27): the civilized man cannot be surprised. Second, an absolute court has an influence pernicious to poetry (pp. 57–61); it requires imitation even in the minutiae of life and so does not allow for either a variety of characters or the necessary simplicity of manners. This artificiality in turn affects language, as civilization restricts vocabulary excessively, limiting the use of dialect terms and requiring euphemisms and circumlocutions, lest we offend. Civilization and poetry contradict each other, and a gulf separates us from Homer.

This cultural analysis includes a linguistic theory which reinforces Blackwell's conclusions and leads us into allegory. The language of this second or heroic stage of culture was not itself primitive, but it was based on primitive Pelasgic, an affective language. Blackwell draws analogies from the infancy of the individual and from contemporary orientals, Turks, Arabs, and Indians, who lead solitary lives and talk seldom, but when they talk it is with the passion and metaphor which characterize early language (pp. 43–44): passion because language began when exclamations of emotion became song, metaphor because one word or sound had to serve for many things (pp. 38–42). It is this metaphoric component which helps to explain Homer's reputation for wisdom and divine inspiration. Poetry by its nature generalizes, and tropological language reinforces this tendency toward the universal. Blackwell defines metaphor as "a *general Pattern*, which may be applied to many Particulars: It is susceptible of an infinite number of Meanings; and reaches far because of its Ambiguity. It leads, as we found before, even to *Madness*; and wantonly ranges the Corners of the World for Comparisons to fit its fancied Properties" (p. 316). Because it is a general pattern, it has multiple application or meanings, a characteristic which both explains Homer's reputation for wisdom and connects him to allegory or extended metaphor. Any poet of his period would be more or less allegorical,[22] and the most popular genre, the theogony, was allegorical: "It is *a System of the Universe, digested and wrought into an Allegory:* It is a Composition, made up of infinite Parts, each of which has been a Discovery by itself, and delivered as a *Mystery* to the initiated" (p. 98).

The Egyptians turned this natural use of allusions and similitudes into a science and made a fixed system out of tropes and metaphors (pp. 83–84). They used this code to educate the priestly class, making this tropological discourse into a set of myths or fables which, by Herodotus' hypothesis, the Greeks imported into their own religion and elaborated (pp. 50–51). Blackwell argues at length that the pre-Homeric poets in Greece composed Egyptian allegories, that Orpheus and others set up an Egyptian religion whose adherents later looked to Homer for confirmation, something which they could not have done unless Homer's mythology fit their Egyptian beliefs. So the allegories of an Orpheus and of Homer are substantially the same (pp. 167–71).[23] Moreover, Homer himself studied in Egypt (p. 162).[24] His learning was therefore "wholly *fabulous* and *allegorical*" (p. 101), and so was his poetry. We can summarize Blackwell's argument thus: Homer was an allegorist for four reasons—

1. As a poet, he naturally worked with metaphors.
2. The language of his time was predominantly metaphoric.
3. The religion of his time was derived from the scientific mythology of Egypt.
4. The poet himself studied this mythology in Egypt.

Like Pope, Blackwell reads this mythology in standard fashion.

Homer's gods are physical allegory, *"natural Feelings of the several Powers of the Universe,"* or in Eustathius' phrase, "'Εννοιῶν εὐγενῶν σκιαί εἰσὶν ἢ παραπετάσματα, *Shadowings or Wrappers of noble Sentiments"* (p. 142).[25] They express those natural powers which most affect our bodies and minds. And Blackwell's explications are traditional. The *Iliad* begins when Apollo (the sun) sends a plague, and Achilles, warned by Hera (unwholesome air), calls an assembly (p. 207). Such allegories were by now between one and two thousand years old. Blackwell systematizes their historical defense.

This concern with history relates directly to his neoclassical aesthetic. Mimesis must reflect objective truth, and Homer's poems must have the circumstantiality of historical *realia* (pp. 288–90). The poet took his gods from actual practice. His description of the Troad is that of an eyewitness (pp. 283–85), and for the fabulous landscapes of the *Odyssey* Blackwell finds history of an orientalizing sort.[26] The ritual of the dead reflects the funeral and progress of Apis up the Nile, and the Egyptian ceremony explains most of the details in Hades,[27] while burial in the delightful meadows by the Fayum lake helped to model Acheron/Hades and suggested the Elysian Fields promised to Menelaus.

Historicism permeates Blackwell's critical biography and suggests the beginnings of a reorientation in Homeric criticism. D'Aubignac and Pope had tried to use aesthetic categories, but Blackwell turns mimesis into history and so makes possible the change necessary for the disintegrationist hypothesis. Robert Wood, whose *Essay on the Original Genius and Writings of Homer* (1767) had such an influence on Wolf, worked from much the same set of assumptions.[28] Blackwell himself strengthens rather traditional assumptions, because he uncritically accepts his sources, particularly the late classical evidence. He draws on the Pseudo Plutarch and the Herodotean *Life* to construct Homer's biography; and, while he admits that the Orphic hymns are forgeries, he dates them early and assumes that they contain the poet's real opinions (pp. 88–89).[29] Here he contrasts sharply with Pope, who is suspicious of his sources, thinks we have only opinion on Homer's life (*"Essay,"* p. 27), and carefully classifies the evidence.[30] Despite his historicism and his portrait of the rhapsode, Blackwell resembles more the old Renaissance critics: he displays a reverence for written sources, a conviction that allegory was the earliest form of poetry, the Egyptian hypothesis. Vico, while himself conservative on many questions, was critical of *his* sources and so could begin the new age in Homeric criticism.

Vico

Homeric allegory had been linked to a devolutionary historiographi-
cal model. Homer and the deepest, most philosophical poetry were
phenomena of the beginnings, achievements which later writers, born
in declining times, could emulate but not equal.[31] Homeric allegory
ceased to exist when historians turned to an evolutionary model and
found such notions irreconcilable with their conceptions of primitive
beginnings. The two patterns coexisted uneasily in Blackwell's *Enquiry*
because, though conceiving of Homeric Greece as a rude, uncivilized
place, he believed that its inhabitants reflected the long-established
culture of Egypt. Vico both denied this influence and classified Egypt
itself as primitive. The evolutionary model had won.

Many helped to demythologize Egypt. In *Le sterminate antichità*
Paolo Rossi lists and analyzes finely the principal figures.[32] The effort
had begun a century earlier with Casaubon and Bacon, whom Vico
cites by name, and concluded with Warburton (1742) and Vico himself
(1744). Blackwell thus was perhaps the last to argue for Egyptian wisdom. We can summarize Rossi's findings under four headings (pp.
121–22):

1. The earliest men were incapable of abstraction and so used
   hieroglyphs or direct pictures of objects and of emotions.
2. The alphabet—the use of conventional signs to indicate
   words—came later, as civilization became more sophisticated.
3. The Egyptians used a hieroglyphic writing comparable to
   that of the Mexican Indians. They therefore existed at a
   primitive, unphilosophical level of culture.
4. The wisdom of Egypt is a Neoplatonic projection backward.

In Homeric criticism the rejection of Egypt depended upon a change
in historical methodology. Here the connection with Egypt was not one
invented by Neoplatonists but a hypothesis enunciated by the early
writers. Herodotus had accepted the great antiquity of the country and
argued that the Greeks had borrowed their cults from Egypt.[33] His
reasons highlight the contrary principles of the new anthropological
historiography practiced by Vico. Herodotus denied coincidence; if
Egypt and Greece worshiped Dionysus in the same way, one was the
originator and the other a borrower of the cult. In this case Greece was
the debtor, as the younger nation (*Historiae* 2.49). Similarly, if the
Colchians and the Egyptians, two people remote from each other,
practiced circumcision, one must have borrowed the custom from the

other, and again the Egyptians were the originators (2.104). Vico, on
the other hand, can accept coincidence because he assumes a general
pattern of cultural development, behind or above the particular histories of nations. Similarities between Greece and Egypt confirm that
pattern, indicate its reliability. They do not point to the historical influence of one culture on another, for such would be a contamination
and would alter the pattern in the younger culture. If two places indicate a correspondence to each other and to the ideal pattern, that
correspondence shows, rather, that the two places were unaffected by
each other.[34] Homer never visited Egypt (*SN* 89, 803).

This ideal pattern includes an evolutionary historical model, and the
controlling analogy for the early period is the childhood of the individual. With Blackwell, Vico thinks that the sublime poets belong to the
infancy of the world. Such poetry animates objects with sense and
passion, as boys who play with things talk as if they were living persons
(186–87). Because of this model, Vico regularly rejects all classical
testimony to the antiquity of wisdom.[35] The ancients judged earliest
man by their own standards, as magnificent rather than as uncivilized
(121–23). The principle is Tacitean: "Omne ignotum pro magnifico est"
(cited by Rossi, p. 153). We honor what we do not know: hence the
veneration for remotest antiquity. Classical writers exaggerated the
wisdom of their ancestors, found allegories in old fables and mystical
senses in hieroglyphics (*SN* 128). A whole class of literature is therefore apocryphal. The Orphic poems, which Blackwell used to gloss the
preHomeric period, actually breathe the Platonic and Pythagorean
school (ibid., 745). Egypt, that other source for Homeric wisdom, was
likewise primitive, for the reasons I have already listed (*SN* 222–23).
All arguments for profound knowledge in Homer's period are false, and
the poet therefore composed no allegory.

Homeric poetry accordingly reflects a primitive rather than a philosophical understanding of reality. Originally the gods were what early
man considered necessary or useful (7), and the four elements were
civic: the air, through which Jove thunders; Diana, the water of peren-
nial fountains; Vulcan, the fire to burn out the forests; and Cybele,
cultivated land (690). Diana provides an example of this thinking. In the
beginning hell was no deeper than the fountains, so the gods swore by
"Styx," and Diana became Proserpine (714). These original elements
in turn became the basis for divine ceremonies, the water, fire, and
grain at the auspices (690). Traditional Homeric allegory, which pre-
supposed the physical four elements of earth, air, water, and fire, had
to wait for prose discourse or the ability to make genus-species distinctions (460). Philosophers drew on an inherited poetic vocabulary

and wanted to support their thoughts with the wisdom of the poets and the authority of religion (362). The poetic and the philosophical, however, work in opposite directions. One immerses us in particulars where the other would raise us above universals (821). That is, a philosophical or allegorical reading of Homer contradicts the nature of his language.[36]

Like Blackwell, Vico assumes that primitive speakers needed simile and metaphor to supplement their small vocabulary (409, 456, 832). They could not define things properly, could not abstract from a particular to a genus (406).[37] Instead, they enlarged or exaggerated particulars, made images of men and gods grander than ours (816), ideal models. They turned a particular commander into a figure like Tasso's Goffredo and expected other particular commanders to conform to this exaggeration (205). This idealization, plus metaphor, accounts in turn for the phenomenon of *diversiloquia*. Primitive man spoke metaphorically of a single person, but his language had a double application (403). A grandiose particular, Goffredo, modeled other particulars. This double-speak sometimes manifested a social division, as in the case of Venus. Originally the goddess with the cestus, the deity invoked at patrician marriages, she became the nude goddess of the lower classes, which lacked legitimate love unions (569). The plebeians had no names but those used by their patrician leaders, which they employed in different meanings and so gave a double sense to various gods and terms (581). The patrician Venus was also the plebeian concubine of Mars (579). Primitive man talked univocally in a polyvalent language, a phenomenon which explains why the later allegorical readings could exist, why philosophers could see in these grandiose beings abstract genera.

Through this metaphorical language early man uttered his myths, which for him were history. And here Vico both resembles and differs from the euhemerists. Jove was not a historical ruler of Crete. Rather, the stories about the gods reflected general, frequently social conditions and existed in primitive minds as facts.[38] Vico would recount the historical development of the human soul, and in this respect any resemblance he might bear to a euhemerist like Blackwell is superficial. On the other hand, Vico constantly uses euhemerist methods in his practical criticism. Hera or Juno provides an example. Her traditional range of meanings included marriage, air, the people of Argos and Sparta (see chap. 1 above). Vico selects one of those meanings, marriage, and eliminates the others.[39] He thus confines the goddess to her cultic significance and explains that marriage in the heroic period was limited to patricians and thus differentiated noble from plebeian (652).

Juno is therefore "jealous"; she objects to marriage with "strangers" (656). A later period of effeminate customs distorts this story, and Juno becomes the sterile goddess who hates Jupiter's children and shows herself an enemy to heroes and to virtue (514).[40]

This use of euhemerist sources likewise involved Vico in strained readings remarkably similar to the traditional euhemerism of a Boccaccio. The story that Jupiter tied up his wife in mid-heaven, for example, symbolizes the civilizing process (514)! The binding is matrimony, and it occurs in the sky because marriage required auspices. She is tied by the neck because early man overcame his wife by force; her bound hands are the wedding ring; and the anvils on her feet, the stability which marriage creates. This fantastic explanation reveals how close Vico remained to the old ways. While euhemerism searched for historical *realia* behind fable, it commonly served as the first stage in *allegoresis* and used much the same techniques. Vico would deny allegory to Homer and has a new conception of fable, but his practice resembles that of the old mythographers.[41] The revolutionary fights with outmoded weapons.

The story of Juno illustrates another difficulty. Vico argues that the present or Homeric version comes from the corrupt customs of a later time. The scandal of Homer's gods, which generated allegory in the first place, in fact reflects a society already dissolute, the end of the heroic age (221, 808). That is, Vico denies the conscious literary meaning of the myth, Homer's version, not that of some late Neoplatonist. Some of the errors carefully noted by his editor, Fausto Nicolini, are actually reinterpretations of this sort. Vico says, for example, that Calchas explained the portent of the serpent which devoured nine birds (*Il.* 2.300–330) as the Trojan land which would come under Greek dominion in the ninth year (*SN* 541). Actually the capture of Troy occurred in the tenth year, and Calchas read the birds as the years of siege. Vico, however, equates the dragon or serpent with the land which must be cleared when, in the heroic age, the *pater familias* makes his farm and the aristocratic republic develops[42] He cites the text more as example than as proof, how he, not Calchas, would read the portent.[43]

As we go through the *Scienza nuova*, Vico must deny authorial intent again and again. Homer, Ovid, Livy did not understand their stories; Vico does. We can accept these otherwise damaging admissions only if we accept his overall theory, his reinterpretation of early myth, to which he returns repeatedly.[44] Vico's hypothesis about Homer stands or falls with his ideal pattern. It would not convince someone who did not share his entire set of assumptions and mode of thought.

Vico works from a cyclic model, which he sees reflected in his data. Each nation goes through a pattern of development and relapse into barbarism. Homer's poetry came in an early, evolutionary phase which repeated itself later in the Dark Ages. In this sense we can say that Vico is unhistorical. Behind the flux of history he sees an unchanging schema,[45] and with this vision he can correct the very authors who supply him with the evidence. We cannot therefore accept or reject parts of his argument. They always depend upon his model. Whether we are drawn to one or another idea in his system, we find in specific cases that we are always responding to the whole system. Acceptance or rejection is total.

The dialectic and the pattern, on the other hand, made sense of the disintegrationist data. Vico presents the same evidence as d'Aubignac's, far less than Blackwell assembled, but that evidence now automatically tells its story in an evolutionary model. Josephus had said that Homer did not write down his poems (*SN* 23, 66), and the long debate over hieroglyphics had shown that such sign writing referred to things and not to words and so could not preserve poetry. The σήματα in the letter which Bellerophon carried across the Aegean could not mean anything more than hieroglyphics (433, 859),[46] and Homer does not mention writing anywhere else. Vico dates use of the alphabet for writing at a late period shortly before Herodotus, corresponding to the growth of prose (442–43). The Phoenicians had brought the alphabet to Greece much earlier, but the Greeks had initially used the letters only for mathematics and geometry and continued to use them for numbers throughout antiquity (440). There are then three stages, as always in Vico: the use of hieroglyphics, the use of the alphabet for numbers, and finally, many years later, its use for words. A gap separates the introduction of the alphabet and its use for writing. The *Iliad* and *Odyssey* could not have been written down for hundreds of years, not before Pisistratus in the mid-sixth century (854–55).

Vico next dissolves the single poet into the rhapsodes who transmitted the poem before Pisistratus. He plays on the two etymologies for Homer: the blind man[47] and "ὁμού-εἴρειν," "simul connectere," a man who weaves things together. Homer is any rhapsode or all rhapsodes, and the oft-repeated anecdote that he was poor and went through Greece singing songs describes rhapsodes generally (872, 877–78). Being blind, they had good memories (871) and collected songs based on popular or fabulized history, which had developed over centuries. This long gestation period would explain the confusion of mores and cultural stages which Vico found in the poems.[48] When Pisistratus later systematized these collections, the common term "homer" became a proper name. Homer was a fiction, the heroic character responsible for all the stories (873). All the Greeks contended for Homer's birthplace because the people themselves were Homer (875). The individual was a projection of the collective.

Vico uses the same thinking in other cases. In the Homeric period the deeds of the single hero are equivalent to that of the *socii*, who defend their lord and give him the glory of the combat (559).[49] It is not Ajax alone but Ajax and his followers who hold off the Trojans during the retreat. The hero thus becomes the persona or mask for his family, and his exploits the deeds of his house (1033). Vico probably devised this hypothesis for problems in Roman law (416–22). There he shows how laws under a certain category were ascribed to a person or group which at some time was concerned with that category. The *decemviri* receive credit not for one but for all the laws which establish popular liberty. The heroic character (Homer, Lycurgus, the *decemviri*) again substitutes for the abstraction process, and all the acts or poetry which we might classify by genus and species become attributed to a single persona.

The argument is tight knit. Vico's developmental model demanded primitive beginnings. These in turn could not allow for anything so sophisticated as allegory, and the absence of writing made the preservation and composition of poetry a group effort. The Homer of the biographies and the inspired poet of the *Iliad* and the *Odyssey* never existed. The poems therefore lacked conscious intention, another reason why they had no philosophy or allegory. They became instead historical documents, visions of our dark past.

The hypothesis, while brilliant, lacks proof or, rather, is another of Vico's reinterpretations of traditional data. He adduces no new evidence and does not attempt to refute the principal counterthesis, that of Aristotle, which defeated d'Aubignac earlier and Wolf later called the Medusa's head of the *Poetics*.[50] The philosopher had praised the unity and design of the *Iliad* and the *Odyssey* and had contrasted Homer's art with that of the Cyclic poets, whom Vico dates very late, after Pisistratus. He thinks that they were rhapsodes and derives their title from the *circle* of listeners which ringed them during performances, as people still surround the Neapolitan *cantastorie*.[51] Vico would have to show why rhapsodes should exist after writing came into general use and why they ignored or were unable to imitate a complex unity like that of the *Odyssey*, whether arranged by Pisistratus or developed anonymously in the preceding period of primitive culture. The sophistication necessary for *in medias res* rivals that which Vico presumes for allegory and shows that for the Homeric question the two matters were linked. Without this proof, Vico's analysis remained mere hypothesis. It was Wolf who fifty years later completed Vico's argument, confronted the aesthetic with the historical evidence, and chose for the latter. As he said to Heyne, it is one thing in history or mathematics to dream a theory, quite another to prove it.[52]

Wolf

Vico's name is familiar to students of cultural history, but many have never heard of F. A. Wolf, though we still grapple with the consequences of his hypothesis and follow his example when we edit texts. And until recently the preference of the classical student for history and his suspicion of literary criticism reflected 200 years later Wolf's long war with neoclassicism. His influence, though now anonymous, affects many areas besides Homeric studies, and in his *Prolegomena ad Homerum* (1795) he examined many questions which we must ignore. Our concern is with Homeric allegory and because of that, with the disappearance of the poet, which will take up almost the whole of my discussion. I will return to a direct discussion of allegory at the end.

Wolf gave to the disintegrationist evidence a reading different from Vico's, and the difference indicates a methodological break. They were both historicists who assumed evolutionary models, and they both stressed the consequences of an analphabetic Homer and the memorial transmission of poetry by rhapsodes. The lawyer responded to these data with a hypothesis, that Homer was a fiction or projection of any and all rhapsodes and the *Iliad* and *Odyssey* collections. Wolf gave no explanation. Instead, he said that we could get no closer to Homer than 700 years later, that we could reconstruct only the Alexandrian text, which was stabilized in the second century B.C.

The difference is not only that between the theorist and the editor, or between what we crudely call deduction and induction. Vico relates everything to a single, complicated system of interconnecting hypotheses. As Wolf complained in his review of Vico, the Italian explains everything,[53] especially that vague area of prehistory, where the records are few and inaccurate. Wolf accumulates and carefully analyzes much more evidence than his predecessors, but the more he argues, the more we realize our necessary ignorance of the classical world. He enlarged the area of the unknown and located Homer far within it, beyond the reach of the neoclassical aesthete and the allegorical interpreter, both of whom assumed some form of assured communication with the poet. Allegory received its appropriate quietus: an accurate history.

Wolf effected this removal of the poet in two ways. He oriented speculation not to the poet or his poem but to the media of its preservation: rhapsodes and alphabets, editors and scholiasts. Second, a negative dialectic replaced, where possible, rational guesswork and established a methodological *docta ignorantia*.

We can illustrate the first by his analysis of writing. D'Aubignac and Vico had repeated Josephus' claim that Homer was analphabetic; Wolf gives an analytic history both of the alphabet and of writing materials, which shows conclusively that Homer could not have written the *Iliad* even if writing existed prior to his period. Writing was not practical until the introduction of papyrus in the sixth century. Early laws had been inscribed on hard materials like stone, wood, and metal, while the Syracusans used leaves to exile citizens. None of these provided practical materials for recording long poems (*Pro.* 15). Skins were better but came to Ionia later, during the Olympic periods (after 776–75 B.C.), and the fact that they gave way to parchment indicates that they were not much used (16.47–48). Even if they were, the early alphabets were too clumsy (16). The Cadmean sytem had only eleven or sixteen letters, those of Palamedes would have added only three or four. Simonides and Epicharmus were credited with completing the system, which occurred during the sixth and fifth centuries, while the Athenians adopted the full twenty-four-letter Ionic alphabet only in 403. No alphabet existed which would make writing practical before the sixth/fifth centuries. Homer would have had for his poems neither the means of writing nor the materials on which to write.

Moreover, it is doubtful in such a situation, when poetry was communicated by memory through rhapsodes, that Homer would even *think* of long poems (26), like a man who would build a ship without a sea. If he had, the medium of communication would have defeated his purpose. A long poem would have become fragmented through rhapsode performances. And such a medium encourages interpolation (25). The rhapsodes were themselves poets and inspired by Homer. The verse form with its lack of rhyme and brevity of phrase made interpolation easy. Such changes and additions, of lines or of whole episodes like the Catalog of Ships or the κόλος Μάχη (*Il.* 8), would be legitimate, the normal way a poem grows and lives through rhapsodes.

This exhaustive analysis of media gradually changes our notion of how the *Iliad* could exist. Its laws differ from those which govern texts, the poems we know from the later manuscript and print cultures. In an oral civilization the poem and its medium are not separable. Unlike

Virgil or Demosthenes, Homer and Hesiod thus present a unique problem for the editor and critic,[54] a problem which we cannot solve. We know little or nothing about rhapsodes (25.82) and little or nothing about the poems themselves for this early period. This is Wolf's most far-reaching discovery and, as we shall see, the basis for his quarrel with the genre critics, who lumped Homer with later epic poets and generally thought they understood the *Iliad* and the *Odyssey* much too well.

This discovery mirrors itself in a dialectic of negation, which betrays its presence in Wolf's concessive clauses and exhaustive argumentation. Here is an abstract model of what we have already seen. The standard position assumes *A*, then *B*. I deny *A*. But even if I should accept *A*, *B* still does not follow. The object of this dialectic is a learned agnosticism, and its source may be Plato. Wolf got his university post through his edition of the *Symposium* (1782) and remained interested in editing Plato all his life.[55] Not that Wolf was a Platonist, but his editorial problem called for a negative dialectic. He wanted to recover the true form of the *Iliad* (*Pro.* 11.27) but had to work through corrupted copies which came from a period two millennia later. He had to sift his evidence, classify the manuscript families, and by his own analogy imitate the physician who uncovers the wounds to judge the hidden illness (1.2). He found that the *vera forma* was irrecoverable and probably never existed.

This learned "agnosticism" particularly marks his discussion of the Alexandrian editors, where he can draw on the Venice scholia, recently published by Villoison (1788).[56] The Venice scholia cite 250 writers, all since lost (*Pro.* 41.146). Wolf infers that what we have from antiquity is no more than a few bookcases from a library (4.9). And what we have frequently eludes us. A scholiast will cite a variant reading but give no rationale for it. Or he will provide one, but the explanation is his own guess. The scholiasts, for example, belabor Zenodotus, the first Alexandrian editor of Homer, for his emendations and supply his reasons. Nowhere, however, do they state that he did a commentary on Homer's text (*Pro.* 43.166 and n. 84), so Wolf wonders where they would get their "reasons," especially when we remember that the scholiasts worked not from primary texts but from compendia put together no earlier than the Augustan period (42.152). They did not have Zenodotus' edition of Homer, nor did he write a commentary. We thus cannot gauge the intelligence or methods of Zenodotus[57] or of the Alexandrians generally, a point Wolf makes several times (41.147, 42.152, 44.170–71). And there are the additional questions of the clean text and the evidence of erasures.

Homer's text has none of the problems that troubled Apollonius of Rhodes or Quintus of Smyrna, who composed much later and left written copies. Wolf asks why Homer's text in contrast should be so perfect, when no text in any sense existed for hundreds of years and when the scholiasts record so many variant readings? Presumably, many of the vulgate readings may be no earlier than the grammarians, who went about cleaning up Homer's language. They obliterated whatever did nòt correspond to their more elegant laws (*Pro*. 43.164 n.82). The scholiasts cite, for example, *Iliad* 15.71 as the unique case where Ἴλιον is neuter, but we know that Zenodotus had two other such readings, at 16.92 and 18.174. Is this uniformity genuine or the result of silent correction? Who might corrupt Homer more than a grammarian, who emends the poet by his own wit (*Pro*. 46.181), especially when grammatical theory was just in its beginnings? Many of Zenodotus' errors can be attributed to the primitive state of grammar in his time. He had trouble with duals, the use of the article, the powers of plural substantives, pronoun declension, and dialect distinctions, and he did not allow for anacoluthon (*Pro*. 43. 158–62). Yet he emended Homer's text.

Then there is the evidence of erasures. We have traces of Homeric verses cited by others which have vanished from the vulgate text and from the scholia (*Pro*. 49.202–3). Aristarchus deleted four verses from Phoenix' speech in *Iliad* 9 and transferred another phrase from *Iliad* 18 to *Odyssey* 4.[58] Casaubon remarked of the latter that the silence of the ancients on this transfer indicates that our text is the one which Aristarchus emended. That is, we must accept the Alexandrian text of Homer, and we cannot estimate what has been eliminated. We do not have the manuscripts and data to evaluate their editorial procedures and can get no nearer Homer than the second century B.C.

This necessary dependence on the Alexandrian editors in turn forced Wolf to battle with the literary critics, neoclassical and allegoriacal. All his effort concerned the first, and we must understand this polemic if we wish to understand the end of Homeric allegory, which had survived as a minor matter within the neoclassical synthesis and died along with it.

The evidence of the scholia and the grammarians reinforced Wolf's own historical conclusions, namely, that Homer could not have put together long and sophisticated designs like the *Iliad* and the *Odyssey*. Aristophanes of Byzantium and Aristarchus, the two great Alexandrian editors, had doubts about the endings of *both* poems (*Il*. 24, *Od*. 23.297ff.). Likewise Quintus Calaber assumed that the *Iliad* was left unfinished (*Pro*. 29.97–98; 31.103), and Eustathius remarked that the

Doloneia (*Il.* 10) came into the *Iliad* only with the Pisistratid recension (*Pro.* 33.112). This class of evidence, historical and grammatical, contradicted the assumptions of the neoclassical critics, who, following Aristotle, praised Homer's unity and recommended the *Iliad* and *Odyssey* as models for imitation. If the epics are well designed, then the historical evidence seems faulty. If the historical data is correct, then we must revise or discard our aesthetic assumptions. D'Aubignac had tried to argue both alternatives and had failed. Wolf opted for the historical and attacked the aesthetic.

He refuted Aristotle in classic Platonic fashion, taking the assumptions of his opponent and using them to prove his own case. The aesthetic defense of the *Iliad* and the *Odyssey* depended upon chapter 8 of the *Poetics*:

Μῦθος δ' ἐστὶν εἷς οὐχ ὥσπερ τινὲς οἴονται ἐὰν περὶ ἕνα ᾖ· πολλὰ γὰρ καὶ ἄπειρα τῷ ἑνὶ συμβαίνει, ἐξ ὧν [ἐνίων] οὐδέν ἐστιν ἕν· οὕτως δὲ καὶ πράξεις ἑνὸς πολλαί εἰσιν, ἐξ ὧν μία οὐδεμία γίνεται πρᾶξις. διὸ πάντες ἐοίκασιν ἁμαρτάνειν ὅσοι τῶν ποιητῶν Ἡρακληίδα Θησηίδα καὶ τὰ τοιαῦτα ποιήματα πεποιήκασιν· οἴονται γάρ, ἐπεὶ εἷς ἦν ὁ Ἡρακλῆς, ἕνα καὶ τὸν μῦθον εἶναι προσήκειν. ὁ δ' Ὅμηρος ὥσπερ καὶ τὰ ἄλλα δια‾ φέρει καὶ τοῦτ' ἔοικεν καλῶς ἰδεῖν ἤτοι διὰ τέχνην ἢ διὰ φύσιν· Ὀδύσσειαν γὰρ ποιῶν οὐκ ἐποίησεν ἅπαντα ὅσα αὐτῷ συνέβη, οἷον πληγῆναι μὲν ἐν τῷ Παρνασῷ, μανῆναι δὲ προσποιήσασθαι ἐν τῷ ἀγερμῷ ὧν οὐδὲν θατέρου γενομένου ἀναγκαῖον ἦν ἢ εἰκὸς θάτερον γενέσθαι, ἀλλὰ περὶ μίαν πρᾶ‾ ξιν οἵαν λέγομεν τὴν Ὀδύσσειαν συνέστησεν, ὁμοίως δὲ καὶ τὴν Ἰλιάδα.

Unity of plot does not, as some persons think, consist in the unity of the hero. For infinitely various are the incidents in one man's life which cannot be reduced to unity; and so, too, there are many actions of one man out of which we cannot make one action. Hence the error, as it appears, of all poets who have composed a Heracleid, a Theseid, or other poems of the kind. They imagine that as Heracles was one man, the story of Heracles must also be a unity. But Homer, as in all else he is of surpassing merit, here too—whether from art or natural genius—seems to have happily discerned the truth. In composing the Odyssey he did not include all the adventures of Odysseus—such as his wound on Parnassus, or his feigned madness at the mustering of the host—incidents between which there was no necessary or probable connexion: but he made the Odyssey, and likewise the Iliad, to centre round an action that in our sense of the word is one.   [1451a15–30][59]

For the historian this isolation of Homer from his contemporaries is itself striking. Wolf digs up in Photius an observation by Lycius Proclus, who says that the other early epic poems had a natural order, of the kind Aristotle slighted:

> Quippe fuit ille multorum ἐπῶν ab initiis rerum usque ad mortem Ulyssis deductorum, collectio, omnem prope fabularem historiam *perpetua et naturali serie* complectens.

> Certainly that collection of many epics, drawn from the beginnings even to the death of Ulysses, embracing in a continuous and natural series all the near-fabulous history.[60]

Were the Cyclic poets then ignorant of Homer's organization, or were they unable or unwilling to use the single action with its sophisticated accoutrements, the retrospective narration and interwoven episodes (*Pro.* 29.96)? Now if Homer alone among the oral epic composers has an Aristotelian unity, this fact by itself should make us suspicious, should suggest that the order might be artificial, something created in later ages.[61] And in fact there is all the evidence for the ordering of the poems by Pisistratus (*Pro.* 33.109). So the celebrated unity of the *Iliad* and the *Odyssey* argues for a late reworking of the epic material and proves multiple authorship. Wolf reverses the Aristotelian norm (order follows from "intention") and appeals instead to the atomists for an analogy, those philosophers who argued that this ordered cosmos was the product of chance.

Wolf reinforces this argument by two others, likewise reversals of Aristotelian norms. First he looks for awkward passages which show how different rhapsodies were sewn together (30.99–102). To do this, he must first separate the poem into parts. He says he recognizes the difficulty of such an attempt. How could anyone forget Aristotle and the other critics who much later drew from the wholes their precepts (28.93)? The archaeologist, however, may find a complete house but must be careful not to attribute additions to the first builder.[62] In other words, Wolf works from diametrically opposite assumptions for which he supplies appropriate evidence. Second, as we have seen, he casts doubt on the endings of both epics. Wolf sets up this, his most extreme argument, with another Aristotelian notion. In a well-unified poem the critic should not be able to add or to subtract anything. Wolf shows that complete rhapsodies were added later to Homer's epics and suggests they could be subtracted now. With this final blow he concludes his

analysis of unity and his subversion of neoclassical principles
(31.103–4).

Wolf had opposed the aesthetician on three grounds, all historical.
His data convinced him that the *Iliad* was a unique case; that genre
criticism, though it might set up the *Iliad* as a model for later imitation,
was itself not germane, as it did not recognize the peculiar status of
Homer's poem (12.33). Second, the aesthete used atemporal
categories. Wolf complained to Heyne that such a man glosses words
by an art of self-deception. He does not know their meaning and proj-
ects backward the viewpoint of his own time. He is not just ahistorical
but antihistorical.[63] Third, to follow Aristotle or an imitator like
Horace violates normal procedure in research. The historian must not
choose one leader and reject other witnesses but must follow a con-
sensus:

> In universum autem habet hoc historicum genus hanc legem, ut
> nihil effiiciatur ex singulis voculis et sententiis scriptorum,
> atque omnia ex perpetuitate quadam et nexu testimoniorum
> rationum et argumentorum suspensa sint.

> The historical kind has this general law that nothing should be
> effected by single little comments and opinions of writers. Ev-
> erything should depend on a certain continuity and binding
> together of testimonies, reasons, and arguments. [Preface to
> *Iliad,* xix]

Against Aristotle are all the old grammarians who find a different subject for the *Iliad,* the deeds of the Greeks and Trojans before Ilium,[64]
and the proem promises nothing beyond *Iliad* 18: all the deaths occasioned by Achilles' anger (*Pro.* 27). The ancient evidence contradicts
the philosopher (*Pro.* 29.94–95 and n. 91).

The historian analyzes change, in this case the fortunes of Homer's
poems from prehistory to the Hellenistic period.[65] The developmental
historian looks for a movement from simple to complex forms. Wolf
assumes that a bard chanting single rhapsodies could never have produced the complex unity of an *Odyssey.* That was done by a later
polished compositor (28.92). The same model applies to aesthetic
theory. If we put together all the sayings on art by the Greeks, we
would see that they came to theories of complex unity late. The *Poetics*
is a special case and not representative. It suffices to contrast actual
Greek drama with Aristotle's precepts (*Pro.* 29.95 and n. 91). Aesthetics, like the literary forms which it studies, grows and develops.[66] So
does allegory, which in a developmental model must come late.

Wolf hardly discusses allegory, allowing it only one chapter out of fifty-one, but the chapter breathes the new spirit. He gives us its first history. Allegory originated much later than the Homeric period, in response to a given cultural problem. The philosophers were arguing whether Homer was impious. Pythagoras, Xenophanes, and Heraclitus of Ephesus attacked the poet, while he was defended by Theagenes of Rhegium, Anaxagoras of Clazomenae, Metrodorus of Lampsacus, and Stesimbrotus of Thasos (*Pro.* 36.124). The spirit of this defense was conservative. Veneration persists for what everyone accepts and in which all were educated. These rhapsodes and philosophers thus credited Homer with their own learning (12.33), and subtle exegesis became a religious act (36.125). This projection backward, while a normal development for sacred books, contributed nothing to true or historical interpretation and was in fact anachronistic, as Homer's stories were connected to contemporary physical and moral doctrine (36.123–24). The movement reached its acme in the late Empire, when Favorinus, Oenomaus, and Longinus debated whether Homer was a philosopher or a poet, and the allegorical *morbus* or disease became general. Everyone looked in Homer for allegory, anagogy, and history.[67] With this survey, Wolf dismisses allegory by a history of its growth and development. It is a datum of later culture and has no intrinsic relationship to Homer.

Allegory had been a medium of truth. It had died mostly with neoclassicism but lingered on in Homer because it was considered to be historical truth. It was appropriately removed by historical research, which at the same time undermined neoclassicism. Both assumed universals. Allegory conveyed truths about man and the universe; neoclassicism worked with generic rules. Neither survived a historicism concerned with change through time.[68]

Wolf's analysis fittingly closes my own discussion of allegory as a historical phenomenon. To continue, I would need to expand his paradigm and include all those writers who came after Homer, some of whom I have discussed in this book. Still the beginning and the ending would be same, the poetry of Homer, which both occasioned the growth of allegory and kept it alive longest. And so this book comes full circle.

Appendix: Landino's
Camaldulensian Dialogues

The Commentary Itself

Landino cast the *Camaldulensian Dialogues* in Ciceronian form, in
which a principal speaker gives connected lectures on a particular
subject. The speaker in this case is Leon Battista Alberti, the distinguished architect and theorist, while the interlocutor is the young
Lorenzo de' Medici. Landino thus both compliments his patrons and
makes an artistic point (he began his career in Alberti's circle and
married into the family, but it was the Medici who got him the pro-
fessorship in 1458).[1] Landino puts together the vernacular writers who
for him were supreme in the Quattrocento, supreme partly because of
their thorough training in Latin letters;[2] Alberti and Lorenzo were
therefore appropriate discussants for an analysis of Virgil. Landino
spaces the lectures over four days. On the first Alberti praises the
contemplative over the active life, against Lorenzo's severe rebuttal.
On the second he analyzes the *summum bonum* and on the third and
fourth the *Aeneid,* utilizing the themes and positions he worked out on
the previous two days. The setting is near the monastery of Camaldoli,
high in the Apennines east of Florence.

In his commentary Landino presents Aeneas as the struggling hero,
painfully working his way toward perfection despite many mistakes
and moral failures:

> Poeta enim non ipsum a principio sapientem fingit: et vera
> virtute ornatum: sed eum qui a perturbationibis animum vendi-
> care cupiens / se paulatim a viciis redimat: et post varios er-
> rores in Italiam: id est ad veram sapientiam perveniat.

> For the poet does not imagine him as one wise and adorned
> with true virtue from the beginning, but as one who, desirous
> of freeing his soul from disturbances, gradually redeems him-

197

self from vices, and after various wanderings, reaches Italy,
that is, true wisdom. [GiV]

In this process Aeneas goes through four stages of development:
(1) the innocent sensuality of childhood = Troy; (2) a gradual weaning
from sensual values = the journey to Sicily; (3) the temptations of the
civic life = Sicily and Carthage; (4) the life of contemplation = Italy.
In Troy Aeneas first realizes the human dilemma, when he sees the
gods destroying his city. Human mortality makes the sensual values
which he has espoused and defended completely inadequate. But recognition is only a beginning, and Aeneas makes many errors before he
can find a genuine alternative to mortality and begin the contemplative
way. Initially there are problems with various kinds of avarice (Thrace,
the Harpies) and mistakes over the ends proper to men, as when he
searches out his mortal origins in Crete. By the time he visits Helenus,
however, Aeneas has reached a kind of plateau and can avoid
altogether the occasions of sensuality. Accordingly he does not approach Scylla and Charybdis, monsters which recapitulate the problems of his earlier life, the tempatations to sensual pleasure and to
avarice. He also knows now that his ultimate goal is both remote and
difficult. The *summum bonum* cannot be found in a day. There is a long
journey first.

In the next stage of his development, where the nature of the temptation radically changes, Aeneas nearly fails. While he easily avoids the
abuse of civic responsibility, the temptations to tyranny and to the
exercise of naked power (the Cyclops), he cannot resist ordering an
ideal city state like Carthage. It takes divine intervention to make him
relinquish political power and turn to Italy. And there he must recapitulate yet once more all the dangers and temptations which he had
faced before or which this world can offer. This is his descent into hell,
an intellectual rather than a physical journey, under the guidance of the
Sibyl. And this is the true center of Landino's critique, taking up most
of book 4 and more than half of his total exegesis.

Landino prefaces his exegesis of Hades with an elaborate Platonic
discourse on the descent of the soul through the planets to its bodily
prison and its re-ascent. In Hades itself he carefully explains everything, quite unlike his procedure earlier. One example must suffice out
of many. Landino twice interprets the rivers of hell, and both times he
sees their order as significant of a developing psychological process. In
the first schema the rivers symbolize human birth or the soul's death
(KiV). Lethe, from which the other four come, is forgetfulness. The
others follow in logical sequence:

Acheron—loss of joy (ἀχαίρων): "Nam quod in dei contemplatione purus existens animus gaudium accipiebat / id omne ex oblivione amittit" (KiiR, "For the soul loses in forgetfulness all the joy which it received when it experienced the pure exsistence of the contemplation of God").

Styx—the moroseness which sets in afterward.

Cocytus—the mourning which follows moroseness.

Phlegethon—"ex diuturno autem luctu in furoris insaniaeque ardorem incidere solemus" ("From extended mourning we usually fall into the flames of frenzy and madness").

In the second schema Landino outlines the stages of a particular act of sin. In the first place, "a concupiscentia nostra veluti a fonte manat aqua / quae stygem paludem efficit" (KviV, "From our concupiscence, as from a spring, flows the water which makes up the Stygian swamp"). The thought produces the act, and we have the troubled waters of Acheron. After we have crossed this river, the other two follow: "(id autem est post peccatum) sequitur moeror: quem refert ipsa Styx. Postremo maior luctus / qui est Cocytus" (LiR, "[that is, after the sin has been committed] there follows sorrow, which is what Styx signifies. After that, great mourning, which is Cocytus"). It is clear from these examples (the rivers and Tartarus) that Aeneas' intellectual survey of sensual vice includes a dynamic element. He experiences the process of sin as well as its categories, one reason perhaps why such a survey is dangerous and requires the resources of eduction and wisdom. If the "mind is its own place" (*PL* 1.254) even a controlled experience of hell could be fatal.

What follows is a detailed diagram of Landino's whole exegesis:

Book 3

Prologue (FiR–FiiiV)	Platonic art theory
	methodological preliminaries
Troy (FiiiV–FvV)	innocent sensuality
Paris (FiiiV–FvV)	culpable sensuality (Venus over Pallas)
Its fall (FvV–viR)	recognition of human morality
Wanderings (FviR–GviR)	weaning from sensual vice
Aeneades (FviR–GiR)	newly discovered powers of the soul
Thrace (GiV)	avarice (the acquisitive type)
Delos (GiiR–GiiV)	veiled command to find one's origins

Crete (GiiV–iiiR)	mortal origins, which cannot give happiness
Strophades (GiiiV–ivV)	avarice (the frugal type) which wears virtue's mask
Helenus (GivV)	reason, by which Aeneas learns the road to his true goal
Scylla-Charybdis (GvR–vV)	sex and avarice (so recapitulations of the two chief temptations)
Sicily-Africa (GviR–HviiiV)	temptations of civic virtue
Cyclops (GviV)	perverted desire to rule
Storm (HiR–ivR)	ambition (Juno) rejecting contemplation
	Neptune or reason reasserted
Lybic Bay (HivR–vV)	Aeneas flees monstrous vice but remains in society
Wood (HvV–viV)	*hyle* or matter (the bottom of the chain of being)
Venus (HviV)	veiled because human affairs involve error
Carthage (HviiR–viiiR)	ideal city state
The cave of love (HviiiR–viiiV)	by his commitment to Dido, Aeneas restricts himself to the corporeal realm

Book 4

Apologia (IiR–iiR)	Stoic allegory a matter of imitation
	Federigo of Urbino as art patron
Parting (IiiV–iiiV)	civic life rejected
Mercury (IiiV–iiiR)	soul must return home
Last meeting (IiiiR–V)	politics rejected
Ship burning (IivR–ivV)	sense over inferior reason
Women left behind (IivV)	mind separates itself from the senses
Death of Palinurus (IivV)	all sense desires killed
Sibyl (IvR–viV)	
The outer temple (IvR–V)	allegory of what is rejected
Oracle (IvV–viV)	capsule analysis of *Ae*. 7–12
Underworld (KiR–LviV)	human body

Preliminaries (KiR–iiiV)	theoretical bases for the discussion
Rivers (KiV–iiV)	fall of the soul
Reason for the trip (KiiV–iiiV)	self-education
Golden Bough (KivR–vR)	wisdom
Misenus (KivV–vR)	empty glory
Vestibule (KvV–viV)	shadows (evil as privation)
River crossing (KviV–LiiV)	
Rivers (again) (KviV–LiR)	concupiscence
Charon (LiR–iV)	allegory of free will
Cerberus (LiV–iiV)	body put to sleep
The dead (LiiiR–iiiV)	good and evil mixed
Suicides (eg) (LiiiR–iiiV)	result of soft living
Ultimates (LivR–viV)	good and evil separated
Tartarus (LivR–ivV)	habitual vice
Elysium (LivV–viV)	habitual virtue

Such an exegesis—by its exhaustiveness, its attention to detail, its internal coherence and thematic consistency—is finally very impressive, even though we might feel that Landino has used Virgil's narrative rather as a scaffold for another poem of his own making. Lorenzo's final praise normally applies to art works rather than to critical analyses: nothing can be added or taken away (LvV). And the whole has the familiar ring of medieval allegory, where the hero goes to the Tower of the Seven Liberal Arts or analogous places to receive an education from allegorical personifications. This is part of my point. The interpretation of Virgil has a close interrelationship with medieval creative writing. Eugen Wolf alludes to the critical principle involved.[3]

A Brief Note on Landino's Political Theory

Like other Platonists, Landino uses the same categories for different disciplines. In *De vera nobilitate* the criterion of variety, for example, which Cardini says is a commonplace in Quattrocento literary criticism (pp. 14, 38–39, 154, 195), applies also to politics. Man is by nature social, and the city requires variety (*De vera* 78), a point which Landino confirms by a reference to Virgil's Elysium (*Ae.* 6.660–64), which includes priests, soldiers, prophets, and inventors or benefactors in the arts (*De vera* 107). That is, here he is working with the literal level of the poem and talking politically. However, Landino also argues, especially in his critique of Venice (ibid. 46–47, also 90–91), that one's origins should not determine one's career; and Aretophilus, the main speaker in the dialogue, is himself from a poor and obscure family (43). The Platonic ladder thus has its social reflection, as it allows for a variety of professions, which are distinguished in quality (e.g., the priesthood is a higher profession than that of a merchant), and requires excellence in every class. Landino argues by ideal examples and says that we call *noble* anything perfect or absolute in any discipline. It is noble for exacting reasons, because it fulfills many requirements (ibid. 57–59, 61). Finally, he leaves all these careers open to anyone. This decision makes philosophy, the highest profession, a career available to anyone and is the reason why Landino rejects Scholasticism for a philosophy modeled on Cicero, the great, politically committed Platonist. This choice is already clear in his first prolusion, on the *Tusculan Disputations*. Landino wishes to do philosophy without a technical vocabulary so as to reach everyone[4] and contrasts Cicero with the Scholastics who force with thorny subtlety rather than persuade us to agree: "itaque multo plura ab invitis extorquent, quam a volentibus impetrent" (Tusc. Prol. 307). The city requires us to be both philosopher and orator, as we cannot be of use to the city unless we can both think rightly and express our thoughts clearly (ibid. 308). Cicero is therefore the ideal, perfect eloquence joined to philosophy, and the best in Cicero (again the ideal category) is the *Tusculan Disputations*, where "simul et dicendi et philosophandi genus uberius complexus est" (ibid. 294; it is a rhetorical question). In fiction Landino cites Xenophon's Cyrus and of course Aeneas as the perfect models for imitation (General Proem to 1488 Virgil 215–16).

Notes

Preface

1. Henri de Lubac, *Exégèse médiévale* (Aubier, 1959), 1:202.
2. I have changed my mind from my earlier statement that Milton was both neoclassical and allegorical; see Michael Murrin, *The Veil of Allegory* (Chicago, 1969), p. 197. Whatever mythic depths exist in *Paradise Lost* are in his matter, the Genesis narrative, which Origen long ago classed as allegorical and which Milton read as history: see *Periarchon* 4.3.1.
3. See C. S. Lewis, *The Allegory of Love* (New York, 1958), pp. 44–45.
4. "Two Essays in Renaissance Literary History," *Modern Language Quarterly* 36 (1975): 425.

Chapter One

All quotations from the *Iliad*, the *Odyssey*, and the *Aeneid* are taken from the standard texts in the Oxford series. For the Homeric scholia I have used the *Scholia Graeca in Homeri Iliadem*, ed. Hartmut Erbse, 5 vols. (Berlin, 1969–77). I have likewise used Erbse's abbreviations. For example, ex. indicates the exegetical scholia and b the common source for Venetus B, its related family of manuscripts, and the Townley Manuscript (T) (for the latter, see Erbse's introduction, 1:xxvi–xxviii, xlviii–xlix, and the general stemma, 1:lviii). For *Il.* 20–21, however, I originally had to use the older edition of Wilhelm Dindorf and Ernst Maass (Oxford, 1875–88) vols. 2 (Venetus Graec. 822, or A), 4 (Venetus Graec. 821, or B), and 6 (Townley or Burney 86). I also used Oxyrhynchus papyrus 221 (ancient scholia on *Il.* 21) in vol. 2 of the *Oxyrhynchus papyri*, ed. and trans. Bernard P. Grenfell and Arthur S. Hunt (London, 1899); and *Les scolies genevoises de "l'Iliade,"* ed. Jules Nicole (Geneva, 1891), vol. 1, henceforth cited as Nicole. Geneva has detailed and unique scholia for the Theomachy. I have since checked these citations in Erbse and used his symbols. Oxy. 221, for example, becomes Pap. 12. The older critics, of course, cite from Dindorf and Maass, and I have left their references as they give them. For the D scholia (see n. 3 below) I have used Ὁμήρου Ἰλιάς (Oxford, 1762), 2 vols.; and for the *Odyssey* the *Scholia Graeca in Homeri Odysseam*, ed. Wilhelm Dindorf (Oxford, 1855), 2 vols. For Heraclitus' Ὁμηρικὰ Προβλήματα I have used the edition of Félix Buffière, *Allégories d'Homère* (Paris, 1962), hereafter cited as Buffière, *Allégories,* when I refer to his introduction or notes; citations from Heraclitus will be by chapter and verse. When there are too many notes to a passage, Buffière inserts the extra ones in a later section which he calls "Notes complémentaires." I will cite these as "nc" plus the page number in the *text* of Heraclitus (where the notes actually belong). Buffière's other work, *Les mythes d'Homère et la pensée grecque* (Paris, 1956) I will cite as Buffière, *Mythes*. For Servius I have used *Servii Grammatici qui feruntur in Vergilii Carmina commentarii*, Georg Thilo and Hermann Hagen (Leipzig, 1881–87), 3 vols. For *Aeneid* 1–5 I have checked the Thilo-Hagen readings with the Editio Harvardiana: *Servianorum in Vergilii Carmina Commentariorum*, ed. E. K. Rand (Lancaster, 1946), vol. 2 and A. F. Stocker & A. H. Travis (Oxford, 1965), vol. 3. Where line numbers conflict I cite Thilo-Hagen first, e.g., to 6.322/321. Citations from the Pauly-Wissowa *Real-Encyclopädie der classischen Altertumswissenschaft* (*RE*) will be by author, article, title, and column number, e.g., Eitrem, s.v. "Hera," *RE* 15 (1912), 385. For translations I have used the literal rendering of the *Iliad* by Richmond Lattimore (Chicago, 1961) and for the *Aeneid* that by Allen Mandelbaum (Berkeley, 1971). For the Presocratics I have used the *Vorsokratiker*[5], ed. Hermann Diels and Walther Kranz, 3 vols. (Berlin, 1934–37). I cite by fragment number only. Translations from the Presocratics are normally by John Burnet in his *Early Greek Philosophy*, 4th ed., reprint (New York, 1958). He has most complete collection of the fragments in translation. For the Stoics I cite from the *Stoicorum veterum fragmenta*, ed. Hans von Arnim, 4 vols. (Stuttgart, repr. 1968). Again I cite by fragment number. Translations from the Greek Stoics, from the Homeric scholia, and from Servius are my own, and I have silently altered the translations of others where precision required it. I should warn the reader that when Greek names appear in their Latinized forms, the author in question is using the Latinized form.

1. The Deception of Zeus is the traditional title of the episode.

2. See Buffière, *Allégories*, pp. ix–x.

3. I must describe the various scholia which record Homeric allegories. They have recently been sorted out for the *Iliad* by Hartmut Erbse. Those which concern us are two, the first of which scholars call the D or *scholia minora*, which Lascaris published in 1517. They were erroneously attributed to Didymus and so are called D. These include interpretations and stories which may date back to pre-Hellenistic times and which might represent what Athenian schoolchildren learned (Erbse, 1:xi and lxvii). Pfeiffer thinks that Callimachus may have used a set of Homeric commentaries which later became the D scholia (Rudolf Pfeiffer, *History of Classical Scholarship* [Oxford, 1968], 1:139). In their present form the D scholia are of course later and include quotations from Aristarchus and from his pupil Apollodorus of Athens. D cites Apollodorus at 21.448. For Aristarchus, see M. van der Valk, *Researches on the Text and Scholia of the "Iliad"* (Leiden, 1963), 1:67. The other or exegetical tradition comes to us through the *scholia maiora* or *vetera;* explains names in fable, history, and geography; and uses philosophical notions of the arts and rhetoric (see Erbse, 1:xii). It is a Byzantine collection drawn from various sources and applied to single places in Homer. The compiler did not follow a specific method and often gave the same readings in different phrases (p. li). Erbse thinks that the examples used in the exegetical scholia stem from commentaries written in the first century B.C., that is, from the same period as Virgil (pp. xii–xiii). In the actual manuscripts, however, these two traditions often appear together. The two principal manuscripts in which we have the exegetical scholia, for example, Townley and Venetus B, also contain the D

scholia (Erbse, 1:xvii, xxvii). Buffière dates the Townley (T) as tenth century (see *Allégories,* p. xlviii). In the Venetian codex the eleventh-century scribe did the text of the *Iliad* and wrote in the exegetical scholia as well, while a later hand added D. For us, this practice introduces another caution. Often we seem to have many sources for a particular episode, while we actually have only one or two, because the same sources are in many manuscripts. This is true of the Theomachy. Here we also have, however, scholia in Pap. 12 to *Il.* 21, which scholars date to the first century A.D.

4. Menander the rhetorician (third century A.D.) remarks that the rhapsodes who recite the Hymn to Apollo identify him with the sun, Hera with air, and Zeus with heat (see Parmenides A.20). This remark would place the identification of Hera with air back to the fifth century B.C. For the Stoics, see Zeno in Arnim, 1:154, 169. Cicero has Balbus remark, in *De natura deorum* 2.26, "Aër autem, ut Stoici disputant, interiectus inter mare et caelum, Iunonis nomine consecratur, quae est soror et coniunx Iovis, quod ei similitudo est aetheris et cum eo summa coniunctio." I cite from the Loeb text, ed. and trans. H. Rackham (Cambridge, Mass., 1933). See also the Stoic Cornutus' Περὶ τῶν θεῶν φύσεως 3; he taught Persius in the first century A.D. For another reference, see Julius Firmicus Maternus *De errore profanarum religionum* 4.1.

5. Her chariot takes her over sea as well as land (14.308) and therefore supports the notion that she always travels in the air.

6. Hera calls up the storm with the same term used later in the Theomachy: ὄρσασα (14.254; 21.335). The reference to cyclones is by Zeus and is glossed by D at 15.26. In the same place the exegetical scholiast explains that, while it is unclear whether Hera and Boreas collaborated in the storm or whether Hera alone ordered it (bT), the second alternative is better (b).

7. ἐπὶ δὲ νεφέλην ἕσσαντο / καλὴν χρυσείην· στιλπναὶ δ' ἀπέπιπτον ἔερσαι (14.350–51).

8. Here is the passage and the explanation in Heraclitus, chap. 40:

ἦ οὐ μέμνη ὅτε τ' ἐκρέμω ὑψόθεν, ἐκ δὲ ποδοῖιν
ἄκμονας ἧκα δύω, περὶ χερσὶ δὲ δεσμὸν ἴηλα
χρύσεον ἄρρηκτον; σὺ δ' ἐν αἰθέρι καὶ νεφέλησιν
ἐκρέμω· ἠλάστεον δὲ θεοὶ κατὰ μακρὸν Ὄλυμπον,
λῦσαι δ' οὐκ ἐδύναντο παρασταδόν·

Do you not remember that time you hung from high and on your feet
I slung two anvils, and about your hands drove a golden
chain, unbreakable. You hung in the ether and among the clouds
nor could the gods about tall Olympos endure it
and stood about, but could not set you free.

[*Il.* 15.18–22]

As air, Hera swings between the ether and the clouds, the upper and lower limits of that range. The gold chain is fiery, the zone where air and ether meet. It thus parallels the epithet χρυσόθρονος, or golden-throned, which the D scholiast glosses in the same way: the upper air incandescent with ethereal fire (to *Il.* 1.611). The vertical order in this scene represents the temporal process in which the elements came into existence: ether, air, water, and earth (the two anvils). The movement is from the lightest (fire) to the heaviest (earth), and the motion is toward the center of the cosmos. The elements differ from each other by weight, so air and fire remain at the periphery, and earth and water sink to the center. D uses Peripatetic distinctions (to 15.18): Zeus is the highest, in-flamed air; and Hera its second and lower level, that produced by ocean exha-lations. Anaxagoras perhaps first connected the fiery ether to the Olympians. See N. J. Richardson, "Homeric Professors in the Age of the Sophists," *Pro-ceedings of the Cambridge Philological Society*, n.s. 201, no. 21 (1957): 69. Buffière cites Cornutus 17; Venetus A on 15.18; Venetus B on 15.21; and Probus on Virgil, Eclogue 6.31 (*Allégories,* "nc," p. 48).

9. Richard Heinze noted this etymology in *Virgils epische Technik* (Leipzig, 1915), p. 299n. It is cited among the etymologies in the *Cratylus* 404C.

10. I draw from Macrobius' elaboration of the schema. See *Commentarii in Somnium Scipionis*, ed. Jacob Willis (Leipzig, 1970), 1.6.24–33. However, this analysis of the elements is very old and is assumed, e.g., by Aristotle in the *Meteorologica*. See also Buffière, *Mythes*, p. 99. Basil gives a breakdown identical with that of Macrobius. See *In Hexaemeron* 4.5 in the *Opera omnia quae exstant*, ed. Julian Garnier (Paris, 1839), vol. 1 (henceforth abbreviated as *Hex.*). The Porphyry scholion which Dindorf records for *Il.* 20.67 in Venetus B indicates the logical basis of this analysis. Augustine in *De genesi ad litteram* 3.2 stresses the similarity of water and air. Watery exhalations make the humid zone (*aër*) near the earth's surface. These exhalations thicken and make wind and cloud.

11. Aristotle, e.g., said that dry exhalations from the earth produced winds (*Meteor.* 2.4.359b27–361a23), while the Stoics attributed air generally to moist exhalations from water, and wind was an airstream (Arnim, 2:697–99). They also disagreed on lightning, which Aristotle explained as the ejection of the dry exhalation when a cloud condensed (2.9.369b4–370a34), while Zeno made it the kindling of clouds and thunder the noise when they rubbed together or were broken by winds (Arnim, 1:117). The later Stoics said simply that lightning was the kindling of clouds, rubbed together or broken (ibid., 2:703–5).

12. D to 14.323 cites the Semele story for a parallel. Zeus must come to her as he came wooing Hera, so he arrives in his chariot, flickering with lightning, and blasts her with a thunderbolt. Ex. to 15.17 (bT) adds that the whip of Zeus is a metaphor for thunderbolts (the god threatens to whip Hera after he discovers the deceit) and cites 12.37, where the phrase "tamed by the whip of Zeus" signifies "tamed by fear of yesterday's thunderstorm." In T, ex. also cites 2.782, where Zeus whipped earth and Typhon with his bolts. T, ex. to 14.350–51, says that the golden cloud which veils the lovers is an ether cloud. D, in a long note to *Il.* 15.18, adds a further parallel from the *Theogony*, in which Kronos and Rhea signify the same happening. Kronos is the higher element, gushing out as a thunderstorm, while Rhea is the falling rain. Pope cites two passages (*Georgics* 2.325–27; *De rerum natura* 1.250–52) in which Father Ether rains on the earth (to *Il.* 14.179).

13. Much of this analysis is standard. Buffière cites Cornutus 3; the *Clemen-tine Homilies* 6.8; and refers also to Stobaeus 1.22.2; *The Life and Poetry of Homer* 96; and a citation by Maass in *Aratea* 91 (*Allégories,* "nc," p. 47).

14. Aristotle and the Stoics agreed that air was a combination of dry and wet exhalations (*Meteor.* 1.9.346b, Arnim, 2:563), and Aristotle stressed that the dry and wet exhalations always existed *together* but were called dry or wet depending on which quality predominated (2.4.359b27 ff).

15. It is worse for Athena: in other contexts she is prudence, not earth.

16. The episode of plague, with which the *Iliad* begins, provides another example. Hera moves Achilles to call an assembly. If we assume that the plague came from infected air, then λευκώλενος Hera, she of the white arms, represents the clean air which blows away the fetid vapors and so ends the epidemic (Heraclitus 15.2–6). The exegetical scholiast explains her action slightly differently. Achilles, who has medical training from Chiron, can tell through the air about the plague. Her epithet, λευκώλενος, comes from the fact that the air, being transparent, becomes brilliant in the light of the sun and stars (bT to *Il.* 1.53). Now epithets alone do not make an interpretation, especially in Homer. Hera functions marginally here, yet the scholiasts insist that she is air.

17. So he has the old pun of Kronos/Chronos (41.6), and Hades becomes the dark, lower air by a similar means, Ἀίδης / ἀήρ: Ἀίδης / ζόφον ἠερόεντα (41.4, 9). Perhaps the most strained is Aphrodite, who appears as an adjective in the allegory of the smith at his forge (Hephaestus and Ares): ἐπαφροδίτῳ (69.15). Buffière refers to a dissertation by Robert Münzel and states that the Hermes discussion likewise comes from Apollodorus, though he cites no evidence (*Allégories*, p. xxxiv).

18. For a discussion of Meliteniotes, see Nicole, 1:xix–xxiv. By his argument, the second or B scholia in the Geneva text are fourteenth century.

19. Xenophanes objected to the immoral activity of the gods in Homer and Hesiod and, more fundamentally, to the anthropomorphism involved. He assumed not that God was like man in shape or thought but that man made gods in his own image, blue-eyed and red-haired for Thracians, snub-nosed and dark for Ethiopians. Man cannot know the truth about the gods. Even if he thought correctly, he could not know it. There was development, however, and by striving we find out better through time. In all a sophisticated agnosticism, which could not contrast more completely with Homer's gods in human form; see B.12, 14–16, 18, 23, 25–26, 34. The quotation in our text comes from Sextus Empiricus *Math.* 9.193 and is partially translated in J. E. Sandys, *A History of Classical Scholarship* (repr. New York and London, 1967), 1.29.

20. Cited by Buffière (*Mythes*, p. 241). For Demeter, Kirk and Raven cite a fragment from Aeschylus' *Danaids* (44.1–5), where Demeter is simply corn (see G. S. Kirk and J. E. Raven, *The Presocratic Philosophers* [Cambridge, repr. 1969], p. 29).

21. See the following citations in *Vorsokratiker*⁵: Anaximenes A.18, Xenophanes B.32, Pythagorean School B.37c, C.2, Anaxagoras A.86, Metrodorus of Chios A.17. Burnet (p. 230) remarks that this practice was common among the Presocratics.

22. *Vorsokratiker*⁵ lists this as the reading of Hippolytus, Heraclitus. The Pseudo Plutarch has Zeus instead as heat and is paralleled in Plutarch's *Life of Homer*. Aëtius has a different schema: Zeus-heat, Hera-air, Hades-earth, Nestis-water; while Philodemus has Zeus-fire and Hera-air. Among the moderns Burnet (pp. 228–30) prefers to equate Zeus with air and Hades with fire. He argues that Empedocles had discovered the distinction between air and mist and used αἰθήρ consistently for air, which would be a standard use of the term. The epithet for Zeus favors Heraclitus' reading, however. Ἀργής normally describes the white flash of the thunderbolt, of lightning. So in Hesiod the three Cyclops, who supply Zeus with thunderbolts, are named Βρόντης (thunder), Στερόπης (lightning), and Ἀργής; see *Theogony* 139–41.

23. Buffière (*Mythes*, p. 99) cites Venetus A and B and also *The Life and Poetry of Homer*.

24. See Zeno in Arnim, 1:167, 169 (on the *Theogony*). For the later Stoics on Hera, see Arnim, 2:1066, 1075.

25. See, e.g., Kirk and Raven, p. 212; for his book, p. 184. They cite Diogenes Laertius.

26. B.1 (it introduces his book). See also B.34.

27. The complaint in *Theaetetus* 179E–180B.

28. In *Symp.* 187A Eryximachus remarks that B.51, the bow and the lyre, is absurd because it is contradictory. Probably the most celebrated instance of contradiction would be B.67.

29. See Burnet's argument and citations, pp. 143–46.

30. Kirk and Raven, pp. 196–98.

31. Burnet, pp. 146–50; 165; Kirk and Raven, pp. 190–91.

32. For Joseph Owens, see "The Interpretation of the Heraclitean Fragments," in *An Etienne Gilson Tribute*, ed. Charles J. O'Neil (Milwaukee, 1959), pp. 148–68.

33. *Vita Probiana* 10–12; *Vita Focae* 63; *Vita Donati* 128–29. I follow the numbering in Colin Hardie's ed. for the *Vitae Vergilianae antiquae* (Oxford, 1957). See also Servius to *Ae.* 6.264.

34. For Hera in chains, see n. 8 above. In the other episode Hera intervenes to save Achilles, endangered by the flooding Xanthus. She orders her son not to cease burning without her word, and she herself will cause the south and west winds to blow a whirlwind in from the sea, toward the city walls and into the faces of the Trojans. The fire thus depends on intermittent but violent gusts from the southwest, winds which earlier darkened the Trojan rout (21.6–7). Hephaestus begins burning the corpses scattered on the plain, dries the land, and stops the water flow (ex. to 366, bT, remarks that water flows more slowly when heated). The flood halted, the fire spreads to the trees and foliage along the river bank, heats the water in the river, and causes great suffering to the fish (21.350–55). The river then asks Hephaestus to stop, but his request is ignored, and Xanthus must finally submit to Hera. That is, the fire stops when its fuel is exhausted (the trees and the corpses) and the wind drops. The river can now flow once more within its banks and through to the sea. Since Hephaestus and Xanthus are opposites (fire is hot and dry, while water is cold and wet), they cannot cease fighting except via an intermediary, in this case air, which is hot like fire and wet like water (Basil stresses this point at *Hex.* 4.5). Hera therefore releases the river from Hephaestus.

35. The storm which extinguishes the conflagration in *Aeneid* 5 is a special case and will be discussed separately. When Juno later summarizes her struggle with the wandering Trojans, she says, "Quin etiam patria excussos infesta per undas / ausa sequi: et profugis toto me opponere ponto" (7.299–300); Servius assumes that she refers to storms.

36. *Virgils epische Technik*, p. 299.

37. The variant textual readings for 7.543 still locate the interview in midair.

38. At 12.139 Servius glosses the epithet *diva* as air, citing a passage from Horace. He likewise explains Juno's remark at 7.300 physiologically, where the goddess says that she opposed the Trojans on every sea: "Plus est, quam si diceret tempestates. 'Me' autem per physiologiam imbres, tonitrua, tempestates."

39. The terms are λαῖλαψ, ἀέλλη, and θύελλα.

40. Here too there is one exception, the storm which blows the Trojans back to Sicily (5.8–34), itself modeled on the sole lightning storm in the *Odyssey*, which hits Odysseus' ship off Thrinakia/Sicily. Both storms blow in from the west and begin with identical formulae:

> Ἀλλ' ὅτε δὴ τὴν νῆσον ἐλείπομεν, οὐδέ τις ἄλλη
> φαίνετο γαιάων, ἀλλ' οὐρανὸς ἠδὲ θάλασσα,
> δὴ τότε κυανέην νεφέλην ἔστησε Κρονίων
> νηὸς ὕπερ γλαφυρῆς, ἤχλυσε δὲ πόντος ὑπ' αὐτῆς.

[*Od.* 12.403–6]

> nec iam amplius ulla
> occurrit tellus, maria undique et undique caelum
> olli caeruleus supra caput astitit imber.

[*Ae.* 5.8–10]

The results are completely different. The Trojans evade the storm, which is just beginning, and row into Sicily. Odysseus' ship is hit by a thunderbolt and sunk.

41. Jove, of course, does not take direct part in the storm, but Juno uses his thunderbolts, as she half admits in her initial soliloquy (1.39–49). Kenneth Quinn stresses the visual accuracy with which Virgil depicts storms (see *Virgil's "Aeneid"* [Ann Arbor, Mich., 1968], pp. 102, 386–87).

42. To *Georgics* 1.311.

43. See the explication of the divine conspiracy, pp. 000 herein.

44. See Aristotle *Meteor.* 2.5.361b31–35. Virgil makes the connection of Orion with winter and its storms explicit at *Ae.* 7.718–19: "quam multi Libyco volvuntur marmore fluctus / saevus ubi Orion hibernis conditur undis."

45. The other direct remark is the well-known allusion at 4.193–94: "nunc hiemem inter se luxu, quam longa, fovere / regnorum immemores turpique cupidine captos." Heinze points out that the winter season was already stressed in the *Odyssey*. He also discusses some of the difficulties, if one contends that the whole of *Ae.* 1–6 occurs in winter (pp. 346–47). The problem turns not on events in the narrative but on inconsistent time references to seven years.

46. Polybius had already argued this identification. See Diodorus Siculus 5.7.1–7 and Strabo 1.2.15, 6.2.10–11.

47. See also 365b29–366a5.

48. Though Aristotle and the Stoics have different explanations for storms, they share a common technical vocabulary, one different from that used by Homer. Aristotle classes them in diminishing order of strength (*Meteor.* 3.1.370b5–371a29): κεραυνός = thunderbolt; ἐκνεφίας ἄνεμος = our cyclone or hurricane; τυφῶν = tornado; πρηστήρ = a lighter but inflamed whirling. For the Stoics, Stobaeus gives a list by descending degrees of fire (Arnim, 2:703): κεραυνός, πρηστήρ, τυφῶν. Diogenes Laertius (Arnim, 2:704) and Aëtius (2:705) arrange the terms by wind velocity and size. So a τυφῶν has more wind than a πρηστήρ (Diogenes Laertius), and the latter is slower moving than a κεραυνός (Aëtius). The Stoics understand the ἐκνεφίας ἄνεμος as a thunderstorm; see the scholiast gloss on Hesiod's Cyclops (Arnim, 2:700). For Aristotle, they come in the rainy seasons.

49. According to Servius (to *Ae.* 7.142–43), Virgil suggests two different

theories of thunder. First, the lines at 7.141 indicate that it is caused by burning cloud (a Stoic theory). Second, Servius cites 8.392, which assumes that thunder depends on fraction at the edge of a cloud: "Ignea rima micans percurrit lumine nimbos." Either Stoics or Aristotelians might argue that this line fits their theories (for the distinction, see n. 11 above), but *Ae*. 3.199 suggests more the Stoic: "Ingeminant abruptis nubibus ignes."

50. Servius' gloss: "Nubes enim aëris densitas facit."

51. I borrow this particular from Basil *Hex*. 3.8.

52. Servius to 1.71. He refers appropriately to his commentary to the weather prognostics in *Georgics* 1.

53. Heinze, p. 298–99. Akusilaos remarked that some make Iris the peculiar messenger of Hera; others, of all the gods (B.5).

54. Robin Schlunk notes that Virgil's departures from Homer are often signaled by problems or questions in the scholia. See *The Homeric Scholia and the "Aeneid"* (Ann Arbor, Mich., 1974), pp. 89–90. Here the scholia say nothing, but some such questions were raised, as we can see from the Q scholiast to *Od*. 5.293, where Poseidon, not Zeus, is called the Cloud Gatherer (Q is Dindorf's abbreviation for the scholia contained in Ambrosiana Ms. Partis superioris Q.88). The scholiast notes that Odysseus himself attributes this storm to Zeus and explains that the epithet certainly belongs to Zeus, but the gods can use the power of all things against men. It is this kind of problem which we do not find in the *Aeneid*.

55. Zeno identified Zeus with ether and assumed that fire was mental (Arnim, 1:154, 157). Cleanthes made the cosmos God and applied the term "God" to the mind of all nature and especially to the ether, the burning circle at the height and the periphery, which girdles all things (Arnim, 1:530, also 534). Chrysippus and the later Stoics assumed the same equations of Zeus, ether and intelligence; see, e.g., Arnim, 2:634 and n. 12. The exegetical scholiast can thus say that Hypnos puts to sleep the mind of the cosmos (bTil, to *Il*. 14.252). For Jove and Venus, see Macrobius. *Commentarii* 1.19.20–25.

56. D's long note to *Il*. 15.18.

57. Such cosmological allegory is Heraclitus' major concern. The following stories all present visions of cosmogony: the chaining of Hera in mid-heaven, the gods dividing the world (*Il*. 15.189–93), the shield of Achilles, the binding of Proteus, and, if not the four elements, then Love and Strife creating by their union the harmony of the world (69.8–11). Most of his physical allegory therefore symbolizes creation. Heraclitus finds his most perfect symbol in Hephaestus the demiurge, laboring away at his forge (chap. 43), but he waxes most eloquent over Proteus, where he evokes creation in lyrical prose (chap. 65).

58. We can also include the storm which occurred earlier and drove the Trojans from Crete to the Island of the Harpies. Though the symbolism is different, the meaning is identical. Aeneas narrates the incident and is of course unaware of her agency when he explains the first storm to Dido. The prophet Helenus, however, soon warns Aeneas to appease Juno (3.433–40), and the symbolism of the Harpy episode fits the winter pattern. A storm drives the Trojans blindly for three days (3.194–204). They then arrive at the Island of the Harpies, where they have a frustrating battle with the monster birds and get in return an ominous prophecy from Celaeno. "Physically" they could not win against the Harpies, for the cold season is beginning, and shortly Aeneas will

go into winter quarters. At *Od*. 1.241 Telemachus says that the "Harpies" took away his father, and the scholiasts allow the term to mean either whirlwinds or the mythological birds: B: rapacious winds or the revenging goddesses; E: rapacious winds or birds; V: δαίμονες or rapacious winds. The formula is repeated at *Od*. 14.371. Similarly, a ἁρπάξασα ... θύελλα blows back Odysseus' ship when his companions open the Bag of Winds (*Od*. 10.48). In Hesiod's *Theogony* (265–69) they are Ἀελλώ ("storm fast") and Ὀκυπέτη ("swift fly"), the winds which arise from ocean (Electra) and sea (Thaumas). In Pherecydes (B.5) they are children of the north wind and help storms guard windy Tartarus. In the *Aeneid* episode the famine which the birds suffer and predict in turn for the Trojans comes normally to people at the end of winter, when supplies have run out; and it is just at this time that Celaeno's prophecy is fulfilled, though without danger to the Trojans. The Harpies signify winter and its frustrations as surely as do Juno and Aeolus.

59. Servius at *Ae*. 8.90 suggests, however, that the Tiber once had a different course in Rome.

60. Pope confessed that he did not know the time of year when the *Iliad* occurred; see his note to *Il*. 1.554. Heraclitus has a long argument to prove that the story occurs in late summer; see his chaps. 8–10. Unfortunately, he cannot explain why the Xanthus would be in flood. Hellanicus in *Troïka* 2 argues that storms on Mount Ida sent a flood to the plain. This theory would explain why the Trojans swim about in a river *ford* (*Il*. 21.1). See B* to *Il*. 21.242 in Dindorf and Maass.

61. Heinze, pp. 305–7; Quinn, p. 109.

62. See Murrin, *The Veil of Allegory*, pp. 72, 101–2.

63. Erich Auerbach, *Mimesis*, trans. Willard Trask (Garden City, N.Y., n.d.), p. 4. Or see Giraldi Cinthio's definition in *On Romances*, trans. Henry Snuggs (Lexington, Ky., 1968), p. 135: "[It puts] the thing clearly and effectively before the reader's eyes and in the hearer's ears." The concept is too commonplace to require analysis and normally appears in discussions of epic.

64. Lessing, *Laokoon*, 12:99–100.

65. I am aware, of course, of the hyperbole involved when Virgil has Aeneas cross from Carthage to northern Sicily in a single day. See Heinze, p. 344. Anaxagoras long before had called Iris the sign of a storm because the clouds which form the mirror reflection are surrounded by water which either makes wind or pours down rain (B.19). In Aristotle she is literally a storm coming into being, for a rainbow forms when air from a cloud is turning to rain drops (*Meteor*. 3.4.373b14–34). Basil (*Hex*. 6.4) talks of solar phenomena which precede a storm and which may likewise explain why Iris comes before a storm. Winds or water can cause a solar halo. The rays shoot out among the clouds in straight lines and assume the colors of the rainbow. They predict extraordinary storms or show great changes in the air. Aristotle classes all such phenomena together and likewise regards a solar halo as a weather sign. At full and darkest in color, it indicates rain; broken, a wind coming; and fading, fine weather. See *Meteor*. 3.3.372b16–35. For a rainbow, he says that the sun or an equivalent light must be behind us and the rain not yet begun, so the cloud can act as a mirror. The small water particles reflect color but not shape (3.4.373b14–34). The Stoics seem to presuppose the same definition (Arnim, 2:692): sunbeams bent back from wet clouds. Servius to *Ae*. 4.700/701 explains that a rainbow is a mixture of light water particles, translucent air, and dark clouds irradiated by

sunlight. Hence Iris descends to Carthage with the sun opposite: "Mille tra-
hens varios adverso sole colores" (4.701). Iris can also signify storm winds. In
Hesiod she is sister to the Harpies (*Theogony* 265–69). Empedocles remarks,
ʼΙρις δ' ἐκ πελάγους ἄνεμον φέρει ἢ μέγαν ὄμβρον (B50, "Iris brings wind from
the sea or a great storm"). In the *Iliad* she summons the winds to the funeral
pyre of Patroclus and in a simile swoops from Ida to the Trojan plain like snow
or hail which flies from clouds, cold from the wind rush of Boreas. The simile
indicates for the exegetical scholiast her signification (bT to 15.237–38).

66. Eitrem, s.v. "Hera," *RE* 15 (1912), 399.

67. Heraclitus 31.1–4. Ares represents the irascible out of rational control,
the raging one, μαινόμενος (*Il.* 5.831), an epithet which could never apply to a
god but, rather, indicates battle mania. Virgil's Juno talks this way, or so
Landino assumes in his stylistic analysis of her soliloquy in *Ae.* 7. She speaks
in a disorderly fashion and changes topics abruptly. She begins with
exclamatio, follows with short questions, and uses brief *sententiae* without
copula. Her resolve, to go to hell merely to delay Aeneas, reflects both her
wrath and her desperation; see his remarks at *Ae.* 7.292–93, 301, 315. I cite
from Virgil's *Opera* (Venice, 1489).

68. *Virgil: A Study in Civilized Poetry* (Oxford, 1963), p. 322.

69. Eitrem, s.v. "Hera," *RE* 15 (1912), 398 cites for the signification of Hera
as air the myths of Endymion and Ixion, who love not Hera but a cloud.

70. Viktor Pöschl, *The Art of Vergil*, trans. Gerda Seligson (Ann Arbor,
Mich., 1962), p. 23.

71. Servius explains at 7.529: "Sic bella dicit surrexisse paulatim, sicut ven-
tis flantibus sensim mare turgescit."

72. *The Veil of Allegory*, p. 103.

73. She says, e.g., that her daughter is worthy only of Bacchus and then
sings her marriage to Turnus. See Servius to *Ae.* 7.385, 398.

74. The commentators point to Euripides' influence on the Juno-Allecto
scene. See Servius to 7.320, 337, and Landino to 328; they stress Allecto. I
would add that Virgil found the equation of Juno with *furor* in Euripides'
Herakles, where the goddess sends Lyssa, a violent or martial madness,
against the hero. Euripides also has a set of parallels to the Dionysiac mysteries. Lyssa flutes on a φόβος (fear 871) for Iris and Hera; the hero dances to
fluting manias (875–79); and later his mad dance without tympany is contrasted
to Bacchic revels (887 ff). The literal collapse of the palace roof which occurs
also in the *Bacchae* further supports this set of parallels. Virgil's debt to the
Greek dramatist is of course much more far-reaching. Euripides taught him
how to organize a psychological allegory; and the warring deities Venus and
Juno, desire and wrath, go back to oppositions like that of chastity and love,
Artemis and Aphrodite, in the *Hippolytus*. Virgil also borrowed formal devices, like the soliloquy and dialogue scenes with which Juno opens both parts
of the *Aeneid*.

75. I.e., the Juno of Lanuvium and the Etruscan Deity of Falerii. See Thulin,
s.v. "Iuno," *RE* 19 (1917), 1120–21, 1123. For the incident with the Gauls, in
which she saved the capitol from the barbarian, see Livy, *Ab urbe condita*
5.47.1–6. At Argos a shield was given to the victor at the Heraia, and at Samos
she received one-tenth of the booty. See Eitrem, s.v. "Hera," *RE* 15 (1912),
385, 387. Virgil identifies her with Tanit, the goddess of Carthage, whose image
was brought to Rome in the Punic Wars and later returned to the rebuilt city, now
called Colonia Iunonia. See Cumont, s.v. "Caelestis," *RE* 5 (1897), 1248–49.

76. Pygmalion killed Dido's husband in a *furor* of avarice (*Ae.* 1.343–52).

77. Others, of course, had thought of it before. In the fifth century B.C. Metrodorus of Lampsacus had already interpreted allegorically the human as well as divine personages of the *Iliad*. He read the gods medically and the human beings cosmologically (3–4)—*gods:* Demeter = liver, Dionysus = spleen, Apollo = bile; *men:* Agamemnon = ether, Achilles = sun, Hector = moon, Paris = air, Helen =earth. Buffière reconstructs his reasoning (*Mythes,* pp. 126–31). The love making of Helen and Paris shows that the earth is surrounded and interpenetrated by air. Achilles and Hector, the sun and moon, rule the day and night, but the moon pales as the sun rises. Apollo is the bile because it was then assumed that an excess of bile caused illness. The theory is ingenious, but its specifics were ignored by later interpreters. Homeric allegory remained discontinuous, confined to the gods.

78. Heraclitus explains how Apollo the sun causes plague (chaps. 7–8), and Plutarch interprets the metamorphoses at Circe's as the soul after death choosing another shape. See frag. 200 in the Loeb *Moralia,* ed. F. H. Sandbach (London, 1969), 15:366–75.

79. For Tasso, see chap. 4; for Boileau, see *L'art poétique,* 3.160–93.

Chapter Two

1. See Eberhard Müller-Bochat, "Leon Battista Alberti und die Vergil-Deutung der Disputationes Camaldulenses," *Schriften und Vorträge des Petrarca-Instituts Köln* 21 (1968): 19.

2. For the dating of the manuscript, see Roberto Cardini, *La critica del Landino* (Florence, 1973), pp. 19, 89, 159. It was dedicated to Federigo of Urbino, who was not yet duke. That fact plus his defection to the enemies of Florence gives a *terminus ad quem* of 20 July–20 August 1474. Pietro Cennini's transcription of the emended text is dated late spring 1474. For the record of publication, see Thomas H. Stahel, S.J., "Cristoforo Landino's Allegorization of the Aeneid: Books III and IV of the 'Camaldolese Disputations'" (Ph.D. diss., Johns Hopkins University, 1968), p. 2. I will use Stahel's translation of Landino's Virgil commentary, but for the first two books of the *Camaldulensian Dialogues* the translation will be my own. My base text is *Christophori Landini Florentini libri quattuor* (Strassburg, 1508).

3. Landino and Bernardus Silvestris, e.g., both allow for a discontinuous physical allegory in the poem. Bernardus reads Juno's handmaidens at *Ae.* 1.71–72 physically. See *The Commentary on the First Six Books of the "Aeneid" of Vergil Commonly Attributed to Bernardus Silvestris,* ed. J. W. and E. F. Jones (Lincoln, 1977), pp. 5–9. In the proem to bk. 3 Landino acknowledges its presence in the poem, something which the critics have recognized: see Vladimiro Zabughin, *Vergilio nel rinascimento italiano da Dante a Torquato Tasso* (Bologna, 1921–23), 1:198–99; Cardini, *Critica,* pp. 110–12.

4. See Müller-Bochat, p. 14. For these two critics of the *Odyssey,* see Buffière, *Mythes,* pp. 413–59.

5. For additional discussion of the earlier Neoplatonist critics, see Jean Pépin, "Porphyre, exégète d'Homère," *Entretiens sur l'antiquité classique, xii: Porphyre* (Geneva: Foundation Hardt, 1965), and James A Coulter, *The Literary Microcosm* (Leiden, 1976).

6. Petrarch said that Virgil followed Plato without naming him; see Zabughin, 1:198.

7. The New Academy learned its negative epistemology partially from Chrysippus; see Cicero *Academica* 2.24.75, 2.27.87. For this and for the *De natura deorum* I cite from the Loeb text, trans. H. Rackham (Cambridge, Mass., 1933). Similarly, when Antiochus reacted against his predecessors and tried to get back to Plato, he drew heavily on the Stoics. John Dillon (*The Middle Platonists* [Ithaca, N.Y., 1977]) remarks that Antiochus' theory of knowledge or logic was Stoic, which in turn was the basis for his physics and ethics (pp. 64, 68–69). The testimonies to this Stoic influence are Numenius (pp. 52–53), Cicero, and Sextus Empiricus (pp. 58–59).

8. Philip Merlan, *From Platonism to Neoplatonism* (The Hague, 1968), 3d ed. rev. The thesis runs through the whole book, but see esp. pp. 2, 228, and the whole chapter entitled "*Metaphysica generalis* in Aristotle?"

9. See Buffière, *Mythes*, p. 428.

10. Ficino explains in the preface to his translation of Plotinus that he was later converted to Platonism by Cosimo and Gemistus Plethon. See Cardini, *Critica*, p. 26.

11. For the background, see Cardini, *Critica*, pp. 21–22. Landino got the notion from *Tusculan Disputations* 4–5 and *De finibus* 4.

12. He enunciates the first as early as the "Praefatio in Tusculanis" (hereafter cited as "Pref. Tusc."), Cardini, *Critica*, pp. 301–2. Here Landino quotes Apollo's oracle: Know thyself. For the Stoic equivalent, see Cleanthes, frag. 538 in Arnim, vol. 1. Henceforth I will cite Cleanthes, Zeno, and Chrysippus as they are printed in Arnim, by volume and fragment. Cicero supplies Landino with the notion that through virtue man attains the *summum bonum:* see "Pref. Tusc." 295. The Stoic version was a paradox, which Landino cites at *De vera nobilitate*, ed. Manfred Lentzen (Geneva, 1970), p. 56: all wise men are nobles and kings because the mind alone enobles us. Subsequent references will be to this edition, but see Cardini's review in *Critica*, 246–62) where he argues for the edition by Maria Teresa Liaci (Florence, 1970).

13. Cardini (*Critica*, pp. 21–23) cites Landino's early sketch history of philosophy.

14. On reincarnation (12.20, 13.19), on the notion that the body is the source of passion (14.32), on technical terminology. He rejects Virgil's *dolor*, for example, because the word applies principally to the body (14.7.2). See also Pierre Courcelle, "Tradition platonicienne et traditions chrétiennes du corps-prison," *Revue des études latines* 43 (1965): 412.

15. The third theory concerns reincarnation, a doctrine which has a history too complicated for inclusion within this chapter, as the later Platonists reinterpreted it. Plotinus denied that the first soul participated in a downward metamorphosis (1.1.11, 2.9.2). Porphyry would have liked to deny reincarnation and denied that the purged soul returned to a body (see Augustine's remarks in the *City of God* 12.20.3, 13.19). I cite from the *Opera Omnia*, ed. monks of Saint Maur (Paris, 1838), p. 7. Landino rejected metempsychosis, as is evident in his note on Circe (to *Ae.* 7.12: *cantu*), and assumed that Plato's stories of reincarnation were moral allegory. For Landino's commentary on the text of Virgil's poems (1488), I cite from the *Opera* (Venice, 1489).

16. Socrates also implies it at *Phaedrus* 250C, where he compares the relationship of soul and body to that of an oyster and its shell. Courcelle cites from the later Platonists Maximus of Tyre (7.5), where he says that we should rejoice when our body decays because our jail is breaking down ("Tradition," p. 415); *Hermetica* 7 and the *Asclepius*, where νοῦς, which is divine, returns to its divine state from the prison of this world (p. 418); Plotinus 4.8; Porphyry's

Sentences 40 and the *De regressu animae*, via Augustine *Sermo* 241.7.7 in *Pat. lat.* t. 38, p. 1137 (pp. 420–21). He also has an article on the parallel tradition, the metaphor of the body as a tomb; see "Le corps-tombeau," *Revue des études anciennes* 68 (1966): 101–22. It turns on the pun of σῶμα and σῆμα, cited in the *Cratylus* (p. 101) and ascribed to Homer in the Pseudo Plutarch *Life of Homer* (p. 111). In this article Courcelle cites many of the same writers to the same effect, though they use this other metaphor: Plotinus 4.8.1.30, Porphyry *Sentences*, Maximus of Tyre 10.1, *Hermetica* 7.2. See pp. 105–6, 109. He adds Olympiodorus, who in his commentary on the *Gorgias* equated death with this life, where the body is our tomb (p. 111). Macrobius uses the pun at *Commentarii* 1.11.3.

17. See Courcelle, "Tradition," pp. 411–12. Cicero used either *custodia* or *carcer*. Courcelle cites *Pro Scauro* 3.4, *Tusc.* 1.30.74, and the *Dream of Scipio*.

18. For both Plutarch and Servius, see *Aeneis Buch VI*, ed. Eduard Norden (Leipzig, 1903), p. 32. The poisoning of the soul by the body comes through passion. At *Phaedo* 83D Socrates remarks that pleasure and pain nail the soul to the body. For a Neoplatonist this process occurs as the soul descends to the body. Iamblichus in *De mysteriis* cites the *Phaedo* to this effect. See Pierre Courcelle, "Variations sur le 'clou de l'ame,'" in *Mélanges offerts à Mademoiselle Christine Mohrmann* (Utrecht, 1963), p. 38. See also his original article, "La colle et le clou de l'âme dans la tradition néo-platonicienne et chrétienne (*Phédon* 82E; 83D)," *Revue belge de philologie et d'histoire* 36 (1958): 72–95.

19. Porphyry credits Numenius for much of his interpretation in *The Cave of the Nymphs*, and Proclus cites similar extracts in his *Commentary on the "Republic."* Edouard des Places has collected the fragments of Numenius for the Budé series (Paris, 1973).

20. Buffière (*Mythes* p. 460) cites *Gorgias* 493A and *Cratylus* 400B–C. I would add the myth in the *Phaedrus*, which pictures the soul among the stars, its fall, and its imprisonment by the body.

21. Buffière, *Mythes*, pp. 395, 430–31, 438–42. Plotinus did not take the soul's fall literally. He talked rather in terms of radiation. The first soul, like a fire, lights up the lower, which drinks up the light (2.9.3). This is a continual process, because it is the nature of light to shine, of the good to give. The first soul gives what it has from νοῦς, illuminating and impressing the lower (2.3.17).

22. In the Περὶ Στυγός. See Pierre Courcelle, *Les lettres greques en occident* (Paris, 1943), pp. 29–31. He shows that Macrobius borrowed the same classification.

23. Buffière, *Mythes*, p. 412. It is part of his interpretation of the *Iliad* made in his commentary on Plato's *Republic* (1.108.1).

24. See Courcelle, "Interprétations néo-platonisantes de livre VI de l'*Eneide*," in *Recherches sur la tradition platonicienne* (Vandoeuvres: Fondation Hardt pour l'Etude de l'Antiquité classique, 1970).

25. Müller-Bochat, p. 20.

26. Courcelle ("Le corps-tombeau," pp. 110–11) states that Macrobius defined the human body and the material world as the true Dis. He has the descent of the soul through the spheres (1.12), symbolized by the rivers of Hades (1.10–11), and hence the assumption that the body is the prison house of the soul. Landino learned some of this material directly from his teacher Carlo Marsuppini, who he says (in *De anima* 1.37–38) taught about the soul's fall and whose *Consolatoria* to Cosimo and Lorenzo has a Platonizing passage which anticipates Landino's *De anima*. See Cardini, *Critica*, pp. 71, 80. For Landino

he cites from the edition of Book One by Allesandro Pado in *Annali delle Università Toscane*, 34 (1915).

27. See, e.g., his later remarks in "Pref." 1488 Virgil in *Scritti critici e teorici*, ed. Cardini (Rome, 1974), 1.211–25. Politian also showed great respect for Macrobius when he annotated Virgil. See Zabughin, 1:203.

28. To give one checklist, of the Virgils cited by Hermann Hagen in his *Catalogus codicum Bernensium* (Bern, 1875), half contain Servius.

29. To 6.703–24. The *Georgics* reference is to 4.129 ff. Elsewhere Servius remarks that Faunus is a chthonic deity because nothing is lower than earth (to *Ae.* 7.91). Courcelle thinks that Servius found his comparison of the soul to a lamp flame in Porphyry. He shows that the comparison was originally Stoic and Neoplatonic, cites Marcus Aurelius and Plotinus (*Enneads* 1.4.8.2–5), and points out that Ambrose uses the comparison in *De Jacob et vita beata* 1.36 (*Corpus scriptorum ecclesiasticorum latinorum* 32.2, p. 28.2). Plotinus and Ambrose talk of the lamp outside in bad weather. The wind may blow, but the fire does not go out. See Courcelle, "L'âme en cage," in *Parusia*, ed. Kurt Flasch (Frankfurt, 1965), pp. 111–12.

30. In the *Camaldulensian Dialogues* he is concerned only with the Odyssean *Aeneid*, but he provides a capsule analysis of *Ae.* 7–12 at ivV–viV. In his commentary to the text of the poem, he continues his allegory into the later books. He develops Virgil's presentation of *furor* in Juno (her speech at 7.292–93, 310–13, 315, 323), Allecto (7.571), and Amata (7.405). He especially works out Virgil's simile of water boiling in a kettle (7.466). Blood heats from the kindling of the bile, like water from fire. The blood sends a fume up to the head, and right reason loses control. Earlier, Aeneas' arrival in Latium allows Landino to recapitulate his analysis in the *Camaldulensian Dialogues*. Neptune blows the Trojans past Circe; i.e., *ratio superior* preserves men who have purged themselves of perturbations. The Trojans reach their destination (contemplation) at sunrise, when reason dispels the clouds of ignorance (7.26), and the bird song in the Latian wood intimates the harmony which is contemplation and contrasts with the wood of wild beasts, which Aeneas found in bk. 1.

31. Brooks Otis argues that Aeneas confronts his whole past life, when he descends to hell (see pp. 290–97).

32. Landino may refer to the *Academica* at *Camaldulensian Dialogues* CivV, when the second day of discussion is beginning.

33. *Saturnalia*, in *Macrobius*, ed. F. Eyssenhardt (Leipzig, 1868), 6.4.7. The translation is by Percival Vaughan Davies (New York and London, 1969). Servius at *Ae.* 7.9 likewise remarks that we see the movement of the water.

34. Quinn, pp. 386–87. I will cite two more examples. Servius at 7.794 ("totis agmine / . . . campis") says that the poet sets the scene before our eyes, the mass of soldiers following Turnus. Landino observes that the *subitus tremor* of Turnus (7.446) is the rhetorical figure *notatio*, a description given as if we saw the action.

35. Otis, p. 91. Servius' observations may be drawn from the Homeric scholia, as Homer gives Virgil the model for this hyperbole with the formula ὀρώρει δ' οὐρανόθεν νύξ (*Od.* 5.294, 9.69). The E scholiast to *Od.* 5.295 explains that Homer did not believe that the North Pole was lifted above the ground. Night therefore *rises* from the sky, that is, from the horizon, the way

an approaching storm would *appear* to sailors because of the curvature of the earth. For the second passage, the H scholiast (to 9.69) notes that the formula means darkness because the poet never has night come from Olympus (heaven). Homer here calls the storm a λαῖλαψ. Liddell and Scott note that Aristotle (in *De mundo* 395a7) defines this as an *upward* whirling. For the *Odyssey* scholia, I cite from the *Scholia Graeca in Homeri Odysseam,* ed. Dindorf.

36. So the Stophades: "terra...se attolere...visa" (205–6) and "diva Lacina" (552), which Servius glosses, "quia adpropinquantibus aut recedere montes videntur, aut surgere."

37. Who incidentally appears with the formula "se attolere...visus" (*Ae.* 8.32–33).

38. *Ae.* 3.172–76. Heinze (p. 313) says that Aeneas cannot be certain whether it is dream or vision.

39. The death portents for Dido are of this sort; see *Ae.* 4.460–61 and Servius' remarks for 4.456, 461.

40. For Mercury's previous appearance, Servius says that the god takes a human shape so that he can be seen; see his gloss to *Ae.* 4.277.

41. He does allow that the shape might actually be Anchises' *anima,* dropped from heaven. See also his gloss on *Ae.* 2.271, the dream vision of Hector. I would add the *imago* of Sychaeus, which Dido sees in a dream (1.353–54). Servius also denies that the Penates actually appeared to Aeneas (to 3.148. For Thilo it is Daniel–Servius). Cicero uses this class of spectral experience when he alludes to Iliona waking up in Pacuvius' play. See *Academica* 2.27.88. In a related type of incident, also involving a divine communication, Servius denies that the Delian earthquake actually happened. He follows the Stoics and Academics, who deny that anything contrary to nature can really occur (gloss to *Ae.* 3.90).

42. Otis, p. 304; Nohrnberg, *The Analogy of "The Faerie Queene"* (Princeton, N.J., 1976), p. 64, n. 175.

43. Servius to 6.282. Ausonius likewise connected the two. See Courcelle, "Interprétations néo-platonisantes," p. 118. Virgil expresses this equation in characteristic hypothetical fashion. It is the tree of dreams by common opinion, "quam sedem Somnia *vulgo* / vana tenere ferunt." I owe this last observation to my colleague Robert Kaster, of the Classics Department at the University of Chicago.

44. P. 398. Cicero alludes to the same argument at *Tusc.* 1.16.36–37. The practice of inhumation occasioned the mythology of Hades, and the cremated were put there even though they lacked bodies. Eustathius' argument thus rests on positions familiar in educated circles and developed before Virgil wrote the *Aeneid.* For the *Tusculan Disputations* I cite from the Loeb text, trans. J. E. King (Cambridge, Mass., 1945).

45. Chthonic ritual, moreover, was associated with Avernus, the lake where Aeneas experiences the underworld. Cicero quotes an unknown poem and applies it to the place: "Unde animae excitantur obscura umbra aperto ex ostio / altae Acherontis salso sanguine, mortuorum imagines" (*Tusc.* 1.16.37, "Whence, once the blood has been sprinkled, souls, images of the dead, are called forth in the dim shadow from the open mouth of deep Acheron"). More

specifically, Strabo remarks that local tradition located Homer's Nekyia here, that Odysseus came here to consult the dead (*Geography* 5.4.5). For Strabo I cite from the Loeb edition with trans. of H. L. Jones, 8 vols. (New York, 1917–32). The setting and the epic tradition thus both indicated sciomancy, and Virgil's descriptions correspond to what we know of such rituals. For the Homeric identification, Strabo cites Ephorus, a historian of the fourth century B.C., who assumed that the Cimmerians, whom Homer places next to Hades (*Od.* 11.14–15), lived next to Avernus in underground caves and had a chthonic oracle. Avernus is enclosed in steep crags on which once grew an uncut wood of great trees that darkened the lake and created an appropriate atmosphere. Those who sailed there from the sea first sacrific' d to chthonic powers. A spring near the sea was equated with Styx, and its water was left untouched. The nearby thermal waters and the Acherusian Lake were identified with Phlegethon, the river of fire. Ephorus said that the Cimmerians never came above ground except by night; hence Homer's statement that Helios never shines on them. Agrippa destroyed the mystery of the region when he had a canal cut to Cumae, the wood felled, and the area built up with houses. In other places (*Geography* 1.1.10, 2.9, 2.18), Strabo argues that Homer transferred the Cimmerians, who lived in mist and cloud (*Od.* 11.14–15) in the Crimea, over to the Naples area. Eustathius has a more elaborate analysis (to 11.14). The identification with Avernus rests on several arguments. Odysseus sails in a day from Circe's island (Monte Circeo) to the land of the Cimmerians, where he consults the dead. This mountain is halfway between Rome and Naples, a short sail from Lake Avernus. The name Hades is a pun, ὑπὸ γῆν, which becomes ἀϊδήν ("unseen") as the Cimmerians never came above ground by day. For Eustathius I cite from *Eustathii commentarii ad Homeri Odysseam,ad fidem exempli Romani editi* (Leipzig, 1825), 1:397.

46. For an elaboration of this argument, see also *Tusc.* 1.5.10–6.11.

47. Servius glosses this with characteristic skepticism: "deo plena: aut certe *similis* furenti" (to *Ae*. 6.262; italics mine).

48. Servius has an interesting discussion of *umbrae* at *Ae*. 4.654. The term applies specifically to the body, but he says the poets used it loosely. A similar ambiguity attaches to *imago,* which can refer both to a literal image, be it a statue or portrait, or to the ghosts of the departed. Dido says that her imago will go under ground (4.654). For skiagraphy I draw on J. J. Pollitt's glossary in *The Ancient View of Greek Art* (New Haven, 1974), pp. 247–54. The relevant passages for Plato and Aristotle are 1–2 and 4–9. For an analysis of skiagraphy, see Pollitt's discussion of Apollodorus the skiagrapher (pp. 251–52).

49. P. 408. Homer's term for the dead is ψυχή (e.g., *Od.* 11.141, 150, 205, 222), and the commentators translate it with εἴδωλον, ἴνδαλμα (e.g., H to *Od.* 11.139), and similar terms. That is, they would answer Odysseus' question differently from his mother. Asked whether she were an εἴδωλον (213), she replied that she was ψυχή but then compared the ψυχή hovering over the funeral pyre to a dream (222). For the commentators, she is an εἴδωλον.

50. The inconsistencies between Palinurus' account of his death and that given by the narrator reinforce this skepticism.

51. Servius discusses *umbrae* in a number of places, along with *anima* and *simulacra.* See his remarks for *Ae*. 2.641, 772; 4.654.

52. See Courcelle, "L'âme en cage," p. 103. Plutarch in *Quaestiones convivales* 8.2 [718D] remarks that sensible objects then appear to the soul truer than intelligible objects. See Courcelle, "La colle et la clou," p. 85. The other

philosophical schools, of course, had answers for the Academic critique of perception. Lucretius, for example, argues the Epicurean rebuttal in *De rerum natura* 4, where he inverts the set of assumptions behind the debate (469 ff.). The senses are the criteria of truth, and each has its own function and equal trust. Right reason cannot be based on false sensation, and error therefore resides in the mind rather than in the body. In dreams, e.g., the mind lacks a truth criterion and so imagines ghosts and monsters (749 ff.). He lists all the borderline cases cited by the New Academy (386 ff., 426 ff.): to sailors, the boat seems stationary and other objects seem to move; square towers seen at a distance seem round (353 ff.); etc. He does not, however, explain the phenomena but assumes his general position. In *all* cases the mind misjudges what the body perceives.

53. For Plotinus the first soul, our real self, does not sense objects. It endows a qualified body with life, and this other creature perceives. The first soul receives noetic impressions from the sensations of the composite being (1.1.7), and διάνοια judges sense impressions, contemplating the forms (1.1.9). Sensation then is an εἴδωλον of the soul's perception.

54. See P. O. Kristeller, *The Philosophy of Marsilio Ficino*, trans. Virginia Conant (New York, 1943), pp. 208–9. For Ficino the soul has little forms which correspond to objective species (pp. 236–37).

55. Not that there were no exceptions in so long a history. I cite from Dillon. Antiochus of Ascalon, the founder of the "Old" Academy, insisted with Aristotle on the union of body and soul and included bodily goods in his definition of happiness (pp. 70–73). Antiochus studied under Philo, was a friend of Cicero and Lucullus (pp. 53–54), and taught Varro (p. 62). He seems to have rejected the incorporeal (p. 83) and was later called a crypto-Stoic by Numenius (pp. 52–53).

56. In *Tusc*. 1. Cicero adduces the Platonic arguments for the immortality of the soul, arguing that our minds and the gods are of the same substance (26–27.65–67) and that the meaning of Apollo's oracle, "Know thyself," is that the way to know soul is by soul (22.51–53). Cicero uses the term *animus*, which Landino employs in its narrower sense as mind. See also Dillon, pp. 96–100.

57. Augustine and Claudianus Mamertus preserve this fragment from Porphyry's *De regressu* and Mamertus makes the additional gloss in his *De statu animae*. See the *Opera*, ed. August Engelbrecht (Vienna, 1885), 2.7, p. 128. Augustine returns to this epigram again and again, when he argues with the Platonists in *The City of God*. At 12.26 he remarks sarcastically that such an idea, which presupposes that the lesser gods made our bodies, makes the gods our jailers. Porphyry's treatise does not survive, but from citations Courcelle concludes that there was much about the *Phaedo* in it. See Courcelle, *Lettres grecques*, pp. 229, 28. In "Tradition," pp. 420–21, Courcelle cites a remark from one of Augustine's sermons which makes Porphyry's meaning even more explicit: "Porphyrius dixit, scripsit: 'Corpus est omne fugiendum.' 'Omne' dixit, quasi omne corpus *vinculum* aerumnosum sit animae" (*Sermo* 241.7.7, *Pat. Lat.* t. 38, p. 1137). For a collection of the fragments, see Joseph Bidez, ed., *Vie de Porphyre, le philosophe néoplatonicien, avec les fragments des traités* Περὶ ἀγαλμάτων *et* "*De regressu animae*" (Hildesheim, 1964).

58. For the whole argument, see BviR–V. Landino maintained this notion consistently in his other writings. He reads the first canto of the *Divina commedia* as the opposition of mind and body, where the hero's mind awakes and realizes that it has lost the way, oppressed by ignorance and vices, well sym-

bolized by the *selva* or *hyle:* "perché nettemente Platone come chiama Iddio cagione di tutti i beni, così per l'opposito chiama la selva cioè il nostro terrestre carcere cagione di tutti i mali." Tasso underlined this passage in his edition. See *Dante con lespositione di Christoforo Landino et di Allessandro Vellutello* (Venice, 1564), ivB. And here again the Stoics and Platonists agree. Cleanthes said that man was soul alone (Arnim, 1:538).

59. See Landino's very Scholastic discussion of mental movements as sequential, orbicular, and oblique BiR–V).

60. They were the only sect which could not fit his syncretic Platonism. Cardini shows that through his work on Cicero, Landino concluded that the Stoics, Academics, and Peripatetics agreed on man's moral ends and that they derived this understanding from Socrates, an idea he presents on the second day of the *Camaldulensian Dialogues* (CivV–DiiiV). That is, the ethical-moral system of Aristotle and Zeno had an essentially Platonic matrix, something Landino indicates in his sketch history of philosophy (1460); see *Critica* 21–22.

61. In 1.1.10 Plotinus expresses the same concept in more philosophical terms. Virtue is double, according to the double definition of man as first soul and as synthetic being (first soul, psychic εἴδωλον, and body). The separable or first soul has virtues proper to thought, while the other virtues come by training and custom and apply to the synthetic being, in which vicious passions exist. Landino discusses politics in *De vera nobilitate*. Like other Platonists, he was much committed to political questions, and I have included a brief summary of his ideas in the appendix. We should remember that the student and listener in the *Camaldulensian Dialogues* is the future *princeps* of Florence, whom Landino will identify with the philosopher-king in *De vera nobilitate* 104. Here, however, he does not discuss politics for two reasons. Landino is concerned with the inner sense of the *Aeneid*, while he considers politics part of its literal level. In Pref. 1488, *Ae.* 232, in *Scritti critici e teorici*, vol. 1, he says that the double sense of the *Aeneid* serves the two kinds of men, the contemplative and the active. The allegorical instructs the contemplative, and the literal concerns the active life and moves and instructs its audience in political virtue. Second, here and in *De vera nobilitate*, he argues by ideal categories. There he presents the best merchant, the best priest, the best in each of the social categories; see, e.g., his discussion of merchants and money lenders at 67–69. Here he is portraying the ideal among the ideals, the philosophic contemplative. Accordingly, he must eliminate all the other alternatives. The philosopher can rule a state, for example, but government does not form a necessary part of his definition. Landino therefore rejects politics in the *Camaldulensian Dialogues*.

62. "To prune" is not an analogy but the original meaning. Virgil so uses it at *Georgics* 2.407. I am indebted to Robert Kaster for this note.

63. Plotinus himself did not use the dialogue form, but he preserves its purpose. Often he seems to think out loud. He will survey various opinions, as at 1.1.1–5, or ask a series of questions which together make an analysis, as in his attack on astrology (2.3.2–4). He sometimes concludes hypothetically (1.1) or will bring in an exegesis of a poetic scene or myth. He concludes 1.1, e.g., with a discussion of Heracles in Hades (1.1.12). Plato invented his own myths, which often conclude his dialogues, as in the *Republic* and the *Phaedo*. The Florentines preferred the Plotinian ending. Ficino concludes the *Banquet* with an analysis of Guido Cavalcanti's philosophical *canzone*, "Donna mi prega,"

and Landino ends the *Camaldulensian Dialogues* with the *Aeneid* and the *De vera nobilitate* with the Heracles myth.

64. Cicero reiterates this point frequently in the *Tusculan Disputations*. He cannot speak with the certainty of the Pythian Apollo but, as a *homunculus*, must follow the more probable of many conjectures (1.9.17). The philosopher can decide not what is true but the *verisimilar* (1.11.23), and his model is the Socrates of the *Apology*, who even at the prospect of death refuses to affirm (1.41.99). It is the charitable mode. As the philosopher follows the more probable, he is willing to refute and to be refuted (2.2.5).

65. Critics of Virgil traditionally read the *bivium* to Tartarus and Elysium as the Pythagorean Y. See Courcelle, "Interpretations néo-platonisantes," p. 100.

66. See GviR, where Helenus tells Aeneas that he is on the second level.

67. Landino derived this set of distinctions from Macrobius, who himself credited Plotinus with the schema The Alexandrian had made a more flexible classification of the cardinal virtues, as Plato with a single set of definitions had ruled politicians out of virtue (*Commentarii in somnium Scipionis* 1.8.5–13). Macrobius presents a fourfold hierarchy, of which the fourth is exemplary and limited to the divine mind. So for human beings the classification is the same as that of Landino: political, purgatory, and contemplative. For the second Macrobius merely indicates that this category corresponds to Plato's philosophical virtues, so Landino would have had to look them up in the *Republic*. Courcelle (*Lettres grecques*, p. 22) says that Macrobius in the *Saturnalia* actually found his explanation of the virtues in the *Sententiae* of Porphyry, itself a résumé of Plotinus' teachings. Landino uses a tripartite dialectic in other areas, important and unimportant. Here are three examples:

Antique Theology (HiiiR)		Intellection (IivR–V)		The Three Mouths of Cerberus (LiiR)
(type)	(purpose)			
civic	ethical reform	intelligentia	divine union	food
natural	education	intellectus	superior reason	drink
fabulous	entertainment	ratio	inferior reason (sense directed)	sleep

This triple classification runs through all of Landino's works. So in the Dante commentary, the *Inferno* is political virtue; the *Purgatorio* the purgative; and the *Paradiso* the virtues of a soul already purged. Again, Ficino had used the schema earlier, in his sermon "De laboribus ac aerumnis D. Pauli Apostoli." See Lentzen's remarks in his edition of *De vera nobilitate*, pp. 15–17.

68. "Pref. Tusc." 294–95, Cardini, *Critica,* and also "Pref. Virgil" (1462), also in *Scritti critici teorici,* p. 28.

69. Merlan, p. 185.

70. Murrin, *The Veil of Allegory,* pp. 46–47.

71. The ladder reappears immediately afterward in the proem to Landino's translation of Pliny's *Natural History*. The food of the mind is cognition, and

the best cognition is true science of things. The mind moves from the visible to the invisible, like going up the stories in a tower. Landino illustrates the notion of the ladder by the metaphor we most often use to describe allegory: the ascending stories in a tower. See Cardini, *Critica*, pp. 155–56, where he quotes the passage.

72. See Stahel, p. 28. For a fuller discussion of Camaldoli and its setting, see Tudor Edwards, *Worlds Apart* (New York, 1958), pp. 100–106.

73. I cite from *Fulgentius*, ed. R. Helm (Stuttgart, repr. 1970). The translation is by Leslie George Whitbread in *Fulgentius the Mythographer* (Columbus, Ohio, 1971), p. 64.

74. I cite from *La Règle de Saint Benoît*, ed. Vogüé and Neufville (Paris, 1972), vol. 1.

Chapter Three

I have quoted from standard translations where I could and have so noted them in the footnotes. I have silently emended these passages where the argument required greater specificity or, as in the case of Marco Polo, where the English version was not based on the Italian. Where no translator is cited, the English version is my own, as, e.g., in most of the extracts from Boiardo.

1. Aquinas *Summa contra Gentiles* 2.14.921, quoted from the revised Leonine text. See *Liber de veritate catholicae fidei contra errores infidelium*, rev. C. Pera, P. Marc, and P. Caramello (Rome, 1961), vol. 2.

2. To cite examples, Ettore Paratore, "L'*Orlando innamorato* e l'*Eneide*," in *Il Boiardo e la critica contemporanea*, ed. Giuseppe Anceschi (Florence, 1970), pp. 347–75 (Anceschi edited the papers given at the Boiardo congress at Scandiano in 1969, and henceforth I will cite the volume as Anceschi). Paratore argues that in his epic Boiardo drew mostly on the Iliadic *Aeneid* for military details and genealogies. Giovanni Ponte remarks that Virgil was the great model for Boiardo's Latin pastorals; see *La personalità e l'opera del Boiardo* (Genoa, 1972), p. 37. In the Latin eclogues Giulio Reichenbach noted the Virgilian imitations in 3, 4, and 7 and argued that the mixture of political and recreational-amatory subjects was itself Virgilian: see *Matteo Maria Boiardo* (Bologna, 1929), pp. 24, 28, 32. I would add that the structuring of the whole resembles that of Virgil. Eclogues 1, 4, and 9 are political; 2–3 and 7–8, recreational. The changes are at 5–6 and 10; here too, though the subject matter differs, the form in 5–6 is Virgilian: paired songs in 5 and mythic history in 6. Boiardo writes more independently in the later Italian pastorals but still keeps the Virgilian model alive. The oracular tenth eclogue recalls Virgil's fourth; the ninth depends on both the Corydon and the eighth eclogue; and Boiardo regularly frames his poems with dawn and sunset. The facts of Virgilian influence are undeniable. For the Italian eclogues and for the *Amorum Libri* I cite from the *Opere volgari*, ed. Pier Vicenzo Mengaldo (Bari, 1962).

3. See Ponte, *La personalità*, p. 37.

4. In a brilliant article, Antonia Benvenuti connects the *Amorum libri* both to the International Gothic style of painting in the late Quattrocento and to the earlier troubador poetry which the poet could have found in the Este library. That is, his poetry is medieval and French, not classicizing and Italian. See "Tradizioni letterarie e gusto tardogotico nel canzoniere di M. M. Boiardo," *Giornale storico della letteratura italiana* 137 (1960): 533–92.

5. See *De' romanzi delle comedie e delle tragedie,* ed. Giulio Antimaco (Milan, 1864), vol. 52 in the Biblioteca rara, pp. 80–82. As the Italian is not readily available, the reader might consult the English translation by Snuggs in Cinthio, pp. 60–61. For an example of this difficulty, consider the comic scene in the *Innamorato* where an old man gives a lecture on patience to a chained Orlando at 1.6.17–22. The friar comforts the paladin with a martyrology, but Orlando replies that he needs help, not comfort, and he is correct, as there is a cyclops coming around the corner. All citations from the *Innamorato* are from Luigi Garbato's edition, 4 vols, (Milan, 1970).

6. Normally the comparison with dreams indicated a negative response to the *Innamorato.* Angelandrea Zottoli's classic essay for his edition of the *Opere* (Milan, 1936), vol. 1, is the best modern example; see esp. pp. xxiii–xxv. He argues that Boiardo molded the fantasies of his aristocratic audience and hence lacked depth. Carlo Dionisotti cites various negative judgments from the Renaissance; see "Fortuna e sfortuna del Boiardo nel cinquecento," in Anceschi, pp. 221–41. In the Renaissance the charge applied to a whole class of fiction which included Arthurian romance and the popular tales of Charlemagne's knights. For such critics this type of fiction lacked truth, did not present a historical reality, and hence could be dismissed as empty imaginings. Domenico de Robertis defends the dream, seeing in it a manifestation of the creative imagination; see "Esperienze di un lettore dell'*Innamorato,*" in Anceschi, pp. 197–220.

7. See Dionisotti, p. 226, whose argument Ponte repeats in *La personalità,* p. 79. The *Teseida* with dei Bassi's commentary was printed at Ferrara in 1475 and may have suggested to Boiardo the notion of a romance in ottava rima with two lovers battling over a woman.

8. It was twice inserted into the 1467 booklist, and there are two notices that Ercole kept it in his study. See Giulio Bertoni, *La biblioteca estense e la coltura ferrarese* (Turin, 1903), pp. 222, 262.

9. Giulio Reichenbach proved this point in the first chapter of his *"L'Orlando innamorato" di M. M. Boiardo* (Florence, 1936). It has become a commonplace among critics.

10. The Falerina episode extends from 2.3.48 to 2.5.24. There are also two descriptions of the garden, by Fiordelisa at 1.17.38–46 and by Angelica at 1.28.28–33. For Alcina, see 2.13.59–60; and for Morgana's initial plot, 2.7.43–45, the whole business with Manodante being her second. For Marfisa's action, see 1.19.35–54, 20.37–41.

11. If we take the hyperboles seriously, 2–3 million died at Albracca, and Gradasso burned the kingdom of Granada, the cities of Seville and Valencia; captured Gibraltar, Seville, and Toledo; and ruined Valencia and Aragon; see 1.4.24; 1.3.4.8–9. For Reichenbach, see his "Matteo Mario Boiardo," in *Letteratura italiana: i minori* (Milan, 1961), pp. 682–83.

12. In his *rifacimento* Berni softens Boiardo's line. "Questo è un spirto d'abisso veramente" becomes "Un Diavol veramente esser si crede." For Berni I have used the 1542 edition (Milan).

13. We never know what happens to these prisoners because Orlando and Falerina, journeying to the Old Man's Castle, come to Morgana's lake first. Orlando, struggling with the giant, disappears under the water, and Falerina runs away in terror.

14. See his speeches at the Second War Council, 2.3.25–33.

15. See Bertoni, pp. 192–95. This emphasis on fortune and astrology has parallels in the tarot game, for which Boiardo composed verses. In one version the game begins by chance, and Fortune was included among the face cards and illustrated politically with Pompey on the wheel. Zottoli prints the verses, together with the commentary by Pier Antonio Viti, at the end of vol. 2 of the *Opere*.

16. See the allegories prefixed to 2.3 and 2.4. The second point he makes into a general moral reflection of an optimistic sort: "Ne mostra che doviamo sempre sperar bene, percio che spesso quando manco è aspettato allora ne aviene, liberandone di molte gravi calamità." He prints, of course, Domenichi's *rifacimento* of the *Innamorato* (Venice, 1576).

17. See 1.17.38–46. "Tramontana" indicated the north.

18. Berni's allegory is included by Domenichi in his own *rifacimento* of 1545 and so would have formed part of the text read by anyone in the late Renaissance. The Vatican Library has seven editions for this text between 1545 and 1576, and after a comparison of all three versions, I can say that Domenichi keeps Boiardo's allegory intact (at least in this episode). This fact suggests that, as texts of the *Innamorato* were numerous in the period, while a Spenser or a Milton might get a distorted image of Boiardo's language, he would have had his allegory properly presented. Berni himself, who ruins much of the finer allegorical details in his version, was not reprinted after 1545. I will note, as I proceed, where he distorts Boiardo's symbolism.

19. Boccaccio so defines Dido: "Et sic intendit pro Dydone concupiscibilem et attractivam potentiam" and places it among the various passions to which human fragility is subject and which he considers to be Virgil's theme. See *Genealogie deorum gentilium* (henceforth cited as *GDG*), ed. Vincenzo Romano (Bari, 1951), 14.13, p. 723. Bks. 1–8 are in vol. 1, 9–15 in vol. 2.

20. "Ad intelligenzia della qual cosa è da sapere che in ciascuno uomo sono due principali appetiti, de' quali l'uno si chiama appetito concupiscibile, per lo quale l'uomo disidera e si rallegra d'avere le cose che, secondo il suo giudicio, o ragionevole o corrotto ch'egli sia, sono dilettevoli e piacevoli; l'altro si chiama appetito irascibile, per lo quale l'uomo si turba o che gli sieno tolte o impedite le cose dilettevoli, o perché quelle avere non si possano." See *Tutte le opere*, ed. Vittore Branca (Verona, 1964), 2:454. Alberto Limentani edited the *Teseida*, and the note is to 7.30.

21. See Andrea di Tommaso, *Structure and Ideology in Boiardo's "Orlando innamorato"* (Chapel Hill, N.C., 1972), p. 47. He gets the definition of ire from Aristotle.

22. See Bertoni, pp. 194–95, where in a footnote he quotes verses from the *Sphera*, a manuscript in the Este library. Likewise recall the narrator's opening remarks as well as Orlando's constant choice of Angelica over his duties in France.

23. *Summa contra Gentiles* 2.47.1237. See also his conclusion at 2.60.1374.

24. Both terms are used. See, e.g., Iroldo's discourse at 1.17.9 and 14.

25. Berni unfortunately drops this point in his version!

26. All translations from the *Teseida* are by Bernadette Marie McCoy in *The Book of Theseus* (New York, 1974).

27. *Teseida*, ed. Limentani, pp. 462–72. Pinturicchio put similar animals in the garden where the elders tempt Susanna. The picture is in the Sala dei Santi

of the Apartamento Borgia in the Vatican. Antonia Benvenuti remarks that such "gothic" scenes, though allegorical, present natural detail with minute realism (p. 557).

28. See *Amorum libri* 82, 130, 179.

29. For the Lusignans, see Jean D'Arras, *Melusine*, ed. M. Ch. Brunet (1854; reprint ed. Nendeln, Liechtenstein, 1972), pp. 9–11, 36–65, 332–35, 352–60. For the Angevins, see Amy Kelly, *Eleanor of Aquitaine and the Four Kings* (New York, 1950), p. 160.

30. The difference, however, is not clear. Ariosto classes Falerina with the fays in the *Cinque canti;* and in Bonelli's 1576 edition of the *Innamorato*, she is a *fata* in the verse argument for 2.5.

31. Here is Berni:

> Et quella Fauna, e quell'altra Serena,
> Mille altri van piacer, ch'alle brigate
> Mostran bel viso, e hanno poi la coda
> Di velen pieno, e di puzza, e di broda.

[2.5.5]

For Boccaccio's analysis, see *GDG* 7.20.

32. Berni had already identified her temptation with gluttony (2.5.5).

33. It likewise appears in 43, the *Somnium.*

34. See also 94 (Tetrasticus Cantus). In *Pastorali* 3 it is the lady's hair, the "lacio d'oro," which binds the lover Dafnide. In the same eclogue Dafnide talks of his love as a white deer which he has lost. In the *Innamorato* Morgana tries to decoy Orlando with a white stag (1.25.1–15).

35. Reichenbach long ago noted that reality normally produced comic scenes in the *Innamorato.* See his *"Orlando innamorato,"* pp. 237–42. For Boiardo's financial and familial battles, see Zottoli, 1:xii–xiii.

36. In his article on Juno (*GDG* 9.1, p. 440), Boccaccio basically expands Fulgentius' analysis. See *Mitologiae* 2.1: *De Iunone,* in the *Opera,* ed. Rudolf Helm (Stuttgart, repr. 1970). For the peacock woman Ponte cites a passage from the elder Pliny (*Naturalis historia* 10.2), which Boiardo incorporated in his Ricobaldo. In my opinion the parallel is not very close. See *La personalità,* p. 92.

37. See his gloss to *Ae.* 3.218.

38. See *Mitologiae* 1.9.

39. In *Tractatus et opuscula,* ed. J. Leclerq and M. M. Rochais (Rome, 1963), vol. 3. Bernard is one of the few theologians whose work is kept in the Este library, though I could not determine whether they have his *De gradibus.*

40. Fulgentius and Boccaccio give these readings. See *GDG* 9.1. and *Mitologiae* 2.1: *De Iunone.*

41. In *GDG* 4.30 he turns the apples of the Hesperides into rich herds of sheep, plundered by Hercules. Again the medium is the pun ("mēlon"): "nam oves a Grecis male seu mala dicuntur."

42. Her lover is Ord*auro,* she says that wisdom is worthless without money (1.22.19), and her brother was originally named Brama*doro.*

43. Gloss to *Ae.* 3.218.

44. Likewise in *Teseida* 7.33 the *Ire* are "rosse come foco." The convention is as old as *Il.* 1.103–4, where the eyes of an enraged Agamemnon seem to flash fire.

45. Note to *Teseida* 7.30, "ne' campi trazii." I cite from University of Chicago MS 541V and give the line number in Boccaccio, as pagination differs in the various manuscripts and printed texts of dei Bassi's commentary.

46. Dei Bassi, of course, does not say that *all* sanguine and choleric types come from the north. Orlando grew up in Italy, and Rodamonte is the other warrior prone to wrath.

47. In the long note to *Teseida* 7.30, p. 454.

48. Note to 7.30, "ne' campi trazii."

49. Herodotus associated such stories mostly with the Persians, while cannibalism was often attributed to the Tatars. See Denis Sinor, "Le Mongol vu par l'occident," *1274, année charnière: mutations et continuités* (Paris, 1977), p. 61.

50. See the remark on *ire rosse* and *discordia* in the note to 7.30: "guazzosi verni," and likewise the initial sequence outlined for 7.30: "ne' campi trazii."

51. Boccaccio used Ovid and Macrobius here. See *GDG* 4.68, pp. 222–26.

52. See his speech at the Second War Council (2.3.20–24). At Monaco Rinaldo dismounts to fight him because Rodamonte tries to kill Baiardo; see 2.14.46–51 for the interchange. Rodamonte there is "la anima di foco . . . E per grande ira non trovava loco" (46).

53. See *Argonautica* 3.1278–1407 for the bulls and for the armed men. For the serpent, see 2.1208–10; and for the capture of the fleece, 4.123–82.

54. *Metamorphoses* 3.32. The adjective may mean that the serpent belonged to Mars or simply that it was warlike, or (probably) both. Its children, the armed men, die with a similar verbal ambiguity "suoque / Marte cadunt subiti per mutua vulnera fratres" (122–23).

55. *GDG* 2.63. The Dorians originally lived in the area before the conquest of the Peloponnesus, so the original Spartans could have been neighbors.

56. "Un furioso toro si vede, che pericolo significa, percioché egli con le cornua ferisce non vedendo il modo, il che al feritore e periculosissimo." This is printed at the end of Zottoli's edition of the *Opere*, vol. 2.

57. Reichenbach, "Boiardo," p. 668.

58. See Giovanni Paccagnini, *Pisanello e il ciclo cavalleresco di Mantova* (Venice, 1972), p. 51. The extract is from a letter to his wife Barbara, written in 1453. It was at Mantua that Pisanello did *sinopie* for an Arthurian cycle, which is the topic of Paccagnini's study. Here is the passage: "E qui lo facto d'arme durò circha doe hore molto stricto et asparo, et à sta morte persone e cavali asay de l'una parte e de l'altra, et fu de li più belli facti d'arme che may vedessemo, et era in bel vedere, che li non era arbore, frate ne' fosse che ci desse impazo. . . ."

59. *Il libro di Marco Polo detto Milione*, ed. Daniele Ponchiroli (Turin, 1954), chap. 56, p. 59; chap. 54, p. 58; chap. 65, pp. 76–77. All future references will be to this edition, which is of the "ottimo," a medieval Tuscan translation of the French original. The parallels are not so surprising when we remember that the romancer Rusticiano of Pisa wrote the book from Marco Polo's dictation. For the English translation I have used that of Sir Henry Yule, which keeps to the phrasing of the original. This is of course based on the French text, so I have brought it closer to the Italian and modernized it where necessary. See *The Book of Ser Marco Polo* (London, 1903), vol. 1.

60. See "Storicità e immaginosità del Boiardo nella versione di Ricobaldo Ferrarese," in *La rassegna della letteratura italiana* (Florence, 1972), pp.

203–13. I accept Ponte's thesis. By Occam's razor, we should assume that Boiardo did his own interpolating and adding, rather than posit a lost source. For the *Istoria imperiale* or *Chronicon Romanorum imperatorum*, see the text edited by L. A. Muratori in *Rerum Italicarum scriptores* (Milan, 1726), 9:405, henceforth cited as *Istoria*.

61. See his remarks and footnotes in "*L'Orlando innamorato* nella civiltà letteraria del quattrocento," in Anceschi, pp. 418–19. The article has since been reprinted as chap. 5 of *La personalità*. He also suggests Balkh for Albracca, but this identification would not work, since Bactra-Balkh is Origille's town (1.29.6) and thus has a different history. See *La personalità*. For the capture of Bukhara, Samarkand, and Urgench, see W. Barthold, *Turkestan Down to the Mongol Invasion,* 2d ed. (London, 1928). pp. 409–14, 433–37.

62. Marfisa wants to conquer the world, and Agramante's remote ancestors won victories by courtesy (2.1.11). Here is the entire passage: "Costui fue uomo di grande valenza e di senno e di prodezza; e sí vi dico che, quando costui fu chiamato re, tutti gli Tartari, quanti n'erano al mondo, che per quelle contrade erano, si vennoro a lui a tennolo per signore. E questo Cinghys Cane tenea la signoria bene e francamente; e quivi venne tanta moltitudine di Tarteri, che non si potrebbe credere. Quando Cinghys si vidde cotanta gente, apparecchiossi con sua gente per andare a conquistare altre terre. E sí vi dico ch'egli conquistò in ben poco di tempo otto provincie. E non faceva male cui egli pigliava, né no' rubavano, ma menavaglisi dietro per conquistare l'altre contrade; e cosí conquistò molta gente. E tutta gente andava volentieri dietro a questo signore, veggendo la sua bontà. Quando Cinghys si vidde tanta gente, disse che voleva conquistare tutto il mondo. Allora mandò suoi messaggi al Presto Giovanni, e ciò fu nel 1200 anni, e mandògli a dire che voleva sua figliuola per moglie . . . [Prester John refuses with insults].

"Quando Cingys Cane udío la grande villania che 'l Presto Giovanni gli aveva mandato a dire, enfiò sí forte, che per poco, che non gli crepò lo cuore in corpo, percioch'egli era uomo molto signorevole. E disse che conviene che cara gli costi la villania che gli mandò a dire, e ch'egli gli farebbe sapere s'egli era suo servo. Allora Cinghys fece il maggiore isforzo che mai fosse fatto; e mandò a dire al Presto Giovanni ch'egli si difendesse" (*Il milione* 53–54).

"When Chinghis Kaan heard the brutal message that Prester John had sent him, such rage seized him that his heart came nigh to bursting within him, for he was a man of a very lofty spirit. At last he spoke, and that so loud that all who were present could hear him: 'Never more might he be prince if he took not revenge for the brutal message of Prester John, and such revenge that insult never in this world was so dearly paid for. And before long Prester John should know whether he were his serf or no!'

"So then he mustered all his forces, and levied such a host as never before was seen or heard of, sending word to Prester John to be on his defence" (1.47–48).

63. That is, the lands of the so-called Golden Horde rather than the larger empire of the thirteenth century. The Golden Horde controlled Urgench till 1379. I am indebted for this point to John Woods of the History and Near Eastern Languages and Literature departments at the University of Chicago. Boiardo adds Scandinavia. For the map, see Francesco L. Pullé, "La cartografia antica dell'India," *Studi italiani di filologia indo-iranica* (Florence, 1905), 5:125. He cites a *postilla* mentioned by Bertoni (*Biblioteca*, p. 261),

which would date the map at 1488 and put it in the duke's study.

64. 1.1.26. Cathay is described both as a city and as a district; see 1.1.52–53 and 1.10.14. Marco Polo talks of it as a district in north China (he does not equate the two). See, e.g., chaps. 89–90. We know that Albracca is a day's journey *west* of this area (1.6.42). On Marino Sanuto's world map (ca. 1306–21), Cathay is on the Silk Route east of Hyrcania (northern Iran) and somewhat north of a squashed Caspian. For a reproduction, see C. Raymond Beazley, *The Dawn of Modern Geography* (Oxford, 1906), 3:520–21. This location would explain their description in Ricobaldo as long-haired warriors who come from Scythia and ride great horses; see *Istoria,* p. 409. For a discussion of the Silk Route in this area, see Giorgio Pullé's introduction to his translation of Friar Giovanni da Pian del Carpine's *Viaggio a'Tartari* (Milan, 1929), pp. 183–213 (henceforth cited as *Viaggio*).

65. By Ariosto's time the area was already becoming an empty space on the map. Girolamo da Verrazzano's *Grande planisfero* (1529) carefully shows the new Spanish and Portuguese discoveries but moves the Caspian far to the east and places Bactriana *north* of Sogdiana. The map is on display in the Vatican Library.

66. Orlando and Astolfo both go via the Tana and Circassia to Orcagna and Albracca. In Circassia Astolfo meets Sacripante, who is assembling his army for the war, while Orlando's first duel is with a giant servant of the Circassian monarch (1.5.64). Rinaldo on his return also passes through southern Russia (2.14.9–10). The limits of Circassia are defined in the catalog of Sacripante's forces at 1.10.37–41, and it is on the border of his realm (Media) that Falerina's agent arrests Angelica. This location is confirmed by the itinerary of Orlando and Angelica when they return west (2.19.51–52). Leaving Armenia on the right, they travel through Iran and Mesopotamia.

67. Iroldo journeyed twenty days from Babylon before he was arrested in Orcagna (1.17.2); and Orlando, when Origille steals his horse at Ninus' tomb, is three days away from Nineveh (1.29.53). Both towns appear on Ercole's *mappamondo*. See Pullé, "Cartografia," pp. 126–27.

68. The Aral was unknown to both classical geographers and contemporary mapmakers. See Guy Le Strange, *The Lands of the Eastern Caliphate* (Cambridge, 1905), pp. 455–57. The Oxus flowed into the Caspian during classical times; hence the Greeks did not know of the Aral. In the early Middle Ages and since the sixteenth century, it has flowed into the Aral. Ercole's *mappamondo* shows the Oxus flowing into the Caspian. See Pullé, "Cartografia," p. 128. Morgana has her lake near a navigable sea and plots with Manodante, whose city of Damogir (or Damosyr) is fifteen days' sail *northeast* (2.10.50–51, 2.13.30). These directions could not apply to the Black Sea but work reasonably well with the Caspian. "Damo-syr" suggests a location on the Jaxartes or Syr Darya (in Persian, the River Syr). For these names, see Le Strange, pp. 434, 476. Ellsworth Huntington (*The Pulse of Asia* [Boston, 1907], pp. 342–47) speculates that the Caspian was higher and larger in the later Middle Ages and may have included the Aral. Its southern shore would have been longer: hence its squashed appearance on the maps. It was after the Mongol siege of Urgench (1221) that the Oxus was diverted to the Caspian. See Barthold, *Turkestan,* pp. 436–37, and "K Istorii Orosheniya Turkistana," *Sochineniya* 3(1965): 97–233. For the classical period see also Huntington, pp. 330–41.

69. See chap. 5 below.

70. Haggard's heroes wandered about in the African inter;or; later, when everything in Africa was known, H. P. Lovecraft, Talbot Munday, and James Hilton turned to Antarctica and Tibet. See also C. S. Lewis' remarks in *Of Other Worlds* (London, 1966), pp. 68–69.

71. E esta huerta avia una portada muy grande e alta e fermosa e fecha de ladrillo, labrada de azulejos e de azul e de oro amuchas maneras ... e esta huerta es grande mucho, e enella avia muchos arboles frutals e de otros que fazian Sonbra ... e las paredes del estavan guarnidas de unos paramentos de paño de seda de color Rosado; e estos paramentos estavan guarnidos de chapas de plata sobre doradas, e enllas engastonadas esmeraldas e aljofar e otras piedras, bien puesto ... e en medio desta casa, antla puerta, estavan dos mesas de oro sobre quatro pies ... enllas estavan syete Redomas de oro; e las dos dellas guarnidas de aljofar bien grueso e de esmeraldas e turqueas, e enllas, de partes de fuera, estavan engastonadas, e cada una dellas avia e tenia çerca dela boca un balax; E otrosy avia seys taças de oro Redondas; e la una dllas estava guarnida de partes de fuera de aljofar bien grueso, Redondo e claro; e en medio avia un balax enfiesto tan ancho commo dos dedos e de buen color proprio (*Embajada,* pp. 162–64).

"Where before its entrance gate was a high portal very finely built of brick ornamented with tiles wrought variously in gold and blue.... The garden where this festival took place is very large and it is planted with many fruit-bearing trees with others that are to give shade.... The walls here about were all hidden being covered by silk hangings of a rose coloured stuff, that was ornamented with spangles of silver plate gilt, each spangle set with an emerald or pearl or other precious stone....

"In the center of the palace before the doorway to the alcoves were placed two tables made of gold, standing each on four legs, and the table top and the legs were all made in one piece of metal.... On the one table were set seven golden flasks, and two of them were ornamented outside with great pearls and emeralds and turquoises, set in the metal, while at the mouth there was a balas ruby. Beside these seven flasks there were standing six cups of gold circular in shape, and one of them had set within the rim a very big round pearl of fine orient, while at the centre point of the cup was encrusted a balas ruby of beautiful color that measured across two finger breadths." I cite from the *Embajada a Tamorlán,* ed. Francisco López Estrada (Madrid, 1943). The translation is by Guy Le Strange, *Embassy to Tamerlane* (London, 1928), pp. 227–28. Even before the Italians knew of Tamerlane's empire, Boccaccio could say of Tatary, "Estimano essere adunate le maggiore ricchezze e moltitudine di tesori, che oggi in alcuna altra parte sopra la terra si sappiano ... imperadori de' Tartari (le magnificenze de' quali e le ricchezze appo noi sono incredibili)." See *Il comento de Giovanni Boccacci sopra la Commedia,* ed. Gaetano Milanesi (Florence, 1863), 1.6.194.

72. Morgana and Dragontina also have their paradises in Orcagna. When Falerina and Orlando stumble on Morgana's lake, they are traveling from Falerina's own garden to the border fortress, where she trapped prisoners. Similarly, Rinaldo breaks up one of Falerina's death brigades when he is traveling from the Rocca Crudele to Dragontina's garden.

73. I am indebted for most of this particular translation to Joseph Connors of the Art Department at the University of Chicago.

74. Marco Polo talks about the rubies from Balacsian (chap. 35), a moun-

tainous region on the upper Oxus. Boiardo himself uses "carbone" for the gem in a necklace; see *Pastorale* 10.116. Clavijo also mentions them in the description just quoted. Le Strange quotes Magdisi, who says that this region produced a luminous stone which in a dark room lighted up nearby objects. See *The Lands of the Eastern Caliphate*, pp. 436–37. The area and its gems are mentioned on Duke Ercole's map. See Pullé, "Cartografia," p. 129.

75. "Narra con poca verisimilitudine" ("He says with little verisimilitude"). Here is the whole passage: "Narra con poca verisimilitudine, questo Vecchio in una parte del Regno suo avere avuto un giardino, il luogo del quale ancora si vede, di circuito di sette mila passi tutto d'alti monti & inaccessibili circondato, fuori che da un luogo solo, il quale di muro altissimo è munito. Qui dentro alberi di molte maniere per tutto il tempo verdi con odoratissimi fiori e frutti di diversa fazione; esservi ancora bellissimi casamenti edificati di colorati marmi, e d'oro tutti risplendenti: fontane, che per alcun giorno or vino, or latte, & ora mele artificiosamente gittavano; & oltre a ciò di mansuetissimi animali, e per formositade a riguardanti piacevoli, tutto il chiuso circuito essere stato ripieno con vari uccelli insieme, che per vaghezza di penne, e per diversi canti rendeano il luogo molto più lieto. L'aria tutta e nelle case, e fuori con aromatici incendi soavissimo odore in ogni parte spirava. Erano queste cose guardate, e tenute in cura da fanciulle di scelta bellezza, e dottrina nell'arte Musica incomparabile, dalle voci delle quali con quelle de' dolci strumenti in parte risonava tutto il dilettevole giardino. Dentro a questa gioiosa prigione scrive il Tesoriere avere il Vecchio posti fanciulli, prima che la ferma memoria, e il naturale conoscimento fosse in loro, e con delicati cibi in sommo diletto facendoli allevare, di Lingue diverse, e di ogni buon' arte appartinente a guerra & a pace istruire li facea; e poiché alla perfetta età fossero pervenuti, con medicata bevanda fattoli di quivi trarre, in una orribile prigione senza luce, e di cose fetide ripiena porre li facea, e con molto disagio alcun giorno nutrirli; e da poi con quel medesimo beveraggio trattoli ancor di quivi, e fattoli a se venire loro persuadea, quello primo essere stato il Paradiso, nel quale lietamente furono accresciuti, vedendo esso Vecchio loro Signore alcuna fiata; e questo secondo luogo essere stato l'Inferno, nel quale fame, sete, e tenebre patito aveano. Questo Inferno di nuovo loro minacciava, quando a' suoi comandamenti fossero avversi; e il Paradiso loro promettea, quando quelli fidatamente, e senza alcuna paura adempissero; affermando loro, che qualunque in servigio di lui morisse, eternamente quel Paradiso possedea" (*Istoria imperiale*, pp. 407–8).

"He says with little verisimilitude that this Old Man had in one part of his kingdom a garden, the place of which can still be seen, surrounded for seven miles by high and inaccessible mountains, except for one place alone, which was protected by a very high wall. Inside there were evergreens of many kinds with most sweet-smelling flowers and fruits of diverse fashion; also there were the loveliest palaces, built with colored marble and all resplendent with gold. Fountains each day artificially spouted now wine, now milk, and now honey, and beyond this there were the gentlest animals, pleasing for their outward beauty. The whole enclosed area was filled with various birds together, which by the charm of their plumage and by their diverse songs made the place much more cheerful. All the air, inside the houses and outside, blew with aromatic incense the sweetest scent in every part. These things were guarded and tended by girls of particular beauty and incomparable training in the art of music. All the delightful garden resounded from their voices and from the part music of sweet instruments. The Treasurer writes that the Old Man put boys inside this joyful prison, before they had certain memory and natural understanding, and, having them reared with delicate foods in the highest delight, he had them instructed in different languages and in every good art pertaining to war and to peace. And, when they had grown up, he drugged them, took them from there and put them in a horrible, lightless prison, filled with stinking things and had them fed each day with much discomfort. Then with the same drugged drink, having drawn them again from there and made them come before him, he persuaded them that the first place was Paradise, in which they had grown up, where they had sometimes seen the Old Man as their Lord, and that the second place was hell, in which they had suffered hunger, thirst, and darkness. This hell threatened them again, whenever they were hostile to his orders, and he promised them Paradise, when they fulfilled his commands faithfully and fear-lessly, affirming that whoever died in his service possessed that Paradise eter-nally." Marco Polo's version is quite similar. He does not have a "hell," and the boys are twelve when they are brought into the garden. See chap. 31.

76. Sinor, "Le Mongol vu par l'occident," pp. 61–62. Paul Pelliot argues that Friar Giovanni used *Tatar* in his first redaction, but that the text was later normalized to Tartar. See *Recherches sur les chrétiens d'Asie centrale et d'Extrême-Orient* (Paris, 1973), p. 14. For Friar Giovanni, see n. 77. For Giorgio Pullé see *Viaggio*, p. 155. These are typical views of nomadic invaders. See Otto J. Maenchen-Helfen, *The World of the Huns,* ed. Max Knight (Berkeley, 1973), pp. 1–17.

77. John Boyle says of Friar Giovanni's analysis of the Mongols' military system that it was "written with an acuteness of observation that would do honour to a modern military attaché." See *The Mongol World Empire (1206–1370),* reprint ed. (London, 1977), chap. 1, p. 7. He later bases his own analysis on that of the friar. See Boyle, chap. 5, p. 342. Giovanni Ponte thinks Boiardo inserted a passage from Friar Giovanni into the *Istoria imperiale;* see his remarks in Anceschi, p. 419. There are few manuscripts of the second redaction, the one which includes Friar Giovanni's account of his journey, but Vincent of Beauvais digested the second redaction in his *Speculum historiale,* of which eighty manuscripts survive. See P. Anastasius van den Wyngaert, O. F. M., *Sinica Franciscana. I: Itinera et relationes Fratrum Minorum saeculi xiii et xiv* (Quaracchi, 1929). 13–14. This volume contains Wyngaert's edition of Friar Giovanni's *Ystoria,* and all quotations are taken from it.

78. Friar Giovanni, 6.16. Hakluyt's used the first redaction of Friar Giovanni and lacks these comments. See Wyngaert, *Sinica,* p. 13. For the Mongol intention to conquer the world, see Eric Voegelin, "The Mongol Orders of Submission to European Powers, 1245–55," *Byzantion* 15(1940–41): 378–413.

79. See e.g., the description of his itinerary in chap. 9.6, 9–10, 15. He paid so much at the borders that he had little left to offer the newly elected grand khan (9.34).

80. Beazley, 3:346.

81. Friar Giovanni, 7.2. Marco Polo relates that the Mongols paid an animal tax to Prester John of one-tenth (chap. 52), and Giorgio Pullé says that Chinggiz exacted this tax even in the youthful days of his exile. See *Viaggio,* p. 129. The Mongol system changed and was more complicated than these European reports indicate. See I. P. Petrushevsky, "Rashid al-Din's Conception of the State," *Central Asiatic Journal* 14(1970): 148–62, and "The Socio-Economic

Condition of Iran under the Ilkhans," *Cambridge History of Iran* 3:483–537; H. F. Schurmann, "Mongolian Tributary Practices of the Thirteenth Century," *Harvard Journal of Asiatic Studies* 19(1956): 304–89; John Masson Smith, "Mongol and Nomadic Taxation," *Harvard Journal of Asiatic Studies* 30(1970): 46–85.

82. The town of "Sakint" best exemplifies this system. After the destruction of Bukhara and Urgench, its terrified inhabitants surrendered voluntarily and did not offer battle. Nevertheless, the Mongols sacked the town, killed many, deported the rest, and filled the city with replacements. See Friar Giovanni, 5.26. The Mongols completely destroyed Khurasan, with its great cites of Merv, Herat, and Nishapur. The populations of these cities were systematically massacred. See Boyle, chap. 4.

83. In the second scene (2.3), the people are a "gente villana" (54), and Orlando cries after them, as they flee, "Via! Via, canaglia!" (59). For a more complete discussion, see pp. 31–42 of Eduardo Saccone's "Osservazioni su alcuni luoghi dell' *Innamorato*," *Modern Language Notes* 86 (1971): 31–60.

84. *Herodoto Alicarnaseo Historico delle guerre de Greci & de Persi* 5.7, pp. 168V–169R (Venice, 1533).

85. G. L. Kittredge, *Witchcraft in Old and New England* (New York, repr. 1956), pp. 185–203; see also pp. 57, 165. Similarly, there is Merlin's glass in *Faerie Queene* 3.2.17–25. I am indebted for the first reference to Charles Ross.

86. For the whole sequence, see 1.12.23–41; for Alexander, 2.1.27.

87. For her, Falerina is "quella regina, brutta incantatrice" (2.4.6).

88. I am indebted for this interpretation to Charles Ross. The Italian words suggest the rest of her career: *fallare*, to err, be mistaken; *fallire*, to fail.

89. Tacitus *Annalium* 15.42; quoted from the edition by C. D. Fisher (Oxford, 1906). Suetonius also passes a negative judgment on the project: "Non in alia re damnosior quam in aedificando domum" (*De vita Caesarum* 6.31, ed. Maximilian Ihm [Stuttgart, repr. 1967], vol. 1 of the *Opera*). For the English version of Tacitus, I have used that by A. J. Church and W. J. Brodribb, *The Complete Works of Tacitus* (New York, 1942), p. 379. Suetonius appears in the 1467 booklist (29) and the 1495 list (209, in Italian; 448, in Latin). Tacitus also appears twice in the 1495 inventory (90, in Italian; 76, in Latin). There is no indication what works of Tacitus are contained in these volumes. See Bertoni, Appendices I and II².

Chapter Four

All quotations from *Gerusalemme liberata* are taken from Lanfranco Caretti's edition, vol. 1 of *Tutte le poesie di Torquato Tasso* (Verona, 1957). Caretti's text is that of B₂ (the second text edited by Febo Bonnà in Ferrara in 1581), and his critical appendix cites the variants in B₁ (Bonnà's first edition, also 1581) and O (published by Francesco Osanna in Mantua, 1584). For Tasso's manuscripts and the Prose Allegory as well as the allegories of Guido Casoni and Francesco Birago, I have used the three-volume edition of the poem by Angelo Solerti and his collaborators (Florence, 1896) (cited here as *GL*). For the discourses and dialogues I have used, where possible, Ettore Mazzali's edition of the *Prose* (Milan, 1959). For *Le considerazione sopra tre canzoni di M. Gio. Battista Pigna intitolate Le tre sorelle,* I have used *Le prose diverse di Torquato Tasso,* ed. Cesare Guasti (Florence, 1875), vol. 2. I have also used Guasti for the Poetic Letters in vol. 1 of *Le lettere di Torquato Tasso* (Florence, 1853). For Tasso's books with their *postille,* see the descriptive bibliography for the Barberini collection in the Vatican by A. M. Carini: "I postillati 'Barberiniani' del Tasso," *Studi tassiani* 12 (1962): 97–110. For Dante I have used Natalino Sapegno's three-volume edition of the *Divina commedia* (Florence, 1955–57). I have used the following translations and have silently emended them wherever I needed a more exact correspondence with the original text. For *Jerusalem Delivered* I have used the Renaissance translation by Edward Fairfax (New York, n.d.). This edition unfortunately does not include Fairfax' translation of the Prose Allegory, for which I have used Henry Morley's edition of the Fairfax-Tasso *Jerusalem* (London, 1890). For *Discorsi dell' arte poetica. I,* I have used the translation in *Renaissance Philosophy: The Italian Philosophers,* ed. and trans. Arturo E. Fallico and Herman Shapiro (New York, 1967). For the *Divine Comedy* I have used the translation by Carlyle, Okey, and Wicksteed (New York, n.d.). Other translations are my own, unless another source is cited.

1. Lucretius *De rerum natura* 2.55–58. In his edition, Tasso had the passage underlined. For an analysis and reproduction of Tasso's *postille* to Lucretius, see B. Basile and C. Fanti, "Postille inedite tassiane a un Lucrezio aldino," *Studi tassiani* 25 (1975): 75–168. The translation of Lucretius, *On the Nature of the Universe,* is by Ronald Latham (Baltimore, 1964).

2. *The Veil of Allegory,* pp. 168–73, 196–97.

3. For the Prose Allegory I have also consulted M₃, the te:.. in Celio Malaspina's printing of the *Liberata* (Venice, 1582), as well as for the allegories of Guido Casoni.

4. They were first printed together with the *Liberata* in 1587.

5. We need a new critical edition of the *Liberata* for two reasons. Solerti was unable to see a number of manuscripts, and the quality of his editing has been severely criticized. Walter Bullock first pointed out that Giovanni Gentile, one of his collaborators, was careless; see "Carew's Test of the *Gerusalemme liberata,*" *PMLA* 45 (1930): 330–35. Ralph Nash then examined some of the printed texts and concluded that Solerti's apparatus criticus was not good enough to reconstruct those texts; see "Errata in Solerti's Critical Edition of *The Gerusalemme liberata,*" *Italica* 27 (1950): 241–44. Herein the situation is not so desperate, as I am concerned with major changes which affect interpretation and not with the fine points of stylistics. For more recent comment, see Caretti, p. 653. The manuscripts which have since been examined were partially done by Solerti himself, in two articles for the same journal. For the Marciana (Mc), see "Un nuovo manoscritto della *Gerusalemme* con correzioni autografe," *Revista delle biblioteche e degli archivi* 10 (1899): 29–30; and for the Cavalieri (Cv), see "Un altro manoscritto della *Gerusalemme* ritrovato," ibid. 17 (1906): 65–69. For San Pantaleo 81 (P) and Naples, Biblioteca Nazionale codice xiii.c.28 (N), see Giorgio Petrocchi, *I fantasmi di Tancredi* (Caltanissetta, 1972), pp. 225–58. In the reconstruction of manuscript revisions, I have used all the foregoing. The fundamental discussion is Solerti, *GL,* 1:93–130. I warn the reader, however, that there are misprints in it, especially a confusion between An and Al (Viotto's ed. at Parma 1581, containing *lezione varie* collected by Aldo Manuzio the Younger). For the printed texts,

Caretti presents B₂ and a clear critical appendix for B₁ and O, which latter two I have checked in copies at the Biblioteca Apostolica Vaticana.

6. The *Gierusalemme*, or MS Urbinate-Latino 413, is reproduced by Caretti in the appendix to his edition of the *Liberata*. The other manuscripts which Solerti dates at this stage are An, Am, and Vo, which together contain cantos 4–5, 8–9, 12, and 15. ("An" is a manuscript edited by Ignazio Angelini [Rome, 1877]; "Vo" is Vaticano-Ottoboniano 1355; and "Am" is Ms Ambrosiani Q.120 sup. & R.99 sup.) The titles in An are still the originals, so Ubaldo rather than Rinaldo is the hero. Solerti gets the date 1566 from one of Tasso's letters, where the poet says that he has finished canto 5; see Solerti, *GL,* 1:6.

7. Mc has a reworked version of cantos 9 and 12. 15 is now stanzas 1–56 of the vulgate version, from 4–43 of Am. Bm has 1–4, 9, and 15.1–56. It is the first to have the *novella* of Sofronia and Olindo, but the numbering of the cantos presupposes that it does not exist. Br₁ provided Malaspina with his text for the incomplete *editio princeps* (Venice, 1580) and contains cantos 1–10, 12, 14.1–50, 15.4–43, and 16.1–62. In addition, it contains plot summaries for cantos 11, 13, and the rest of 14. It has the original and reworking for cantos 1 and 12, the shorter (and earlier) version of 15. Canto 10 ends with Goffredo's dream. Solerti dates it earlier than Fr, the first manuscript of the final series. Cv is a mixed manuscript, and I will discuss it in n. 11 below.

8. Fr is the first to have cantos 11, 13, and 17–19. It and Ol (Oliveriana de Pesaro) have 20. Solerti dates Fr earlier than Au and Es₂ because it has more of the early readings for 12 and 17–18, with revisions on four autograph folios. Cantos 14–15 were docked in later. Au has the *Aminta,* and its *Liberata* text in its revisions reflects the Poetic Letters. There are lacunae in 15, and like the other manuscripts of this stage, it lacks 20.121–37 (the reconciliation of Rinaldo and Armida). Es₁ lacks some stanzas in Au and preserves some of the earlier readings, but its critical signs betray the Poetic Letters. The second hand in Es₂ makes it more up-to-date than Es₁. Some of its critical signs were made by Tasso and his friend Flaminio Nobili and reflect the Poetic Letters. For the later manuscripts, Es₃ has the conclusion to canto 15, the episode with the two women at the Fountain of Laughter where Au, Fr, Es₁–₂ stop (see Solerti's textual notes to 15.56–57), and has fewer early readings than the other Este manuscripts. It lacks, however, 20.121–37. It has many notes and queries by Tasso to his readers. Br₂ has the 1575 version set up for press with all the later corrections. Petrocchi dates Naples between Es₃ and B₁. It is closer to the 1575 than to the vulgate text and has agreements with Es₃.

9. I have compared these three versions for the wood.

10. Ol has cantos 1, 2.7–90, 3.7–36, 12.13–16, 16.1–72, and 20. Solerti says it has the primitive version for canto 1, but 2.7–90 is the novella of Sofronia and Olindo (1572–73), 12.13–16 comes in at the same period, and 20 was not finished in November 1574 (Solerti cites a letter; see *GL,* pp. 10–11. So Ol has both early and late material. Cv in its first hand predates Bm, as its numeration presupposes there is no novella of Sofronia and Olindo, and its versions of cantos 8–9 are early (Sveno is still Dano). The second hand, however, is the Bm/Br₁ version of cantos 1–3, and its version of 16 (1–72) is the longest in any manuscript prior to the full versions of 1574–75. Finally, Br₁, which is the most developed manuscript of the 1572–73 series, has an earlier version for canto 15.

11. Letter 48, p. 118. B. T. Sozzi has noted that in the Poetic Letters the

defense of love and magic are interconnected; see *Studi sul Tasso* (Pisa, 1954), p. 334.

12. To Scipione Gonzaga: Letter 79, pp. 192–93: "perché ciascuno de gli interpreti suole dar l'allegoria a suo capriccio, né mancò mai a i buoni poeti chi desse a i lor poemi varie allegorie; e perché Aristotele non fa più menzione de l'allegoria ne la Poetica e ne l'altre suo opere che s'ella non fosse *in rerum natura*." In regard to Aristotle, he made the same point earlier in Letter 48, p. 118.

13. His earlier references in the Poetic Letters are generally condescending. Likewise the passage in *Inferno* 9.61–63, where Dante referred directly to allegory and which Tasso often used later, gets the following *postilla:* "Nissun poeta ch'io mai visto fuor che Dante fa professione de l'allegoria anzi sempre la dissimulatio." See *Dante con lespositione di Christoforo Landino et di Alessandro Vellutello* (Venice, 1564), hereafter cited as Landino-Vellutello. Tasso's copy is part of the Barberini collection in the Vatican: Stamp. Barb. Cr. Tass. 28.

14. See, e.g., Tasso's remark to Luca Scalabrino: Letter 32, 2 June 1575, p. 89. For Sozzi, see *Nuovi studi sul Tasso* (Bergamo, 1963), p. 37.

15. See his argument in the First Discourse, *Discorsi dell' arte poetica*, pp. 354–55.

16. He was defending the wood and other marvels in the *Liberata*. See Letter 47, p. 114.

17. I have discussed such an episode in Boiardo. It suffices to add that Alcina's isle drew most of the attention from Ariosto's allegorizers.

18. Caretti dates them among Tasso's academy lectures, between 1567 and 1570. See p. xlix. They were included in the manuscript of Pigna's verses to Lucrezia Bendidio, which Guarini prepared and dedicated to Leonora d'Este (May 1572). See Angelo Solerti, *Vita di Torquato Tasso* (Turin, 1895), 1:168–71.

19. Letter 36, pp. 94–95. In his edition of the *Liberata* (Milan, 1974), 1:xxv, Marziano Guglielminetti states that in the Poetic Letters the marvelous was one of the principal subjects for argument among these Aristotelians. Sozzi also makes this point. See *Studi.*, p. 336.

20. See Solerti, *GL*, p. 35. He concludes that the published poem is essentially the original draft as it stood in late 1576 (p. 56). Many of the changes discussed in the Poetic Letters, however, were made for the *Conquistata*. There Tasso deleted the episode of Sofronia and Olindo, the ship of Fortune, and much of the mago's underground abode (pp. 57–58).

21. See his epistle of 1 October 1575 to Scipione Gonzaga: Letter 47, pp. 113–14. He assumes that the episode of the wood will move nausea in his friend.

22. There are, e.g., almost no changes for cantos 13 and 18 in Br2, which contained the later corrections to the original draft. See n. 8 above.

23. I cite from Br1 (Barb. Lat. 4052 in the Vatican): "i cristiani vanno al bosco, e per li incanti suoi i quali son tutti illusioni" (155R).

24. The nightmare simile is missing in the manuscripts which represent the original draft and contain canto 13: Fr, Au, Es1, and Es2.

25. See also his remark in Letter 48, p. 118: "non mi spiacque però di parlar in modo, c'altri potesse raccogliere ch'ella vi fosse."

26. See Tasso's remarks to Luca Scalabrino in Letter 84, p. 214.

27. See Letter 79, p. 194, to Gonzaga; and the undated June letter to Scalabrino: Letter 76, p. 185.

28. See Solerti's remarks in the *Vita*, 1:128–30.

29. See Solerti, *GL*, 1:112–13. His source is a marginal note to canto 13. Most of the critical marks in this manuscript concern language revision.

30. Flaminio, for example, cites with respect both Sperone Speroni and Alessandro Piccolomini. He was part of Cardinal Ippolito d'Este's set in Rome, along with more illustrious personages like Muret and Palestrina. See Solerti, *Vita*, 1:155.

31. In the same dialogue Flaminio gives a short sketch of his career. He studied dialectic and philosophy first under Remigius Melioratus at Pisa, after whose death he went to Ferrara, where he became the student of Vincentius Madius and friends with Giraldi Cinthio, Bartolomeo Ricci (the teacher of Silvio Antoniano), and Baptista Pigna. He later returned to Pisa as a teacher of logic. See *De hominis felicitate, De vera et falsa voluptate, De honore* (Lucca, 1563), pp. 321–23. The printer repeats many page numbers in this book. The Vatican number for Tasso's copy is Stamp. Barb. Cr. Tass. 10.

32. In *Dell'amore humano*, ed. Pier Desiderio Pasolini (Rome, 1895), Plato and Aristotle each supply definitions for the ends of love, but the technical detail and language is Aristotelian and Scholastic. Flaminio uses Aristotle's method in constructing a definition (6V) and the four causes (see, e.g., 29V). For the group of three treatises, Tasso brings more Platonic material into the *postille*. He notes carefully in *De felicitate* where Flaminio disagrees with Ficino (pp. 181, 242) and refers to Ficino's commentary on Plotinus for a more complex opinion on how to diminish the affection (p. 89). Similarly, in *De voluptate* he will bring in Plotinus and Dionysius the Pseudo-Areopagite to annotate Flaminio's discussion of the mind (p. 347). In general, Tasso read Flaminio with care but also with critical detachment. In *De felicitate* he can disagree with the philosopher's expression (p. 44). This sympathy and detachment also mark his reaction to Flaminio's ideas on allegory.

33. In bk. 1 of *De voluptate* the speaker, Flaminio, so refutes Bartolomeo Ricci's condemnation of all pleasure. Ricci argues from historical examples.

34. *Discorsi del poema eroico*, pp. 498–99. Poetry is especially recommended for the instruction of youth. Tasso discusses the moral end first and stresses it over pleasure.

35. See Letter 84, p. 214. For Maximus I cite via microfilm from Tasso's personal copy of the *Sermones*, which is Stamp. Barb. Cr. Tass. 50 in the Vatican Library. The numbers in parentheses are those of the modern Teubner edition of H. Hobein (Leipzig, 1910). Maximus' *Sermones* first appeared in a Latin translation by Cosmus Paccius, bishop of Florence, and Tasso's copy was the *editio princeps* (Rome, 1517). By his *postille* Tasso demonstrated special interest in the following lectures: 7(17), "Whether Plato Would Have Been Right to Expell Homer from His Republic;" 15(25), "Words Which Correspond to Deeds Are the Best;" 19(29), "What Is the End of Philosophy?" 21(37), "Whether General Studies Contribute to Virtue;" 22(38), "Whether Man Becomes Good by Divine Assignment;" 40(6), "What Is Science?" Tasso also read Cosmus Paccius' preface, where he discusses Maximus' life and literary style. Cosmus has the reference to Commodus.

36. This is Tasso's note. Maximus says that philosophy and poetry are "rem

quidem nomine duplicem / simplicem substantia / minimeque re ipsa differentem" (lxxiR).

37. See *De rerum natura* 4.11–17. Tasso's simile does appear in Cv, marked with a serpentine line. Solerti conjectures that it displeased his readers (*Rivista delle biblioteche e degli archivi* 17. [1906]: 67). Cv is a manuscript which registers two different periods of composition. The second hand did this canto, and it corresponds closely to the final version. Where it varies from the vulgate, however, it agrees with Bm and M₁ (which has behind it Br₁).

38. In Sermo 21(37), where he discusses *musica,* Maximus cites a list of ancient poets who support this argument. Hesiod drew the Boeotians from flute music to the humanities; Tyrtaeus worked at Sparta; through his odes Alcaeus educated the people of Lesbos on politics; Anacreon and Orpheus softened the hearts of a tyrant (Polycrates) and brigands (the Thracians); see lxV.

39. xlviiiR. Tasso read Maximus in Latin, so I cite from this translation rather than from the Greek. Tasso postillated Maximus' application of *ars* and *virtus* to Homer.

40. As usual, the cosmological is duly cited and then ignored. Maximus refers to the conflict of Hephaestus and Xanthus to illustrate the battle of the elements (ilR).

41. He does not mention most of the women (Clorinda, Erminia, and Sofronia), nor does he discuss the Saracen heroes. Of the episodes, he passes over Armida's castle on the Dead Sea and her garden in the Isole Felici. On the other hand, his analysis of Armida would give sufficient clues for these episodes, and many of the characters are more or less allegorized in the text. One thinks of Argante, e.g., who is regularly identified with *furore* (e.g., 6.25, 7.87, 9.53, 9.67).

42. Letter 84, p. 214. Later in *Discorsi del poema eroico,* p. 515, he will say of the two, "e Virgilio ed Omero ci descrissero non solamente le cose che sono sotto la terra, ma quelle ancora che a pena con l'intelletto possiamo considerare; ma le recoprirono con un gentilissimo velo d'allegoria." For Homer he read Maximus of Tyre, and in *Discorsi . . . eroico* 671 he refers to Porphyry. For Virgil he had a copy of Servius. See the 1587 inventory, which Solerti prints as document 43 in *Vita,* 3:59.

43. Solerti cites Bm for variant readings, which place this stanza in 1572–73. Br₁ has it.

44. Solerti cites Au and Es₁ for variants for both stanzas, Es₂ and Es₃, as well for 14.24. Br₁ has the first stanza with one minor change in line 2: "tè rettor de le squadre, e capitano."

45. For 7.62 Solerti cites a variant in Au (1572–73). Br₁ has a minor variant in line 8: "altri ponga l'ardire, e 'l ferro in opra." Canto 11 existed then only in a prose sketch. For 11.22 the only variant is Es₃, a manuscript of the revision period.

46. In Es₃ the sense, although the same, is weaker; "mente" is corrected to "mentre," a variant likewise recorded in Al.

47. Aladino recalls such an exploit in France at 3.60.

48. In 17(27) Maximus uses Plato's fable as an analogy. He uses it in the same way as Plato, as the analogy clarifies a psychological and ethical state. He compares the corrupted mind, now irrational and ruled by contrary desires, to a state in which the plebs rule: "quod quidem fit quotiescumque in civitate

probitas victa multitudinis penitus licentiae / atque audaciae serviat. Necesse est enim eiusmodi civitatem dissonantem / ac multarum partium esse: eandemque innumeris affectionibus / ac variis cupiditatibus refertam: In voluptatibus quidem intemperantissimam / In iracundia praecipitem / In tribuendis honoribus immodicam in foelicitatibus elatam: In calamitatibus abiectissimam esse" (liR). His historical example is Athens during the Peloponnesian War.

49. Caretti by implication identifies the wood of canto 7 with the enchanted wood of cantos 13 and 18. See his note to *GL* 3.74. Tasso identified two woods, one six to seven miles from Jerusalem, where the crusaders found material which they used in their initial assault, and one much farther away, the Wood of Sharon, where they found better wood. For the first see William of Tyre, *Historia rerum in partibus transmarinis gestarum* 8.6, in *Recueil des historiens des croisades: historiens occidentaux* (Paris, 1844), 1:i. Before Caretti many scholars identified Tasso's wood with that of Sharon. See, e.g., Petrocchi, pp. 32, 69. Vivaldi started this error; see *Sulle fonti della "Gerusalemme liberata"* (Catanzaro, 1893), 1:142. I add the following evidence to support the identification. The crusaders were so desperate for timber that they sent a military company to the Wood of Sharon, a mountainous area considerably north of Jerusalem, near Samaritan Nablus. Tasso, however, locates the wood near the city, six miles away, and thus identifies it with the grove originally used by the crusaders, the first wood referred to by William of Tyre. Tasso is also careful to define the surrounding topography. The Jerusalem area does not have the landscape of medieval romance, where the wood extends in every direction. There is only one grove with trees fit for siege material, the one the demons later inhabit. The rest is desert (3.56, 74). In the last century Chateaubriand suggested plausibly that this particular wood must be east, not north of Jerusalem; see *Itinéraire de Paris à Jérusalem* (Paris, 1968), p. 346. Rinaldo goes there directly from Mount Olivet, and the narrator makes no mention of a preliminary detour past Jerusalem or around the crusader camp, which was situated north of the city. In the *Conquistata* Tasso makes the location specific, and Ismeno goes toward the rising sun, when he wishes to enchant the wood: "Incontra l'Sol, ch'a l'Orizonte ascende" (16.2). I cite from the *Gerusalemme Conquistata,* ed. Luigi Bonfigli (Bari, 1934), vol. 2. Now Erminia and Tancredi, once lost, similarly end up east of Jerusalem, at the Jordan and the Dead Sea. The reasonable assumption then is to identify the two woods, for otherwise we would have to accuse Tasso of a gross error in his fiction, the sort of thing he took such care to prevent. The man who wanted a map of Jerusalem and who would rewrite an entire passage because he was told that his wooden siege tower could not be stable would hardly contradict his own statements and allow two woods near the city; not when the plot turns on the need for timber (see his remarks of 2 June 1575 to Luca Scalabrino: Letter 32, p. 86; and of 11 June 1575 to Scipione Gonzaga; Letter 35, p. 92). What would become of Ismeno's enchantment, the burning siege tower, and the elaborate recall of Rinaldo if the crusaders had two woods from which to construct siege engines? Tancredi gets lost looking for Clorinda in the same wood where he later fails before her demonic image. Tasso thus keeps our attention on the wood throughout the poem.

50. For Boccaccio I have used Vincenzo Romano's edition (Bari, 1951), vol. 1. We can see Tasso's concern for the logic of this thought process when we see the changes he made in his classical model, *Thebais* 4.419–42. Here is the

order in Statius: the darkness, euhemerist belief (about Diana the huntress), and the local person fleeing in fear with his ox. He thus ends dramatically, while Tasso concludes instead with the euhemerism and follows a logical order: the darkness, the consequent fear, and subsequent fantasy.

51. In *FQ* 1.1.7 ff. Spenser directly combines the two views, the epic tree catalog and the allegorical *significatio,* as he wishes to stress quite a different theme: fair-seeming evil.

52. Casoni stresses the illusory nature of the demonic defenses in his argument and says that Tancredi succumbed to a fiction:

> Illusioni di fallace incanto
> Rendon munita ombrosa selva antica.
> Vinto è Tancredi: ei cede al finto pianto
> Della sua bella e sospirata amica.

53. Getto would see in the Christian movement a full circle. The woodcutters fled, afraid of the unknown. By his analysis, so does Tancredi; see *Nel mondo della "Gerusalemme"* (Florence, 1968), pp. 292, 297.

54. The source hunter normally would point not to the wood of *Inferno* 1 but to that of the suicides, which Dante visits in canto 13; and this scene along with the corresponding episode in *Aeneid* 3 certainly provided the technical model for Tancredi's temptation. In his *postille* to the three editions of Dante which he possessed, Tasso demonstrates a continuing interest in the mechanism of the scene: how the tree bleeds, how it speaks, and the physical manifestations of fear. When in Venice, Tasso marked up the first twenty-four cantos of the *Inferno* in a text now in the Angelica in Rome (Venice, 1555) Aut. 1.23. The second and third texts are in the Vatican. The second had commentaries by Landino and Vellutello (see n. 13 above); the third, one by Bernardino Daniello (Venice, 1568). In his *postille* Tasso generally ignores the commentators except for Landino. There he notes how the tree talks as well as Landino's explanation at canto 9 of pallor in the face caused by fear (53Rb). In the Daniello Dante he notes again the mechanism of speech and at the beginning of the *Inferno* the physical effects of *timore* (p. 9). Tasso, however, drew his understanding of the wood from the dark wood of *Inferno* 1. He was careful to make his own wood dark as well. We have seen that fear of the dark initiated misleading reports about the wood, and Tasso notes that it has so many trees that they create a permanent shade (13.2). Bright moonlight cannot filter through its branches (7.23), and at midday the sun makes at best an uncertain light (13.2).

55. When Dante flees back into the dark wood: "ritrovandosi ancora nella selva, figurata per l'ignoranza, e cecità della sua mente" (p. 4).

56. Tancredi also fails through fear. The poet once thought of changing canto 13 to make Tancredi surrender to terror and so be overcome in a case "pertinente a la fortezza" (27 June 1575 to Scipione Gonzaga: Letter 37, pp. 95–96). Tasso wanted to transpose here the earthquakes and storms which Rinaldo later experiences. He did not carry out his design, but in the printed texts he describes Tancredi's failure in the language of fear. The sound in the trees instills "dolor" (13.40), a technical term in Flaminio for a revulsion from pain (though he can use it elastically: in its broader sense it contrasts directly with "voluptas"; see *De voluptate,* pp. 307–8). Once the tree speaks, the hero shows the physical symptoms of fear (13.44–45). His heart trembles and becomes like ice, and he is compared to a man in a nightmare, fearful of chimeras.

Lovers, of course, experienced fear. Flaminio explains that it contrasts with hope and accompanies love prior to union (*Dell'amore humano* 33R–V). Its subvariety, reverence or respect, does not fade away but continues, when the love is sincere, pure, and free of jealousy (36V). Tasso underlined and postillated this observation. This kind of fear would also apply to Tancredi. The lover forms such an excellent image of the beloved in his mind that he adores the image and feels fear, astonishment, and a coldness in his limbs when he comes into the actual presence of the beloved (34R).

57. The mere recollection of the "selva selvaggia" causes fear in Dante (1.4–6); it is situated in the valley of fear (14–15); no one ever escaped from it (22–27); and, when Dante has been chased back there by the wolf, his veins and pulse pound, and he is crying (88–92). Virgil's explanations are at 2.43–48, 118–26; 3.10–15. In a passage in which he denies that the lover lacks freedom of choice, Flaminio cites the first of Virgil's explanations. By denying his freedom the lover avoids self-reform, the long struggle to overcome love (*Dell'amore humano* 38R). Tasso, however, did not mark this passage.

58. Flaminio cites Aristotle: "Aristoteles autem studiorum radices amaras esse, quamvis fructus sint dulcissimi, dicere solitus erat" (*De voluptate,* p. 352). See also his remark in *De felicitate,* p. 93: "sed potius sit forma quaedam, ut diximus, a ratione per consuetudinem in appetitu impressa, ex qua moderatae semper, et rationi obedientes affectiones emergant."

59. Tasso modeled this scene on Dante's burning city of Dis (*Inferno* 8.70–75). Demons line its walls and deny entrance to the two travelers. Dante, seeing his guide upset and hearing the demons' threats, experiences terror and must be guarded from the Furies and the Gorgon Medusa.

60. Maximus of Tyre argues that the same point in a different fashion. The mind attains *sanitas* only after it has been educated, developed good habits, and learned the art of virtue. Tasso postillated his conclusion: "His maxime modis animus efficitur beatus: vitaque hominis sanitatem assequitur. Hinc rectae opiniones harmonica quadam corporis atque animi compositione coordinatur" (Sermo 17[27]liiR).

61. Pigna, pp. 83, 102.

62. Vellutello glosses the wood out of the *Convivio* (Landino-Vellutello, 2Va), while Daniello points to Horace (p. 2). Landino gives it a Platonic reading. The soul, infected by the body, has lost the right way and is now infected with vice and oppressed by ignorance (1Vb).

63. See the Landino-Vellutello Dante, 267V.

64. May 22, 1576; Letter 75, p. 181. *Feritas* in love indicates a state where the intellect serves the sense of touch. Flaminio compares it to the love experienced by bulls and horses. See *Dell'amore humano* 21R.

65. *Palanteis* becomes *palantis* in the modern text (49).

66. I stress the submerged metaphor of *discorda/s'accorda* and so lose the other analogy of musical harmony, the strings in and out of tune. See Pigna, p. 90.

67. I put together two remarks at Pigna, pp. 90–91.

68. During the battle in which Charlemagne confronts the united powers of Spain and Africa, the wizard Atlante, fearful for his nephew Ruggiero's life, lures Orlando out of the battle. The hero hears Charlemagne cry for help, sees Oliviero dragged off and Rinaldo struck to death. Quite naturally he chases after the mirage until in a laurel wood the vision smokes off into nothing.

Doubly frustrated, for he believes that he has lost Angelica during the battle, Orlando enters the grove to drink at a pool. Through the water he sees a crystal palace and women, dancing and singing. Beside himself, "fuor di se stesso e fuor di sentimento" (3.7.9), he jumps in. He meets the nymphs in a flowery meadow and with them leaves this world through a gold and sapphire door, forgetting everything. His exit signals the Christian rout, which occurs simultaneously.

In bk. 3 Brandimarte arrives from Africa to rescue his friend. He comes upon Mandricardo and Gradasso in a battle of clubs and is informed by a laughing Ruggiero that these warriors fight for what they will never have, Orlando's sword Durindana. Brandimarte interrupts the duel, and a party of three is selected: Ruggiero, Gradasso, and Brandimarte himself, accompanied by Fiordelisa. Meanwhile, the nymphs of the fountain, elated over their illustrious "guest," have constructed an elaborate defense: a magical wood, so thick that a knight cannot ride through, one which mirrors one's psychological preoccupations and longings. Ruggiero and Gradasso fail in the attempt and are in turn victimized. The one has been looking for his love, Bradamante; the other, for a sword and horse. That is, they are both distracted from their official objective and liable to temptation. When Ruggiero cuts a laurel, the beautiful naiad who emerges leads him to the pool, where he loses his mind, "de lo animo usato al tutto il priva" (3.7.22), and jumps in. When Gradasso cuts an ash, he finds a marvelous horse, with a gold bridle and covering of gems and pearls. He immediately mounts "quella bestia vana" (3.7.27), and it flies off through the air and drops him in the pool, where he joins the dance, forgetting everything like the others. Brandimarte alone wins through, as his concern is Orlando. When he arrives at the pool, Fiordelisa gives him a crown of roses and herbs, which protects him from the enchantment. He goes into the water with three other garlands and rescues the heroes. It seems to the victims, as they emerge from the fountain, as if they have been jerked out of a dream. They can remember nothing of the enchantment and are instantly expelled from the wood, like a wind blowing a butterfly from the fire, where it wants to go and where it would be destroyed.

69. Maximus makes the same point. The mind, swayed by the affections, falls into false opinions, like the mind of drunks, in whom intoxication generates an inner disease (Sermo 17[27], IV–liR).

70. The poem begins when in a dawn vision God inspires Goffredo to reopen the military campaign, and the rising sun gilds the armor of the departing army (1.72–73) and greets the crusaders on arrival at Jerusalem (3.3).

71. They have, however, passed over or denigrated the interrelation of his Platonism and his allegory. Sozzi, e.g., constantly stresses Plato, as at *Studi,* p. 270, but finds the Prose Allegory a tragicomic episode, a manifestation of the exhaustion which followed the poet's great creative drive (*Nuovi studi,* p. 76). Sozzi admits that it demonstrates the poet's continuing Platonism but prefers to emphasize other aspects of that tradition, in particular the poet's possible connections to Renaissance hermeticism and magic. And this has been the general tendency. See, e.g., Getto's remarks at pp. 47, 184; or Eugenio Donadoni, *Torquato Tasso* (Florence, 1920), 1:366–67. Both argue that magic meant more than religion to Tasso. Contemporary scholars prefer to separate the poet's Platonism from his allegory for several reasons. The first is historical, the assumption that the allegory was a posthumous act, detached from the

poem and not particularly helpful as interpretation, the argument which I have tried to refute in the earlier part of this chapter. The second, if we follow Petrocchi's review of the criticism at pp. 189–90, would stem from Benedetto Croce, who attacked the equation of poetry and philosophy which the poet learned from Maximus of Tyre and which foreign critics emphasized. In its place Croce stressed the poet of sentiments or would argue, in *Storia della età barocca in Italia* (Bari, 1929), pp. 236–37, that *Gerusalemme liberata* is more than a product of Tasso's conscious or literary mind. This suspicion of the conscious in turn goes back to Donadoni, who distinguished the poet from the literary culture of the period (1.7–8, 14–15), the imagination from logical schema. In later critics these dichotomies could verge on a cult of antimeaning. So Sozzi talks about *fortuna* in Tasso, the inexplicable behind human events (*Studi*, pp. 270–73). Such a position would obviously negate any rationalizations of the *Liberata;* hence the contempt or disinterest in the Prose Allegory. In effect, Sozzi has found a Plato for Tasso which never existed in the Renaissance. It is Plato with his mystery but deprived of his rational dialectic, a Plato fit for the romantic and not for the historical approach to criticism. The notion of *fortuna,* e.g., did not in the Renaissance necessarily conflict either with reason or with Tridentine Catholicism, and the magicians whom he stresses practiced what we might call operational allegory, as everything for them turned on analogy. Platonism since the late Roman period had often been tied to magic, which was a *rational* operation. We might agree with Eugenio Garin's rather Freudian analysis (see the two chapters in *Medioevo e rinascimento* [Rome, 1973], pp. 141–77), that magic in the Renaissance by its existence manifests the abyss, the irrational; but in its mechanism and theory it is logical, and Garin's long list of learned books for the learned only goes to support this rational side of magic (p. 159).

72. See Buffière, *Mythes,* pp. 393–582.

73. Proclus carefully applies Plato's quadruple distinctions of knowing (ἐπιστήμη, διάνοια, πίστις, and εἰκασία) and works out further details on his own. When the hero looks at the night sky, he perceives the spheres (generals, the gods sung in hymns), circles (generals together with named particulars), and stars (individually named particulars). See *In Platonis rem publicam,* ed. Wilhelm Kroll (Leipzig, 1899), 1:294.

74. *Prose,* pp. 325–27. Here he is not paraphrasing the *Greater Hippias,* his Platonic model.

75. William of Tyre *Historia* 8.18.

76. Sozzi quotes Getto: "Una poesia che alla fine sembra lasciare nella memoria come un vago suggerimento religioso: illusioni e delusioni sempre, perché la verità di questa vita è l'altra vita" (from Getto's *Interpretazione del Tasso* [Naples, 1951], p. 417). See *Nuovi studi,* pp. 181–82.

Chapter Five

1. Samuel Taylor Coleridge, lectures of 1818, cited in John R. Elliott, Jr., *The Prince of Poets* (New York, 1968), p. 15.

2. In his brilliant and suggestive *Source and Meaning in Spenser's Allegory* (Oxford, 1971), J. E. Hankins points to Natalis Comes and prefers three levels: historical, physical, and ethical (p. 19). In practice, however, his ethical includes the psychological, so his categories are close to those which I derived

from Harington. The theological level is the one open to debate, and I present it here as hypothesis only. Hankins further stresses the Aristotelian side of Spenser, and his book can be seen as a useful corrective to this Platonic book. Tasso still awaits a thorough analysis of this sort. His Barberini book list breaks down evenly among Platonists, Aristotelians, and authors on rhetoric and poetic. The best approach probably will be via the *De anima* commentaries which were available to him. There are three on his list, and all the Aristotelians lectured on it, as we can see from the bibliography which Charles H. Lohr is compiling (see "Renaissance Latin Commentaries," *Studies in the Renaissance* 21 [1974]: 228–89, and *Renaissance Quarterly* 28 [1975]: 689–741; 29 [1976]: 714–45; 30 [1977]: 681–741). It is one of the great fields for future research. I should add that Tasso heavily annotated the *Universa philosophia de Moribus* of his old teacher in Padua, Francesco Piccolomini, a text which Hankins considers fundamental for *The Faerie Queene*. The two kept in contact, and Tasso visited him in Padua in 1575; see Solerti, *Vita,* 1:57, 94, 201. For the Barberini book list, see Carini.

3. In *Theories of Comedy,* ed. Paul Lauter (Garden City, 1964), p. 45. Spenser may have read Trissino's *Italia liberata.* For recent remarks on this possible source, see A. B. Giamatti, *Play of Double Senses: Spenser's "Faerie Queene"* (Englewood Cliffs, N.J., 1975), p. 31; and Nohrnberg, who points to Trissino's Acratia at pp. 440, 499. Ariosto, of course, would talk to his patrons, but always as narrator of the poem. See the discussion of the rhapsode convention in Giraldi Cinthio, pp. 7–8, 36–37. See also Robert M. Durling's analysis of Ariosto and Spenser as narrators in *The Figure of the Poet in Renaissance Epic* (Cambridge, Mass., 1965), chaps. 5, 7.

4. For Donatus and Trissino, see *Theories of Comedy,* pp. 29, 46 (the quotation from Terence is p. 46).

5. 2.Pro.1. All quotations from Spenser are taken from the three-volume edition by J. C. Smith and Ernest de Sélincourt (Oxford, 1909–10). This is one of the many remarks by Spenser which Isabel MacCaffrey would have had to explain away. The initial chapter of her study, *Spenser's Allegory* (Princeton, 1976), shows how dangerous Coleridge and romantic theories of the imagination can be when the critic tries to accommodate historical data to them. She begins with a vague definition: " 'Imagination' for Wordsworth includes nearly everthing that the mind does except immediate perception in the present moment, and even that readily gives way to the inward-turning gaze" (p. 74). This vagueness allows for a strategy of misquotation, in which she says "imagination" where others were talking about other and more particular things: Mulcaster, who speaks about reason (pp. 7, 31); Spenser himself, who in the extract from the *Tears of the Muses* (505–10) does not even mention the imagination (p. 9) Drayton, who talks about the mind's capability for direct inspiration (p. 13); Boethius, for whom perception of simple forms parallels imagination, which sees things *sine materia* (p. 17); Milton, whose old quotation (simple, sensuous, and passionate) is presented as if it were not a comparison with rhetoric (pp. 17, 129); Sidney, on erected wit (p. 17); Yates, on magical imagination (p. 19); and Tasso, on the mystic intellect which is above ratiocination (p. 19). She thus equates the imagination with reason, Neoplatonic inspiration, wit, and magical image making. That is, the authorities hardly go together, even when the same topic is involved, as Wordsworth with his associational psychology meant something quite different about reason than

did Mulcaster. MacCaffrey would have served her romantic theory better if she had argued from a universalist position and simply ignored history, or if she had accepted the fact that Spenser had a low opinion of the imagination, separated the man from the poem, and simply assimilated *The Faerie Queene* within her romantic aesthetic.

6. See, e.g., Gianfrancesco Pico della Mirandola, *On the Imagination,* ed. and trans. Harry Caplan (New Haven, 1930), pp. 50–53 (solipsism), 56–57 (demonic action), 60–61 (madness). Chap. 12 details remedies to be taken against evil spirits. For another discussion of this same point, see Michael Murrin, "The Varieties of Criticism," *Modern Philology* 70 (1973): 342–56.

7. See Giraldi Cinthio, pp. 12, 49–51. He argues that feigned works are better than those based on history and completely reinterprets Aristotle's remarks on Agathon's feigned tragedy, *The Flower.*

8. Like Ariosto, he also appeals to the experience of travelers and to the wise. See *Melusine.* See also A. K. Donald's ed. of the English for EETS, Extra Series 68 (London, 1895), pp. 2–6, 370–71.

9. I have used the Loeb text for the *Confessions,* which is essentially that of Knöll for Teubner (1909). For the translation, however, I have used that of R. S. Pine-Coffin (Baltimore, 1961), p. 267.

10. See *Orlando innamorato* 2.8 for Orlando's first visit to Morgana's realm.

11. Pierre Ruelle, in the most recent edition of *Huon* (Brussels, 1960), dates the *chanson* between 1216 and 1229 but admits that the latter date cannot be determined precisely; see pp. 92–93. I will cite, however, from the translation of Lord Berners, ed. S. L. Lee, EETS, Extra Series 40–43, 50 (London, 1882–87), which is the only available version of the whole prose text. Spenser would have known the prose rather than the poetic version. Material added to the original *chanson de geste* will be called the Huon Continuations. For Hyrcania, see pp. 595, 603.

12. See Isabel Rathborne, *The Meaning of Spenser's Fairyland* (New York, 1937), p. 111.

13. *Historia verdadera de la conquista de la Nueva España* (Madrid, 1968) 87 (pp. 178–79). The translation is by A. P. Maudslay (New York, 1956), pp. 190–91.

14. See Rathborne, p. 240.

15. *The Allegorical Temper* (New Haven, 1957), pp. 107–11, 113–14. I disagree, however, with Berger's sharp distinction between elves and human beings and between classical and Christian heroes.

16. Huon himself, however, disobeys Oberon three times: when he first blows the ivory horn, when he lies to the guard at the First Gate of the Muslim Admiral Gaudy's palace, and when he sleeps with Esclaramonde before the marriage service; see *Huon,* pp. 81, 152, 257.

17. The references are all in canto 8. The argument calls them "paynim," and so does the narrator in 10 and 54, while the brothers swear by "Termagaunt" and "Mahoune" (30, 33).

18. An appropriate passage in Tacitus shows the other side of this process (*Annalium* 15.31): "Concerned for Tiridates' interests, the Parthian king had sent envoys to Corbulo asking that his brother should not be exposed to any external signs of subjection—that he should keep his sword, be entitled to embrace governors, not be kept waiting at their doors, and at Rome receive a consul's honours. Vologeses was accustomed to foreign ostentatiousness.

Clearly he did not understand how we Romans value real power but disdain its vanities" (trans. Michael Grant [Baltimore, 1956], pp. 347–48).

19. See *Huon*, pp. 72, 489. The impreciseness of Spenser's reference is also typical of this method. Only on his first visit did Huon technically come to fairyland *with* Oberon, and then he did not knight anyone. The second time he found Oberon dying in Momure and had traveled there by himself.

20. See *Huon*, p. 601. For a number of similar examples, see Rathborne, pp. 186, 188, 212–14.

21. In the Middle Ages "India" was often used loosely for all of Asia. Francesco L. Pullé, "Cartografia," pt. 2, 5:6, 11, 26, 61, cites Alcuin, Theodulf of Orleans, Honorius Augustudinensis, and Roger Bacon for this usage. This loose terminology also appears in the romances. Angelica, as Indian princess, lives on the Northern Silk Route (Turkestan, not modern India). See chap. 3 above.

22. See *FQ* 2.1.6 for the reference to Huon and Guyon. Arthur reads English chronicle history in the House of Alma (2.10).

23. One could make some case for *Huon*: Guyon's treatment of Tantalus resembles Huon's methods with Cain. They both elicit information from a damned person and then refuse to help him, out of respect for divine justice. Also, the first episode in Guyon's voyage recalls the beginning of Huon's second voyage east, where he passes over the Perilous Gulf and shipwrecks at the Castle of Adamant. What Huon experienced sequentially Guyon does simultaneously, as he sails between the Gulf of Greediness and the Rock of Reproach (*FQ* 2.12.3–9). There the resemblance ends. Guyon escaped what Huon had to suffer.

24. Rathborne, pp. 172–73. Furthermore, Rathborne likewise points out on p. 142 that the genesis of fairyland is euhemeristic. It reflects Ovid's story of Prometheus in the *Metamorphoses*, which Golding sees as an analogue of the Genesis story of man's creation (see his Epistle to Leicester, 419–54). For additional information, consult Rathborne's remarks on E. K., on Burton's *Anatomy* (p. 164), and on the way Melusine was euhemerized by Spenser's French contemporaries (p. 170).

25. For this distinction, see Murrin, *The Veil of Allegory*, pp. 95–96, 127.

26. We know that Guyon was at Cleopolis when Red Cross set off on his quest (2.1.19) and that he has been on his own quest for three months after he meets Red Cross again (2.2.44). Therefore he left Cleopolis shortly after the Red Cross Knight. Arthur's chronology supports these inferences. When he rescues Red Cross, he has been searching nine months for Gloriana (1.9.15), but he has been out a year when he meets Guyon (2.9–7). Likewise, we know that the adventures of Red Cross occur in high summer, as Alastair Fowler points out (*Spenser and the Numbers of Time* [London, 1964], pp. 70–71). But again our most pervasive feeling is that of the absence of seasons and specific times in *The Faerie Queene*.

27. I am indebted for this remark to Lynda Bundtzen of the English Department at Williams College. I have also discussed this matter in "The Varieties of Criticism."

28. See Murrin, *The Veil of Allegory*, pp. 146–48, 149–50.

29. Rathborne has her own suppositions on this problem; see p. 145. I think the same objection applies to Hankins' recent discussion of the Briton-faery distinction. He cites a discussion by Francesco Piccolomini in *Universa*

philosophia 6.2: the Greeks thought of the islands around Britain as places of kindly spirits and heroes (p. 49). He also euhemerizes the heroes with help from Aristotle. Divine parentage is a fiction which registers the fame a hero enjoyed in life or after death or a sense of divine afflatus, a supreme delight in divine things. Francesco goes on to distinguish daemons of the Platonic sort and heroes, the souls of the famous or men who, though still alive, are earning fame (p. 48). The distinction is suggestive and fits a euhemeristic scheme but cannot explain why there is no difference between faery (daemon) and Briton (hero). Moreover, Spenser does not locate fairyland near Britain.

30. See n. 21 above.

31. This we may take as a representative example of this kind of discourse: "We say then that since eternity is the measure of a permanent being, in so far as anything recedes from permanence of being, it recedes from eternity. Now some things recede from permanence of being, so that their being is subject to change, or consists in change; and these things are measured by time, as are all movements, and also the being of all things corruptible. But others recede less from permanence of being, forasmuch as their being neither consists in change, nor is the subject of change; nevertheless they have change annexed to them either actually, or potentially. This appears in the heavenly bodies, the substantial being of which is unchangeable; and yet with unchangeable being they have changeableness of place. The same applies to the angels, who have an unchangeable being as regards their nature with changeableness as regards choice; moreover they have changeableness of intelligence, of affections, and of places, in their own degree. Therefore these are measured by aeviternity, which is a mean between eternity and time" (*Summa theologica* 1.10.5; the translation is the older one by the Fathers of the English Dominican Province [New York, 1947], 1:43–44).

32. P. 264, in Coffin.

33. I use the term "eternal" loosely here, as not-time, and will avoid technical, Scholastic vocabulary like "aeviternity."

34. *Epistularum* 2.3.119–27. I cite from *Horace: The Complete Works*, ed. Charles E. Bennett and John C. Rolfe (Boston, 1956). The translation is by Smith Palmer Bovie in the *Satires and Epistles of Horace* (Chicago, 1959), p. 276. His first sentence is an interpretation.

35. A number of critics have done studies of characters in *The Faerie Queene*, something which would be impossible if Spenser had constructed inconsistent personalities. The most notable example is that of T. K. Dunseath, *Spenser's Allegory of Justice in Book Five of "The Faerie Queene"* (Princeton, 1968).

36. See Aristotle's criticisms in *Poetics* 1454a27–33 concerning the needless degradation of a famous character. His remarks involve two plays of Euripides.

37. For a reference to Spumador, see *FQ* 2.11.19; for Morddure, see 2.8.21.

38. See the beginning of Geoffrey's bk. 9.

39. To argue that Spenser needed creative freedom in his handling of Arthur and Saint George is nonsense. He could always have used invented characters like Britomart.

40. The proverb concludes many Greek tragedies besides *Oedipus Rex* and is paraphrased by Solon in his discourse with Croesus. See Herodotus *The Persian Wars* 1.32.

41. Augustine makes a similar observation about time as the measure of a sound: "In fact, what we measure is the interval between a beginning and an end. For this reason a sound which has not yet come to an end cannot be measured"; see *Confessions* 11.27, p. 275 in the Penguin translation.

Chapter Six

1. See *De doctrina* 1.11, in *The Works of John Milton* (New York, 1933–34), pp. 14–17. For the English translation by Bishop Sumner, I cite by page number from *The Student's Milton,* ed. Frank Allen Patterson (New York, 1930), pp. 996b–97a. All quotations from *Paradise Lost* will also be taken from this edition, as it contains practically all of Milton in one volume and is more available than the Variorum, Columbia, or Yale Milton. All quotations from the Bible are from the Authorized Version. This notion of coresponsibility explains the Father's contrast between man and angels in *PL* 3.129–32: "The first sort by thir own suggestion fell, / Self-tempted, self-deprav'd: Man falls deceiv'd / By th'other first: Man therefore shall find grace, / The other none." In *Paradise Lost* it is clear, of course, that they fell before the creation of the world. At the conference in hell the demons know only rumors about man, and God expressly states at 7.150–161 that this creation will now function as a response to the defection of Satan and his angels.

2. Xenophanes argued that God is not like man either in shape or in thought but that man invariably images Him anthropomorphically—Thracians think of God as blue-eyed and red-haired; the Ethiopians, as snub-nosed and dark—and that if animals had hands, they would make animal deities. See frags. 170–174 in Kirk and Raven. For Getto, see p. 38.

3. For the angels, see *De doctrina* 1.7, p. 978a, and also his remark in the argument to *PL* 1: "For that Angels were long before this visible Creation, was the opinion of many ancient Fathers." For heaven, see *De doctrina* 1.7, p. 977b. Milton uses the old analogy of light from a luminary, when he argues that heaven, as the place of God's throne and habitation, must have existed long before.

4. Satan is arguing with Abdiel: "Who saw / When this creation was? remember'st thou / Thy making, while the Maker gave thee being?" (5.856–58). Calvin, speaking of the angelic fall, anticipated Milton: "Because this has nothing to do with us, it was better not to say anything, or at least to touch upon it lightly, because it did not befit the Holy Spirit to feed our curiosity with empty histories to no effect" (*Institutes* 1.14.16). Here and elsewhere I use the translation of the *Institutes* by F. L. Battles, vols. 20–21 in the Library of Christian Classics, ed. John T. McNeill (Philadelphia, 1960); this quotation is from p. 175. The principle involved is one of the major lessons in *PL:* man must know to know the appropriate. Calvin clarifies this attitude when he discusses the angelic creation: "Let us remember here, as in all religious doctrine, that we ought to hold to one rule of modesty and sobriety: not to speak, or guess, or even to seek to know, concerning obscure matters anything except what has been imparted to us by God's Word" (*Institutes* 1.14.4, p. 164).

5. *PL* 5.719–37, 6.56–60. For Patrides, see "*Paradise Lost* and the Theory of Accommodation," in *Bright Essence,* an anthology of essays by Patrides, W. B. Hunter, and J. H. Adamson (Salt Lake City, 1971), esp. p. 163, but I

recommend the whole article. R. M. Frye likewise discusses the doctrine of accommodation and cites Calvin; see *God, Man, and Satan* (Princeton, 1960), pp. 3–14.

6. See chaps 1–2 of the *Itinerarium Egeriae*, ed. Otto Prinz (Heidelberg, 1960). Egeria five times exclaims over the immense size of the Sinai plain, four miles wide and sixteen miles long: "vallem infinitam, ingens, planissima et valde pulchram" (1.1).

7. The angels have their permanent dwellings elsewhere. In Exodus (15.27) we remember the camp by Elim with its twelve water fountains and seventy palm trees.

8. Manna is described in Exod. 16:13–15, 31. After the dew had melted, the Israelites found something round and little, like hoar frost, something white which resembled coriander seed.

9. Jerome makes this parallel to Exodus; see his comments on Ezek. 1:22–26 in his *Commentaries on Ezekiel*, bk. 1, chap. 1. I cite from *Sancti Eusebii Hieronymi stridonensis presbyteri operum*, edited by the monks of Saint Maur (Venice, 1768), 5.1.21. Hereafter I will cite Jerome's and Calvin's *Commentaries* first by the biblical passage, and then by the commentary. I omit Jerome's chapter divisions, as they correspond to Ezekiel's. Jerome also talks of the vision as a storm (Ezek. 1:14; bk. 1, p. 7) and later says that the movement of the cherubim resembles lightning (ibid., 13–14; p. 15). Calvin compares the vision to the hail storm sent upon Egypt in Exod. 9: 24; See his *Commentaries on the First Twenty Chapters of the Prophet Ezekiel*, Lecture 2, in the translation by Thomas Myers (Edinburgh, 1849), 1:68. J. H. Adamson points to the ancient Syrian gods who rode animals or stood on thrones carried by animals. He also states what some in Milton's circle and among the Cambridge Platonists made of this vision; see "The War in Heaven: The Merkabah," in *Bright Essence*, pp. 104, 109–12.

10. *A Commentary upon the Divine Revelation of the Apostle and Evangelist John*, trans. Elias Arnold (Amsterdam, 1644), p. 86: "He saw heaven opened & within the heavens an open Pavilion or stage, alluding to the custome of commoediants." Ezekiel had already gone far in this direction because he subsequently refers back to this initial vision as a kind of fixed, emblematic presentation of God's glory; see 3:23, 10:15. In the latter vision especially, where the glory of the Lord departs in wrath from Jerusalem, the iconography is kept strictly the same; see chaps. 8–11 generally.

11. In Rev. 4 the candlestick appears as the seven torches burning before the throne, while later the altar (under which are the martyrs) is mentioned constantly (e.g., 6:9), and the incense offering appears twice (5:8, 8:3–5), while in 11:1–2 the prophet is told to measure the altar and Temple but not the forecourt, which is consigned to the heathen. In *PL* the following are references to the courts and Temple of the Father: 6.889–90, 7.148–49; to the lamps, 5.712–14; and to the incense offering, 11.17–25.

12. Jerome, e.g., has the same phrase in both his versions of Ps. 23, "Quis ascendit in montem Domini?" (23:4), while the Authorized Version has "Who shall ascend into the hill of the Lord?" (24:3). But the parallel should not be overstressed. In Ps. 2 God proclaims His Son *after* the heathen armies rebel, and the topography differs. Moriah is a hill among hills, overlooked by Mount Olivet. Jerusalem stands in the uplands, not in a plain, and in *PL* Milton never alludes to houses near the Mountain of God. Satan's palace rather resembles a

city, "High on a hill, far blazing, as a mount / Raised on a mount, with pyramids and tow'rs" (5.757–58).

13. Milton describes the sky as jasper when the sun is behind a cloud (11:209), which he identified just before as *blue* (11.206). Because Milton uses "jasper" in reference to the sea and the cloudy sky, one can guess that he means blue-green. For Allen's opinion, see *The Harmonious Vision* (Baltimore, 1954), p. 98. The confusion exists also in Servius' commentary on Virgil, where both he and the anonymous commentator say that the "yellow" jasper in Aeneas's ornamental sword is *green*. See *Servii grammatici qui ferunter in Vergilii Carmina commentarii*, ed. Georg Thilo (Leipzig, 1881), to *Ae.* 4.261. Jackson Cope points out the essential problem, the indeterminacy of the *substance:* "The trouble lies in the depiction of heaven as place. Lying outside of space, it cannot be captured in any metaphors of substance. The jasper before the throne is now a 'bright / Pavement' (III, 362–3); now it 'flows' around Jacob's Ladder (III, 518–9); in another moment it is even indeterminate whether 'a bright Sea flow'd / Of Jasper, or of liquid Pearle' (III, 518–9). Like details are only echoes of the uncertainty of the whole prospect of heaven as it lies 'extended wide / In circuit, undetermin'd square or round' (II, 1047–8), *The Metaphoric Structure of "Paradise Lost"* (Baltimore, 1962), p. 54.

14. See Pareus' remarks on pp. 90–91. He notes these additional interpretations: the multitude of angels and of heavenly powers, the gospel fulfillment of Solomon's brazen sea, confession, and the people of this world seen clearly from God's throne. Pareus prefers the last.

15. D. C. Allen says finely, "As a consequence, this flower, beyond the things of earth, has neither color nor form: it is an emblem of immaculateness enhancing the visual interpretation of the accompanying panels and lifting them above a mundane commentary" (p. 99). In addition, the term "purple," if a translation of *purpura,* could cover a range of colors.

16. *PL* 4.554. Satan comes to battle "arm'd in Adamant and Gold" (6.110), "adamant" being another term for "diamond." Adramelech and Asmodai wear rock of diamond (6.364–65), and as the second day of battle begins, the good angels advance shining in golden arms (6.527).

17. 3.595–97, 606–8; italics are mine except for *"Elixir."*

18. Milton may have imitated Virgil in this elastic use of terms. *Ae.* 10 begins with a heavenly council at which Venus herself and Jove's throne are "golden" (16, 116).

19. So, e.g., few similes are used to describe the Messiah's chariot; Ezekiel clusters them in the manner of the narrator's initial description of heaven.

20. Hints that the two are very close include Raphael's opening remark (5.574–76) and his observations that time exists in heaven (5.580–83); that heaven has hill and dale and a soil with entrails like earth's (6.639–41, 516–17); that angels make love (8.620–30) wear armor, and are able to eat human food. Finally, there is the Father's statement that heaven and earth will merge in the apocalypse (7.160–61). On the other side, the narrator states that the gates of heaven are inimitable by model or pencil (3.508–9); Raphael says that not even angelic tongues can describe the encounter of Michael and Satan (6.296–301); and Adam judges the things of heaven and the war to be matters far differing from those of his world (7. 70–71). For the latter point see William Madsen, *From Shadowy Types to Truth* (New Haven, 1968), p. 88. Adamson argues that Milton wrote in the mystical tradition and conceived of creation *ex Deo;* that is,

God contains matter *virtually*. If so, we can understand why Raphael should both suggest and deny that heaven is like earth, as the mystics denied the distinction of matter and spirit. It depends for them, rather, on one's standpoint. *B* may be simultaneously "form" to *C* (an inferior) and "matter" to *A* (a superior). See "The Creation," in *Bright Essence*, pp. 81–102.

21. Addison's discussion is of course in the *Spectator* papers' see esp. no. 333. He agrees essentially with the implied argument of Samuel Barrow's Latin poem to which I referred earlier. For Stein, see *Answerable Style* (Minneapolis, 1953), pp. 17–37. Charles Williams, in his preface to the *English Poems of John Milton* (London, 1940), World's Classics Series, pp. vii–xx; and C. S. Lewis, in *A Preface to "Paradise Lost"* (1942; reprint ed., New York, 1969), pp. 94–103, originally argued this position. Stanley Fish quotes Stein and accepts his analysis; see *Surprised by Sin* (New York, 1967), p. 179. In a good article, W. B. Hunter reads the heavenly scenes theologically. See his distinction of virtual and actual and his threefold application of the heavenly war in "The War in Heaven: The Exaltation of the Son," in *Bright Essence*, pp. 122–23.

22. Calvin and Melancthon asserted that the typological was the literal sense. See Madsen, p. 29.

23. Milton paraphrases Wollebius; see Madsen, p. 49.

24. The Protestants normally read "Michael" as "Christ." Catholics likewise used the interpretation, and the heavenly war was a popular topic for the baroque ceilings of Roman churches, where Michael might or might not appear, but the stress went to Christ. It began with Giov. Dom. Cerrini's painting for Santa Maria della Vittoria (1608–20) and received classic form in Baciccia's fresco for Il Gesù, where all bow, willingly or unwillingly, before the name of Jesus. The splendor of the divine name gives total joy to the blessed and damns the others, who turn into monsters below. Jacinto Brandi kept Michael in the scene but used Il Gesù as a model for his own version, which he did for San Carlo al Corso in the 1670s. Again, there is no battle. The rebel angels fall before the glory.

25. Thus far and no farther the literal sense of Luke's gospel required that Milton read the heavenly war typologically. Attempts to develop that reading further have not been persuasive. A Catholic exegete, e.g., could have drawn a detailed comparison between the three-day battle in heaven and Christ's three days in the grave, when He descended to hell and freed Satan's prisoners. Milton, however, was a mortalist and did not believe in the harrowing of hell. Michael makes no mention of such an event in *PL* 12. Hunter parallels in strained fashion the angelic banquet in *PL* 5 with the Last Supper, Satan's departure by night with that of Judas, Abdiel with Paul (*Bright Essence*, pp. 126–27). Nor are parallels to the war at the end of time more persuasive. Hunter and Madsen both assume erroneously that Milton read Rev. 12 prophetically. The parallel should rather be to Rev. 19, which Milton did so read, where Christ, though accompanied by an angelic army, defeats the enemy alone. Unfortunately, this parallel is too general and appears in other places. Yahweh, not Israel, wins the military victory. Milton's own presentation of the Last Judgment differs substantially from his presentation of the heavenly war (see *PL* 3.321–41; 12. 539–51; and *De doctrina* 1.33). Jesus comes on the clouds. He judges both men and angels, while the world burns and is remade. In these passages Milton reads Rev. 19–21 literally, not typologically.

26. Madsen argues for a contrary position: "It is therefore difficult to understand what it means to say that Milton uses the *method* of accommodation in *Paradise Lost,* since he would hardly arrogate to himself a mode of understanding and expression that he denies to the human authors of the Bible and reserves to God alone. He of course uses the biblical *language* by which God has accommodated Himself to our understandings, but this does not make him a Moses who has 'looked on the face of truth unveiled'" (p. 74). I am not, however, making theological claims concerning Milton's inspiration. If, as Madsen admits, Milton uses the *language* of accommodation, then he creates the problems I have just discussed, whether he is inspired or not. Moreover, to support his claim, Madsen must dismiss the narrator as fictive and distinguish Raphael's method from Milton's, a distinction which we have seen does not really hold. Shortly thereafter, Madsen makes a different point, one which I accept and consider fundamental: "*Paradise Lost* is a fiction... analogous to the Bible not in its structure but in its modes of discourse" (p. 82). In this chapter I explore one of those modes.

27. See, e.g., Calvin's statement on the epiphany in Exod. 34: "Thereupon his powers are mentioned, by which he is shown to us not as he is in himself, but as he is toward us: so that this recognition of him consists more in living experience than in vain and high-flown speculation" (*Institutes* 1.10.2 [p. 97]).

28. Quoted by Pareus, p. 286, and applied to Rev. 13:2.

29. For a parallel example, consider the figure which introduces Daniel's last vision (10:6), whose body was *like* a turquoise, face *like* lightning, eyes *like* burning torches, arms and feet *like* shining brass, and speech *like* the noise of a multitude. This figure is a variant of Ezekiel's and is presented by the same method. It in turn models the One among the candlesticks who introduces Apocalypse: *like* a man, with head and hair white *as* white wool or *as* snow, eyes *like* fire, feet *like* brass glowing in an oven, and a voice *like* a great water (Rev. 1:12–16). For beastly examples, there are the monsters of the fifth and sixth trumpets, the "locusts" and "horses" of Rev. 9.

30. The fire goes before the Jewish army and destroys the inhabitants of Palestine (Deut. 9:3), a point repeated in Moses' song, where the fire is also seen as arrows coming from an archer (Deut. 32:22–23). Milton combines the two images for the Messiah in his chariot (*PL* 6.763–66, 844–52).

31. I quote from the Columbia Milton, because Patterson's edition eliminates Milton's biblical quotations. See *De doctrina* 2.5 (17:137–39).

32. The image is from Jer. 13:10.

33. *Institutio Christianae religionis* (Geneva, 1618), 5R. For the English, see Battles, p. 47. See also Zwingli, *On True and False Religion,* trans. Henry Preble with the assistance of Charles Tupper Baillie in the *Latin Works and the Correspondence of Huldreich Zwingli,* ed. Samuel Macauley Jackson, William John Hinke and George Warren Richards (New York, 1912–29), 3:332: "For this is the distinction between the worshippers of the one true God and idolaters, that we worship a God who is invisible and who forbids us to make any visible representation of Him, while they clothe their gods with any shape they please."

34. *De vera et falsa religione* 18, in *Sämtliche Werke,* ed. Egli, Finsler, and Köhler (Leipzig, 1914), 3:774–75. For the English, see the *Latin Works,* p. 199. Zwingli is talking of the Lord's Supper.

35. See also Calvin: "Indeed, whatever they afterward attempt by way of

worship or service of God, they cannot bring as tribute to him, for they are worshiping not God but a figment and dream of their own heart'' (*Institutes* 1.4.1 [p. 48]). This situation is the other side of the prophetic dilemma I discussed in *The Veil of Allegory*, pp. 22–32.

36. Calvin is quoting Augustine. See p. 113 in Battles. In *Institutes* 1.11.6 Calvin gets an appropriate quotation from Varro out of Augustine: ''That the first men to introduce statues of the gods 'removed fear and added error''' (p. 106).

37. *Milton's Epic Voice* (Cambridge, Mass., 1967), pp. 128–40.

38. *De doctrina* 1.30 (p. 1040a): ''No passage of Scripture is to be interpreted in more than one sense; in the Old Testament, however, this sense is sometimes a compound of the historical and typical.''

39. Cited by Frye, pp. 10–11. For the application to Gen. 1–2, I am indebted to Bernard McGinn, professor in the Divinity School at the University of Chicago.

40. See *Heptaplus*, second proem, in *De hominis dignitate, Heptaplus, De ente et uno*, ed. Eugenio Garin (Florence, 1942), pp. 188, 192.

41. I cite from the epitome by Genser, as translated by Thomas Taylor; see ''An Apology for the Fables of Homer,'' in *Thomas Taylor the Platonist*, ed. Kathleen Raine and George Mills Harper (Princeton, 1969), pp. 462–64, 469.

42. In this respect Patrides cites a passage from Louis A. Reid: ''The characteristic of religious poetry as such is that it is forever attempting to express the trans-phenomenal or the transcendent, and forever failing to do so. Perhaps it is fairer to say that it is always partially succeeding and partially failing. It must fail to do so in the sense that the trans-phenomenal, the transcendent, the infinite, can never be more than hinted at by phenomenal, finite symbols. Yet on the other hand, it can in its own symbolism suggest or express this very inexpressibility'' (*Ways of Knowledge and Experience*, pp. 117–18); see ''*Paradise Lost* and the Language of Theology,'' in *Bright Essence*, p. 175.

43. Josephus, *Antiquities of the Jews* 14.4.4; *Jewish Wars* 1.7.6; Tacitus, *History* 5.9.

Epilogue

1. For a full discussion, see *Conjectures académique ou dissertation sur "l'Iliade,"* ed. Victor Magnien (Paris, 1925), pp. xi–xxvi; henceforth cited as *CA*.

2. Otherwise the evidence of these late biographies is mutually contradictory; see *CA*, pp. 28–32.

3. I here am paraphrasing F. A. Wolf, *Prolegomena ad Homerum*, ed. Rudolf Peppmüller (Hildesheim, repr. 1963), chap. 33, pp. 111–12. Peppmüller included in this edition *Briefe an Herrn Hofrath Heyne* (1797). I will cite from the latter by individual letters, from the former by chapter, including page number where necessary, as, e.g., *Pro.* 33.111–12.

4. In his attack on the characters he cites Erasmus and J. C. Scaliger; see *CA*, p. 19.

5. See Magnien's discussion at *CA*, pp. xxxviii–xxxix.

6. He also cites a reading of Plato which applies to the episode where Zeus sleeps with Hera on Mount Ida and the battle before Troy gets turned around. God leaves the universe to the conduct of the celestial intelligences, and most

creatures act against orders and are confounded by their own negligence. D'Aubignac asks who would ever see this reading for themselves, and whoever thought of it in the 400 years before Plato; see *CA*, pp. 86–87.

7. Giraldi Cinthio (pp. 67–71) had made the same argument a century before and likewise used ridicule rather than a direct refutation.

8. See Murrin, *The Veil of Allegory*, pp. 171–74.

9. The first argument comes from Plato *Republic* 2. 380–81. For the third he adds that the gods are always eating, first in Ethiopia and then on Olympus (*CA*, p. 114).

10. See, e.g., Tasso, *Discorsi dell' arte poetica* 1.357–58, and *Discorsi del poema eroico* 2.533–41, 554.

11. He presents the evidence for the composition of the poems in a more scholarly fashion. So for Pisistratus he cites Cicero, Aelian, Libanius, the anonymous *Life*, and a scholion to Dionysius Thrax; see his "Essay on the Life, Writings, and Learning of Homer," p. 58 in *The "Iliad" of Homer, Books I–IX*, ed. Maynard Mack (New Haven, 1967). Vol. 7 of the Twickenham edition. All references to Pope's translation of the *Iliad* and the *Odyssey* and to his scholarly paraphernalia are to vols. 7–10 of the Twickenham edition. Elsewhere Pope remarks on the simpler manners of Homer's time ("Postscript," 10:394) and states that no arts except medicine existed in Homer's time ("Essay," 7:74). He credits the poet, however, with the initiation of history, geography, and rhetoric. Pope there explains that Homer drew his notions from nature and truth, some of which were the same as those the scientists later discovered.

12. This is the beginning of his notes to the *Iliad;* 7:82.

13. For the Juno scenes I have cited Pope occasionally in chap. 1. He normally uses Eustathius, e.g., at *Il.* 1.74 (the plague), 5.978 (Juno disguised as Stentor), and 20.44 (the theomachy). Heraclitus the allegorist explains Juno in chains (*IL.* 15.23).

14. Before the *Odyssey* Pope printed extracts from René Le Bossu's *Traité du poème épique*, and Bossu remarked that the epic poet serves a moral end which is achieved through allegories. See section 1 (9:5).

15. "Essay," 7:69. He once more cites Maximus of Tyre. We have already seen how important Maximus was for Tasso. Le Bossu puts the matter succinctly—the gods stand or fall as allegory: "*Homer* and the Ancients have given to their Deities the Manners, Passions and Vices of Men. Their Poems are wholly Allegorical; and in this view it is easier to defend *Homer* than to blame him" (sec. 7, [9:22]). The translation which Pope used for Bossu is adapted from that of "W. J." (1695).

16. Pope later cites Diodorus Siculus' Egyptian reading for the lovemaking of Jove and Juno on Mount Ida (to 14.179).

17. The marvelous is essential to epic poetry (*Enquiry* [London, 1735], pp. 24–27), which Blackwell defines more as plot than as the fabulous (p. 118). He stresses the mimesis of external truth and assumes the accuracy of the catalog of Ships (pp. 284–90) and the historicity of Homer's characters (pp. 301–4, 324–25, 329–31, 333).

18. He explains Homer's uniqueness under five categories. The poet had the happiest climate, the most natural manners, the boldest language, the most expressive religion, and the richest subject. The hypothesis is clumsier and more elaborate than that of inspiration; and he assumes the confluence of so

many superlatives from different areas that the whole is at least as doubtful as the supernatural explanation. Miracles produce more economical hypotheses.

19. He cites the lives by Pseudo Plutarch and "Herodotus."

20. This is part of an argument that manners determine literary culture.

21. In what Croce calls Vico's confusion of the philosophical and the empirical; see *La Filosofia di Giambattista Vico* (Bari, repr. 1965), pp. 58–59. For Croce Vico confounds the philosophical notion of poetry and the empirical conception of a barbaric civilization and so converts a dark age into an age ideal for poetry.

22. Blackwell then connects allegory and inspiration, when he cites 2 *Alcibiades* and suggests that this mythological faculty best deserves the descriptions of inspiration, when the poet sees things in various lights (pp. 151–52).

23. Blackwell's proof comes from Justin Martyr and Clement of Alexandria, who argue that certain Homeric passages were derived from Orpheus and Musaeus.

24. He bases an elaborate proof on references to Egypt in the *Iliad* and the *Odyssey*. E.g., he follows Herodotus and Diodorus Siculus and assumes that Helen went to Egypt; that her nepenthe is opium, currently popular there; and that the rest of the Near East borrowed the opium habit from Egypt (pp. 132–36).

25. Blackwell also cites Strabo, who says in his gods Homer organized ancient opinion and fable. These conceptions were "physical" and concerned with causes for actions. Blackwell closes with a reference to Vincenzo Gravina's *Della ragion' poetica*, which claims that the ancients gave a popular dress to theology, physics, and ethics.

26. He follows the Phoenician hypothesis of Samuel Bochart; see, e.g., pp. 226–30.

27. He cites the gates of the sun, the deme of dreams, the fields of asphodel, and the εἴδωλα of *Od.* 24, the Temple of Gloom, the brazen gates of Cocytus and Lethe, Charon's boat and his name (pp. 131–32). His source is Diodorus Siculus.

28. See Rudolf Pfeiffer, *History of Classical Scholarship from 1300–1850* (Oxford: Clarendon, 1976), p. 161. Wood appeared first in a German translation (Frankfurt, 1773) and then in English. See Mark Pattison, *Essays by the Late Mark Pattison*, ed. Henry Nettleship (Oxford, 1889), 1:379. For Wood I cite from *An Essay on the Original Genius and Writings of Homer, with a Comparative View of the Ancient and Present State of the Troade* (Dublin, 1776). Wolf cites Wood in the English edition of 1775 at *Pro.* 12 and reconfirms his arguments on the alphabet at *Pro.* 14–19. He states that Wood was a formative influence on his theory in the Fourth Letter to Heyne (pp. 276–77, 283–84). Wood shares with Blackwell the following assumptions. First, Homer is a mimetic artist who copies nature (p. 4) and talked with eyewitnesses of the siege of Troy (p. 186). Second, Wood uses euhemeristic analysis where necessary and follows Heraclitus the allegorist on the plague in *Il.* 1 (p. 195): "Because, in a marshy situation, like that of Troy, unwholesome at this day in the hot season, nothing could be more probable and natural than the fever of a crowded camp, when the sun was most powerful; ... this I take to have been the plague which Apollo sent among the Greeks." For Heraclitus, see *Homeric*

Problems 8–14, in Buffière, *Allégories*. Third Wood and Blackwell accept Thucydides' portrait of Homeric society as primitive and piratical (*Essay,* pp. 33–34, 141–42, 270). Wood differs from Blackwell in that he visited Troy himself, ignores the Egyptian hypothesis, and develops the primitive model. He thus makes Homer analphabetic and denies him allegory. It was his discussion of writing which particularly influenced Wolf, and he, not Vico, was the influential critic in the 1770s and 1780s. His *Essay* quickly appeared in German (1773), and Villoison cites the French version by Cl. Demeunier (1777) in his *Prolegomena;* see Ὁμήρου Ἰλίας, (Venice, 1788), p. lviii. If this were a study of influence and not an analytic study, I would devote many pages to Wood, but for analytic purposes Vico and Wolf include his position and much more.

29. He likewise accepts as authentic the "Hymn to the Delian Apollo" (pp. 108–10). He does point out where Herodotus is inconsistent (pp. 98–99) and realizes that outside sources on Homer's heroes must be derivative (pp. 320–21).

30. Pope remarks that Homer's poems occasioned much of his biography ("Essay," 7:40–41) and classes as "envious" the story in Diodorus Siculus that Homer plagiarized the Delphic oracle (ibid., p. 32), which Blackwell considers probable (pp. 177–78).

31. See Murrin, *The Veil of Allegory,* pp. 86–90. This notion of the Gold, Silver, Bronze, and Iron Ages had been reinforced by biblical decline patterns in Genesis and the apocalyptic visions. For a Renaissance example, see George Herbert's "Church Militant."

32. See "La religione dei geroglifica & le origini della scrittura," pp. 81–131 in *Le sterminate antichità* (Pisa, 1969).

33. For the antiquity of Egypt, see *Historiae* 2.143–45, where Herodotus explodes the notion of divine ancestry in Greece; for the borrowing of deities, 2.49–52.

34. Vico insists on the parallel, uninfluenced growth of nations; see *Principi di scienza nuova* (hereafter cited as *SN*), 3 vols., ed. Fausto Nicolini (Turin, repr. 1976), pars. 435–36. I cite by Nicolini's numbered paragraphs. See also his denial of Athenian influence on Roman law, especially the "Ragionamento primo d'intorno alla legge XII tavole venuta da fuori in Roma," printed by Nicolini in the appendices to vol. 3.

35. In his two central chapters Rossi has worked out the historical backgrounds in late Renaissance and early eighteenth-century thought for Vico's thinking; see *Le sterminate antichità,* pp. 81–164. Croce said that Vico drew no clear lines between myth and poetry (*La filosofia,* pp. 66–67) and that he confined poetry to barbaric times and so could not explain how poetry could be a phenomenon for all ages (pp. 58–61).

36. At 836 Vico states that the reasons which make Homer the greatest of poets deny him *any* philosophy. With reflection sensation declines, a change which explains why later writers cannot imitate Homer's descriptions (707).

37. Vico assumes that all early literature was poetry (438, 470).

38. Croce, *La filosofia,* p. 65. Friedrich Meinecke remarks that Vico stresses the typical and ignores the individual in historical development. In his picture of the evolving Roman state, he leaves no part for leading personalities and external wars. This would be another reason why Vico rejects a personal Homer. See *Historism,* trans. J. E. Anderson (New York, 1972), pp. 46–47.

39. Pope connects Juno to marriage at *Il*. 20.44, citing Eustathius, and the *A* scholiast at 20.67 contrasts Juno and Paris, marriage and adultery. Both notes concern the theomachy.

40. The example is Heracles, the "glory of Hera" or Juno.

41. Croce remarks that, when Vico moves from original ideas to particulars, he stumbles precisely for reasons like this; see *La filosofia*, p. 56. Rossi points to his use of emblem literature (*Le sterminate antichità*, pp. 181 ff.).

42. See his analyses of Heracles, the dragon of the Hesperides, and the Hydra at *SN* 539–40.

43. Another example: At *SN* 558 Nicolini faults Vico because he says that the slaying of Misenus proves Aeneas' power over the *socii*, though Virgil had to adjust the events to contemporary morals. Triton kills Misenus, but the Sibyl somehow knows of it and demands that the burial take place *before* Aeneas visits Hades. Actually, Vico cites Servius' *interpretation* of the passage (6.107).

44. In his discussion of poetic physics, for example, he simply repeats his standard paradigm for sociopolitical history (*SN* 688).

45. Meinecke points to Polybius and Machiavelli as predecessors in this thinking, whom Vico transforms; see *Historism*, p. 41.

46. See Rossi, *Le sterminate antichità*, pp. 81–131. For Vico's discussion of hieroglyphics, see *SN* 429–35 and the analogy to medieval military ensigns at 1051.

47. The etymology accepted by d'Aubignac at *CA*, p. 38. I pass over Vico's revival of the Separatist hypothesis. He assumed that direction terms and geographic zones were originally local and only later applied to the wider world (*SN* 741). So Homer's "ocean" was any broad water around an island (724). He likewise assumes the locale of a poem indicates a man's area of habitation (881). The *Odyssey* presents western and southern Greece, and Alcinous on Corfu talks of Euboea as infinitely far away. Therefore its poet could not have composed the *Iliad*, which presupposes the other end of Greece, the northeast (789). The social conditions reflected by the poems likewise differ (879–80): the *Iliad* with its passionate heroes mirrors a youthful Greece, while in the *Odyssey* the passions of that society had cooled, and people preferred luxury and pleasure to violence. The *Iliad* thus preceded the *Odyssey* by many ages. Vico here does a variation on Longinus' young and old Homer (9.11–15).

48. See Croce, *La filosofia*, pp. 175–77. He thinks that for Vico the following hypotheses would have had equal value, as documentation was lacking: one or many poets, many poets or an able collector of their poems. In his review of Vico for the *Museum der Alterthums-Wissenschaft* (1807), vol. 1, Wolf also points to Vico's emphasis on the confusion of cultures in the two epics. See the reprint in *Kleine Schriften*, ed. G. Bernhardy (Halle, 1869), 2:1160.

49. Croce points to Tacitus as the originator of this principle. (*La filosofia*, p. 160).

50. In the Fourth Letter to Heyne, p. 273.

51. Wolf summarizes this without comment in his review of Vico (*Kleine Schriften*, 2:1163).

52. Fourth Letter, p. 284. He uses the same image for Vico in his review (*Kleine Schriften* 2:1166), where he repeats the judgment of Cesarotti that what Wolf methodically proved another had *dreamed* before (2:1157).

53. At *Kleine Schriften* 2:1158 Wolf simply lists the topics which Vico discusses and lets the list tell its own story: coins, the origin of language, cosmography, Aeneas, hieroglyphs, etc. Croce and Nicolini, in their *Bibliografia vichiana* (Naples, 1947), 1:395–99, make an unsuccessful plea for Vico's indirect influence on Wolf. Three of the four texts cited date after 1783, the year Wolf first published his essential ideas in his edition of Hesiod's *Theogony,* and the *Gazette littéraire de l'Europe* (1765) article which they summarize concerns matters which Wolf ignores in the *Prolegomena.* Of the other three, Wolf is explicit that he did not know any work by Heyne on Homer in 1790 (see *Bibliografia vichiana,* 1:394–95) and cites remarks from 1792 which show that Heyne was still using genre categories for Homer (that is, he did not understand that Homer was a unique problem). See the Fourth Letter, pp. 290–92. Wolf read Merian's *Mémoires depuis l'avénement de Frédéric-Guillaume II au trône* (1793) only while the *Prolegomena* was at the press and would not have been in Berlin to hear the original lectures in 1789; see *Bibliografia vichiana,* 1:388–90. Croce and Nicolini cannot be certain whether Wolf read Cesarotti's *Ragionamento storico-critico au Omero* (1787) before or after the *Prolegomena,* (1:391–93).

54. A point made by Wolf's historians; see Pattison, 1:378; and Pfeiffer, *History of Classical Scholarship from 1300–1850,* p. 174

55. Pattison, 1:352, 354. Wolf never forgave his student Heindorf for editing Plato's *Opera omnia;* see Pattison, 1:409. In 1812 he did an edition of the "*Euthyphro,*" "*Apology,*" and "*Crito*" (Berlin) and an essay on the *Phaedo* (Berlin). See "Verzeichnis der Schriften Wolfs," in *Friedrich August Wolf: Ein Leben in Briefen,* ed. Siegfried Reiter (Stuttgart, 1935), 3:258–60. He also had started work on the *Menexenus, Meno, Ion, Amatores, Clitophon,* and *Phaedrus.* See the "Vollständiges Verzeichnis von Wolfs reservirtem litterarischem Nachlasse," Beilage 14, nos. 62, 65–67, 69–70, 72 in Wilhelm Körte, *Leben & Studien Friedr. Aug. Wolfs, des Philologen* (Essen, 1833), 2:281–82. Meinecke stresses how the Platonic tradition influenced the developing historicism, e.g., in Herder (p. 299), who in a review claimed Wolf's thesis for his own (see Pattison, 1:386–87). In this respect, Meinecke emphasizes Goethe who was a friend of Wolf and praised his "almost magical skill in giving present reality to the past in the highest degree" (p. 484, where Meinecke quotes from the *Annals* for 1805). Meinecke sums up his argument by saying that Neoplatonism was the *greatest* of the forces which led to historicism generally and in Goethe (pp. 492–93, 510).

56. Villoison did much in his *Prolegomena* to encourage this agnosticism. He stressed the corrupt state of the *Iliad* text and borrowed arguments from Wolf, which he used in his edition of Hesiod's *Theogony* (pp. lvi–lvii). The problem was not just corruption but incorrect emendations, and Villoison lists some outside examples (Aristotle, the Bible); see pp. xxxiv–xxxv. Homeric grammar was looser and got "corrected" by later grammarians, who followed rigid rules (pp. lviii–lix). Venetus A reveals the terrible problem of the modern editor: "Vides igitur immensam variarum lectionum copiam ex antiquis optimorum Criticorum, et Editorum libris, e vetustissimis Codicibus depromptam, et judicio interposito notatam, nunc primum lucem adspicere" (p. xxvi).

57. Pfeiffer agrees with Wolf. See *History of Classical Scholarship,* (Oxford: Clarendon, 1968), pp. 105, 108. P. M. Frazer says that the work of the ancient

commentators was already lost in the Ptolemaic period and notes that Didymus cites Zenodotus indirectly; see *Ptolemaic Alexandria* (Oxford, 1972), 1:476 and n. 238.

58. In nn. 47 and 49 Wolf cites Plutarch, *Quomodo adolescens poetas audire debeat,* for the first and Athenaeus for the second. The latter is a reference to a lyre which now adorns the wedding feast of *Od.* 4.3–20.

59. The translation is by S. H. Butcher, in *Aristotle's Theory of Poetry and Fine Art* 4th ed. (New York, 1951), pp. 32–35.

60. *Pro.* 29.97. On p. 96 he refers directly to the passage from Aristotle just quoted.

61. *Pro.* 31.102. So the unity of the *Odyssey* was accomplished by a later redactor, born in an age more polished and prolific in the arts, who wove together separate rhapsodies; see *Pro.* 28.92.

62. Preface to the *Iliad* in *Homeri opera omnia,* ed. Wolf (Halle, 1794), 1:xxvii.

63. Fourth Letter to Heyne, p. 275.

64. Moreover, Wolf assumes that an Aristotelian action relates everything to a single hero. This conception works with Odysseus but not with Achilles, for whom a few battles would suffice (*Pro.* 27).

65. The *Prolegomena* was the first attempt at the history of an ancient text; see Pfeiffer, *History of Classical Scholarship from 1300–1850,* p. 174.

66. It is appropriate that Friedrich Schlegel, in "Über die Homerische Poesie" (1796), developed in response to Wolf a historicist aesthetic. I cite from the reprint in *Friedrich Schlegel (1794–1802): Seine prosaischen Jugendschriften,* ed. J. Minor (Vienna, 1882), 1:215–29. For Schlegel the genre rules do not apply to Homer, for the artist of epic works simply, making a unity through similarities in a material of endless variety. As long as the material is of the same type, the story can be extended, and the epic poet will not stop before he has made a picture of his whole surrounding world. The beginning of an epic poem is unfixed, *in medias res,* because each event is a limb in an endless row, which extends before and after (pp. 222–23). Aristotle mingled epic and tragic notions and so erred. His concern for unity applies, rather, to episodes in the epic (p. 229 and n. 2). So Schlegel unites Aristotle's aestheticism and Wolf's notion of historical development.

67. *Pro.* 36.126. Pope also criticizes these late allegorizations ("Essay," 7:64.

68. In Meinecke absolute standards and the supposition of an unchanging human nature were the greatest impediments to the development of historicism, whether they were concepts of natural law (p. 3) or the perfectionist ideas of the Enlightenment, which later became notions of progress (p. lvii). The Enlightenment judged men by an absolute standard of ultimate human aims, not by the standards which the men themselves held (p. 445). For this see also Carl Becker, *The Heavenly City of the Eighteenth-Century Philosophers* (New Haven, 1932), who argues with wit and venom that the Enlightenment historians thought unhistorically, in terms of moral "oughts." See, e.g., his remarks on Hume, Montesquieu, and D'Alembert (pp. 109, 114–15). Historicism, in contrast, relates to relativism, its vulgar equivalent (Meinecke, p. lvii), and its originators insisted on a fluid conception of human nature, like, e.g., Vico (*Historism,* p. 44). Goethe said that one could not write universal history from a moral viewpoint (p. 445) and made metamorphosis a general principle.

Meinecke cites Ottilie in Goethe's novel *Elective Affinities:* "Everything perfect and complete after its own kind must transcend its own kind and become
something else, something unique" (*Historism,* p. 473). Specific characters
result from metamorphosis (Goethe's diary for May 17, 1808). Each perfection
must be superseded, and there is no final stage (*Historism,* pp. 472–73).

Appendix

1. See Manfred Lentzen's note to his edition of *De vera nobilitate,* p. 39.
2. See Cardini, *Critica,* pp. 92, 203, 219–20, 224–25. For Landino Lorenzo
would not have been a great poet without his knowledge of Latin literature and
rhetoric. See Pref. 1488 Virgil. 224. Cardini in *Critica* further explains. Landino
ruled Cavalcanti out of the first rank of poets because he lacked a grounding in
Latin letters (pp. 215–16). Alberti was known for his Latinate prose (pp.
142–43), and Landino dedicated his *Xandra* to him (pp. 1–2) and praised especially his *De architectura* (pp. 127–28).
3. See Eugen Wolf, "Die allegorische Vergilerklärung des Cristoforo Landino," *Neue Jahrbücher für das klassische Altertum Geschichte und deutsche
Literatur* 43 (1919): 464. This article is the major early study of the *Camaldulensian Dialogues* and relates Landino to his sources.
4. See Cardini's introduction to the Tuscan Prolusion, p. 290.

Index